blue
rider
press

spin·glish

ALSO BY HENRY BEARD AND CHRISTOPHER CERF

The Pentagon Catalog

The Book of Sequels
(with Sarah Durkee and Sean Kelly)

The Official Politically Correct Dictionary and Handbook

The Official Sexually Correct Dictionary and Dating Guide

Encyclopedia Paranoiaca

spin·glish

The Definitive Dictionary of

Deliberately Deceptive Language

HENRY BEARD *and* CHRISTOPHER CERF

BLUE RIDER PRESS

New York

blue
rider
press

An imprint of Penguin Random House LLC
375 Hudson Street
New York, New York 10014

Copyright © 2015 by Henry Beard and Christopher Cerf

Library of Congress Cataloging-in-Publication Data

Beard, Henry, author.
Spinglish : the definitive dictionary of deliberately deceptive language /
Henry Beard, Christopher Cerf.
p.   cm.
Includes bibliographical references.
ISBN 978-0-399-17239-7
1. English language—New words—Humor.   2. English language—Dictionaries—
Humor.   3. English language—Terms and phrases—Humor.   4. Vocabulary—Humor.
5. Figures of speech—Dictionaries.   6. Exaggeration (Philosophy)—Dictionaries.
I. Cerf, Christopher, author.   II. Title.
PN6231.W64B43   2015   2015007373
818'.5407—dc23

Printed in the United States of America
1   3   5   7   9   10   8   6   4   2

Book design by Gretchen Achilles

Line drawings by Ryan G. Smith

For Katherine and Gwyneth

contents

Introduction .... *xiii*

Spinglish–English *1*

English–Spinglish *203*

Acknowledgments *237*

Notes *243*

introduction

Do you speak Spinglish? Well, if you speak *English*, chances are you've been using Spinglish for a long time, most likely without even knowing it. For example, have you ever overslept and missed a meeting and blamed your absence on a "scheduling error"? Tried to weasel out of a parking ticket because of an alleged "meter malfunction"? Explained that a bounced check was merely the result of an "unanticipated negative cash-balance accounting issue"?

Or, when you noticed that your hospital had billed you for a "disposable mucus recovery system," did you figure out they were charging you fifteen bucks for a box of Kleenex? Are you aware that whenever companies say "for your convenience," they actually mean "for *our* convenience"?

If you answered yes to even one of these questions, you're already on the road to mastering the devious vocabulary of verbal distortion, and with our indispensable bilingual dictionary as your guide, odds are you'll soon be earning your B.S. in B.S.— or, better still, a coveted Spin Doctorate. And even if you're a rank beginner, don't despair: *Spinglish: The Definitive Dictionary of Deliberately Deceptive Language* is virtually guaranteed to teach you how to succeed in business, politics—and everything else— without really lying!

But what precisely *is* Spinglish? Well, in spite of its polyglot-sounding name, it isn't some foreign language. It's just our native tongue, transformed into a sophisticated method of judicious miscommunication through the use of careful word choice and the artful rephrasing and reframing of familiar terms. To put it another way (which, of course, is what Spinglish is designed to do), it all comes down to making me sound better, or you sound worse, or both. I'm a freedom fighter, you're a terrorist. I want to enhance revenues, you want to raise taxes. My product is artisanal, all-natural, and organic; yours is mass-produced, synthetic, and contains artificial additives.

Needless to say, any language can be used to convey or conceal all sorts of meanings and messages, but English is unparalleled in its capacity for creative misdirection, thanks to a couple of unique linguistic features. First, with over a million words, it has the largest vocabulary of any language in the world, and with more than a billion speakers, it is the most widely spoken.

And second, English basically consists of two completely separate and complementary sub-languages: Latin, from the Romans who conquered England and bequeathed us mostly polysyllabic (and often nicely evasive) formulations like "exterminate" and "circumlocution," and the Anglo-Saxon, Celtic, Nordic, and Germanic vernaculars of our barbarian ancestors on the wrong end of the catapult who gave us short, simple, cut-to-the-chase words like "kill" and "bullshit."

Of course, using language to control a narrative is nothing new. Long before George Orwell wrote *1984*, our nation coined Orwellian terms like "Manifest Destiny" to rationalize a transcontinental land grab, "Indian reservations" to refer to forced relocation sites for Native Americans, and "Benevolent Assimilation" to describe the violent seizure of the Philippines after the Spanish-American War, to name just a few.

It's also important to distinguish between slang and jargon, which are spontaneously generated, and loaded language and weasel words, which are premeditated. Saying that a bunch of people who were fired were "given the boot" or that someone who died "kicked the bucket" is just colorful; describing mass layoffs with euphemisms like "downsizing" or "rightsizing," or a death due to malpractice as a "negative patient care outcome," is deliberately deceptive.

The fact is, not only has Spinglish been around for a long time, it's everywhere: on Wall Street and Madison Avenue, inside the Beltway, in Silicon Valley and Hollywood, in the fields of Law, Medicine, the Arts—you name it, and if you can name it, someone can rename it to make it sound a whole lot better and promote it with a flurry of press releases flogged by a host of professional Spinocchios and hundreds of highly paid liars with fireproof pants ready to pull the genuine imitation faux wool over your eyes.

But now, thanks to this shoot-from-the-lip glossary of time-tested, tried-and-untrue terminology, you, too, can have just the right self-serving phrase at the tip of your forked tongue, and no matter how embarrassing the situation or awkward the silence, you'll never be at a loss for misleading words again!

So apply some Sock-Puppet News-Job nose-growth-control cream, shown to be of significant value in limiting topical, prevarication-related nasal lengthening (your results may vary), put on that pair of Poppy-Khaki brand combustion-resistant trousers (certified 100% effective when worn with approved carbon-fiber undergarments), and issue a statement, run an ad, or just offer a simple explanation that tells it like it isn't, it wasn't, and it couldn't ever have been.

spin·glish– en·glish

a

abortion machines. A term coined by radio host Rush Limbaugh to bemoan what morally lax Democratic pro-choice policies are "turning women into." Example: *Meryl Streep earned an Academy Award nomination for her performance in* The French Lieutenant's **Abortion Machine.**[1]

above critical. A relatively soothing term used by nuclear engineers to describe a reactor that is out of control and in danger of melting down, or worse still, blowing up.[2] [See also: **core rearrangement; super-prompt critical power excursion.**]

abuse. Torture, especially when it's conducted by the United States or its allies. Consider, for example, this quote from Secretary of State Donald Rumsfeld, responding to a reporter's question about photographs showing U.S. troops torturing prisoners at Abu Ghraib during the Iraq War: "I'm not a lawyer. My impression is that what has been charged thus far is abuse, which I believe technically is different from torture. . . . I don't know if it is correct to say what you just said, that torture has taken place. . . . And therefore I'm not going to address the torture word."[3] [See also: **enhanced interrogation techniques; human rights abuses; pain compliance techniques; repetitive administration of legitimate force; special methods of questioning; stress and duress tactics.**]

academically fragile. A term used to describe student athletes whose poor grades or lack of class attendance threaten their accreditation for a college sports team.[4]

ACC (aggressive carbon copy). A copy of a business e-mail message sent to a third party (e.g., the CEO of your company) in hopes of undermining the recipient.[5]

Accelerated Pacification Campaign. See: **pacification**.

acceptable. Unacceptable, except to those using the term. For example, as author Paul Dickson explains, the phrase "acceptable unemployment" describes an employment level that is acceptable only "to those who have a job."[6]

access controller. A doorman.[7]

An **access controller.**

accidental delivery of ordnance equipment. Bombing something other than your intended target—a civilian hospital, for example, or your own troops.[8] [See also: **friendly fire; incontinent ordnance.**]

accommodator. Anyone who's willing to compromise when *you* don't want to. (The term was coined in 2013 by a Georgia Tea Party U.S. senatorial candidate, David Perdue, to characterize congressional Republicans willing to meet the Democrats halfway on budget issues.)[9]

accounting irregularity. Fraud.[10]

accreted morphological obstacle disruptor. Pick axe.[11]

acluistic. Clueless, and according to *Dangerous Logic*'s "Office Jargon for the 21st Century" web page, "extraordinarily clue-resistant." Example: *Jason is so* **acluistic** *that*

An **accreted morphological obstacle disruptor.**

you can call him **"acluistic"** *to his face without his being offended.*[12] [See also: **reverse infallibility.**]

acolytes. A dismissive political term used to characterize the supporters of an opposing politician or political movement.[13]

acquired taste. Food writer Nick Heady describes this as "something people only ever say about foods that are horrible."[14]

"acting only with all the facts in hand." Something that political strategist Frank Luntz advises Republicans to say they're in favor of, as a substitute for declaring their unyielding opposition to any and all measures designed to alleviate global warming. This tactic will only work, of course, with audiences who still believe there's a good chance that global warming isn't really occurring. Therefore, Luntz advises his GOP clients, "you need to continue to make the lack of scientific certainty a primary issue in the debate."[15] [See also: **"making the right decision, not the quick decision."**]

action (verb). To make something a priority (and possibly even work on it). As the invaluable website CheesyCorporateLingo .com points out, this term is particularly useful when reassuring your boss that whatever he or she is talking about is right at the top of your to-do list.[16]

active. An adjective, commonly used in teacher evaluations, to describe children who are disruptive or who have an attention deficit disorder.[17]

active consideration. See: **under active consideration.**

active defense. The National Security Agency's term for the computer surveillance and cyberattack programs it implements. The phrase was first used in response to the disclosure that the agency had secretly implanted radio transmitters, hidden in USB plugs and tiny circuit boards, in more than 100,000 computers worldwide, and then used them to collect and/or alter software data.[18]

activist. A term favored by conservatives for anyone they disagree with. ExtremelySmart.com's Jerry Merchant and Mary Matthews offer the following examples: "Activist" unions, "activist" school boards, and "activist" homosexuals.[19] [See also: **activist judge.**]

activist judge. A judge who interprets the law in a way that recognizes and guarantees someone else's constitutional or legal rights in a manner of which you don't approve.[20] [See also: **activist.**]

address. To devote at least a minimum amount of attention to. As the *Office Life* blog points out, when you offer to "address" a problem brought to you by a customer or a superior, you're making no actual commitment to solve it—a commitment for which you might later be held accountable.[21]

adhere more closely to a special forces philosophy. Phraseology used in 2008 by Tesla founder and CEO Elon Musk to describe what he was doing when he laid off 10 percent of his company's workforce.[22] [See also: **modest reduction in near-term head count.**]

adjunct professor. A part-time college teacher with one or more advanced degrees but no job security or health benefits and few if any prospects of full-time university employment. When an adjunct professor loses his job, he becomes an adjunct professor *emeritus*.[23]

adjust. Reduce downward. Example: *"We're adjusting our revenue projections," Mr. Creighan enthused, "which gives us a rare opportunity to engage in some long-overdue workforce imbalance rectification."*[24]

administrative professional. Secretary. Also called, with slightly less euphemistic effect, an "administrative assistant."[25] [See also: **area associate; executive assistant; office manager; personal assistant.**]

adorable. A real-estate term for an extremely small house.[26]

adult beverage. Beer, wine, or liquor.[27]

adult entertainment. Pornography.[28]

adverse event. A U.S. Federal Drug Administration term for drug reactions resulting in "death, life-threatening outcomes, hospitalization, persistent or significant disability, or congenital anomaly/birth defects."[29]

An **adorable** property featuring a unique roof design.

advice. A term used by New York governor Andrew Cuomo to characterize the political pressure applied by his office and his aides as part of a well-documented pattern of interference with the Moreland Commission, a government anti-corruption panel that the governor himself had established but then abruptly shut down after it began investigating his own ethics.[30]

aerodynamic personnel decelerator. A U.S. Army term for parachute.[31]

aesthetic procedure. Face-lift.[32]

affected by material error. A phrase used by European Union accountants to designate money stolen from a budget.[33]

affirmative action. Preferential treatment; racial quotas; reverse discrimination.[34]

affluenza. A term favored by members of the anti-consumerist voluntary simplicity movement, who define it as a social malaise caused by rampant materialism and consumerism. The "disease" gained national attention after sixteen-year-old Ethan Couch, the son of a Fort Worth sheet metal magnate, pleaded guilty to killing four pedestrians in a drunk driving episode fueled by beer he'd helped steal from a local Walmart, but was let off without prison time after a psychologist, hired as an expert witness by his defense lawyer, convinced Judge Jean Boyd that the youth was an affluenza victim, whose background of wealth and privilege had robbed him of the ability to take responsibility for his behavior. Instead of being sent to jail, Couch was sentenced to twelve months of inpatient treatment at a $450,000-a-year rehab center paid for by his parents. "In other words," wrote neuroscience journalist Maia Szalavitz, because Couch "never learned that there are consequences to his actions," he was rewarded with an opportunity to "learn again that there are none—and that money can always buy an easier, softer way."[35]

affordable portable lifestyle beverage. A phrase used by Michael Bellas, CEO of the Beverage Marketing Corporation, to describe bottled water. Lucy Kellaway of the *Financial Times* chose Mr. Bellas's term as the 2013 winner of the annual Golden Flannel Award for the finest example of "corporate guff" in the "rebranded common object" category. "To call something free 'affordable,' and something that is necessary for life itself a matter of 'lifestyle,'" Kellaway wrote, "represents the idiocy and verbosity the Flannel Awards were established to recognise."[36]

after-death care provider. Undertaker.[37] [See also: **bereavement care expert; post-health professional.**]

after-sales service fees. Kickbacks.[38]

aggravated bovine ejection. A term used by medics to pinpoint the cause of injuries suffered by a professional bull rider who was thrown from his ill-tempered two-ton mount during a rodeo performance.[39]

aggressive accounting. Accounting practices that inflate revenues and hide potential shortfalls to make a company appear more attractive to investors. According to *Investopedia*, "some forms of aggressive accounting are illegal, others are not. Regardless of the legality, however, aggressive accounting practices are universally frowned upon, as they are clearly designed to deceive." **Aggressive accounting** is also sometimes called **creative accounting** or **innovative accounting**.[40]

aggressive cash management. Business dealings of borderline legality.[41]

aggressive defense. A U.S. military term for an aggressive offensive attack.[42] [See also: **preemptive.**]

"ahead of its time." A book publishing euphemism for "It bombed."[43]

air support. Bombing.[44] [See also: **armed reconnaissance.**]

Alaskan divorce. Murdering your spouse. As PlicketyCat, a correspondent on Chris Martenson's *Peak Prosperity* Web forum, phrased it, "The typical Alaskan Divorce follows the same 3 S rule as hunting off season . . . shoot, shovel, shut up."[45]

"aligning cost, culture and capabilities to enhance customer service and satisfaction levels for shoppers, patients and payors." What Walgreens announced it was doing when it eliminated approximately one thousand corporate and field management jobs from its workforce in 2009.[46]

-ality. A suffix that, as British artist and writer Penny Tristram points out, can be added to absolutely any word to make the speaker or writer sound academic. Among the examples she offers are "materiality" (the quality of being real rather than

digital) and "baconality." (The
suffixes -**icity** and -**osity** work
equally well.)[47]

alleged. An adjective to use when
you're required to discuss
something terrible you actually did.[48]

all natural—nothing artificial.
A pair of terms that, until
2014, appeared on packages of
the Kellogg Company's line of
Kashi breakfast foods, which

*Flag, a watercolor by Polish artist
Monika Malewska displaying an
unusual degree of* **baconality.**

actually contain several artificial ingredients, including pyri-
doxine hydrochloride, calcium pantothenate, and a soy oil processed with hexane, an industrial solvent found in gasoline.
The cereal company agreed to stop using the misleading
descriptors as part of a settlement in a consumer fraud class-
action lawsuit.[49]

all-out strategic exchange. A U.S. Department of Defense term
for a nuclear war.[50]

ally. Vassal state.[51]

almost. A word that comes in handy when you're trying to make
a numerical result sound better than it actually was. Instead
of saying, "57 percent agreed," for example, say, "almost six out
of every ten."[52] [See also: **more than**; **only**.]

"almost new." A real-estate advertising term that, according to
sales agent Kate Cocuzzo, is "kind of like 'almost pregnant.'"[53]

alternative dentation. False teeth.[54]

aluminum shampoo. A police euphemism for subduing an unruly
suspect by hitting him over the head repeatedly with a metal

flashlight, a tactic also sometimes referred to as **flashlight therapy.** If a baton or nightstick is used, it's a **walnut shampoo.**[55]

ambient noncombatant personnel. Refugees.[56]

ambient replenishment assistant. Shelf stacker at a Safeway supermarket.[57]

ambulation. An impressive-sounding medical term that means, simply, "walking." The word is commonly used by doctors when they prescribe strolling up and down hospital corridors as a therapeutic activity. Example: *Sure, you can talk the talk, but can you* **ambulate** *the* **ambulation?**[58]

"America's longest-standing civil rights organization." How the National Rifle Association defines itself on the home page of its website.[59]

American Council on Science and Health. A nonprofit "consumer education consortium" whose stated mission is to "ensure that peer-reviewed mainstream science reaches the public, the media, and the decision-makers who determine public policy." The council, which has been funded largely by chemical, petroleum, pharmaceutical, and food corporations (including, among many others, Dow Chemical, Monsanto, Chevron, Georgia-Pacific, Coca-Cola, General Mills, and Nestlé USA), has advocated strongly for the safety of pesticides, PCBs, and artificial sweeteners and against mandatory nutrition labels.[60]

amply proportioned. Fat.[61]

analysts. A term that is frequently used by journalists to gloss over the fact that the unidentified news sources they are citing are actually their close friends or coworkers, or perhaps even more likely, themselves. The word **"observers"** is often employed in a similar fashion.[62]

anchor babies. A term used by Representative Steve King (R–Iowa), among others, to describe children born in the United States to illegal immigrants who take advantage of the Fourteenth Amendment's guarantee of automatic birthright citizenship to secure permanent legal status for a son or daughter and, presumably, some protection against their own deportation. King has introduced legislation to "close the anchor baby loophole."[63]

anecdotal evidence. A convenient phrase to use when you want to discredit actual eyewitness accounts of embarrassing events in which you were involved or for which you were responsible as unreliable or nonserious secondhand information.[64]

angel dusting. A misleading marketing practice in which manufacturers add a minuscule amount of a substance known by consumers to be beneficial—a quantity far too small to have any therapeutic effect—solely so it can be advertised as an ingredient. The practice is also known as **fairy dusting.**[65]

angeled eggs. A term for deviled eggs, favored by those Christians who believe that it is important not to give Satan or his minions a foothold by even so much as speaking their names.[66] [See also: **sanctified eggs.**]

animal relief area. A space in an airport, or other public facility, set aside for animals to urinate or defecate in.[67]

annual leave. A more professional-sounding, and less hedonistic, term for "vacation." Example: *Stanley elected to spend his well-earned* **annual leave** *in Las Vegas with his mistress.*[68]

anomaly. An accident. In the aftermath of the *Challenger* disaster in 1986, for example, NASA spokesperson Kay Parker stated that the agency was using flight simulators in the course of its "anomaly investigation," and a Virgin Galactic corporate spokesman termed the explosion and fatal crash of the company's SpaceShipTwo space tourism craft during a test flight in 2014 "a serious anomaly."[69] [See also: **major malfunction.**]

An artist's rendering of the RMS *Titanic*, depicting the aftereffects of an **anomaly** it experienced in 1912.

anti-fascist bulwark (antifaschistische Schutzmauer). The official East German Communist name for the Berlin Wall. As Walter Ulbricht, the East German leader at the time the Wall was built, explained to his people, the wall was intended to keep Western "enemies of the German people" out, rather than to keep its own citizens from fleeing.[70]

anti-life legislation. Any law that supports a woman's right to have an abortion.[71]

anti-prohibitionist. A less judgmental contemporary term for 1920s-era rum runners.[72]

anti-terrorist fence. See: **Apartheid Wall.**

Apartheid Wall. The Palestinian name for the barrier that, since 2003, Israel has been building in and around the West Bank. Israeli government officials prefer to use the terms **"anti-terrorist fence"** or **"security fence"** to describe the structure, the largest construction project in their country's history, because, they say, it was designed solely to protect their populace from Palestinian suicide-bombing attacks. Others, including the Israeli Center for Human Rights in the Occupied Territories, point out that more than three-quarters of the barrier has been, or will be, erected within the West Bank itself, not along the Green Line that separates Israel from the lands it occupied after the Six-Day War in 1967. Thus, they argue, the wall seems to be intended as much to perpetuate the existence of Israeli settlements on Palestinian territory, and facilitate the construction of new ones, as it is to protect Israeli citizens.[73]

Appalachian Trail devotee. An adulterer. The term was coined by blogger John Gruber in a post about South Carolina governor Mark Sanford, who famously explained an extended absence from the executive mansion by saying he was "hiking the Appalachian Trail." It later turned out he had been in Buenos Aires having an extramarital affair.[74] [See also: **hiking the Appalachian Trail**.]

Appalachian trail devotees
Mark Sanford and María Belén Chapur.

apparently. A qualifier that, like **evidently, presumably, seemingly**, and **supposedly**, is useful to throw into a sentence whenever you want to assert something you fear—or know—might not be true.[75]

appropriation of nonessential items from businesses. A phrase used by New Orleans police spokesperson Marlon Defillo to describe the alleged actions of members of the force who were observed stripping items from the shelves of a Walmart store in the Lower Garden District of the city during the height of Hurricane Katrina. Mr. Defillo emphatically rejected the use of the term "looting" to describe the officers' behavior.[76]

arbitrary deprivation of life. Murder. The U.S. Department of State devised this term in 1984 to describe assassinations by "friendly governments" such as the military regimes then in power in El Salvador and Guatemala, because, as Elliott Abrams, Ronald Reagan's assistant secretary of state for human rights, told reporters at the time, "we found the term 'killing' too broad."[77]

area associate. What the Kohler company, for one, calls its part-time secretary-receptionists.[78] [See also: **administrative professional; executive assistant; office manager.**]

area denial munition. Land mine.[79]

areas of concern. Objections. This phrase is particularly useful when you want to undermine someone else's proposal without being overly obvious about it.[80]

arguably. A good adverb to use when making a strong assertion that you know is unsubstantiated and quite possibly unfounded.[81]

armed reconnaissance. A U.S. military term for bombing.[82] [See also: **air support.**]

arrogant. A convenient term to use when you want to disparage a female colleague or employee who would be admired for her self-assurance if she were a man.[83]

artisanal. A term widely used to imply that almost any product, like toasted bread, or service, like pencil sharpening, involved the hands-on contributions of highly skilled workers and is therefore worthy of a significantly enhanced retail price.[84]

"As everyone knows . . ." As philosopher Robert Todd Carroll has pointed out, this is a convenient phrase to insert before any dubious assertion you intend to make. "One way to keep anyone from thinking about your statement is to assure them that what you have to say need not be questioned," Carroll explains.[85] [See also: **"Common sense tells us that . . ."**]

"As it turns out . . ." A phrase that Apple Store employees are instructed to use as a more positive-sounding substitute for the word "unfortunately" whenever they are unable to solve a customer's problem. "Bet that really soothes the guy whose iPhone has exploded next to his ear," surmises *Gizmodo*'s Adrian Chen. "As it turns out, you have a shard of glass embedded in your ear drum."[86]

"as little as . . ." A descriptive, and often deceptive, phrase used by advertisers to suggest that the price or monthly cost of, or annual charge for, a particular product or service is unusually low.[87]

aspirational goal. The National Council of Teachers of English defines this as "a goal to which one does not aspire all that much." "The goal of 'aspirational goal,' clearly, is to disguise inaction and thwart legitimate aspirations," NCTE continues. (The term was used by George W. Bush to avoid setting a deadline for withdrawing troops from Iraq, and also by members of the Asia Pacific Economic Cooperation forum to sidestep setting hard limits on carbon emissions.)[88]

aspirational picture. A disclaimer frequently found, often in very small type, next to the photographs in cosmetics print advertisements. It means that the image of the model depicted has been so heavily digitally manipulated, or otherwise retouched, that it no longer accurately depicts any actual positive effect of the product being featured.[89]

aspiring citizens. Illegal aliens. The term is preferred by some advocates of immigration reform over **undocumented workers**, because, as Anat Shenker-Osorio writes in *Salon*, it describes immigrants by "what they bring," not "what they lack."[90]

assertive disarmament. War. Example: *The Great* **Assertive Disarmament** *of 1914–1918 was, as it turned out, mistakenly* *billed as the* **assertive disarmament** *to end all* **assertive disarmaments.**[91]

asset with optionality. A nonperforming asset, or, as *Wired*'s Ryan Tate prefers to define it, a corporate holding that's ticketed for "possible death." The term was coined by AOL's CEO Tim Armstrong in 2013 to describe Patch, a money-losing company division he founded that, despite his continuing dream of finding options to save it, had no apparent prospects for profitability.[92]

assets. A Pentagon term for weapons.[93]

assign ownership. Transfer responsibility and/or shift the blame to someone else.[94]

assistance for the poor. Welfare.[95]

assisted living. Nursing home care. Similarly, what used to be called an "old-age home" is now called an **assisted living facility.**[96]

asterisk (*). A symbol used in advertising to indicate that a particular statement is false, incomplete, or contradicted by qualifications in a fine-print notice at the bottom of the page or screen image.[97]

astroturf organization. A fake grassroots organization created for the express purpose of making the goals and messages of a political or corporate sponsor appear to have arisen spontaneously from an independent group representing the public interest. The term was coined by the late U.S. senator Lloyd Bentsen.[98] [See also: **flog.**]

astrotweeting. Blogger Rick Hasen coined this term to describe the creation of fake Twitter accounts for the purpose of "demonstrating" nonexistent political support (or lack of support), often from unexpected sources. According to Bill White, who ran unsuccessfully for the Texas governorship against Rick Perry in 2010, Perry's campaign used the technique against him. "They wanted to question my support in the African-American community," White told *Texas Monthly*, "but they couldn't recruit an African-American person to do it, so on Twitter they used a stock photo of a black person. One of the people who supported my campaign clicked on the image and found out it was a singer from Atlanta."[99]

asymmetric warfare. British author Steven Poole defines this as "a U.S. military term for fighting people who don't line up properly to be shot at."[100]

at risk. Poor. (In 2010, Washington state senator Rosa Franklin, declaring that this phrase still stigmatized the economically disadvantaged, recommended that they be described as "at hope" instead.) Example: *If he were writing today, Benjamin Franklin would almost certainly have titled his famous pamphlet* **At-Risk** *Richard's Almanac.*[101]

atmospheric deposition of anthropogenically derived acidic substances. Acid rain.[102] [See also: **poorly buffered precipitation.**]

"attracting a younger demographic." Terminology used by ABC/Disney executives to explain why they fired the Dancing with the Stars Big Band after its seventeen seasons of playing on the hit TV show and replaced twenty-eight musicians, singers, and arrangers with preexisting sound recordings and a "small electronic" ensemble.[103]

attrit. Kill. Specifically, "attriting" enemy forces means killing as many of them as possible.[104]

attritioned. Fired.[105]

audible verbal self-reinforcement. Talking to oneself.[106]

austerity measures. Government policies that British author Steven Poole suggests might more properly be called "Give-Us-More-Of-Your-Money-And-We'll-Spend-It-On-Fewer-Of-The-Things-That-You-Want Measures." "What is perhaps worse," Poole adds, "is the implicit demand in 'austerity measures' that citizens not only acquiesce to the policies in question, but actually agree that they are good for them."[107]

automatic amusement device. A more dignified term for an arcade game or a pinball machine.[108]

aversion therapy. Shock treatment; torture.[109]

avoidant personality disorder. One of the things the American Psychiatric Association calls "shyness." They also call it **"social anxiety disorder" (SAD** for short).[110]

b

baby carrots. Carrots that would have been too misshapen to market had they not been cut into bite-sized chunks to hide their original deformities. The new name was coined in 1986 by California carrot grower Mike Yurosek, and is credited with almost immediately raising annual U.S. consumption of the orange vegetable by almost two pounds per person.[1]

backdoor draft. See: **stop-loss program.**

backfill position. A job vacancy that came about as a result of someone's being fired (as opposed to a newly created post). *The Guardian*'s Steven Poole wasn't able to resist noting that the term sounds "like something an adventurous type might adopt at an S&M club."[2]

backhoe fade. A telecommunications industry term for the sudden loss of a telephone or data signal that occurs when an underground cable is accidentally damaged or severed while it's being dug up.[3]

bad bottle. A useful term to invoke when someone tells you that he or she wasn't at all impressed by a wine you recommended. (If your friend actually encountered a "bad bottle" of the wine you hailed, then your original praise could well have been merited.)[4]

bad citation. Plagiarism.[5]

badger watching. See: **watching badgers**.

ballistically induced aperture in the subcutaneous environment. Bullet wound.[6]

banausic. A term used by critics to characterize artworks that are dull, ordinary, or just plain lousy.[7] [See also: **International Art English**.]

Two Trees in Love, by Julie Seelig, a prototypical example of **banausic** art.

bangalored. Fired after your job was outsourced to India.[8]

banger. A euphemism used by sports commentators to describe basketball players whose only talent is to stand under their team's basket and absorb physical punishment from more skilled opposing players. As Cracked.com's Christina Hsu points out, this term "seems like a compliment until you notice that nobody who can actually, you know, shoot, ever gets called a 'banger' no matter how much pushing they do in the paint."[9]

Barack Hussein Obama. Here's a "pop quiz" from the *New States-man*'s Alex Hern: "What's Barack Obama's middle name? . . . It seems pretty likely that you know it's Hussein. Now, do you know John McCain's? (It's Sidney.) What about Mitt Romney's? (Trick question. Mitt is his middle name, and his real first name is Willard.) There is a reason you know the former's but not the last two. It's because reminding everyone that Barack Obama has, not just a scary foreign-sounding name, but a scary foreign- and Islamic-sounding name which is the same as that nasty dictator plays really well with a Republican audience."[10]

barista. A coffee server (at Starbucks and elsewhere).[11]

barnyard. A sophisticated wine taster's euphemism for the distinct odor of **dairy nutrients** found in many prized vintage pinot noirs. A similar descriptive term—***pipi de chat*** (French for "cat pee")—is used by wine cognoscenti to describe the signature pungent aroma of a fine sauvignon blanc.[12]

basis for nonactional orientation. A reason for not doing something. The phrase was used by the U.S. Tariff Commission in the course of explaining why it was refusing to fill out a questionnaire.[13]

bath salts. A deceptive label used on packages of synthetic narcotics—also known as "designer drugs"—so they can be sold in gas stations, convenience stores, and other retail outlets without arousing the suspicions of local authorities.[14] [See also: **jewelry cleaner; phone screen cleaner; "not for human consumption"; plant food.**]

bath tissue. Toilet paper.[15]

behavioral health. A kinder, less stigmatic term for "mental health." Elana Premack Sandler, MSW, MPH, notes that since

our behavior is something we can at
least theoretically change, "'behavioral health' might be a more hope-
ful concept for those who experience
mental illness or addiction and who
may have felt that these diseases
were permanent parts of their
lives."[16]

World Wrestling
Entertainment stalwart Mark
William Calaway, better
known by his ring name, the
Bereavement Care Expert.

bereavement care expert. Undertaker.[17] [See also: **after-death care
provider; post-health professional.**]

bespoke. A word that once was used
only by exclusive Savile Row tailors to describe their custom-
made suits but that now is being adopted by scores of other
service providers, including software consultants, surgical
clinics, SAT tutors, cracker bakeries, and even janitorial contractors, to describe absolutely anything that you might imagine has been tailored to your specific needs.[18]

best efforts. A pledge that relieves you of all responsibility for
meeting a deadline or, indeed, for ever successfully completing
the task in question. Example: *"I am absolutely committed to
using reasonable* **best efforts** *to roll this rock up the hill," said
Sisyphus.*[19]

between jobs. Unemployed.[20]

beverage host. A more refined term for bartender or cocktail
waiter.[21] [See also: **mixologist.**]

bias. Someone else's tendency to believe something you disagree
with.[22]

bibliophilistic pilferage. Stealing books from a library. According to author William Lambdin, the term was coined by

a psychologist who "couldn't bring himself to say that people who steal books are thieves."[23]

Big Pharma. A nickname for the pharmaceutical industry, useful whenever you want to criticize it.[24]

bilateral suborbital hematoma. Black eye.[25]

binocular deprivation. Sewing shut both eyes of a laboratory animal for research purposes. (Sewing shut one eye of a laboratory animal is called "monocular deprivation.")[26]

biographical leverage. An intelligence agency term for information that can be used to blackmail somebody.[27]

A popular wildflower, the Susan with **bilateral suborbital hematoma.**

"biological changes over time." In an attempt to "avoid controversy," the state of Georgia struck the word "evolution" from the proposed official biology curriculum it presented to the press in January 2004 and inserted this phrase in its place. (Less than a month later, confronted with what she termed "an even greater controversy," Georgia superintendent of schools Kathy Cox restored the word "evolution" to the document.)[28]

bio-robot. A human being assigned to a task so dangerous that it was originally intended to be performed only by mechanical devices. The term was coined by the Soviet managers of the Chernobyl cleanup.[29]

Bio-robots on the roof of Chernobyl Reactor 3, shortly after the anomaly there in 1986. (Note: The white smudges near the bottom of the photo were a consequence of intense radiation emanating from the rearranged core in the chamber below.)

biosolids. Sewage sludge.[30] [See also: **dairy nutrients; organic biomass.**]

"birth pangs of a New Middle East."
U.S. secretary of state Condoleezza Rice's confidence-inspiring characterization of the Israeli–Hezbollah conflict of July 2006, during which thousands of troops and civilians were killed or injured, an estimated 500,000 Israelis and almost 1 million Lebanese citizens were displaced, and $4

The **"birth pangs of a New Middle East."**

billion of damage was inflicted on Lebanon's infrastructure. The secretary's remarks were part of a statement explaining why the United States was not supporting calls for a cease-fire in Lebanon.[31]

black sites. The CIA's term for secret prisons it operates in locations overseas—outside United States legal jurisdiction—where "enhanced interrogation techniques" are used to extract information by force from "illegal combatants."[32] [See also: **enhanced interrogation techniques; rendition.**]

blamestorming. Discussing why a deadline was missed or a project failed and deciding who (other than oneself, of course) is to be held responsible.[33]

blind obedience. Loyalty to a cause you don't agree with.[34]

bloc. An alliance or coalition of nations of which the speaker or writer disapproves. For example, Western leaders commonly characterized the group of countries allied with the USSR as the "Eastern Bloc" or the "Communist Bloc" but almost never as the "Eastern Alliance" or "Communist Coalition."[35]

Bombay duck. A fish featured in Indian cuisine that according to food writer Nick Heady is not only "really ugly" but also characterized by a "fishy stink that ensures that nobody will be confused by the inaccurate name." "I've never tried Bombay duck," Heady concludes, "but I've seen it described as 'an **acquired taste'**—something people only ever say about foods that are horrible."[36]

Bombay duck.

boots on the ground. Men or women sent to a combat zone to kill or be killed.[37]

booze-fueled rampages. British journalist Robert Hutton describes these as "what vile thugs go on, to the dismay of revelers."[38]

branded accommodation product. A service offered by a hotel chain. The concept was "pioneered" by ITC Hotels, which offers not only "three brands of accommodation," but also "a mouthwatering array" of "highly evolved branded cuisines."[39]

bravery. See: **fanaticism.**

"bright sunny home." A description, frequently used in real-estate advertisements, that Luke Mullins of *U.S. News & World Report* translates as "There's not a tree in sight."[40]

"brilliantly defies categorization." A publishing industry copywriters' phrase that, according to James Meader, publicity director at Picador USA, means, "Even the author has no clue what he's turned in."[41]

budget reinforcement. Raising taxes and/or cutting public services. For example, "budget reinforcement measures" were a centerpiece of the Swedish government's official "budget policy framework" for 2013.[42]

burly. Obese, fat.[43]

business manager. A kinder and gentler term for pimp. "I never considered myself to be a pimp," one convicted panderer told an interviewer from the Urban Institute. "I just considered myself to be a part of the urban lifestyle."[44] [See also: **companionator.**]

A sex care provider, accompanied by her **business manager**.

businesslike. An adjective useful for describing any discussion or meeting in which, to quote the London *Times* literary editor Philip Howard, "no business is done, and no agreement is reached."[45]

"But it would be wrong." A classic self-immunizing legal phrase attributed to President Nixon by his chief of staff, H. R. "Bob" Haldeman, during Haldeman's July 30, 1973, appearance before the special Senate committee investigating the Watergate break-in. Haldeman testified that Nixon responded to an apparent hush-money blackmail demand from the burglars by saying, "There is no problem in raising a million dollars—we can do that," but asserted that the president added the now infamous disclaimer "But it would be wrong" immediately thereafter. There is no unimpeachable evidence that Nixon actually made this remark, but it's such a historic—and infinitely useful—equivocation that we felt that, arguably, it would be wrong not to include it.[46]

"by our foreign staff." As Bloomberg correspondent and journalistic jargon connoisseur Robert Hutton points out, most newspapers don't have foreign staffs anymore. When you see this byline, it means: "We lifted this from the newswires."[47]

C

Cadillac-driving welfare queens. See: **strategic racism.**

calamari. Fried squid testicles.[1]

campaign contribution. Bribe.[2]

can be. A pair of words useful to insert before an adjective when you want to make a claim about a product or service that is most likely not true. For example, saying that a toothpaste "can be effective" in fighting tooth decay is a pretty good indicator that it probably isn't.[3] [See also: **may be.**]

canine control officer. Dogcatcher.[4]

"cannot be ruled out." A journalistic phrase that precedes or follows one or more sentences containing pure speculation.[5]

canola oil. A more family-friendly term for rapeseed oil.[6]

cap-and-tax. A term used by Republicans, Tea Party groups, and the coal industry to describe cap-and-trade programs designed to limit carbon emissions by creating a market-based system of government-issued pollution permits. Some more vocal opponents of such proposals prefer the term **crap-and-trade.**[7]

capital punishment. The death penalty.[8]

carbon-based error. A tech term for a failure caused by a human being rather than a machine.[9]

card-carrying. Belonging to an organization the speaker or writer doesn't like. For example, Senator Joseph McCarthy continually ranted about "card-carrying Communists." As authors Paul Dickson and Robert Skole point out, people who belong to organizations the speaker *likes* "do not carry cards, but are dedicated advocates."[10]

career alternative enhancement program. What the Chrysler Corporation announced it was "initiating" in 1988 when it terminated the jobs of more than five thousand employees at its plant in Kenosha, Wisconsin. Example: *"Clean out your desk and hit the bricks, toots," said Ms. Jones's superior as he handed her a pink slip. "We're initiating a* **career alternative enhancement program** *tailored specifically for you."*[11] [See also: **career-change opportunity.**]

career associate scanning professional. A grocery store checkout clerk. The term was coined by Wegmans Food Markets, a regional supermarket chain based in Rochester, New York, for use in its help-wanted advertisements.[12]

career-change opportunity. What the president of Clifford of Vermont, Inc., a wire and cable distribution company, announced he was offering fifteen of his employees when he dismissed them in 1990. "It was not a cutback or a layoff," he explained.[13] [See also: **career alternative enhancement program.**]

careful. Cowardly. Example: *After a convivial dinner with the government relations professional from Second Amendment Sisters, Senator Tierney decided to adopt a* **careful** *position on assault weapons control legislation.*[14]

carefully crafted, nuanced responses. Lies of omission. The term was used by Admiral John Poindexter in describing Oliver North's testimony during the Iran-Contra affair.[15]

cash-flow problem. Bankruptcy, or, at least, near-bankruptcy.[16]

catastrophic longevity. Insurance terminology for every actuary's worst nightmare: that too many people will live for too long, jeopardizing insurers' profits.[17]

categorical inaccuracy. Lie. Example: *Representative Joe Wilson might have avoided a formal rebuke if during President Obama's State of the Union Address in 2009 he had shouted, "You have uttered a* **categorical inaccuracy!**" *instead of "You lie!"*[18]

celebration of knowledge. A more positive, less intimidating term for an exam or test.[19]

center of excellence. An outsourcing location with low labor costs. Example: *After the collapse of the Rana Plaza in Bangladesh during which 1,129 people died, the once-thriving garment factory was no longer able to serve as a* **center of excellence.**[20]

A learning facilitator administering a **celebration of knowledge**.

challenge. Problem.[21] [See also: **issue.**]

character lines. Facial wrinkles.[22] [See also: **expression lines**; **laugh lines**; **maturity tracks.**]

characterful. A real-estate advertising term that, according to *The Economist*, means, "The previous owner was mad or squalid."[23]

chemical dependency. A term defined by journalist Norman Solomon as "drug abuse among the upper classes."[24] [See also: **compulsive self-medication**; **substance abuse.**]

chemical-free. A term widely used in advertisements for personal care and beauty products that, obviously, conveys the impression that they contain no chemicals and, therefore, are safer to use than those that do. But as Perry Romanowski of *Chemists Corner* points out, every cosmetic formulation is composed *entirely* of chemical compounds like $C_{16}H_{34}O$ (alcohol), $C_{38}H_{74}O_4$ (wax), and H_2O (water). Indeed, absolutely everything in the whole world is made of chemicals. What a company that claims its products are "chemical-free" is probably trying to tell us, suggests "skin-care biologist" Lorraine Dallmeier, is that there aren't any *synthetic* compounds in them—that is, every ingredient exists at least *somewhere* in nature. But does this mean that such products are "safer"? What do you think?[25]

Chief Happiness Officer. See: **happiness heroes.**

child abuse. What, according to Wisconsin state senator Glenn Grothman, single parents are guilty of simply by being, well, single parents. In fact, he feels so strongly about this that, in 2012, he introduced Senate Bill 507, which, if passed, will compel state agencies to "emphasize non-marital parenthood as a contributing factor to child abuse and neglect."[26]

Chilean sea bass. Patagonian toothfish. The name "Chilean sea bass" was invented by fish wholesaler Lee Lantz in 1977 because he knew that no one in the United States would ever order Patagonian toothfish for dinner. Lantz's rebranding was so successful that, by 2002, the National Environmental Trust found it necessary to create the "Take a Pass on Chilean Sea Bass" campaign to save the previously ignored species from extinction.[27]

chitlins. Boiled pig intestines.[28]

citizen disarmament. Gun control.[29]

Citizens for Asbestos Reform. An industry-sponsored lobbying group dedicated to protecting asbestos manufacturers from health-related lawsuits.[30]

Citizens for Objective Public Education (COPE). A not-for-profit Kansas organization that is challenging the legal right of the state's public schools to teach the theory of evolution. Their argument: Darwinism is a "nontheistic religious worldview," and, therefore, the First Amendment prohibits the use of taxpayer funds to impose it on students.[31] [See also: **nontheistic religious worldview.**]

"civil rights organization." How the National Rifle Association defines itself on the home page of its website. Indeed, the NRA proudly points out, it is *"America's longest-standing* civil rights organization."[32]

civilian contractor. Mercenary.[33] [See also: **security contractor.**]

claims. A verb used by reporters when they quote a source that they don't like or believe. As Paul Dickson and Robert Skole point out in their invaluable book *Journalese*, "A person who likes a source never says he or she 'claims' something. Instead, it is 'firmly stated.'"[34]

clarify. To render a previous statement inoperative.[35]

class warfare. A phrase invoked by Republicans to deflect Democratic Party demands for tax reform and Wall Street regulation.[36]

classic rock. A term coined by radio stations, because, as columnist Dave Barry explains, "they knew we'd be upset if they came right out and called it what it is, namely, 'middle-aged-person nostalgia music.'"[37]

clean coal. A catchy oxymoron coined by the coal mining and electric utility industries to describe expensive and complex technologies used to capture and store underground a small portion of the considerable carbon emissions produced by coal combustion.[38]

clean up the historical record. To falsify official documents. This terminology was used by Oliver North in his congressional testimony about the Iran-Contra affair.[39]

cleanse. To clear an area of enemy troops (presumably by killing most or all of them).[40]

Clear Skies Initiative. Legislation, drafted by the George W. Bush administration, designed (among other things) to weaken controls on smog- and soot-forming gases in the atmosphere.[41]

clerical inadvertence. A term used by Darrell Buchbinder, general counsel of the Port Authority of New York and New Jersey, to explain, two years after the fact, how the official minutes of a February 2012 board meeting had come to show that the Port Authority chairman, David Samson, had voted to approve a project that benefited one of his clients—a clear conflict of interest. Buchbinder proceeded to "correct" the minutes to reflect that Samson had recused himself, rather than voting yes.[42]

client. Mortuary workers' term for corpse.[43]

client engagement. Talking to customers.[44]

climate change. A term that political guru Frank Luntz recommends Republicans use instead of "global warming," on the grounds that "global warming" has such "catastrophic connotations" that voters might actually insist that something be done about it.[45]

climate destabilization. A substitute for **"climate change,"** handy for reinforcing the point of view that it's caused by human industry rather than by nature.[46]

clothing optional lifestyle. Nudism.[47]

Coalition for a Democratic Workplace. An alliance of industry groups organized to fight legislation that would make it easier for workers to unionize, and that seeks to defeat U.S. Congress members who advocate such measures.[48]

Coalition of the Willing. The alliance of "49 countries" that the

George W. Bush White House announced, in an official March 27, 2003, press release, had already "begun military operations to disarm Iraq of its weapons of mass destruction and . . . liberate the Iraqi people from one of the worst tyrants and most brutal regimes on earth." Among the countries listed were Tonga, which deployed forty-nine soldiers in July 2004 and withdrew them the following December; Kazakhstan, which contributed twenty-nine ordnance disposal engineers; Iceland, whose deployed forces, at maximum strength, numbered two; Mongolia, whose total annual defense budget is lower than the cost of one of the Tomahawk cruise missiles the United States launched on the first night of the war; Costa Rica, which sent no troops at all and requested, in 2004, that it no longer be considered a coalition member; Micronesia, the Marshall Islands, and Palau, none of whom could have sent troops even if they'd wanted to, since they have no military forces; and the Solomon Islands, which, upon hearing that it had joined the coalition, announced that it was "completely unaware" of this action on its part and "wished to disassociate itself from the report."[49]

Coalition of the Willing and Unable. A term coined in September 2014 by historian and former Bill Clinton speechwriter Jeff Shesol to characterize the partners on whom President Barack Obama's strategy to "degrade and ultimately destroy" the Islamic State in Iraq and Syria (ISIS) depends. The two main pillars of this coalition, Shesol reminds us, are the Iraqi Shiite militias (who, he points out, have "terrorized the [Sunni] population we intend to protect") and the Syrian anti-Assad rebels (who, since they "have been unable to keep their weapons out of the hands of ISIS," give him cause to wonder, "Which side will we be arming?").[50]

coercive diplomacy. Bombing.[51]

coercive humanitarianism. A term coined by syndicated columnist Mona Charen to characterize a ruling by a public school in Chicago that all students would be required to eat cafeteria food on the grounds that it was likely to be more nutritious than lunches packed at home.[52]

collateral damage. Civilian casualties.[53] [See also: **regrettable by-products.**]

collected. A term that, as the U.S. National Security Agency has chosen to define it, refers *only* to data that has actually been "processed into intelligible form" and "received for use" by a live Department of Defense intelligence employee. This definition permits the agency to intercept untold millions of domestic communications, store them in its databases, and use computer algorithms to search them all for key words and phrases, while still denying that any of these communications were ever "collected."[54]

collective indiscipline. Mutiny; riot. Example: *One of Stanley's all-time favorite movies is* **Collective Indiscipline** *on the* Bounty.

colorblindness. A noun, favored by opponents of affirmative action, embodying the principle that government must never take race into account, even if the goal is to redress racial injustice.[55]

combat emplacement evacuator. A U.S. Army term for shovel.[56]

comfort station. A public toilet.[57]

Committee for Prudent Deregulation. A group formed by Hollywood studios, independent producers, and non-network television stations to lobby against the deregulation of television broadcasting.[58]

"Common sense tells us that . . ." As author and philosopher

Robert Todd Carroll explains, this phrase relieves the speaker of the responsibility for offering facts to support any assertion he or she is about to make. "Who would dare . . . contradict common sense?" Carroll asks.[59] [See also: **"As everyone knows . . ."**]

companionator. Pimp. The term became popular after Nero Padilla, an escort-service proprietor played by Jimmy Smits on TV's *The Sons of Anarchy*, used it to describe his profession.[60] [See also: **business manager.**]

compassion zone. A term first used in Kansas City to describe a location to which homeless persons could be forcibly transferred after a citywide roundup.[61] [See also: **compassionate disruption.**]

compassionate conservatism. A term popularized by historian Doug Wead in his 1977 book *The Compassionate Touch* and embraced—with demonstrable success—by George W. Bush during his initial campaign for the presidency in 2000. University of California linguist Geoffrey Nunberg defines it as "paying lip service where lip service is due."[62]

compassionate disruption. A term used by Honolulu mayor Kirk Caldwell to describe a program under which homeless persons are expelled from the parks and streets of the tourist zone of Waikiki and their personal belongings are seized.[63] [See also: **compassion zone.**]

compliance assistance officers. The U.S. Environmental Protection Agency's term for its enforcement personnel.[64]

compulsive self-medication. Drug addiction.[65] [See also: **chemical dependency; substance abuse.**]

concatenation. An art critic's term that means, basically, "a bunch of things linked together."[66] [See also: **International Art English.**]

concentration deficit disorder (CDD). See: **sluggish cognitive tempo (SCT).**

condition. A term recommended as a substitute for "problem" in a 2008 company memo sent by management to General Motors employees instructing them to choose their words carefully when referring to any automotive defect or failure that "had potential safety implications." The memo also instructed employees to avoid using the words "defect," "failure," and "safety."[67]

confirmed bachelor. A traditional British euphemism for homosexual.[68]

conflated. A term employed by NBC News anchor Brian Williams to account for what he conceded was an embellished claim that he had come under fire during a helicopter ride in Iraq in 2003, when he was in fact riding in a different helicopter trailing safely some distance behind. In an on-air apology for what appeared to be a fabricated story, Williams explained that, over time, he had carelessly confused the two helicopters and combined them, in his accounts of the incident, into a single aircraft.[69]

conflict. A war that is deliberately not called a war because, if it were, the legal provisions of the Geneva Conventions would apply.[70]

confrontation management. Riot control.[71]

confused. Senile.[72]

conglobate. An art critic's term that means to make something into a ball.[73] [See also: **International Art English.**]

congregate care facility. Orphanage.[74] [See also: **group home.**]

Two police officers displaying their **confrontation management** skills during a 2012 anti-austerity demonstration in Madrid.

conscious uncoupling. A term for "divorce" coined by Los Angeles psychotherapist and relationship expert Katherine Woodward Thomas to help couples "turn breakup grief into personal breakthrough." The phrase gained international currency when Gwyneth Paltrow and her husband, Coldplay cofounder Chris Martin, used

Gwyneth Paltrow and Chris Martin, photographed while still **consciously coupled**.

it in a post on Paltrow's website, Goop, to characterize their impending breakup. Example: *One of Marcello Mastroianni's best-remembered roles was his portrayal of an at-risk Sicilian nobleman in* **Conscious Uncoupling** *Italian Style, familiar to Italian audiences as* **Disaccoppiamento Consapevole** *all'Italiana.*[75]

conservationist. A term political consultant Frank Luntz recommends that Republicans use instead of "environmentalist" when describing their green strategy. "Most people," Luntz explains, think environmentalists are "extremists" who indulge in "some pretty bizarre behavior . . . that turns off many voters."[76]

consolidating leadership. Laying off administrators; firing middle management executives.[77]

constabulary duties. As authors John Stauber and Sheldon Rampton point out, this phrase, coined by the neoconservative Project for the New American Century to describe the potential role of American forces in Iraq and elsewhere, constitutes "a vague way of transforming U.S. soldiers occupying foreign countries into friendly neighborhood cops."[78]

consultant. Recruiter Michael Spiro suggests this is a good answer to give if you're unemployed and someone asks you what you do for a living.[79] [See also: **freelancer.**]

consumer sciences. The college-level course that used to be called "home economics."[80]

content curation. Tom Chatfield, author of *Netymology*, offers this phrase as a more dignified alternative to "stringing together a few images from Flickr."[81]

content strategist. An editor, copywriter, or editorial assistant.[82]

contingency workforce. Employees hired on a short-term basis without benefits or job security.[83]

contingent operating difficulty. A major corporate screwup.[84]

"continues in the proud tradition of J.R.R. Tolkien." Author Jason Pinter observes that this phrase, when encountered on a book jacket or cover, promises nothing more than "This book has a dwarf in it."[85]

contractor. See: **civilian contractor**; **security contractor**.

contrast ad. A negative political ad made by *your* side.[86]

controlled access entry. A real-estate term used to call attention to the presence in an apartment building of a lockable front door that someone who doesn't possess a key (or, as Visual Thesaurus columnist Mark Peters calls it, a **"controlled access entry module"**) can't open.[87]

controlled flight into terrain. A U.S. National Transportation Safety Board term for an airplane crash.[88] [See also: **failure to maintain clearance from the ground.**]

Controlled flight into terrain.

controversial. An objective-sounding adjective that, as essayist John Leo points out, is ideal for describing "someone or something the writer finds appalling." Example: *Adolf Hitler will be remembered for, among other things, his* **controversial** *racial policies.*[89]

convenience fee. A surcharge, typically for the "privilege" of paying for an item with a credit card or ordering something over the phone.[90]

"conversation with the British people." A phrase frequently used by the Blair government to invoke what journalist Patrick Cockburn of *The Independent* calls "a phoney sense of participation" in policy decisions that had already been made.[91]

convivial. Habitually drunk, or when used to describe an occasion, overflowing with alcohol. The term was a mainstay of the obituaries written by the acknowledged master of the form, Hugh Massingberd of London's *Daily Telegraph.*[92]

COPE. See: **Citizens for Objective Public Education.**

cordless rechargeable power plaque removers. What Conair calls its Interplak brand of electric toothbrushes, which, the company proudly points out, feature "two brush heads with patent-pending technology."[93] [See also: **home plaque removal instrument.**]

core rearrangement. A nuclear power industry term for the explosive destruction of the core of a nuclear reactor.[94] [See also: **above critical; super-prompt critical power excursion.**]

A reactor building at Chernobyl, April 26, 1986, showing the side effects of a **core rearrangement** event.

Cornish sardine. A fashionable new name for the pilchard, a humble

British fish that, until it was rechristened by fish merchant Nick Howell, was, according to *The Independent*, known principally for being "the dowdy, tinned meal-of-last-resort of impoverished students." The rebranding has led to skyrocketing sales, *The Independent* reports, and the Cornish sardine is now "the darling of British fish counters."[95]

corporate welfare. A term for government policies that favor big business, popularized by those who oppose them.[96]

correction. A drop in the stock market.[97]

correction officer. A prison guard.[98]

correctional facility. Jail.[99]

cosmetorium. Beauty shop.[100]

cost certainty. National Hockey League commissioner Gary Bettman's term for the league-wide salary cap on hockey teams that NHL owners sought to implement at the start of the 2004–2005 season. (Why not call it a "salary cap"? Because salary caps are illegal under U.S. antitrust laws unless labor and management collectively agree to them, that's why.)[101]

cost containment. The reduction of expenditures (by firing or laying off employees, for example).[102]

cost sharing. Making employees pay more for medical insurance, for instance.[103]

coterminous stakeholder engagement. Talking to people. The term was coined by town council officials in the United Kingdom to encourage government employees to converse with the citizenry.[104]

A happiness hero displaying his **coterminous stakeholder engagement** skills.

counseling. A corporate term for administering a warning or tongue-lashing to an employee.[105]

counterfactual proposition. A lie. Example: *One of Sarah's favorite films was* Sex, **Counterfactual Propositions,** *and* Videotape.[106]

courage. Paul Dickson and Robert Skole, authors of *Journalese: A Dictionary for Deciphering the News*, define this as a "universal attribute of people with problems who have not attempted suicide." As an example of such usage, they offer the following: *"Despite a failed face-lift and bust enhancement, and the onset of middle age, she mustered the* **courage** *to continue her career as a belly dancer."*[107]

courtesy call. An unsolicited phone call from a telemarketer.[108]

courtesy disconnect. The Internal Revenue Service's taxpayer help line is programmed to hang up automatically on callers if their wait time to speak to an agent is likely to exceed thirty minutes. The IRS refers to these involuntary call terminations, which number in the millions each year, as "courtesy disconnects."[109] Example: *When Herb tried to call Alice to apologize, she* **courtesy** *disconnected him in a huff.*

courtesy overdraft protection fee. A bank fee for bouncing a check.[110]

covert activity. Spying.[111]

cozy. A real-estate advertising term meaning "tiny" or, according to Minnesota realtor Ross Kaplan, "possibly claustrophobic."[112] [See also: **intimate**.]

A **cozy** faux log cabin currently occupied by a dog.

crap-and-trade. See: **cap-and-tax.**

creating a fiction. A phrase used by Mark Sanford, the married governor of South Carolina, to explain what he was doing (as opposed to lying) when he informed his

staff that he was taking a few days off to "hike the Appalachian Trail" instead of telling them the truth—that he was
heading off to Argentina to visit his mistress.[113]

creation science. The biblical explanation of human evolution
through "intelligent design," based on Christian religious
texts rather than on any scientific theory or data.[114]

creative accounting. Tax evasion.[115]

credibility assessment. A Department of Defense Polygraph
Institute term for using a lie detector on a suspect.[116]

crew member. Low-level, underpaid McDonald's worker with few
or no benefits.[117]

crew transfer containers. A term used by NASA in the days following the *Challenger* incident to refer to the coffins that held
the remains of the three dead astronauts.[118]

Critical Incident Stress Management Group. The Pentagon's
name for the mental health team assigned to treat military
mortuary workers at Dover Air Force Base in Delaware, the
principal processing facility for the bodies of American soldiers killed during the Iraq War.[119]

critically acclaimed. A publishing copywriter's phrase handy for
pitching books with extremely disappointing sales.[120]

"Critics say . . ." An all-purpose introductory phrase used by
journalists to ascribe a purely personal opinion or belief to
unnamed sources.[121]

crop dusting. According to David Sedaris, "crop dusting" is what
flight attendants call the practice of dealing with belligerent
passengers by farting in their direction while walking down
the aisle.[122]

culturally deprived environment. A slum.[123]

culturally disadvantaged. A term for "poor" that's even more euphemistic than **disadvantaged** without the qualifying adverb. As *The Wall Street Journal*'s Grace Hechinger has written, "Poor children have disappeared, if not from the slums, then at least from the language. First, they became 'deprived,' then 'disadvantaged,' and finally 'culturally disadvantaged,' as though they lacked nothing more serious than a free pass to Lincoln Center."[124]

curb appeal. A real-estate term that, according to agent Kate Cocuzzo, means that the inside of the building being advertised is "a nightmare."[125]

curiosity delays. Traffic jams caused by rubbernecking.[126]

curvy. Fat.[127]

customer assistance account manager. A title used by the MBNA Bank (since merged into the Bank of America) to describe its debt collection agents.[128]

customer solution specialists. What the TechSmith Corporation calls its salespeople.[129]

d

dairy nutrients. Cow manure. Example: *Where were you when the* **dairy nutrients** *hit the high-velocity multipurpose air circulation device?*[1] [See also: **biosolids**; **organic biomass**.]

"damp basement in the spring." A real-estate advertising phrase that Luke Mullins of *U.S. News & World Report* defines as "prone to frequent flooding."[2]

data collection. Surveillance.[3]

data storage specialist. A filing clerk.[4]

deacquisition. A more genteel term for "sell," favored by museums and art collectors who elect to consign items from their collections to the auction block.[5]

dead checking. A colloquial term used by U.S. military personnel during the Iraq War to describe the practice of killing any wounded men they found alive after an attack on a suspected insurgent household.[6]

dead tree edition. An environmentally sensitive term for the paper version of a publication that can be found online.[7]

death panels. Government tribunals, which former U.S. vice presidential candidate Sarah Palin claimed were mandated by President Barack Obama's Affordable Care Act, that would decide whether sick and elderly individuals were entitled to continued health care services. "The America I know and love," Palin wrote on her Facebook page in 2009, "is not one in which my parents or my baby with Down Syndrome will have to stand in front of Obama's 'death panel' so his bureaucrats can decide, based on a subjective judgment of their 'level of productivity in society,' whether they are worthy of health care. Such a system is downright evil." One problem with Palin's assertion, which fanned a firestorm of opposition to Obama's proposed legislation, is that it was utterly false: There was, and is, no provision in the Affordable Care Act which suggests the formation of such panels. Indeed, Palin's statement earned her PolitiFact's coveted Lie of the Year award.[8]

death squads. Rush Limbaugh's term for Planned Parenthood and NARAL Pro-Choice America.[9]

death tax. A "usefully derisive" new name invented by Jim Martin, president of the **60 Plus Association,** for what was once more commonly called the "estate tax" or the "inheritance tax." Ever since polls conducted by political strategist Frank Luntz demonstrated that the phrase "death tax" stirs up far more voter resentment than either "estate tax" or "inheritance tax," Republicans campaigning for abolition of the tax have been using Martin's coinage whenever the opportunity presents itself.[10] [See also: **"taxation without respiration"; wealth tax.**]

death with dignity. Assisted suicide; euthanasia.[11]

decapitation strike. Bombing a location where enemy leaders are believed to be hiding.[12]

deceptionist. An office receptionist trained to discourage potential visitors.[13]

decommissioned aggressor quantum. Pentagon terminology for the number of enemy troops killed in a bombing attack.[14]

decruit. To fire a senior employee.[15]

dedicated fan base. Novelist Mat Johnson explains that this phrase, when used in a publisher's sales pitch, means "the author's spouse and mother."[16]

deferred maintenance. Failure to paint, clean, or perform minor repairs on a building, machine, or vehicle. Example: *The structural integrity of the Parthenon has been disenhanced by over 2,400 years of* **deferred maintenance.**[17]

The Parthenon, after nearly two and a half millennia of **deferred maintenance**.

deferred success. A term useful for describing a project that is currently (and most likely will remain) a failure. Example: *The War on Drugs, initiated by*

Richard Nixon in 1971 and still going strong, is one of the landmark **deferred successes** *of U.S. global policy.*[18]

deficit enhancement. Loss.[19]

deficit water situation. Drought. Example: *John Steinbeck's classic novel* The Grapes of Considerable Indignation *describes the great migration triggered by the* **deficit water situation** *in Oklahoma in the 1930s.*[20]

degrade. To severely damage or destroy something. (U.S. Department of Defense terminology used in describing bombing runs.) Example: *"I didn't total your car, I merely* **degraded** *it."*[21]

degrew. What a corporate analyst at India's Religare Enterprises said United Spirits Limited's profits had done when they dropped by 23.3 percent.[22]

dehire. Fire.[23]

deinstall. Fire; lay off.[24]

delayering. Firing middle managers.[25]

de-lifed. A term for "killed" found in the logs of the Arcata, California, police department. Example: *Davy Crockett* **de-lifed** *a bear when he was only three.*[26]

delivery experience specialists. What auto maker Tesla calls its salespeople.[27]

deltiologist. "Artspeak" for someone who collects picture postcards.[28]

demising human capital. What bankers at HSBC announced they were doing when they fired 942 "relationship managers."[29]

dependency. Addiction.[30]

depopulation. A term used by the U.S. government to describe the mass euthanasia of seven million chickens in Pennsylvania in 1983, in an effort to help contain an outbreak of influenza.[31]

deprived. See: **culturally disadvantaged.**

descope. To narrow the goals or scope of a project, frequently so one can declare it successful without having to complete the original mission.[32]

deselect. To fire or lay off an employee.[33]

destaff process. The Fairfax County, Virginia, Public Schools issued a press release in January 2014 defining this as the methodology "being used to determine which positions to eliminate" from its employee rolls during what they identified as a "sensitive budget year." "Looking ahead," they announced hopefully, "the goal is to maximize the use of the destaff process."[34]

destination counselor. Travel agent.[35]

"destruction of property." The crime that four Ferguson, Missouri, police officers charged Henry Davis with in 2009 after they mistakenly apprehended him (they apparently thought he was *another* Henry Davis) and then beat him to the point where his blood spattered messily all over their nice clean uniforms.[36]

detailed. Verbose; rambling; containing more words than necessary.[37]

detainee. A prisoner of war—especially one who, at least according to George W. Bush administration lawyers John C. Yoo and James C. Ho, is not entitled to the protections offered "prisoners of war" under the terms of the Third Geneva Convention.[38]

detention center. Prison; prison camp.[39] [See also: **correctional facility.**]

deterrent, nuclear. See: **nuclear deterrent.**

developing nations. Poor nations. As *The Economist* has pointed out, such nations are often stagnating, or even regressing.[40]

diagnostic misadventure of high magnitude. A medical term for
the accidental death of a hospital patient caused by malpractice during the examination process. (An accidental death that
occurs during the treatment itself is called a **therapeutic
misadventure.**)[41]

"did not suffer fools gladly." A phrase popularized by the London
Daily Telegraph's legendary obituary editor, Hugh Massingberd, that, loosely translated, means "[was] monstrously foul-
tempered."[42]

differentiated beings of startling variety and complexity. A
term to replace "animals," coined by the editors of the recently
founded *Journal of Animal Ethics*, on the grounds that "the
odd notion that animals are only a species and not individuals
should not be perpetuated in our language. Even 'animals' is
itself a term of abuse (which hides the reality of what it pur-
ports to describe, namely a range of differentiated beings of
startling variety and complexity)." However, as *St. Louis Post-
Dispatch* columnist Kevin Horrigan has pointed out, the editors'
distaste for the word "animal" was not strong enough to per-
suade them to strike it from the title of their new magazine. Why?
Perhaps they felt *"Journal of a Range of Differentiated Beings
of Startling Variety and Complexity Ethics* would be a lousy
name," Horrigan surmises. Example: *Anthony's favorite Nine
Inch Nails song was the one that goes, "I want to fuck you like
a* **differentiated being of startling variety and complexity.**"[43]

difficulties. A handy euphemism for "scandal."[44]

digital fever computer. Medical thermometer.[45]

direct flight. A non-nonstop flight. The term is used by United
Airlines (among others) to refer to flights that stop at least
once en route to their final destination but during which the

same flight number is retained from start to finish and passengers are never required to change aircraft at intermediate locations.[46]

direct mail. Junk mail.[47]

directionally accurate. Mostly, somewhat, or at least sort of correct.[48]

directive improvement. Discipline; punishment.[49]

Fyodor Dostoyevsky, author of the Russian literary masterpiece *Crime and **Directive Improvement**.*

director of first impressions. Receptionist.[50] [See also: **deceptionist; telephone intermediary; welcoming agent.**]

disadvantaged. Poor.[51] [See also: **culturally disadvantaged.**]

disambiguate. An impressive way of saying "clarify" that itself frequently needs clarification.[52]

A **director of first impressions**.

discount for using cash. A phrase used to disguise the fact that the firm or establishment offering it is actually charging folks *more* for the privilege of paying with a credit card. Such surcharges, often euphemized as **convenience fees**, are illegal in many states, but "discounts for using cash" typically are not.[53]

discriminate deterrence. A U.S. military term for "pinpoint bombing."[54]

discriminatory taxation. The Cato Institute's James A. Dorn's preferred term for the progressive income tax, which he claims should more correctly be called **tax socialism.** "Envy," he

argues, "not justice, is at the root of the argument for discriminatory taxation. . . . Under such a system, neither persons nor
property are safe from the hand of the state."[55]

discussing Uganda. Engaging in illicit sex, especially while carrying out one's official duties. The term was popularized by
the British satirical magazine *Private Eye*, which first used it
in a report about renowned Irish journalist Mary Kenny, who
had been "discovered" during a party "in the arms" of a former
Ugandan cabinet minister.[56]

discussion partner. Phone sex operator.[57]

disgruntled former employee. Any former staffer who generates
unfavorable publicity about you or your company.[58]

disposition matrix. A term coined by the Obama administration
to describe a sophisticated digitized "kill list" of suspected
terrorists targeted for drone strikes and other clandestine
"disposal" methods.[59]

disputed territories. A term that the Israeli government insists
should be used to describe the West Bank and other Egyptian,
Jordanian, and Syrian lands that its military captured during
the Six-Day War in 1967. Perhaps because the International
Court of Justice, and even Israel's own High Court of Justice,
have ruled that these zones are being held under "belligerent
occupation," the rest of the world more frequently uses the
terms "occupied territories," "occupied Palestinian territories," or "Israeli-occupied territories" when referring to these
regions. But the Israeli Ministry of Foreign Affairs strongly
objects. "Occupied territories are territories captured in war
from an established and recognized sovereign," the ministry
argues on its website. "As the West Bank and Gaza Strip were
not under the legitimate and recognized sovereignty of any

state prior to the Six-Day War, they should not be considered occupied territories."[60] [See also: **liberated territories.**]

disruptive mood dysregulation disorder (DMDD). If your child is sometimes irritable, or has a tendency to have temper tantrums, he or she could well be suffering from this newly identified mental condition, included for the first time in the 2013 update of the American Psychiatric Association's influential *Diagnostic and Statistical Manual of Mental Disorders (DSM).*[61]

distressed produce. Spoiled fruits and vegetables.[62]

diversity. Columnist Dave Barry offers the following definition: "Regardless of what color or hue of state we live in, we are all, deep down inside our undershorts, Americans. And as Americans, we must ask ourselves: Are we really so different? Must we stereotype those who disagree with us? Do we truly believe that *all* red-state residents are ignorant, racist, fascist, knuckle-dragging, NASCAR-obsessed, cousin-marrying, roadkill-eating, tobacco juice–dribbling, gun-fondling, religious-fanatic rednecks; or that *all* blue-state residents are godless, unpatriotic, pierced-nosed, Volvo-driving, France-loving, left-wing communist, latte-sucking, tofu-chomping, holistic-wacko, neurotic, vegan, weenie perverts? Yes. This is called 'diversity,' and it is why we are such a great nation—a nation that has given the world both nuclear weapons *and* SpongeBob SquarePants."[63] [See also: **elites; "tax-hiking, government-expanding, latte-drinking, sushi-eating, Volvo-driving,** *New York Times*–**reading, body-piercing, Hollywood-loving, left-wing freak show."**]

DMDD. See: **disruptive mood dysregulation disorder.**

"doctor portrayal" and "patient portrayal." Prescription-drug manufacturers typically include these text disclaimers in their TV and print ads to protect themselves against legal actions that might arise from their practice of showing actors dressed in physicians' white coats recommending their products to other actors playing sick, depressed, or happily cured patients.[64]

A data storage specialist implementing a **document management** policy.

document management. The now-no-longer-economically-viable Enron Corporation's term for shredding paper evidence.[65]

documenting weight loss. When several naked photographs of Robert Arango, a member of the Senate of Puerto Rico, turned up on a gay meet-up website in 2011, Arango didn't deny that he'd recently taken a series of pictures of himself without his clothes on. However, he claimed, he'd done so only to document the progress of a diet he'd been following. "Even as implausible as that explanation already seems," commented *New York* magazine's Dan Amira, "it becomes *even more implausible* when you consider that one of the photos is a direct shot of Arango's asshole."[66]

"does not provide medical advice." A legal disclaimer that appears in small type at the bottom of every page of WebMD, arguably the Internet's best-known provider of medical advice.[67]

domestic dispute. Common police terminology for a wife-battering incident.[68]

doubled eggs. See: **angeled eggs; sanctified eggs.**

down alternative blanket. Which would you be more likely to buy:

(a) a "down alternative blanket" or (b) a "polyester-filled blanket"? The marketers of polyester-filled blankets are betting the majority of customers will choose (a).[69]

downshifting into a platonic relationship. A phrase used by the British *Sunday Mirror* to describe what Hugh Grant and his girlfriend Elizabeth Hurley were "thinking about doing" after Grant was arrested for "indecent conduct with a prostitute" on Sunset Boulevard in Los Angeles.[70]

downshifting language. A phrase used by General Michael Hayden, the former director of the National Security Agency, during testimony before a congressional committee in 2006, to characterize his calculated substitution of the word "conversations" for the far more general term "communications" in order to obscure the true extent of the agency's warrantless domestic surveillance program.[71]

downsize. To lay off a significant percentage of one's employees.[72] [See also: **rightsize**.]

draconian. A political term used by politicians and journalists to describe some action, often involving budget cuts, with which they disagree.[73]

dried plums. Prunes.[74]

duality. A term used by artists and art critics to describe a painting or other work of contemporary art that has two colors or materials in it, or addresses two different subjects or themes at the same time, or depicts two objects, or, oh, whatever. "I think duality comes up when you don't know what else to say," observes painter Jason Brockert. "'I love it, your art is just so full of . . . duality!'"[75] [See also: **International Art English**.]

"duplicate of a paper that has already been published." Less judgmental terminology for a "plagiarized document." The phrase was used in a retraction notice published by the *International Journal of Cardiology*.[76]

dynamically address. A term for "kill" favored by members of Task Force ODIN, a U.S. Army unit set up during the Iraq War to "win back the roads" from insurgents using IEDs.[77]

e

early retirement opportunity. Dismissal.[1]

earned benefits. A term for "entitlements" coined by Democratic Party media strategists to emphasize the fact that Social Security and Medicare benefits have been paid for by recipients through deductions from their paychecks and are not "gifts" from the government.[2]

"easy access to everywhere." A real-estate advertising phrase roughly translatable as "backing up to an expressway."[3]

eccentric. Weird.[4]

eco-evangelical hysteria. Efforts to curtail global warming. Former House majority leader Dick Armey first unveiled this terminology in 2009 while testifying before a Republican bicameral hearing on climate change legislation.[5]

econometrics. According to *The Office Life*, consulting firms typically market econometric analysis as "a highly scientific

Eccentric Al Yankovic.

mathematical modeling exercise performed by economists and industry-specific experts." In practice, the blog points out, the actual work delivered involves little more than the routine entry of numbers into a standard Excel spreadsheet.[6]

economic freedom. A substitute for the more familiar label "capitalism" that political strategist Frank Luntz urges Republicans to use whenever they discuss the U.S. economic system. "The public . . . still prefers capitalism to socialism," says Luntz, "but they think capitalism is immoral. And if we're seen as defenders of quote, Wall Street, end quote, we've got a problem."[7]

economical with the truth. Prone to lying.[8]

economically depressed neighborhood. Slum.[9]

economically disadvantaged. Poor; destitute.[10]

economically inactive. No longer holding or seeking a job.[11]

economy size. A container of a product that costs more than the "regular size."[12]

ECU. An abbreviation for Eternal Care Unit, a euphemism for a hospital mortuary. Example: *After determining that Samantha had been the victim of an iatrogenic therapeutic misadventure, Dr. Jones ordered her transferred to the* **ECU.**[13]

education transport module. School bus.[14]

effecting modifications. A more impressive-sounding way of saying "making changes."[15]

"efficient" use of space. Severe overcrowding. The phrase was used in a "space utilization plan" issued by Chicago Public Schools in December 2011 that designated school buildings with thirty-six students per "allotted homeroom" as "well-utilized." By contrast, buildings with under twenty-four kids per classroom, no matter

An **education transport module.**

how educationally successful, were classified as "under-
utilized," a first step toward their being targeted for closing by
Chicago mayor Rahm Emanuel.[16]

EITs. An abbreviation for **"enhanced interrogation techniques,"**
introduced by Central Intelligence Agency director John Brennan during a December 2014 press conference. Brennan apparently felt that the fully spelled-out version of the term was not
euphemistic enough to help him rebut charges, detailed in a
Senate Intelligence Committee report, that, between 2002 and
2007, CIA operatives had routinely tortured detainees it suspected might have links to al-Qaeda.[17]

electronic intercepts. Eavesdropping.[18]

eliminate redundancies in the human resources area. Lay off
or fire employees.[19]

eliminating a tax decrease. Then Speaker of the House Nancy
Pelosi's phrase for the tax increase that would result from
allowing the Bush tax cuts to expire.[20]

elites. People defined by former Reagan administration official
and Fox News commentator Linda Chavez as "learned souls"
who "maybe should spend less time at Starbucks sipping double-
lattes over the Sunday *Times* and more time at church or the
local high school football game or in line at a Wal-Mart. They
might actually learn something about the values that drive
most Americans." Such uses of the word "elites," comments linguist Geoffrey Nunberg, transfer suspicion "from the genuinely
powerful to the people who used to be regarded merely as their
clerks and factotums, and in the process suppresses real dispar-
ities of wealth and power. There are only the people who shop at
Wal-Mart and the people who don't, with the people who own
the operation presumably away for the weekend."[21] [See also:

diversity; "tax-hiking, government-expanding, latte-drinking, sushi-eating, Volvo-driving, *New York Times*–reading, body-piercing, Hollywood-loving, left-wing freak show."]

elitist. An adjective used by Fox News and other politically conservative media outlets and members of the Republican Party to describe any liberal or progressive politicians or public figures who, somewhat counterintuitively, support government programs that benefit economically and socially non-elite groups.[22]

embarking on a journey of self-discovery. Unemployed.[23]

emblematic. A term used by the Koch brothers' political action group, Americans for Prosperity, to characterize campaign ads that professed to show Louisiana residents receiving notices telling them their health insurance had been canceled because of Obamacare, when in reality the "residents" were portrayed by paid actors and the scenes they were featured in were not based on actual events.[24]

embryo reduction. The abortion of one or more fetuses in a multiple gestation pregnancy.[25]

emergency exit lights. A Pentagon term for "flashlights" that proved extremely helpful when the U.S. Air Force had to justify paying $214 apiece for them back in July 1985. "We're not going to put good American boys out there with things that can only run on the streets of New York," Lieutenant General Leo Marquez, the USAF's deputy chief of staff for logistics and engineering, explained.[26]

emerging. A term used in Nevada's Clark County School District (Las Vegas) to replace the word "failing" on student report cards. In other words, students who formerly would have received F or D grades are now labeled "emerging."[27]

emotionally disturbed person (EDP). A more sensitive New York City Police Department term for an individual who used to be referred to as a "psycho."[28]

Janet Leigh in the unforgettable "shower scene" from Alfred Hitchcock's classic horror film *Emotionally Disturbed Person.*

en plein air. An impressive French art term signifying nothing more, and nothing less, than that the painting being referred to was "done outside." What's the point? "Imagine two identical paintings side by side and one was labeled '*En Plein Air*' and one was labeled 'Done Outside,'" explains artist Jason Brockert. "Which one would you buy?"[29] [See also: **International Art English.**]

encore presentation. A term used by TV broadcasters to describe a rerun.[30]

enemy combatants. What the George W. Bush administration decided to call Guantánamo detainees so they could be denied the legal protections afforded "prisoners of war" under the Geneva Conventions. In 2010, after the Obama administration had announced it was going to stop using this term, syndicated columnist Mona Charen volunteered a new one: **"former clients of Obama Justice Department lawyers."**[31] [See also: **unprivileged enemy belligerent.**]

energetic disassembly. An explosion, especially an accidental one. Example: *The* **energetic disassembly** *of the zeppelin* Hindenburg *has left plans for lighter-than-air passenger*

The **energetic disassembly** of the *Hindenburg*, 1937.

travel in the early stages of finalization for over three-quarters of a century.[32]

energized fence. A fence designed to electrocute—or at least provide an "unsafe" electric shock—to any person or animal who attempts to cross it.[33]

energy exploration. Drilling for oil or using hydrofracturing techniques to extract natural gas.[34]

engaging the enemy on all sides. A U.S. Department of Defense phrase for getting ambushed, or surrounded, by hostile forces.[35]

English Plus. An upbeat term for "bilingual education," coined by the Spanish American League Against Discrimination (SALAD) in response to the "English Only" movement, which seeks, among other things, to prevent U.S. schools from presenting academic content to non–English speaking children in their native languages as well as in English.[36]

enhanced interrogation techniques. Torture.[37] [See also: **EITs; pain compliance techniques; repetitive administration of legitimate force; special methods of questioning; stress and duress tactics.**]

enhanced light truck. Since sport utility vehicles have come under attack for being gas-guzzlers, a growing number of environmentally aware folks who are embarrassed they drive them—not to mention the car companies that market to them—have started using this term as a substitute for "SUV."[38]

enhanced radiation weapon. A U.S. Department of Defense term for the neutron bomb.[39]

enhanced screening procedures. The Transportation Security Agency's name for new airport security measures it implemented in 2010 that, at many airports, required passengers either to pass though "back-scatter scanners" with the ability to X-ray you through your clothes or to be subjected to a full-body pat down. Lexicographer Erin McKean calls the TSA's new terminology "aggressively bland," and points out that travelers have been far less timid than the agency in providing names for both the scanners (**nude-o-scopes** and **strip-search machines**, for example) and the body pats (**gate rape** and **freedom fondles** are two of the more creative suggestions).[40]

enhanced underwriting acknowledgments. The official name for the advertising spots that, if they were actually *called* "advertising spots," the Federal Communications Commission would prohibit public radio and television stations to run.[41]

"enhancing the customer experience." How Gerrit Zalm, chairman of the Dutch bank ABN Amro, characterized his firm's plan to sack 650 to 1,000 retail banking employees. How would the wholesale elimination of personal service representatives "enhance the customer experience"? By "accelerat[ing] end-to-end digitisation of the key customer processes," that's how.[42]

"enjoy sun showers, and spectacular scenery." If you run across a real-estate advertising pitch like this one, excerpted from an ad for a cabin in the Montana woods, you can be pretty certain there's no bathroom inside the house. (The line "non-potable water available to subdivision," later in the ad, might have been a giveaway, too.)[43]

entertainment options. What fertility clinics call the items they offer to men to help them along with the sperm donation process.[44]

entitlement reform. A Republican term for what Democrats more commonly refer to as "gutting Social Security, Medicare, and Medicaid."[45]

entitlement society. Fox News commentator Bill O'Reilly's term for the people who rely upon government programs that provide health care, unemployment insurance, and food stamps. Those who don't, O'Reilly says, are part of the "self-reliant society."[46]

entrance solutions. Doors. A company called Record UK Limited came up with this imaginative term to describe the products it manufactures and markets. Example: *Angela's favorite song is "Facilitate My Rapid Oxidation,"* recorded by the **Entrance Solutions** *in 1966.*

environmental hypochondriac. Anyone, according to former Republican House majority leader Dick Armey, who believes that global warming is actually occurring.[47]

epic. An adjective frequently used by publishing houses to market books that are too long.[48] [See also: **extraordinary breadth; multilayered.**]

equity retreat. Stock market crash. Example: *After the Great* **Equity Retreat** *of 1929, a number of investment professionals took advantage of career change opportunities to reposition themselves in the apple marketing field.*[49]

erectile dysfunction disorder. Impotence.[50]

erotic film. A pornographic movie.[51]

escort. Prostitute.[52]

escort from the premises. Kick out.[53]

Eternal Care Unit. See: **ECU.**

ethical oil. A term coined by the Alberta tar sands bitumen refining industry to distinguish its environmentally devastating petroleum product from the "conflict oil" produced in unstable countries like Venezuela and Nigeria and in restive states of the Middle East.[54]

ethical positionality. A phrase useful for implying that anyone outside your immediate circle or group cannot possibly be objective enough to pass judgment on you. For example, Reem Fadda, an associate at the Guggenheim Abu Dhabi, employed the term to dismiss growing international condemnation of human rights violations in the treatment of laborers building the museum. Such criticism, she proclaimed, represented an unacceptable form of neo-colonial bias directed at the United Arab Emirates by "non-native" activists.[55]

ethics reform. This is a term that *sounds* wholesome and moralistic but has the subtle advantage of not actually specifying whether the reforms in question are making it harder or easier to get away with inappropriate behavior. Consider the following news item, which appeared in the *Los Angeles Times* on June 18, 1991: "Until recently it was illegal for top administration officials to accept free travel from American corporations. But the law was changed to permit such trips . . . as part of the so-called Ethics Reform Act, enacted in late 1989."[56]

ethnic cleansing. Genocide.[57]

"ethnic jokes as a teaching tool" defense, the. When Ronald Reagan was chastised, while campaigning in New Hampshire in 1980, for telling an "insensitive" joke about a Pole, an Italian, and a duck, he explained that his only purpose had been to provide his audience with an example of the kind of ethnic humor that people (and, presumably, ducks) find offensive.[58]

evaporated cane juice. A term for "sugar" employed by food manufacturers to downplay the use of sugar in their products.[59]

Former welterweight and middleweight boxing champion **Evaporated Cane Juice** Ray Robinson.

eviction technician. Bouncer.[60]

evidentiary deficiency. Lack of evidence.[61]

evidently. See: **apparently.**

exceed the odor threshold. Stink.[62]

excessed. A term used by the New York City Department of Education to describe a schoolteacher who is not technically fired but rather dismissed from his or her position because of a lack of resources.[63]

executary. A *very* important (or at least important-sounding) secretary.[64]

executive action. A CIA term defined by lexicographer Hugh Rawson as "getting rid of people, especially the leaders of foreign countries, and especially by murder."[65]

An **executary** demonstrating how the involuntary sanitation of an audio recording might have occurred.

executive assistant. Secretary.[66] [See also: **administrative professional; area associate; office manager.**]

exfiltration. A British term for "retreat" that columnist John Leo noted, "is not a great euphemism, but sounds lots better than 'running away.'" Example: *Napoleon's* **exfiltration** *from Moscow in 1812 resulted in 380,000 of his troops becoming nonoperative.*[67] [See also: **redeploying to the rear; strategic withdrawal.**]

exotic dancer. Stripper.[68]

expectants. A Vietnam-era U.S. military term for casualties who were expected to die.[69]

expediting fee. Bribe.[70] [See also: after-sales service fees; facilitation payment; fee for product testing; rebate.]

expense base management. What Merck claimed it was engaging in when it laid off thirteen thousand U.S. employees in 2011.[71]

experiencability. A term used by critics to discuss the capacity of any work of art to be experienced (by being looked at, for example).[72] [See also: International Art English.]

experienced. Old.[73]

expression lines. Wrinkles.[74] [See also: character lines; laugh lines; maturity tracks.]

"exquisite egg pasta." A phrase prominently displayed by Stouffer's on packages of its Veal Tortellini with Tomato Sauce that touts what was referred to in the product's list of ingredients as "cooked noodle product."[75]

ex-resource. A species that has been hunted or fished to extinction. The term was coined by The Guardian's resident language expert, Steven Poole.[76] [See also: natural resources.]

extended. A more politic adjective than "overvalued" to describe a stock that investment analysts feel is priced too high to buy.[77]

extraordinary breadth. A publishing copywriter's phrase that, according to literary agent Jonny Geller, is invaluable for describing books with too many scenes.[78] [See also: epic; multilayered.]

extraordinary rendition. The official U.S. government term for the "extra-judicial" exportation of untried terrorism suspects to foreign countries, especially ones that practice torture, for imprisonment and "enhanced interrogation."[79] [See also: **rendition.**]

extremely vivid nighttime hallucination. Nightmare.[80]

extroverted. Loud.[81]

New Line Cinema is rumored to be freshening up its thirty-year-old Freddy Krueger film franchise with a cutting-edge new sequel, *An **Extremely Vivid Nighttime Hallucination*** *on Elm Street.*

façade protectant. Paint.[1]

facilitation payment. A bribe.[2] [See also: **after-sales service fees; expediting fee; fee for product testing; rebate.**]

facilitator of learning. See: **learning facilitator.**

facility fees. Unspecified generic charges routinely added to medical bills issued by hospital-owned outpatient centers and physician practices that are often much higher than the fee charged by the actual doctor who provides services to the patient.[3]

fact-finding trip. Author William Lambdin defines this as "a mission during which a congressman discovers firsthand the alcoholic content of drinks made in foreign countries."[4]

factual shortcuts. A term for "lies," used by Cal Woodward and
Jack Gillum of the Associated Press in their coverage of Paul
Ryan's speech accepting the Republican nomination for vice
president during the party's 2012 convention.[5]

fail to fulfill one's wellness potential. To die, especially when
under the care of a physician or hospital. (Of course, one can
fail to fulfill *other* potentials, too, like one's career potential,
or one's empathy potential.) Example: *The scheduling difficulties at VA hospitals resulted in a significant number of veterans'* failing to fulfill their wellness potentials.[6]

failure to maintain clearance from the ground. A U.S. National
Transportation Safety Board term for an airplane crash.[7] [See
also: **controlled flight into terrain.**]

**"failure to use quotation marks around material written ver-
batim from another source."** Plagiarism. The editors of *Polyvocia*, a journal published by the School of Oriental and
African Studies at the University of London, used this terminology to explain why an article about apartheid they had
published in a previous issue had been retracted.[8]

"fair and balanced." Fox News Channel's slogan, celebrating the
broad spectrum of divergent political views presented over
the years by such Fox commentators and contributors as Bill
O'Reilly, Glenn Beck, and Mike Huckabee on the one hand, and
Sean Hannity, Karl Rove, and Sarah Palin on the other.[9]

fair trade. A term used to describe a system of collusion between
manufacturing companies and the distributors and retailers
who carry their products to fix prices at an artificially high
level. As lexicographer Hugh Rawson points out, the term "fair
trade" implies "exactly the opposite of its actual meaning"—it
is not fair to consumers, and it involves restraint of trade.[10]

fairy dusting. See: **angel dusting.**

fallen hero. Any American soldier who died while on duty.[11]

family protection consultant. Insurance salesperson.[12]

family responsibility days. What Rosenbluth International, a Philadelphia travel company (since sold to American Express), called the sick days it granted to its employees.[13]

family values. Politically conservative code words for opposition to abortion, same-sex marriage, and gender equality.[14]

fanaticism. What enemy troops display when they storm a well-armed position. When *our* troops storm a well-armed position, they display **bravery**.[15]

fastening device impact driver. Hammer. Example: *One of Judith's fondest memories was hearing Pete Seeger sing, "If I had a* **fastening device impact driver,** *I'd employ that* **fastening device impact driver** *in the morning, I'd employ that* **fastening device impact driver** *in the evening, all over this land."*[16]

A **fastening device impact driver.**

fattractive. A more positive term for "fat," popularized by, among others, blogger Athena MacFarland.[17]

Faulkneresque. A book-jacket copywriters' term that, as novelist Arthur Phillips points out, can be used to tout any author who tends to use long sentences.[18] [See also: **Hemingwayesque**.]

The legendary rhythm-and-blues pianist, singer, and songwriter Antoine **"Fattractives"** Domino.

faux. A term to use instead of "fake," to de-emphasize the fakery. "Faux mahogany" is probably plywood.[19]

fear of becoming a statistic. The explanation given by anti–gay rights Florida state representative Bob Allen for why he agreed to pay twenty dollars for the privilege of performing fellatio on a man who turned out to be an undercover policeman. The cop was a "pretty stocky black guy, and there was nothing but other black guys around in the park," Allen said, and he was terrified that he "was about to be a statistic." "Apparently," notes *New York* magazine's Dan Amira, "being a horrible racist is way better than being gay."[20]

feature. A term used for decades in the computer industry to characterize a software malfunction or peculiarity that users typically refer to as a "problem." Also called an **undocumented feature.**

federal family. A self-referential term favored by U.S. government officials who realize how unpopular U.S. government officials have become. After Homeland Security Secretary Janet Napolitano announced, in August 2011, that the "entire Federal Family" was "working as one" to protect affected states from the ravages of Hurricane Irene, the Fox News Channel's Ed Henry tweeted, "FEMA is like an uncle to me."[21]

fee for product testing. A bribe or kickback.[22]

feels like. A phrase frequently employed by advertisers to imply that their product is comparable to something infinitely better. Former marketing executive Gordon Pritchard offers the following example of this usage: *"This fabric* **feels like** *the finest silk."* To counter "feels like," he suggests that you remind yourself that it may feel like the finest silk—"but it isn't."[23]

female sexual interest/arousal disorder. Frigidity.[24] [See also: **hypoactive sexual desire disorder (HSDD).**]

feminazi. An active and committed feminist. The term was popularized by talk radio show host Rush Limbaugh, who gives credit for its coinage to his "good friend" Tom Hazlett, a former economics professor at the University of California, Davis, who now teaches at George Mason University.[25]

festival marketplace. A shopping mall, especially one designed to attract tourists.[26] [See also: **lifestyle center.**]

festival seating. No seats at all. Holders of "festival seating" tickets are invited to bring a blanket, find an open area, and hope for the best. As the late writer and language expert Hugh Rawson has noted, "It was holders of festival seating tickets who stampeded while trying to get into a rock concert in Cincinnati, Ohio, in 1979, killing 11 people and injuring at least eight more."[27]

"Fewer people will be wearing more hats." A convenient phrase to use instead of "We're laying off a bunch of employees."[28]

fewer than. A phrase that's extremely useful when you're trying to downplay a number. Instead of saying "65 percent of the people agreed," for example, say "fewer than two out of three people agreed."[29] [See also: **less than.**]

fiancée. According to the conservative blogger Andrew K. Dart, "fiancée" is "libspeak" for "this month's roommate."[30]

fictitious disorder syndrome sufferer. Liar.[31]

"filled with natural light." A real-estate advertising phrase meaning "not totally windowless."[32]

financial engineering. Accounting fraud.[33]

First Nations summer. A more culturally sensitive term for "Indian summer."[34]

fiscal responsibility. The website DemocraticUnderground.com defines this as "the systematic destruction of social programs such as education, research, healthcare, social security, disability, welfare, etc."[35]

fixer-upper. A real-estate advertising term for a property that might more accurately be described as a "tearer-downer."[36]

fixing Medicare. Cutting health care benefits for the elderly.[37]

flashlight therapy. See: **aluminum shampoo.**

Superstorm Sandy left a significant number of **fixer-uppers** along the Jersey shore.

fleeing a thieving police state. Libertarian News's preferred term for American companies' increasingly frequent practice of relocating their headquarters offshore to avoid having to pay U.S. corporate income taxes.[38] [See also: **inversion.**]

flog. A fake blog, created surreptitiously by a corporation or other organization in order to promote a product or a point of view.[39] [See also: **astroturf organization.**]

floral tribute. Flowers sent to a funeral home.[40]

flotation device. Life preserver. The term was created by the airline industry to help you forget that your life, while it's in their hands, might actually need preserving.[41]

A **flotation device.**

focus-free. A marketing term used to cajole potential camera purchasers into believing that nonadjustable lenses are a benefit rather than a drawback. As advertising copywriter Randy Parker points out, focus-free lenses result "in many pictures that really aren't in focus."[42]

focused obstruction. The translation of a term used by the Israeli military for targeted killings of Hamas operatives in Gaza.[43]

food. A code word used by baseball player Alex Rodriguez and his drug supplier, Anthony P. Bosch, to describe any banned performance-enhancing substance.[44] [See also: **gummies**; **liquid soap**; **pink cream**; **rocket.**]

food insecurity. Hunger. Example: *Suzanne Collins's 2008 science fiction novel* The **Food Insecurity** Games *spawned a huge multimedia franchise.*[45]

"for fans of [insert bestselling author name]." Crime Writers' Association judge Rhian Davis decodes this frequently encountered publishing advertising copy line as "Normally eat smoked salmon? Try some tinned."[46]

for your convenience. For *our* convenience. Example: **For your convenience,** *please wait outside in the pouring rain until our employees conclude their lunch break.*[47]

force cups. What the U.S. Army, among others, calls toilet plungers.[48]

force package. One or more bombers or other warplanes.[49]

A piping technologist brandishing a **force cup**.

force protection. Combat. A term used by Barack Obama's deputy national security adviser, Ben Rhodes, to explain that the American troops the president had sent on a noncombat "humanitarian mission" to Northern Iraq in the summer of 2014 would, in fact, be permitted to engage militants of the Islamic State should it become necessary for them to defend themselves. "The role of U.S. forces is not one of reentering combat on the ground," Rhodes explained. "[But] force protection is always a mission for U.S. personnel in any country in the world."[50]

forest thinning. Commercial logging.[51]

former clients of Obama Justice Department lawyers. Columnist Mona Charen's updated term for what the Bush adminstration used to call **enemy combatants.**[52]

four-point restraint. See: **place in a four-point restraint.**

"four years of unfortunate misunderstandings between the two nations." A phrase used by the Japanese government, in a 2002 advertisement heralding friendship between the United States and Japan, to describe the period between 1941 and 1945.[53]

fourth-quarter equity retreat. One broker's description of the October 1987 stock market crash.[54]

fraction of the original price. Terminology frequently used in advertising that implies that the new price is significantly lower. But in fact, the fraction could be 99/100.[55]

frail. Doddering, senile.[56]

Frankenscience. A term for genetic engineering, and animal-human transplants, popular with those opposed to such practices. Similarly, those seeking regulations banning genetically modified crops call them "Frankenfoods."[57]

A poster "promoting" **Frankenfoods**, produced by the Project for the Old American Century.

free. "Rarely is anything actually free," writes Canadian marketing expert Gordon Pritchard. "Free usually just means that [something] is included in the total price rather than listed as a separate item."[58]

free enterprise. A term coined more than a century ago by economist Alfred Marshall as a softer, friendlier synonym for "capitalism."[59] [See also: **free market economy.**]

free market economy. Like "free enterprise," this is a more congenial term for "capitalism," a word Republican media strategist Frank Luntz advises conservatives never to utter because it "reminds people of harsh economic competition that yields losers as well as winners." "Conversely," he adds, "the free market economy provides opportunity to all and allows everyone to succeed."[60]

free seminar. Free sales pitch. Example (from Walter Wiekes's *Dictionary of Management Jargon*): *"Come to our free seminar to learn how to buy our product."*[61]

freedom fighter. A terrorist who happens to be on the side you're supporting.[62]

freedom fondles. See: **enhanced screening procedures.**

freedom fries. French fries. The term was coined in 2003 by Beaufort, North Carolina, restaurateur Neal Rowland in response to France's refusal to join the **Coalition of the Willing** that the United States was assembling to institute regime change in Iraq. The U.S. House of Representatives, apparently inspired by Rowland's patriotism, promptly ordered the House cafeteria to rename the French fries and French toast available on its menu "freedom fries" and "freedom toast."[63]

freedom toast. French toast.[64] [See also: **freedom fries.**]

freelancer. According to recruiter Michael Spiro, this is a good answer to give if you're unemployed and someone asks what you do for a living.[65] [See also: **consultant.**]

freemium. A bare-bones product or service that companies offer for free, knowing they can charge you a bundle when, inevitably, you upgrade to a more usable version.[66]

friendly fire. An inadvertent attack on one's own troops.[67] [See also: **accidental delivery of ordnance equipment; incontinent ordnance.**]

friendly reminder. Urgent warning.[68]

frothy. A term used by European Central Bank president Mario Draghi to describe market conditions in an effort to assure members of the European Parliament that, although the premiums paid for risky assets like high-yield Greek bonds had plunged dramatically, he saw no evidence of the kind of full-scale "asset bubbles" that typically presage a market crash.[69]

fugitive emissions. Natural gas industry nomenclature for the pollution that is released into the atmosphere as a result of equipment leaks.[70]

full and frank discussion. A conversation or negotiation that accomplished absolutely nothing (and was probably quite unpleasant as well).[71]

full-figured. Fat.[72]

"full-time job." A phrase used by McDonald's to describe a no-benefits position at its restaurants that typically pays $8.20 per hour for a workweek of no more than thirty hours.[73]

fun-loving bachelor. A euphemism for "gay man" commonly used by obituary writers.[74]

fun-loving woman. A euphemism for "promiscuous female" commonly used by obituary writers.[75]

funnel money. To make a cash contribution or any other monetary transfer that benefits a person or organization of whom the speaker or writer disapproves.[76]

furlough day. A non-optional unpaid holiday for workers.[77]

future endeavor. A verb meaning to "fire" or "dismiss." Example: *After* **future endeavoring** *Mr. Rosenthal, his boss warmly well-wished him.*[78]

g

gallerist. Art dealer.[1]

game improvement clubs. Golf equipment manufacturers' term for a set of "easy-to-hit" hybrid irons and slice-proof woods designed for hopeless hackers. Such clubs tend to have extra-large heads or faces, and to be shorter than normal, design features that lessen the odds that striking the ball improperly will result in a bad shot.[2]

game management. The hunting or mass slaughter of wild animals.[3]

The passenger pigeon, a paragon of successful **game management**.

gaming. Gambling, as described by spokespeople for the "gaming" industry. Although "problem gambling" is widely recognized as a psychological disorder, there is apparently no "problem gaming."[4]

garden of remembrance. A cemetery.[5]

gaseous intestinal by-product. Fart.[6]

gate rape. See: **enhanced screening procedures.**

gender reassignment. Sex change surgery.[7]

generational ferment. A term used by a senior executive at the William Morris Agency in Hollywood to account for the abrupt departure of five important young agents who later explained their mass defection as simply a matter of wanting more money than the notoriously stingy firm was willing to pay.[8]

gentlemen's club. Strip joint.[9]

genuine imitation leather. Vinyl.[10]

genuine synthetic fiber. What, according to the online magazine *VotreArt*, the linings of Amble Footwear's Costa Brown loafers are crafted from.[11]

getting lean and mean. Firing people.[12]

Global Climate Science Communications Action Plan. A strategy devised by the American Petroleum Institute, and largely funded by ExxonMobil, designed to raise "serious questions about the scientific underpinnings" behind proposed climate change legislation.[13]

Global War on Terror. See: **War on Terror.**

going to Switzerland. A term for assisted suicide, based on the fact that legally sanctioned euthanasia is more readily available in that country than in most others.[14]

good-natured grunts. Booing and hissing when you or your colleagues or associates are the ones being booed and hissed. The term was coined in 1989 by David Beckwith while he was Vice President Dan Quayle's press secretary to describe the reaction his boss received from cadets at the United States Military Academy when the subject of Quayle's service in the Indiana National Guard during the Vietnam War came up.[15]

good-neighbor policy. Invading a nearby country. For example, George Will wrote that the U.S. invasion of Panama in 1989 was "a good-neighbor policy. America's role in Panama—in effect, administering a recount of last May's election—is an act of **hemispheric hygiene**." Example: *"¡Caramba!" shouted the National Guard major as American paratroopers began landing in Panama City. "Twenty thousand of our* **good neighbors** *have decided to pay us an unexpected visit!"*[16]

goodwill. A term on a financial balance sheet indicating the amount of overpayment for a corporate acquisition.[17]

goodwill payments. Compensation payments. The term was used by the Peverel Group to describe the money it paid back to customers, most of them elderly, who had been hoodwinked by one of the company's subsidiaries into paying grossly inflated prices for burglar alarm upgrades. As *The Guardian* points out, calling the payments "compensation" would have been "an admission of guilt."[18]

government option. What Fox News Channel vice president Bill Sammons, in 2009, instructed his on-air staff to call the "public option" originally included in President Obama's Affordable Care Act, which was then under debate in Congress. Sammons issued his directive the day after Republican strategist Frank Luntz, appearing on Sean Hannity's Fox News program, scolded Hannity for using the term "public option" to describe the government-run (but *not* government-funded) health insurance program that would have been set up by President Obama's legislation, as originally written. "If you call it a 'public option,' the American people are split," Luntz explained, but "if you call it the 'government option,' the public is overwhelmingly against it." In June 2010, President Obama signed the Affordable Care Act into law, but only after the Senate had stripped the public option from the bill.[19]

government relations professional. Lobbyist. According to the *Hill* newspaper, the American League of Lobbyists is considering rebranding itself "The Association of Government Relations Professionals" as part of its mission to "enhance the standing and reputation" of its members.[20] [See also: **legislative leadership advocate.**]

great and good friend. The classic journalistic euphemism for

"mistress," coined by *Time* magazine to describe the relationship between Marion Davies and William Randolph Hearst.[21]

"great nightlife." A real-estate advertising term that, according
to agent Kate Cocuzzo, means "you live above a bar." "Stock up
on earplugs," she suggests. "Or Scotch."[22]

great restraint. What police officers always exercise up until the
moment they are forced to shoot someone.[23]

green-on-blue violence. A U.S. military term for the disturbingly
common, and often fatal, attacks made by Afghan military or
police trainees on the American or other NATO advisers who
have been assigned to mentor them.[24]

greenbacking. Hiring mercenary troops.[25]

Greening Earth Society. An "astroturf" group organized and
funded by the coal industry to promote the idea that increasing
levels of carbon dioxide in the atmosphere caused by fossil fuel
combustion are encouraging the growth of plants and forests.[26]

greenwashing. Adopting what are promoted as environmentally
friendly policies purely for public relations purposes.[27]

gremlins. In 2009, Eliot Spitzer, the governor of New York, was
discovered to be "Client 9" of a high-priced call girl named
Ashley Dupré, a revelation that quickly led to his resignation
from office. Shortly thereafter he appeared on the *Today* show,
and when host Matt Lauer quizzed him about his habit of consorting with prostitutes, he replied, "I have tried to address
these gremlins and confront them." To help him in his quest,
the *New York Post* published side-by-side photos of a creature
from the hit 1984 horror movie *Gremlins* and a hooker so that
Spitzer could study the difference between the two.[28]

ground-mounted confirmatory route markers. A term for "road signs" favored by Scott L. Pickard, a spokesperson for the Massachusetts Department of Public Works.[29]

A **ground-mounted confirmatory route marker.**

group home. Orphanage.[30] [See also: **congregate care facility.**]

group therapy. A Vietnam-era military term for the indiscriminate firing by more than one soldier of M-16 rifles set on full automatic for the purpose of quickly clearing an area of enemy soldiers.[31]

Guardian Deity of the Planet. One of the approximately 1,200 official titles carried by Kim Jong-il, Supreme Leader of North Korea, until his death in December 2011. According to North Korea's Central Broadcasting Station, "160 prominent leaders from across the world" used this and some of Kim's other 1,199 titles "to honor our Great General."[32] [See also: **Lodestar of the 21st Century.**]

Kim Jong-il, former **Guardian Deity of the Planet.**

gummies. A code word used by baseball player Alex Rodriguez and his drug supplier, Anthony P. Bosch, to describe testosterone lozenges, a banned performance-enhancing substance.[33] [See also: **food; liquid soap; pink cream; rocket.**]

gun grabber. A term for someone who supports gun control legislation favored by those who don't.[34]

h

habitability improvements. A convenient phrase to use when you're forced to talk about furniture that you squandered ridiculous amounts of money buying. The U.S. Navy used the term when it spent $32,672 to purchase a sofa, a love seat, and twenty chairs for the destroyer USS *Kidd*.[1]

hair management system. What Speedo International Ltd. calls its Fastskin3 swimming cap.[2]

handcrafted. Handmade, but it sounds more impressive, doesn't it?[3]

hands-off management style. A term used to describe Ronald Reagan's approach to the presidency. Columnist John Leo says it means "out to lunch." Example: *Louis XVI and Marie Antoinette's* **hands-off** management style *was a major factor in their being rendered nonviable by French Revolutionary heads-off managers.*[4] [See also: **"leaves details to subordinates."**]

hands-on mentoring. Sexual relations with a junior employee.[5]

handyman's special. A real-estate industry term for a dilapidated house.[6]

happiness heroes. What Buffer, a company that helps folks schedule and manage their social media updates, calls its customer-support employees. The top banana among Buffer's happiness heroes, as of this

Bill Clinton, a noted **hands-on mentor**.

writing, is "Carolyn," who holds the title of **Chief Happiness Officer** and reveals, on the company's website, that she's "truly grateful when a customer reaches out to us because it gives us an opportunity to learn something about our product or simply talk to someone really darn cool. I love the warm-fuzzies that come from helping people use Buffer in a more awesome way."[7]

hard landscaping. Paving something over.[8]

hardworking taxpayers. A phrase that political strategist Frank Luntz urges Republicans to use instead of "the middle class" when extolling the virtues of tax cuts and less stringent government regulation. "We can say we defend the 'middle class,'" he warned in a speech to GOP governors in 2011, "and the public will say, I'm not sure about that. But [talk about] defending 'hardworking taxpayers' and Republicans have the advantage."[9]

harvest. A traditional agricultural term used as a euphemism for the industrial slaughter of economically valuable species such as seals and other fur-bearing animals or for the large-scale cutting of trees.[10]

harvest party. An inclusive term for a Halloween party, designed to appeal both to atheists (who, while repelled by Halloween's connection to All Saints' Day, are apparently more than willing to join celebrations of Earth's plenty) and to Christians (because it doesn't call to mind the demonic rituals commonly associated with Halloween).[11]

head count realignment. Firing or laying off people. Also known as "head count management" and "head count reduction."[12]

headwind. An all-purpose corporate term used to suggest that a company's poor economic performance was due to cyclical factors beyond its control (high fuel prices, for example, or a colder-than-average winter). By contrast, if financial results

improve, the turnaround is invariably attributed to innovation, product quality, or "customer-centricity" and rarely if
ever to a "tailwind."[13]

health alteration. Assassination. During the 1960s, an internal
CIA group charged with determining potential "termination"
targets was called the "health alteration committee."[14]

health event. Being stricken with terminal cancer, for example.
The term is a staple of the corporate announcements and press
releases issued by Sun Life Financial Canada.[15]

health impact fee. Cigarette tax. In 2005, Tim Pawlenty, the
Republican governor of Minnesota, imposed a 75-cents-a-pack
"health impact fee" on his citizens, an action that permitted
him to honor his 2004 campaign pledge to balance his state's
budget without raising taxes.

health care procurement specialist. Insurance salesperson.[16]

Healthy Forests Initiative. A program initiated by President
George W. Bush to protect America's national forests by, among
other things, permitting and promoting the large-scale logging of ancient trees. Skeptics dubbed the proposal, which
became law in 2003, the **"No Tree Left Behind"** Act.[17]

heartwarming. According to essayist and critic Katha Pollitt,
this adjective, when used by a publisher in an ad, alerts potential readers that "no one in the book has an IQ over 100, with
the possible exception of a dog, who dies."[18]

heavenly deceptions. What the Reverend Sun Myung Moon's Uni-
fication Church calls the "justifiable" lies it encourages its
members to tell nonmembers in service of the church.[19]

heavy landing. A plane crash on an airport runway.[20]

heck of a job. A total screwup. As *Political Wire*'s Taegan Goddard
explains, the phrase entered the language after President

George W. Bush visited Louisiana during the bungled Hurricane Katrina rescue effort and told FEMA director Michael Brown, "Brownie, you're doing a heck of a job." A little over a week after being praised by Bush, Brown resigned.[21]

"helping us with our inquiries." A phrase used by British police to describe a suspect who is in custody but has not yet been charged with a crime. As lexicographer R. W. Holder explains, the wording was devised to avoid the appearance of a presumption of guilt that could doom any subsequent attempt at a conviction.[22]

helpless creatures crawling around incapable of controlling their libidos. Women. (Well, to be fair, this is Mike Huckabee's term for what the "Democrat Party" *thinks* women are. The Republican Party, Huckabee hastens to point out, feels "women are far more than Democrats have made them to be.")[23] [See also: **victims of their gender.**]

helps. A ubiquitous **"weasel word"** that permits advertisers to suggest that a product might be beneficial without promising that it will actually have any effect. Consider, for example, the claim that a certain brand of shampoo "helps control dandruff symptoms with regular use," in which not only the word "helps" but also the phrase "with regular use" are weasels.[24] [See also: **"in conjunction with diet and regular exercise."**]

hematophagous arthropod vectors. What the University of North Dakota School of Medicine, among others, calls fleas. Example: *Eddie tuned the strings of his ukulele to match the first four notes of "My Dog Has* **Hematophagous Arthropod Vectors.***"*[25]

Hemingwayesque. Novelist Arthur Phillips observes that this book-jacket-blurb staple is useful for promoting any author whose work features short sentences.[26] [See also: **Faulkneresque.**]

hemispheric hygiene. See: **good-neighbor policy.**

hemp activism. Championing the legalization of marijuana.[27]

hexiform rotatable compression units. The U.S. Navy's name for common threaded metal hex nuts, which, according to a 1984 Senate committee report, apparently justified their buying them from the McDonnell Douglas Corporation for $2,043 apiece.[28]

A **hexiform rotatable compression unit.**

high-net-worth individual. A great way to say "rich person" without having to say "rich person."[29]

high-velocity multipurpose air circulation device. Fan.[30]

highly leveraged. Hopelessly in debt.[31]

hiking the Appalachian Trail. Committing adultery. The term entered the language in June 2009 after South Carolina chief executive Mark Sanford used it to account for an unexplained six-day absence from the governor's mansion. It soon turned out that he'd actually been having an extramarital affair

A **high-velocity multipurpose air circulation device.**

with a woman in Buenos Aires.[32] [See also: **incredibly intense conversation; serious overdrive.**]

histrionic personality disorder. The American Psychiatric Association's official name for the behavior displayed by a fucking asshole.[33]

"Hitler's grand-nieces once removed." Liberals. The term was coined by *National Review Online* editor Jonah Goldberg, author of the *New York Times*–bestselling book *Liberal Fascism.* Here's how he explained the phrase to an appreciative Heritage Foundation audience: "I'm not saying today's liberals are Hitler's cousins. They're more like his grand-nieces once removed."[34]

holiday tree. A more inclusive, less potentially offensive term for a Christmas tree.[35]

home plaque removal instrument. What the Dental Research Corporation called its Interplak brand of "next generation" electric toothbrushes. Dental Research was acquired by Bausch & Lomb and subsequently sold to Conair, which continues to market Interplak home plaque removal instruments under a spiffy new name: **"cordless rechargeable power plaque remover."**[36]

homicide bomber. A synonym for "suicide bomber" preferred by the George W. Bush White House on the grounds that the words "suicide bomber" validate the terrorist who committed the attack. In 2002, the Fox News Channel made it official policy to say "homicide bomber" instead of "suicide bomber," and it still does so today, even though, as RationalWiki points out, the phrase is, "at best, completely redundant."[37]

hordes. Troops who *oppose* the British Army. British Army troops are called **lads.**[38]

horizontality. A sophisticated art criticism term for the quality of a particular work of art that permits it to be viewed in a left-to-right or, alternatively, right-to-left manner (as opposed to, say, from up to down or down to up).[39] [See also: **International Art English.**]

HSDD. See: **hypoactive sexual desire disorder.**

Human Resources Department. What was formerly known as the Personnel Department. The name change helped clarify the idea that employees were not merely people but valuable corporate assets. Some organizations (the Metropolitan Nashville Public Schools, for example) are making this point even more emphatically by adopting the name "Human Capital Department" instead.[40]

human rights abuses. A gentler way of saying torture and murder.[41]

human shields. Civilians killed by bombing raids on nearby military targets—when it's your side doing the bombing, that is. The term is even more effective if phrases such as **"sacrificed by heartless terrorists"** are affixed to it. When the enemy is the one doing the bombing, of course, the label **"innocent victims"** is far more appropriate.[42]

humiliating U-turn. A change in policy made by someone with whom, at least until now, the speaker or writer passionately disagreed.[43]

hydration engineer. The waterboy on a football team. The term became popular after it was used in Adam Sandler's film *The Waterboy.*[44]

hypoactive sexual desire disorder (HSDD). A new name, introduced by the American Psychiatric Association in the fourth edition of its *Diagnostic and Statistical Manual of Mental Disorders (DSM),* for what used to be called "frigidity." In the fifth edition, the APA substituted an even *newer* name, **female sexual interest/arousal disorder.**[45]

i

"I appreciate your contribution." Corporate-speak terminology that basically means, "Close the door on your way out."[1]

"I don't doubt your word." A phrase used by banks, airlines, and retail establishments that can be roughly translated as "You're probably telling the truth, but so what?" Journalist Enid Nemy offers the following example: "**We don't doubt your word** *that you reconfirmed your reservation, but it isn't in the computer.*" "Don't bother asking," advises Nemy, "you aren't on the flight."[2]

"I hear what you're saying." "I disagree so strongly that there's no point in even listening to you."[3]

"I hope I've been able to answer all your questions." As Guy Winch, author of *The Squeaky Wheel*, points out, corporate customer service representatives invariably end every phone conversation with this line, even if they haven't answered any of them.[4]

iatrogenic. An official (and comfortingly nonpejorative) medical term for something that wasn't supposed to happen, like an infection after surgery, or a complication following a routine treatment, or any medical error or adverse effect.[5]

-icity. See: **-ality.**

ICPs. See: **impaired combat personnel.**

ideation. A business-speak term for having an idea. Someone who has an idea is, of course, an "ideationalist."[6]

idiopathic. A diagnostic term used by doctors to refer to a patient's symptom or condition when, even after conducting a careful examination and a full battery of tests, they don't have a clue as to what it is or what is causing it. Example: *Dr. Amaral determined that Luisa's therapeutic misadventure was both iatrogenic and **idiopathic**, a diagnosis that earned her a special commendation from the hospital director.*[7]

idiot cheese. What, according to Tina Fey, the French started calling "American cheese" after the French fries and French toast served in the House of Representatives cafeteria were renamed "freedom fries" and "freedom toast" to protest France's refusal to support the U.S. invasion of Iraq.[8] [See also: **freedom fries.**]

IDLE. See: **indolent lesions of epithelial origin.**

ill-advised. An adjective that comes in handy when you're trying to explain away a really dumb or terrible idea or action.[9]

illegal alien. An undocumented worker who happens to be employed by your competitor, or who is holding a job that you feel should have been reserved for a native-born American citizen.[10]

illegal combatant. A prisoner of war with no rights under the Geneva Conventions.[11] [See also: **enemy combatants.**]

illiquid. Insolvent. The term was used by the California Historical Society to describe the situation in which it found itself after a decade of multi-hundred-thousand-dollar deficits.[12]

"I'm not sure I agree, but . . ." An introductory phrase that permits you to venture an outrageous opinion, make a baseless charge, or insult or excoriate somebody without taking any responsibility for your words. Consider the following quotation from the United Kingdom's Property Investment Project, which maintains a website for landlords: "I'm not saying I agree, but it's easy to understand why estate agents notoriously receive a bad rap (rightly or wrongly so) for being snake oil parasites that would stab their nans for a fiver."[13]

image adviser. A self-descriptive term preferred by professional political propagandists over the more colorful sobriquet of "spin doctor."[14] [See also: **media consultant.**]

imaginative journalism. A phrase used to characterize an overly sensational or completely fabricated news report. Example: *The influential series of articles about Saddam Hussein's WMD capabilities that Judith Miller*

Judith Miller, a Pulitzer Prize–winning **imaginative journalist**.

wrote for The New York Times *during the run-up to the Iraq War set a standard for* imaginative journalism *that has seldom been equaled.*[15]

immediate consumption channel. Soft-drink vending machine.[16]

immediate consumption outlet. Convenience store.[17]

immediate permanent incapacitation. Death. The term was featured in a document prepared by the U.S. Army to help its commanders "optimize" the targeting of tactical nuclear weapons.[18]

Philip Seymour Hoffman, whose portrayal of Willy Loman in Arthur Miller's *Immediate Permanent Incapacitation of a Customer Solutions Specialist* earned him a Tony nomination.

immigration reform. Oklahoma political blogger Charles M. Phipps defines this as a "euphemism for vote-buying."[19]

impaired. Drunk.[20] [See also: **overrefreshed; overserved; ruddy-faced; tired and emotional.**]

impaired combat personnel (ICPs). A U.S. Department of Defense term for "wounded soldiers." Whenever a Pentagon spokesperson feels this already opaque phrase seems too transparent, the abbreviation comes in really handy.[21]

imperative security internee. A term invented by the U.S. military to classify Cyrus Kar, an alleged "enemy combatant" arrested in Iraq in 2005. As an American citizen, Kar could have successfully asserted his constitutional rights to due process and an impartial hearing unless a new category of detainee had been created especially for him—a category under which, a Pentagon spokesman proclaimed, he could be held indefinitely without being charged with a crime or being given an opportunity to defend himself. Kar, an Iranian-American documentary filmmaker accused of smuggling washing machine timers into Iraq for use in improvised explosive devices, has since been vindicated.[22]

implement a skills mix adjustment. Lay off or fire employees.[23]

improperly dependent. Plagiarized.[24]

improving productivity. Making fewer people do more work without raising salaries.[25]

imprudent. An adjective useful for describing any bungled, failed, mistaken, illegal, reckless, or downright idiotic act you've committed or strategy you've embarked upon.[26]

impulsive. A handy adjective for disparaging a female colleague who, if she were a man, would be applauded for her ability to make quick decisions.[27]

in a rebuilding phase. Sports commentator terminology that, according to Cracked.com columnist Christine Hsu, can loosely be translated as "This team really sucks and isn't worth watching even for laughs."[28]

"in conjunction with diet and regular exercise." Diet pill manufacturers are permitted by the U.S. Federal Trade Commission to extol the potential benefits of their medications as long as this disclaimer is used to qualify any assertions they make. What always goes unsaid, of course, is that "diet and regular exercise" alone will produce the same results, even if they are not used "in conjunction with" the advertised product.[29]

"in harm's way." A euphemistic phrase used by politicians to describe and downplay the extremely dangerous and deadly battlefield conditions that troops whom they are sending to war are likely to encounter.[30]

in the early stages of finalization. Unfinished. Once a project is 50 percent completed, it may be characterized as **semi-finalized.**[31] [See also: **"It's coming along."**]

in transition. Unemployed.[32]

inadvertent disclosure of incorrect information. Lie. (The term was coined by the U.S. Air Force in claiming it hadn't lied in previous testimony about the cost of the B-1 bomber.)[33]

inappropriate. A catchall term useful for minimizing the significance of behavior ranging from sexual misconduct and financial shenanigans to murder.[34]

inappropriate acceleration. A less judgmental term for "speeding," offered by B. G. Milligan of Cockeysville, Maryland, in a letter to *The New York Times* satirizing the newspaper for running a lengthy article about historian Doris Kearns Goodwin's "borrowing" of entire passages from other writers' works without even once identifying her act as "plagiarism." In the same letter, Milligan also suggested that "instead of burglary, one might be arrested for **inappropriate possession of the property of others.**"[35] [See also: **inappropriate copying; unacknowledged repetition.**]

inappropriate copying. How *The New York Times*—in what appears to have been a deliberate attempt to avoid the word "plagiarism"—characterized historian Doris Kearns Goodwin's unattributed "borrowing" of other writers' material in her books *The Fitzgeralds and the Kennedys* and *No Ordinary Time.*[36] [See also: **inappropriate acceleration; inappropriate possession of the property of others; unacknowledged repetition.**]

inappropriate friendship. An affair. Church of the Highlands founder Chris Hodges used this phrase to describe the extramarital dalliance with an intern that forced his longtime friend and colleague, television pastor Dino Rizzo, to take a sabbatical from his ministry.[37]

inappropriate possession of the property of others. Burglary. The terminology was suggested by B. G. Milligan, of Cockeysville, Maryland, in a letter to *The New York Times* poking fun at the fact that the paper had characterized Doris Kearns Goodwin's "blatant pilfering" of other writers' works as **"inappropriate copying"** and **"unacknowledged repetition,"** rather than coming out and calling it "plagiarism."[38] [See also: **inappropriate acceleration.**]

incentive. Bribe; kickback.[39] [See also: **after-sales service fees**; **campaign contribution**; **expediting fee**; **facilitation payment**; **fee for product testing**; **rebate.**]

incestuous amplification. A term coined by noted U.S. military analyst Chuck Spinney to describe the practice of listening to, or being influenced by, only those who already agree with you.[40]

incidentally. *The Economist* translates this as "I am now telling you the purpose of this discussion."[41]

inclusive language. A way of saying "politically correct" that is more politically correct than "politically correct."[42]

income protection. Tax avoidance.[43]

incomplete success. A term for "failure" originally coined in 1980 by President Jimmy

An American C-130 cargo aircraft, photographed in 1980 shortly after participating in an **incompletely successful** attempt to rescue hostages being held at the U.S. embassy in Tehran.

Carter to describe the aborted raid to free the American hostages held in Iran.[44]

incontinent ordnance. Bombs, missiles, or artillery shells that fall on one's own position.[45] [See also: **accidental delivery of ordnance equipment; friendly fire.**]

incorrect promise. A lie. Michael D. Shear and Robert Pear of *The New York Times* used the phrase in 2013 to characterize President Barack Obama's oft-repeated assurance that people who liked their old health plans would have no problem keeping them under the Affordable Care Act. In fact, as soon as the new law took effect, hundreds of thousands of Americans began receiving notices from their health insurance companies telling them that their existing policies were being canceled.[46]

increasing the use of vacancy management. See: **vacancy management.**

incredibly intense conversation. Sex, especially when it's illicit. The term entered the language after South Carolina governor Mark Sanford used it during a press conference to explain what he and an Argentinean woman with whom he'd been having an extramarital affair had been

An **incredibly intense conversation.**

engaged in. Example: *The potential effectiveness of the pick-up line "Hey, baby, let's engage in some* **incredibly intense conversation**" *has, perhaps, been overrated.*[47] [See also: **hiking the Appalachian Trail; serious overdrive.**]

incursion. Invasion.[48]

indefinite idling. Permanent plant closing. Companies that use

the term often do so in hopes of avoiding the severance payments to laid-off workers that the irreversible decommission-
ing of a manufacturing facility typically entails.[49]

individual behavior adjustment unit. Solitary confinement
cell.[50]

individual learning station. U.S. Department of Education terminology for a classroom desk.[51]

indolent lesions of epithelial origin (IDLE). A new term for
slower-growing and generally nonfatal "pre-malignant"
tumors, proposed by a working group of the National Cancer
Institute as a substitute for the scary death-sentence word
"cancer." The suggested name change is part of an effort by the
institute to downgrade negative terminology for the purpose
of curbing overtreatment—and, perhaps not uncoincidentally,
the insurance costs associated with it—triggered by patient
anxiety.[52]

indoor washrooms for dogs. The American Kennel Club's name
for the reusable pee pads it markets under the "Potty Patch"
brand name. According to the official Potty Patch website, the
"indoor washroom for dogs" features a "three-tiered design"
consisting of a mat "made of a soft artificial grass specifically
designed to let liquid flow through," a "stay-dry grate," and an
"easy-clean collection tray."[53]

induced miscarriage. Abortion.[54]

industrial action. A labor strike.[55]

industrial vacation. An all-expenses-paid trip to a resort within
reasonable travel distance of a current or potential client,
vendor, or business partner who is arguably worth visiting.
As *The Office Life* points out, anyone taking an industrial

vacation is typically required to "arrive a few days early to 'prepare' and stay a few days after to 'wrap-up.'"[56]

information adviser. Librarian.[57]

inhalation hazard. The U.S. government's preferred term for poison gas.[58]

initiative. A Washington term defined by comedian George Carlin as "an idea that isn't going anywhere."[59]

inner city. A code word for African-American neighborhoods or, when used as an adjective, for African-Americans themselves.[60]

innocent victims. See: **human shields.**

innocent victims of AIDS. Journalist Norman Solomon defines these as "children, persons with hemophilia, and transfusion victims who have contracted AIDS." Use of this terminology, Solomon points out, is a clever way "to blame other people with AIDS—gay men and IV drug users in particular—who are declared guilty by implication because they are not included in the 'innocent' category."[61]

innovation Sherpa. It's not *totally* clear what William Bunce, the Microsoft staffer who holds this title, actually does for his employers, but perhaps his LinkedIn profile, which describes him as an "experienced change agent" whose "stellar 20-year career" has been "characterized by top-producing sales management in both the B2B and Government arenas," will provide some enlightenment.[62]

innovative accounting. See: **aggressive accounting.**

inoperative statement. A Nixon-era White House press office term for a lie.[63]

inspirational. A term that was invoked by a spokesperson for Darden Restaurants to describe the lavish $152 million, fifty-seven-acre corporate headquarters the "severely under-performing" company, rated highest for "governance risk" by ISS Quickscore, recently constructed for itself in Orlando, Florida. The spokesperson added that the luxurious corporate campus was essential for "showcasing" the company's brands.[64]

instability units. Apartheid-era South African armored police squads that terrorized black townships under the guise of quelling riots.[65]

institutional flexibility. The authority of educational administrators to do anything they want without consulting the faculty about the effect their actions might have on the quality of education offered by their school.[66]

institutional self-help. Cutting salaries or laying off workers to improve profits.[67]

intangible assets. Future write-offs.[68]

integrity control officers. New York Police Department lieutenants assigned to patrol parks, cemeteries, rail yards, and other quiet places where beat cops are likely to be taking an unauthorized nap, catching winks instead of criminals.[69]

intellectual disability. The preferred diagnostic term for what used to be called "mental retardation."[70]

intelligent ventilation points. A phrase conjured up by designer David Blanch to describe the armholes in the shirts he designed for England's national soccer team in 2009.[71]

intense and driven. A euphemism used by journalists to describe a psychopathic public figure.[72]

interdictional nonsuccumbers. Enemy troops who survive a bombing attack. Example: **Interdictional nonsuccumbers**

are always excellent candidates for force package revisitation.[73]

interfacing on substance with sitting congressmen. Lobbying.[74]

intergenerational intimacy. Child molesting; pedophilia.[75]

interior experience. Johnson Controls, Inc., describes itself as a "global leader in interior experience." Former Rutgers English professor and "plain language" guru William D. Lutz translates this as "They sell a lot of thermostats."[76]

International Art English (IAE). According to David Levine and Alix Rule, who coined the term and defined it in a famous and influential article in *Triple Canopy*, International Art English— the "language through which contemporary art is created, promoted, sold, and understood"—"has everything to do with English, but it is emphatically not English." "IAE has a distinctive lexicon," Levine and Rule tell us, "*aporia, radically, space, proposition, biopolitical, tension, transversal, autonomy.* An artist's work inevitably interrogates, questions, encodes, transforms, subverts, imbricates, displaces—though often it doesn't do these things so much as it serves to, functions to, or seems to (or might seem to) do these things. IAE rebukes English for its lack of nouns: *Visual* becomes *visuality, global* becomes *globality, potential* becomes *potentiality, experience* becomes . . . *experiencability.*" So why do people write this way? One reason, Levine told *The Guardian*'s Andy Beckett, is that institutions such as galleries and museums, and those who work for them, "can't speak in simple sentences and be taken seriously. In our postmodern world simple is just bad." Besides, he added, "the more overheated the market gets, the more overheated the language gets. . . . The more you can muddy the waters around the meaning of a work, the more you can keep the value high."[77]

interns. Slave labor.[78]

interspecies communicator. An animal trainer.[79]

intimate. A real-estate advertising term for houses and apartments that are even smaller than the ones described as "cozy."[80] [See also: **adorable; cozy.**]

intricately plotted. Novelist Ruth Harris observes that publishing copywriters and book reviewers fall back on this term when they can't "figure out who did what to whom and why."[81]

Roy Horn of Siegfried & Roy, an incompletely successful **interspecies communicator.**

intrusion detection system. Burglar alarm.[82]

inventory shrinkage. Theft.[83]

inversion. A technical, and conveniently innocent-sounding, term for a form of legal corporate tax evasion in which a company—usually American—reincorporates in a country with a lower corporate tax rate and looser government regulations, often by transferring its assets to a foreign subsidiary and then dissolving the original corporation.[84]

An **intimate** residential property formerly occupied by a clam.

invest. Spend. The *Newspeak Dictionary* points out that politicians never spend money on anything—they invest in it.[85]

investment professional. Stockbroker. Other useful terms for "stockbroker" include "investment adviser" and "investment consultant."[86]

involuntarily attrited. Fired or laid off.[87] [See also: **involuntarily leisured.**]

involuntarily leisured. Fired.[88] [See also: **involuntarily attrited.**]

involuntary career event. Being fired, for example.[89] [See also: **involuntary position eliminations; involuntary reduction in force.**]

involuntary conversion. An accounting term for an accidental fire, explosion, collision, or other "act of God" that "converts" a piece of property from its original state into a pile of rubble. For example, when National Airlines realized a $1.7 million after-tax insurance benefit from the crash of one of its planes in 1978, it announced in its annual report that the net gain in its revenues was the result of "the involuntary conversion of a 727."[90]

involuntary entrepreneurship. Self-employment (or unemployment) as a result of having been fired or laid off. Geoffrey Nunberg, professor of linguistics at the University of California, Berkeley, rates this as "probably my favorite euphemism of the last 20 years."[91]

involuntary position eliminations. Layoffs. The term was used in a 2007 memo from Scott Smith, president of the *Chicago Tribune*, to his employees informing them that approximately one hundred of them were about to lose their jobs.[92] [See also: **involuntary career event; involuntary reduction in force.**]

involuntary reduction in force. A series of layoffs or firings undertaken when not enough employees respond to a request for resignations or early retirements.[93] [See also: **involuntary career event; involuntary position eliminations.**]

irregularities. A term convenient for describing any fraudulent actions that you or your firm have committed.[94]

is. As used by President Bill Clinton, a verb that—in contrast to "was"—refers only to an event that is currently taking place or a condition that exists at the exact moment when an inquiry about that event or condition is made, and not to a prior event that may have happened at some specific point in the past or a previous condition that may have prevailed over an extended period of time. Clinton famously used this definition to explain to a grand jury why he wasn't lying when he assured his staff, after they confronted him with questions about his alleged sexual relations with White House intern Monica Lewinsky, that "there's nothing going on between us."[95]

issue. Problem. (It sounds much better to have an "anger management *issue*" than an "anger management *problem*," doesn't it?)[96] [See also: **challenge.**]

issue ads. Political attack advertisements that skirt regulations preventing political action committees from directly endorsing candidates by assailing unpopular positions that a targeted opponent has taken on controversial issues.[97]

"It came out wrong." A phrase used by a spokesperson for Missouri senator Claire McCaskill to explain how the senator could possibly have claimed (as she had indeed done the previous day) that Barack Obama was the first black figure "to come to the American people not as a victim but as a leader." "And so," commented *The Guardian*'s Steven Poole, "the question of whether it was wrong when it was still in is handily sidestepped."[98]

iterative thinker. A business term for someone who is indecisive. Peter Jones, in a comment reprinted by the late Alexander Cockburn, notes that this trait "no longer appears to be a flaw."[99]

"It's coming along." Lois Beckwith, author of *The Dictionary of*

Corporate Bullshit, translates this phrase as "It hasn't started yet."[100] [See also: **in the early stages of finalization.**]

"It's got a certain acidity." An all-purpose, authoritative-sounding phrase to trot out whenever you're asked to comment on the quality of a bottle of wine and you haven't got a clue what to say.[101]

"It's not about . . ." As Senator Dale Bumpers (D-Arkansas) testified at President Bill Clinton's impeachment trial in 1999, "When you hear someone say, 'This is not about sex,' it's about sex."[102]

j

jack-booted government thugs. A term used by Wayne LaPierre of the National Rifle Association to describe government agents who attempt to enforce federal laws regulating the possession, display, sale, or use of guns.[1]

jet-lagged. A less pejorative way of saying "hungover."[2]

jewelry cleaner. One of the deceptive names under which synthetic narcotics—also known as "designer drugs"—are marketed. Because packages of "jewelry cleaner" are frequently labeled **"not for human consumption,"** they could, at least until recently, be sold at retail outlets or online without being subject to any regulation or oversight.[3] [See also: **bath salts; phone screen cleaner; plant food.**]

job creators. A term that, as *Washington Monthly*'s Jamie Malanowski has noted, turns rich people, "fat cats," and anyone else who hires employees—regardless of salaries paid or
benefits offered—into "gods from whom all blessings flow,"
who therefore must be protected against all attempts to regu-
late, investigate, or tax them.[4] [See also: **job-killing regulations.**]

job-killing regulations. A term widely used by Republican political candidates—its appearance in newspapers increased by
17,550 percent from 2007 to 2011, according to ThinkProgress
.org—to highlight the supposed economic havoc caused by government interventions in the marketplace. In reality, the non-
partisan Bureau of Labor Statistics reports, excessive regulation
was actually cited by employers as the reason for only 0.2 percent to 0.4 percent of all layoffs from 2008 to 2011, as opposed
to weak consumer demand and poor sales, to which the business owners attributed anywhere from 30 percent to nearly 40
percent of all reductions in staffing by their companies during
the same period.[5] [See also: **job creators.**]

job-market researcher. Recruiter Michael Spiro offers this as a
good-natured job description for an unemployed person to use
while seeking a new assignment.[6]

job seeker. An unemployed person.[7]

"jobs at risk from misguided government action." A phrase used
in 2011 by the Sensible Food Policy Coalition (whose members
include PepsiCo, General Mills, and Kellogg's) to warn the
nation about the devastating effect that proposed restrictions
on the marketing of junk food to children could have on food
industry employment. Such restrictions are "the last thing
American families and the U.S. economy needs," said coalition
spokesperson Dan Jaffe.[8]

journey. A business term useful for imbuing even the most tedious task or assignment with (as *The Guardian*'s Steven Poole puts it) "the ersatz thrill of adventurous tourism" and the "therapeutic implications of personal growth." For example, Poole notes, the British government's official set of instructions for claiming disability benefits is entitled "The Claimant Journey."[9]

judicial activism. What judges you don't agree with do. As Jerry Merchant and Mary Matthews of ExtremelySmart.com point out, what judges you *do* agree with do is called "sound jurisprudence."[10]

judgmental lapse. A white-collar crime, especially one that involves a course of conduct. Example: *With the benefit of hindsight, Bernie Madoff's decision to defraud his investors out of billions of dollars might be considered a serious* **judgmental lapse.**[11]

judicial engagement. A term coined by Clark Neily, a senior lawyer at the libertarian Institute for Justice, to characterize actions taken by courts in support of conservative goals. "There does seem to be a willingness on the part of conservatives for judges to be more active in their review," Neily observes. Democratic senator Charles E. Schumer of New York, recalling how vigorously Republicans have attacked **"activist judges"** whenever they rule in favor of progressive causes, is impressed by the GOP's newfound flexibility on the role of the judiciary. "They decry the courts' overruling or implementing things they don't like, but are eager to have the courts implement things they like," he says.[12]

junk science. Any data-driven, fact-based discipline, field of inquiry, or body of knowledge that you happen to disagree with.[13]

"just needs your decorating touches." According to Minnesota real-estate agent and blogger Ross Kaplan, this frequently used real-estate advertising phrase means "needs a general contractor, lots of sub's—and a healthy rehab budget."[14]

juxtaposition. An art connoisseur's term for, as painter/writer Penny Tristram phrases it, "putting shit next to other shit."[15]

JV team. A term used by President Barack Obama in January 2014 to disparage the abilities of the Islamic State fighters who, within the next few months, had succeeded in taking over much of Syria and Iraq. The president later insisted to Chuck Todd on NBC's *Meet the Press* that he had been misquoted, a claim convincingly refuted by the Pulitzer Prize–winning website PolitiFact.com.[16]

k

kinetic military action. War. The term was used by President Barack Obama's deputy national security adviser Ben Rhodes in March 2011 to describe the sustained bombing campaign that was to be directed against the government of Libyan dictator Colonel Qaddafi. Example: *General William Tecumseh Sherman's most famous quotation would arguably have been somewhat less memorable if he had said,* "**Kinetic military action** *is hell.*"[1]

1

laboratory for the written word. An improvement on the antiquated term "publishing house," coined by Blue Rider Press to identify itself on its social media pages.[1]

lads. British Army troops. Troops who *oppose* the British Army are known as hordes.[2]

lagoon. An evocative livestock industry term for an open-pit pond where hog waste is dumped.[3]

land farms. An appealingly rustic phrase coined by the petroleum industry to describe waste dumps where tons of oil sludge are plowed into the ground every day to be decomposed by organisms in the soil.[4]

"language from already published sources without using proper citation methods." Plagiarized content. This terminology has been used more than once in article retraction notices printed in the Taylor & Francis journal *Critical Reviews in Environmental Science and Technology*.[5]

large. A consumer-products industry term for a package that is smaller than "economy size," "family size," "king size," or "super deluxe size."[6]

late developer. A compassionate term for a child who performs academic tasks at a skill level significantly below that of his peers.[7]

laugh lines. Wrinkles.[8] [See also: expression lines; maturity tracks.]

lay paper. To pass bad checks or bogus securities.[9]

leak detection and repair specialist. Plumber.[10] [See also: **piping technologist.**]

lean and mean, getting. Firing people.[11]

lean finely textured beef. The official beef industry term for a processed meat by-product more commonly known as "pink slime."[12]

learning facilitator. A teacher. The term "learning facilitator"— or **"facilitator of learning,"** as some prefer to say—is coming into ever wider use by enlightened educators because, as noted "brain-based learning and simulation" consultant Timothy C. Clapper phrased it in a recent issue of the *Professionals Against Improperly Labeling Active Learners (PAILAL) Newsletter*, they know they must reject the "deliverer of knowledge in a passive environment" model in favor of a new paradigm "where all learners are actively engaged in the construction of their knowledge."[13]

learning opportunity. A mistake or failure.[14]

learnings. Business jargon for things that were learned, such as learning to say "learnings" instead of "what we learned."[15]

least-best. A more compassionate term for "worst" used by United Parcel Service in evaluating its drivers.[16]

least untruthful. During a Senate hearing in 2013, Oregon's Ron Wyden asked James Clapper, President Barack Obama's Director of National Intelligence, whether or not the National Security Agency was collecting data on "millions of Americans." Clapper answered no, a reply that was soon revealed to be an outright lie. When NBC's Andrea Mitchell confronted him about this, Clapper explained that he had responded in what he thought, under the circumstances, was the "least untruthful manner" possible.[17]

leave to pursue other opportunities. Be fired or laid off.[18]

"leaves details to subordinates." A phrase useful for describing a clueless executive.[19] [See also: **hands-off management style.**]

legacy protection. A term designed to make "deficit reduction" sound positively saintly, coined by *Hartford Courant* columnist Rob Kyff.[20]

legislative leadership advocate. Lobbyist. Example: **Legislative leadership advocates** *for the NRA have been remarkably effective in preserving the right of Americans to alter the health of their fellow citizens with automatic weapons.*[21] [See also: **government relations professional.**]

legislatively directed spending. Pork.[22]

legitimate rape. A phrase evoked by former Missouri representative Todd Akin to elucidate his conviction that coitus, when it's truly forcible, almost never results in pregnancy, and that, therefore, the argument that abortion should be legal in rape cases is specious. "If it's a legitimate rape, the female body has ways to try to shut that whole thing down," he explained.[23]

less than. A phrase that comes in handy when you want to "play down" a number. For example, instead of saying "Phoenix has almost half as many people as Los Angeles," say "Phoenix is less than half the size of Los Angeles." [See also: **fewer than.**]

let go. A term for firing someone that's particularly deceptive because it implies that the dismissed person is leaving of his or her own free will, after having been generously given permission to do so.[24]

leverage. To use borrowed money to buy or invest in something.[25] [See also: **levering up.**]

"leverage the drinkables infrastructure." *The Guardian*'s Steven Poole offers this as "a stylish way of saying 'make the coffee.'"[26]

levering up. Spending money you don't have.[27] [See also: **leverage.**]

liberate. To rid a nation, often by forceful overthrow, of a government you don't like.[28]

liberated territories. A term for the West Bank favored by those who maintain that Israel has a historic right to the lands it captured during the Six-Day War in 1967, and that it is therefore incorrect and misleading to refer to them as "the occupied territories," or even, as the Israeli government itself prefers to call them, the "disputed territories." Oklahoma senator Jim Inhofe is a staunch supporter of this point of view. "It is at this place where God appeared to Abram and said, 'I am giving you this land'—the West Bank," he points out. And even if God hadn't been involved, former Pennsylvania senator Rick Santorum agrees that the West Bank now indisputably belongs to Israel. "It was ground that was gained during war," he argues. "Should we give Texas back to Mexico?"[29] [See also: **disputed territories.**]

liberating coalition forces. American and/or allied troops acting as an occupying army.[30]

lifestyle center. A shopping mall, especially an upscale one.[31] [See also: **festival marketplace.**]

like. Canadian designer and former ad executive Gordon Pritchard notes that "like" is a **"weasel word"** intended to "stop the consumer from looking at the actual product being sold and instead start thinking about something that is bigger, better, or different." Pritchard offers three authentic examples of this usage: *"It's* **like** *getting another one free," "It's* **like** *a vacation in Hawaii,"* and *"Cleans* **like** *a white tornado."*[32]

liquid soap. A code phrase used by baseball player Alex Rodriguez and his drug supplier, Anthony P. Bosch, to describe testosterone lozenges in melted or liquefied form, a banned performance-enhancing substance.[33] [See also: **food**; **gummies**; **pink cream**; **rocket**.]

living with mobility impairment. Wheelchair bound.[34]

Lodestar of the 21st Century. One of the approximately 1,200 official titles that the North Korean Workers' Party conferred upon its country's supreme leader Kim Jong-il. Lodestar or not, Kim died in 2011, scarcely 10 percent of the way into the century of which he was preordained to be the guiding celestial presence.[35] [See also: **Guardian Deity of the Planet**.]

Kim Jong-il, erstwhile **Lodestar of the 21st Century**.

long-term nonreligious fasters. The Pentagon's term for the more than one hundred Guantánamo detainees who have gone on hunger strikes to protest their innocence or the conditions of their captivity.[36]

loophole. Any gap in the law that you propose filling with legislation you support. "Because the legal code allows all that it does not prohibit," writes *Slate* editor-at-large Jack Shafer, "loophole prospectors needn't look far to discover new ones. . . . It's a loaded, partisan word, one that implies wrongdoing and scandal where none exists, and inserting it into a political argument gives the inserter the upper hand." Example: *North Carolina's Governor McCrory signed legislation closing a **loophole** that had enabled minorities, and low-income and student voters, to go to the polls without a government-issued ID card.*[37]

"lots of possibilities." A term used by realtors to describe a house that is a hopeless dump.[38]

low-maintenance yard. A yard paved with concrete.[39]

lower ground floor. Basement.[40]

lubritorium. A service station (or a section of one) that offers oil changes.[41]

lyric malfunction. A phrase coined by *New York Times* music critic Jon Pareles to describe the moral calamity that was averted when network censors succeeded in scrubbing two suggestive words from ABC's televised presentation of the Rolling Stones' half-time performance at Super Bowl XL in 2006.[42] [See also: **wardrobe malfunction.**]

m

macaca moment. A racial or ethnic gaffe, caught on video and transmitted to the world, that significantly damages a political candidate's reputation. The term gained currency after Republican senator George Allen of Virginia, stumping for reelection in 2006, famously called S. R. Sidarth, an Indian-American "campaign tracker" employed by Allen's Democratic

opponent, James Webb, a "macaca." The slur is widely considered responsible for Allen's defeat.[1]

Machiavellian. Authors Paul Dickson and Robert Skole define this
as an adjective that describes actions by a politician that the
speaker or writer doesn't support. Politicians the speaker or
writer *does* support, Dickson and Skole note, are "wise, savvy,
strategic, shrewd or astute players of the political game."[2]

made available to the industry. Fired or laid off.[3]

made redundant. Laid off.[4]

"made with real fruit." A term frequently found on the labels for
food products, including Betty Crocker Strawberry Splash Fruit
Gushers, which are made from pear concentrate, contain no
strawberries, and are almost one-half sugar by weight, and
Gerber Graduates Tropical Juice Treats, whose package dis-
plays pictures of fresh oranges and pineapples but lists as principal ingredients corn syrup, sugar, and white grape juice.[5]

Madoff Social Security System. A new name for "Social Security"
proposed by Fox Business Channel host Eric Bolling, on the
basis that it's nothing but a "big Ponzi scheme." It's good, he
adds, that young people "realize they're not going to be able to
suck at the teat of the nanny state too much longer, get off their
butt, work, put some money away, and not have to rely on a
system that's gonna fold, probably by the time they get to collect a check."[6]

major malfunction. A term used by NASA launch commentator
Steve Nesbitt to refer to the explosion of the space shuttle
Challenger, seventy-three seconds into its flight, which
resulted in the death of all seven astronauts aboard.[7]

making enhancements to provide an even better experience. A
phrase used by "service providers" to explain why the service

you're paying them to provide is "temporarily" substandard or, more frequently, not available at all. (Used, for example, by Chase Bank during a computer service outage in 2012.)[8]

"making the right decision, not the quick decision." Something political strategy guru Frank Luntz urges Republicans to "emphasize the importance of" when arguing against immediate government action to clean up the environment.[9] [See also: "acting only with all the facts in hand."]

"males with female features." Saudi Arabia—where the state-funded Permanent Committee on Islamic Research and Fataawa has ruled that all things that "degrade or harm the dignity of women" must be prevented—came up with this description to classify the thousands of American servicewomen who participated in the campaign to liberate Kuwait during the Gulf War.[10]

man-caused disasters. An alternative term for "terrorism," coined in 2009 by Barack Obama's newly appointed Homeland Security secretary Janet Napolitano, and introduced to the public during her first testimony before Congress. "That is perhaps only a nuance," the secretary explained to *Der Spiegel*, "but it demonstrates that we want to move away from the politics of fear toward a policy of being prepared for all risks that can occur." "It is not 'politics of fear' to cite terrorism as the major threat to homeland security," *The Washington Times* observed in an editorial. "It's called reality."[11]

manage expectations. To promise less in the way of profits, salaries, product performance, working conditions, and just about everything else.[12]

manage staff resources. Fire employees at a corporate headquarters.[13]

managed for value. Fired or laid off. Nokia Siemens Networks used the term in a 2011 press release touting a plan to dismiss seventeen thousand employees in areas "not consistent" with the strengthening of its "highly-efficient global delivery system."[14]

mandatory discontinued attendance. A kinder and gentler term used by educators to describe the punitive suspension of a student.[15]

mandatory option. An automobile dealer's term for an option that isn't optional.[16]

marbled. An adjective used to make fatty beef sound more appealing.[17]

market distortion. The World Bank's term for Malawi's program of subsidizing fertilizer for its impoverished farmers, which it ordered the southeast African nation to suspend if it wanted to continue receiving loans. So Malawi did—an action that resulted in widespread crop failures, famine, and a dramatic increase in infant mortality.[18]

marketing representative. Salesperson.[19]

marriage equality. Same-sex marriage, as defined by those who support it.[20]

marriage redefinition. Same-sex marriage, as defined by those who oppose it.[21]

massage the data. Fiddle with the numbers.[22]

maturity tracks. Wrinkles.[23] [See also: **character lines; expression lines; laugh lines.**]

may be. A phrase to employ when making a claim that possibly has merit but equally possibly is utterly false. Example:

Rubbing your face regularly with Smoothify **may be** *helpful in reducing the visible effects of aging.*[24]

A meat technologist.

meat technologist. Butcher.[25]

media consultant. A less pejorative term for "spin doctor."[26] [See also: **image adviser.**]

media watchdog organizations. Pressure groups who happen to be on your side. As former *New York Times* public editor Daniel Okrent phrases it, one guy's "noble guardians" are the other guy's "dishonest advocates."[27]

medical loss ratio. Health insurance company terminology for the percentage of overall corporate revenue that actually has to be paid out to policyholders as benefits for covered medical conditions. The lower this percentage is, the more money the company can retain as profit or use to provide bonuses to top executives.[28]

"meeting the changing requirements of our clients." What IBM claimed it was doing when it instituted mass layoffs in early 2014.[29]

mental activity at the margins. Insanity.[30]

meticulously cared for. A real-estate term for a house where the kitchen appliances and bathroom are technically in working order but are so hopelessly outdated that they'll need to be replaced.[31]

midair passenger exchange. Air traffic controller lingo for a head-on collision.[32]

midnight requisition. Stealing all the good furniture and office supplies from someone's office after he or she leaves the company.[33]

mild irregularity. Constipation.[34]

milieu coordinator. Someone who manages the day-to-day functioning of a drug treatment center or mental health facility.[35] [See also: **behavioral health.**]

Military Information Support Operations (MISO). The U.S. Army's new, more vague, and notably less disquieting term for the psychological operations (psy-ops) and propaganda activities it conducts.[36]

millennial engagement expert. A youth marketer.[37]

miscertification. A Watergate-era term for fraud and criminal conspiracy.[38]

mischievous animals. What Robert Noel and Marjorie Knoller were convicted of "keeping" after their son's two Canary Island fighting dogs fatally mauled their San Francisco neighbor in 2001.[39]

misconnect rate. An industry term for the percentage of passengers' luggage that an airline or airport manages to lose. (They could have called it the "lost luggage" rate, but, of course, they didn't.)[40] [See also: **property irregularity receipt.**]

MISO. The official Pentagon abbreviation for **Military Information Support Operations**—a newly coined term for the U.S. Army's psy-ops and propaganda activities. The acronym—useful because it's even less transparent than the already impenetrable phrase it stands for—prompted the anonymous author of *The Economist*'s *Johnson* blog to observe, "I guess that's what they mean by alphabet soup. (Sorry, couldn't help it.)"[41]

misstatement. Lie.[42]

mistake. A crime, especially one committed by a politician or a corporate executive.[43]

mixologist. Bartender.[44]

mobile estate. Trailer park.[45] [See also: **mobile home.**]

mobile home. A trailer.[46] [See also: **mobile estate.**]

modernize. Jonathan Denn, a board member of the Clean Government Alliance, defines this as "a financial lobbyist's euphemism for destroying vital regulations." On the other hand, nuclear energy advocate Rod Adams warns that "modernize" is an EPA euphemism for *tightening* regulations.[47]

"modernizing Medicare and Social Security." The Business Roundtable's phrase for slashing benefits.[48]

modest reduction in near-term head count. Phraseology used in 2008 by Tesla founder and CEO Elon Musk to describe his laying off 10 percent of his company's workforce.[49] [See also: **adhere more closely to a special forces philosophy.**]

modify one's position. To flip-flop.[50]

molded plastic toilet system cover. A toilet seat. President Ronald Reagan used this term in a 1986 press conference to explain why the Pentagon had paid six hundred dollars for one. "You can go into a mobile home and see something not much different," Delaware senator William V. Roth, Jr., commented at the time.[51]

moment of silence. A prayer rebranded so as not to offend atheists and agnostics.[52]

morale welfare recreation. Consorting with prostitutes. The term was allegedly used by the security contracting firm Blackwater Worldwide to classify, and subsequently bill to the U.S.

government, the salary of a Filipino sex worker who provided services to the company's male employees in Afghanistan.[53]

morally plausible. A phrase describing a policy that seems good and right but is, as a practical matter, too overt to be carried out because it violates the law. William Bennett, for example, when he was America's "drug czar," suggested that beheading convicted drug dealers was "morally plausible," if "legally difficult."[54]

more than. A useful phrase to use when you want to "play up" a number. For example, instead of saying "Only 50.2 percent of the those eligible to vote turned up at the polls," say "More than half of those eligible to vote turned up."[55] [See also: **almost**; **only**.]

motion discomfort receptacle. Air sickness vomit sack.[56]

motor fuel dispensing facility. Gas station.[57]

A **motor fuel dispensing facility**.

"mountains of debt." A phrase frequently invoked by politicians interested in convincing the poor and the middle class that reductions in government spending—and the accompanying cuts in services—will be good for them.[58]

A **mucus recovery system**.

mucus recovery system. A tissue or box of tissues. According to Hugh Delehanty, editor of *Modern Maturity*, this term was devised by a hospital to help justify its charging patients eleven dollars for every box of Kleenex used in connection with their treatment.[59]

mule of the Jews. A phrase employed by Shaykh Abu Muhammad al-Adnani, the official spokesman of the Islamic State, to characterize U.S. President Barack Obama.[60] [See also: **Barack Hussein Obama**.]

multilayered. A phrase that, according to literary agent Jonny Geller, publishing copywriters use to praise books with too many characters.[61] [See also: **epic**; **extraordinary breadth**.]

muse. A word frequently used by authors to acknowledge another writer whose idea they've stolen, or whose words they've plagiarized.[62]

museology. A term, favored by art world cognoscenti, for what museums do.[63]

"My understanding is . . ." *The Office Life* defines this as "a fine bit of rhetoric that avoids committing to a yes/no answer. 'Is it black or white? Well, my understanding is black.'"[64]

n

natural. An FDA-approved food label term that indicates a particular product does not have any artificial or synthetic ingredients. (It may, however, contain pesticides, genetically modified ingredients, and high-fructose corn syrup, and could be heavily processed.)[1]

natural marriage. A more evocative term than "traditional marriage" to describe the formal union between a man and a woman. The phrase has been used to good effect by the Family Research Council in opposing lesbian and gay marriage, most notably in the title of its 2014 National Campaign in Defense of Natural Marriage.[2]

natural resources. Coal, oil, gas, forests, and wild animals that can be mined, drilled for, hunted, or fished to supply energy, food, or other products. The genius of the term, writes British author and political language expert Steven Poole, is that it connotes "an almost sacred right of exploitation," an implication that "everything in the natural world is there to be used by man, and is valuable only to the extent that it finds a place in the human economy." Poole goes on to note that "a species of fish that is fished to extinction is plainly an **ex-resource.**"[3]

needs assessment. A term for "educational testing," embraced by school reformers because it shifts responsibility for any "shortcomings" from a specific student to the educational system itself. Example: *"Darn, I got a grade of 'differently superior' on my final **needs assessment,"** sobbed Naomi.*[4]

negative attention getting. Bad behavior.[5]

negative deficit. A profit, especially when it's earned by an institution such as a foundation or a school that is not authorized to do so.[6]

negative employee retention. The policy of laying off or firing a portion of a company's workforce.[7]

negative gain in measured academic achievement. Decline in reported test scores.[8]

negative growth. Shrinkage of corporate revenue, market share, or stock value.[9]

negative net worth. Bankruptcy.[10]

negative or positive attitudinal orientations. Being sad or happy.[11]

negative patient care outcome. Death. Example: *Just for the record, Patrick Henry did not say, "Give me liberty or give me a* **negative patient care outcome.**"[12]

An icon displaying a **positive attitudinal orientation**.

negative reinforcement. Punishment.[13]

negative start-up synergy. An impressive-sounding business term to use when you're required to explain why your company was screwed up right from the very beginning.[14]

negative wallet biopsy. A coded medical jargon term used by nurses to refer to the discovery that a patient has no health insurance, which invariably results in his or her transfer to a less expensive hospital offering fewer care options.[15]

negatively impact. Hurt. Example: *"Darling, you know I'd never do anything to* **negatively impact** *you," said Sebastian. "But I'm leaving you."*[16]

neighbor procedure. The Israeli Army's term for the use of Palestinian civilians as human shields to protect soldiers during house-to-house searches.[17]

net profits revenue deficiency. A term coined by the Sun Production Company to avoid having to say it suffered a business loss.[18]

neutralize. Kill, destroy. Example: *One of the best-loved American novels of the twentieth century is Harper Lee's classic,* To **Neutralize** a Mockingbird.[19]

"new construction opportunity." Real-estate terminology for a house that's in such bad shape that the buyer will have to tear it down and rebuild it from scratch.[20]

New Middle-Propertied Stratum. "After half a century of denouncing bourgeois middle-class values," writes National Book Award winner Evan Osnos, the Chinese Communist Party "couldn't bring itself to utter the term 'middle class.'" So, Osnos tells us, they came up with a new name instead—"the New Middle-Propertied Stratum"—to describe "the rising ranks of entrepreneurs, intellectuals, and technocrats that the country was increasingly relying upon to drive its economic rebirth."[21]

"new normal, the." A phrase designed to convince the listener that an unacceptable situation is now so customary that it's inevitable and therefore must be passively endured. Bill Allen, in a comment reprinted by the late Alexander Cockburn, offers the following example: *"That our kids are graduating from college with no job prospects and debts approaching a home mortgage is* **the new normal.**"[22]

new-to-you. Used. The term is favored by a growing number of previously owned vehicle dealers, including New to You Auto Sales, LLC, in Waukesha, Wisconsin, and NU 2 U Cars in Chattanooga, Tennessee.[23] [See also: **preloved**; **pre-owned**; **previously enjoyed**; **previously loved.**]

"new Tom Clancy, the." When you encounter this phrase on a book jacket, Scottish novelist Iain Paton advises, you can expect "Jane's Military technical specifications with occasional action."[24]

"next Elmore Leonard, the." A publishing copywriters' phrase that, as Detroit-based crime novelist Bryon Quertermous observes modestly (and perhaps hopefully), can be used to promote the author of any book that "has criminals or Detroit or maybe Florida in it."[25]

no longer a factor. Pentagonese for dead, wounded, or destroyed.[26] [See also: **nonviable.**]

"No Tree Left Behind." See: **Healthy Forests Initiative.**

"nominated for the Pulitzer Prize." As novelist Mat Johnson reminds us, publishers can nominate any book they want simply by paying the fifty-dollar application fee. Remember this fact the next time you see this phrase on a book cover.[27]

noncertified workers. Substitute workers hired for the purpose of breaking a strike; scabs.[28] [See also: **replacement workers.**]

non-core assets. British journalist John Lanchester defines these as the financial equivalent of "garbage."[29]

non-core promise. A promise that, since you didn't keep it, wasn't really important. The term was coined and used by Australian prime minister John Howard to explain why he felt justified in ignoring a campaign pledge not to slash his nation's health and education budgets.[30]

non-facile manipulation of newborn. A medical term for a doctor's or nurse's dropping of a baby at delivery.[31]

non-goal-oriented member of society. Street person; bum.[32]

Nongovernmental International Panel on Climate Change. A global-warming-denying group, founded by the Heartland Institute and financed by the Koch brothers, that issued a report in 2014 titled "Climate Change Reconsidered" extolling the virtues of rising levels of carbon dioxide in the earth's atmosphere. The increased concentrations of CO_2, the document enthused, will not only encourage greater growth of valuable vegetation resources but will also benefit polar bears by providing them with warmer water to swim in.[33]

non-heart-beating donor. A corpse from which body parts have been extracted for transplant use.[34]

nonhuman gratuity receptacle. A term used by the city of Dana Point, California, to specify a container where strip club patrons, who are forbidden by municipal ordinance from directly paying, tipping, or touching an exotic dancer, may legally express their appreciation by depositing cash gifts. The regulations specify that the nonhuman gratuity receptacle must be positioned at least six feet from any area "occupied by the performer."[35]

non-minority-impacted. White only. This phrase, coined by the Beaumont (Texas) Housing Authority, has proven to be especially useful to realtors.[36]

nonoperative personnel. Dead soldiers.[37]

nonperforming asset (NPA). A bad loan.[38]

nonrenew. To lay off or fire. Example: *"You can't* **nonrenew** *me," said Frank as his supervisor handed him a dismissal notice, "because I've already decided to nonremain here!"*[39]

nonsurgical spinal decompression. A chiropractic office's billing term for a therapeutic procedure that is identical to, but more costly than, plain old traction.[40]

nontheistic religious worldview. The science of evolution as defined by **Citizens for Objective Public Education (COPE)**, a group opposed to the teaching of Darwin's theory in public schools. COPE argues that believing in Darwin's explanation of evolution is no more or less "religious" than accepting creationist views, and therefore, if "intelligent design" can't be taught in public schools because of rules governing the separation of church and state, neither can Darwinism.[41]

nontraditional sexuality. Essayist John Leo defines this as "all sexual practices that are either criminal or likely to put large numbers of people into shock."[42]

nontraditional start. A phrase used by Karen Olson, a close friend of former congressional aide Callista Bisek, to characterize the illicit six-year affair with Newt Gingrich that set the stage for Bisek's eventual marriage to the former House Speaker. As Sheryl Gay Stolberg points out in *The New York Times*, Gingrich's dalliance with Bisek helped derail his presidential ambitions by enabling his critics to cast him "as a hypocrite who sought to impeach a president over infidelity while engaging in it himself."[43]

nontraditional violence. Criticism. Lani Guinier, whom Bill Clinton had nominated to be his assistant attorney general for civil rights, helped popularize this term in 1993 when she used it to describe the wave of negative media coverage—much of it distorted and unfair—that led to Clinton's withdrawing her from consideration.[44]

nonviable. Dead.[45] [See also: **no longer a factor.**]

normal involuntary attrition. A term coined by Cisco Systems to describe the process that approximately eight thousand of its workers went through when they were removed from its payroll in early 2001.[46]

nosocomial. Medical jargon for a disease you catch while in a hospital, like a staph infection, as opposed to something you need treatment for that caused you to go to a health care facility in the first place. As Marianne DiNapoli writes in the Albany *Times Union*, "It would be bad for the hospital if you found out that the hospital actually made you sicker, so they use medical jargon instead."[47]

not being able to lift luggage. When it came to light in 2010 that Baptist minister, Family Research Council cofounder, and ardent anti-gay activist George Alan Rekers had engaged an online male prostitute to join him on a fully subsidized ten-day vacation in Europe, Rekers avowed that the only reason he had recruited his traveling companion was that "I recently had surgery and I can't lift luggage." In other words, *New York* magazine's Dan Amira observed, he did what "everyone who needs help with luggage does, he went on Rentboy.com and hired someone with a 'perfectly built 8 inch cock.'"[48]

"not being asked to continue." Language used by a Duke University spokesperson to make it clear that Red Wilson wasn't being fired when his position as head football coach was terminated in 1982.[49]

"not for human consumption." A phrase printed on packages of chemically synthesized narcotics—otherwise known as "designer drugs"—imported into the United States to give the appearance of legitimacy so they can pass through customs. Once inside the U.S., the drugs, which are increasingly being manufactured locally as well as offshore, are marketed, sometimes legally, as **bath salts**; **jewelry cleaner**; **phone screen cleaner**; and **plant food**.[50]

noted authority. A term used by reporters to describe any news source who's willing to return their phone calls or respond to their e-mail inquiries.[51]

nothing artificial. See: **all natural—nothing artificial**.

notion. A useful label for any idea, premise, or theory that you wish to discredit.[52]

novella. Book publicist Larry Hughes defines this as a short story set in very large type.[53]

now-disavowed claim. A euphemism, frequently used in the media, for a lie that has since been "rendered inoperative."[54]

nuclear deterrent. The U.S. arsenal of nuclear bombs and missiles, which, authors John Stauber and Sheldon Rampton point out, would be called **"weapons of mass destruction"** if anyone else owned them.[55]

nude-o-scopes. See: **enhanced screening procedures.**

nutritional avoidance therapy. Diet.[56]

O

OAB. An impressive-sounding medical term for incontinence. OAB stands for "overactive bladder," and, since most people don't know this, it's a good abbreviation to use when you're eager to tell folks that you're suffering from a serious condition but don't want them to know that you have to pee a lot.[1]

object + present participle compounds. See: **"tax-hiking, government-expanding, latte-drinking, sushi-eating, Volvo-driving, *New York Times*–reading, body-piercing, Hollywood-loving, left-wing freak show."**

observers. See: **analysts.**

offer. An advertising term that *The Guardian*'s Steven Poole defines as "a request that you buy something." Poole adds that a request that you buy something the seller really wants to get rid of is called a **"special offer."**[2]

offered a package. Fired.[3]

office manager. Secretary.[4] [See also: **administrative professional; area associate; executive assistant.**]

on vacation. A term used by Russian state television in 2014 to describe Russian troops fighting in the Ukraine.[5]

"one of a kind." Real-estate agent Kate Cocuzzo translates this commonly used advertising phrase as "ugly as sin."[6]

ongoing. A useful adjective for describing a project that is behind schedule.[7]

"ongoing problems." A phrase used by then Vice President Dick Cheney, during a January 2007 interview with CNN's Wolf Blitzer about the Iraq War, to characterize the minor issues (such as unabated sectarian violence, which had so far that month alone killed nearly 1,400 Iraqis and 62 American soldiers) that he felt were distracting attention from the "enormous successes" achieved by the U.S. intervention. "The biggest problem we face right now," Cheney added, "is the danger that the United States will . . . get out of Iraq. If we were to do that, we would simply validate the terrorists' strategy . . . that we don't have the stomach for the fight."[8]

only. A word useful in suggesting that a price, or a statistic, is low even when it isn't. Example: *This beautiful faux-leather coin purse can be yours for only $249.99.*"[9] [See also: **almost; more than.**]

Operation Enduring Freedom. See: **Operation Infinite Justice.**

Operation Infinite Justice. The initial code name used by the George W. Bush administration for the bombing and missile attacks in Afghanistan that launched the **War on Terror** in 2001. When Islamic scholars protested that only Allah was capable of dispensing infinite justice, the campaign was quickly redubbed **"Operation Enduring Freedom."**[10]

Operation Iraqi Freedom. The U.S government's official code name for its military occupation of Iraq, under which, as national security expert Spencer Ackerman pointed out in 2008, "foreign troops have enjoyed the legal right to kill any Iraqi whom commanders deem fit to kill; to search any house commanders deem fit to search; and to detain any Iraqi whom commanders deem fit to detain."[11]

Operation Just Cause. The code name for President George H. W. Bush's invasion of Panama in 1989, during which American military forces succeeded in deposing a former U.S. ally and undercover operative, Panamanian dictator Manuel Noriega, and replacing him with another leader with similar ties to Central American drug trafficking.[12]

Operation Peace for Galilee. The Israeli government's official name for their 1982 invasion of Lebanon.[13]

Operation Rainbow. What Israel called its 2004 incursion into the Gaza Strip. Notes Cracked.com's Paul Abercrombie: "The Israeli PR Agency wanted this to be seen as a friendlier, happier incursion into the Gaza Strip."[14]

Operation Urgent Fury. The Reagan administration's code name for the U.S. invasion of Granada in 1983. As Stanford University linguist Geoffrey Nunberg has pointed out, the moniker "seemed an excessively bellicose title for a mission to rescue some medical students on a Caribbean island whose total armed forces were smaller than the San Jose Police Department."[15]

Operation White Wing. The military code name for a U.S. search-and-destroy mission during the Vietnam War in connection with which 1,352 air strikes were launched, 1,126 fighter sorties were flown, 1.5 million pounds of bombs were dropped, and 292,000 pounds of napalm were used. The campaign was originally dubbed "Operation Masher," but the name was changed after President Johnson complained to General William Westmoreland, the U.S commander in Vietnam, that the word "Masher" didn't reflect the administration's "pacification emphasis."[16]

operational exhaustion. A gentler term for "shell shock," widely used during the Korean War.[17]

operational pause. A military term useful for describing any situation in which one's own troops have become "bogged down."[18]

opportunity scholarships. Political strategist Frank Luntz recommended that Republican candidates use this term instead of "private school vouchers," based on focus group research that showed voters would be far more likely to support them under the new name.[19]

optimizing the consumer footprint across geographies. A phrase used by Citibank in a 2012 press release to characterize its planned layoffs of more than eleven thousand employees worldwide.[20] [See also: **repositioning actions**.]

oral administration fee. What a hospital charges you for bringing a pill in a paper cup to your bedside.[21]

orange roughy. A name used by the fishing and restaurant industries to market a large, relatively unattractive marine species officially known as the "slimehead." The rebranding of the slimehead has been such a stunning success that, in 2006, the Australian government found it necessary to add the fish to its official list of "threatened species."[22]

Or-bam-eos. An alternative name, volunteered by Rush Limbaugh on his August 17, 2011, radio broadcast, for Kraft Foods' newly introduced Triple Double Oreo cookies, which feature layers of vanilla and chocolate cream sandwiched between three chocolate wafers.[23]

organic biomass. Sewage sludge.[24] [See also: **biosolids**; **dairy nutrients.**]

organoleptic analysis. A term for the process of determining whether food or wine is spoiled and should be discarded by sniffing it to see if it smells bad.[25]

original condition. A real-estate advertising term signaling that the owner has done absolutely nothing to maintain the property.[26]

-osity. See: **-ality.**

"our ongoing effort to streamline operations." What Silgan Holdings said their termination in 2006–2008 of more than six hundred employees working at their manufacturing facilities in Alabama, California, Virginia, and Turkey was "part of."[27]

"our society's recognition of the sanctity of life." Capital punishment, as defined by Utah senator Orrin Hatch.[28]

outdoor citizens. The homeless.[29]

outerwear enhancer. Girdle.[30]

outplacement. Corporate layoffs or dismissals, accompanied by a show of help in landing a new job that Michael V. Miller and Cherylon Robinson, writing in *The Journal of Applied Behavioral Science*, liken to the "cooling out" tactics used by confidence game operators to pacify victims whom they've defrauded.[31]

overpriced spare parts flying in close formation. A definition of U.S. Air Force planes used by Pentagon whistleblower A. Ernest Fitzgerald to explain why the cost of procuring them had become so bloated.[32]

Overpriced spare parts flying in close formation.

overrefreshed. Drunk.[33] [See also: **impaired**; **overserved**; **ruddy-faced**; **tired and emotional**.]

overseas contingency operations. A less dramatic and bellicose-sounding phrase adapted in 2009 by the Obama administration as a replacement for "War on Terror," the terminology favored by President George W. Bush to describe ongoing U.S. military and political operations against global terrorist organizations.[34] [See also: **War on Terror**.]

overserved. Drunk.[35] [See also: **impaired**; **overrefreshed**; **ruddy-faced**; **tired and emotional**.]

p

pacification. A term for the military conquest and occupation of foreign territory, originally used in the first century BC by Julius Caesar to describe his bloody victories during the Gallic Wars. Derived from the Latin word for "peace-making," "pacification" took on a more specific meaning during the Vietnam War, just over two thousand years later, when the U.S. Army's Ninth Division launched its **Accelerated Pacification Campaign** in the Mekong Delta region of Vietnam, under which, as Frances FitzGerald has written, they "almost literally 'cleaned out' the [Communist-held] regions of the northern Mekong Delta, bombing villages, defoliating crops, and forcing the peasants to leave their land."[1]

pacify. Subdue by force.[2]

packaging agent. Grocery bagger.[3]

pain compliance techniques. The use of torture to control a person.[4]

palmetto bugs. A euphemism coined by tourism boosters in Florida to make the state's flying cockroaches sound less repellent.[5]

pantry deloading. A consumer-products industry term for the unwelcome profit-depressing phenomenon of customers' actually using some of the items on their cupboard shelves instead of buying more of them.[6]

paper shortage. A problem cited by Eleazar Díaz Rangel, the editor of Venezuela's *Últimas Noticias*, to explain why stories critical of the government of President Nicolás Maduro rarely if ever appear in his newspaper. "There is not enough paper to print everything that comes in," explained Díaz Rangel, "and so we have to pick and choose, and some people call that censorship."[7]

paraphilic coercive disorder sufferer. A sexually violent predator; a rapist.[8]

partially proficient. An unsatisfactory grade on a competence test. To be specific, "partially proficient" is a better grade than "nonscorable," but not good enough to "pass," or to qualify for employment.[9]

partnerless sex. Masturbation.[10]

path to citizenship. Amnesty for illegal immigrants.[11]

"patient portrayal." See: **"doctor portrayal" and "patient portrayal."**

Patriot Act. Legislation enacted in 2001 that granted the U.S. government greater freedom to gather information and in doing so diminished citizens' rights to privacy. (The full name for the law, the USA PATRIOT Act, is an acronym for "Uniting and Strengthening America by Providing Appropriate Tools Required to Intercept and Obstruct Terrorism.")[12]

paycheck protection. A term used in proposed anti-union legislation in Kansas that would "protect" teachers from themselves by prohibiting them from donating to the National Education Association PAC using voluntary payroll deductions.[13]

payroll orphan. A person who has been laid off or fired, and thus will no longer be receiving a paycheck.[14]

Peacekeeper. The name bestowed by the Reagan administration on the U.S. MX ICBM missile, which was capable of delivering ten independently targetable nuclear warheads, each twenty times more powerful than the atomic bomb used to destroy Hiroshima in 1945.[15]

penile insertive behavior. Copulation.[16]

pepperpot soup. Lining-of-hog-belly soup.[17]

percussive maintenance. Dealing with a malfunctioning piece of equipment by banging on it until it begins operating or fails completely.[18]

period of economic adjustment. Recession; depression.[19]

permalancing. Working for an extended period of time as a contract employee with few or no benefits.[20]

permanent pre-hostility. Peace. The use of this phrase earned the U.S. Department of Defense a 1984 Doublespeak Award

Count Leo Tolstoy, author of the nineteenth-century Russian classic *Kinetic Military Action* and ***Permanent Pre-Hostility***.

nomination from the National Council of
Teachers of English, but the Pentagon lost out
in the final voting to the Department of State
for its rebranding of state-sponsored "killing" as the **arbitrary deprivation of life.**[21]

person of interest. A crime suspect—especially
one whom authorities can't level formal
charges against because they lack sufficient
evidence to do so.[22]

**Personal
appurtenance
storage units.**

personal accounts. See: **personalization.**

personal appurtenance storage unit. Locker.[23]

personal assistant. Secretary.[24]

personalization. A term that Republican language guru Frank
Luntz recommended, in a 2005 memo, that GOP candidates use
for the privatization of social security accounts. "Never say
'privatization/private accounts,'" Luntz advised. "Instead say
'personalization/personal accounts.' Two-thirds of America
want to personalize Social Security while only one-third would
privatize it. Why? Personalizing Social Security suggests
ownership and control over your retirement savings, while pri-
vatizing it suggests a profit motive and winners and losers."[25]

personhood. A term characterizing the inherent rights of zygotes
and embryos that is used by anti-abortion forces seeking to
pass state constitutional amendments defining any fertilized
human egg as a legal person. If passed, such amendments
would make many forms of birth control and all instances of
pregnancy termination, even in cases of rape, incest, or medical necessity, the equivalent of murder.[26] [See also: **pre-born
babies.**]

pet-friendly. According to real-estate expert Barbara Corcoran, if you see the words "pet-friendly" in an ad, you can be certain that "the house stinks."[27]

phone screen cleaner. A deceptive name under which synthetic narcotics—also known as "designer drugs"—are frequently marketed online and in convenience stores.[28] [See also: **bath salts**; **jewelry cleaner**; **"not for human consumption"**; **plant food.**]

physical. A hockey and basketball euphemism for a style of play characterized by making punishing, and frequently illegal, hits on opposing players. "There's a lot of nuance to the term, though," notes Cracked.com's Christina Hsu, "so while one fan might really be asking his team to push opponents around and stand their ground in a legal and honorable way, another fan might be asking for nut shots."[29]

physical brand experience. A brick-and-mortar (as opposed to an online) store. Burberry used this phrase in 2013 to describe the company's new retail outlet on Regent Street in London.[30]

physician extenders. Nurse practitioners and physicians' assistants in dermatologists' offices who can do biopsies and chemical peels in place of the actual doctors who run the practices. Whether the physician or the "extender" actually performs the procedure, Elisabeth Rosenthal of *The New York Times* reports, the charge to the patient is generally the same.[31]

pink cream. A code phrase used by baseball player Alex Rodriguez and his drug supplier, Anthony P. Bosch, to describe testosterone creams, a banned performance-enhancing substance.[32] [See also: **food**; **gummies**; **liquid soap**; **rocket.**]

pinkwasher. Breast Cancer Action defines this as "a company or organization that claims to care about breast cancer by promoting a pink ribbon product, but at the same time produces, manufactures and/or sells products that are linked to the disease."[33]

pipi de chat. See: **barnyard.**

piping technologist. A plumber.[34] [See also: **leak detection and repair specialist.**]

pivot. Changing direction quickly and nimbly. As *USA Today*'s Rhonda Abrams points out, the term is a particularly useful one to use after something has gone terribly wrong with your business or with your career. Example*: After our company was cited for numerous food-safety violations, we* **pivoted** *to the manufacture of rat poison.*[35]

place in a four-point restraint. Police terminology for hog-tying an arrestee.[36]

place in a prone position. Police-report terminology for throwing a suspect onto the ground. As law enforcement officer turned novelist Lynda Sue Cooper points out, actions such as this are invariably carried out "for officer safety reasons in accordance with departmental use of force policy."[37]

Planned Parenthood. An organization that provides contraception and abortion services. Blogger Heidi Chapman suggests it might more appropriately be called "Planned Parentless."[38]

planned termination. A suicide or abortion, for example.[39] [See also: **self-deliverance.**]

plant food. A deceptive label used on packages of synthetic narcotics so they can be sold, sometimes legally because they profess not to be intended for human consumption, at retail locations and online.[40] [See also: **bath salts; jewelry cleaner; "not for human consumption"; phone screen cleaner.**]

plasticity. A term used by art experts to describe the telltale three-dimensional shapes displayed by objects like sculptures and other molded or constructed works of art (but strikingly

absent from drawings and paintings).[41] [See also: **International Art
English.**]

plausible deniability. A phrase defined
by noted political blogger Taegan
Goddard as "the ability to deny blame
because evidence does not exist to
confirm responsibility for an action."
The term was coined by the U.S. Central Intelligence Agency during the
1960s, Goddard explains, "to describe
the withholding of information from
senior officials in order to protect
them from repercussions in the event
that certain activities by the CIA became public."[42]

Michelangelo's *Pietà*, a
sculptural masterpiece
that demonstrates
superb **plasticity**, not
to mention stunning
marbleosity.

playing the bamboo flute. A literal translation of the Japanese-
language euphemism for oral sex performed on a man.[43]

playing the blame game. The Center for Media and Democracy
defines this as an accusation "used to dismiss calls for
accountability," particularly in government.[44]

playing the race card. Again according to the Center for Media
and Democracy, a phrase "used to dismiss any concern of
non-whites."[45]

"Please stay on the line. We value your call." See: **"We value your
call. Thank you for your patience."**

pluralistic plan. A euphemistic term for a hiring quota.[46]

Plutoed. Demoted. The term was coined in the wake of the International Astronomical Union's decision, in 2006, to "demote"
the former planet Pluto to "dwarf planet" status.[47]

pockets. A term characterized by Rich Coffey of Vizettes.com as useful for "shrinking bad news." "For example," Coffey writes, "swarming Fedayeen are termed 'pockets of resistance.' Hordes of hungry people are 'pockets of need.'"[48]

"poised to outperform next year." A cheerful financial prediction issued by a company that, Daniel Dunaief of the Long Island (New York) *Times Beacon Record* relates, had failed so badly to meet even its own dismal expectations that there was absolutely no prospect of its posting worse results during the coming earnings season.[49]

police action. What President Harry Truman said U.S. forces would be engaging in when he committed them to combat duty in Korea in 1950. If he had admitted it was a "war," he would have needed congressional authority for sending American troops to fight in it.[50]

political equity. Hypothetical value that accrues to a corporation as a result of its campaign contributions.[51]

poor choice of words. By apologizing for "using a poor choice of words," you can appear to express contrition for a hurtful statement you made while actually standing by the content of your original remarks. Example: *Conservative Republican rock guitarist and confessed sexual predator Ted Nugent conceded that when he described President Obama as a "subhuman mongrel" while campaigning for a Texas senatorial candidate, he had, in effect, made a* **poor choice of words**.[52]

poorly buffered precipitation. Acid rain. "Poorly buffered" could be used in connection with other polluted or otherwise impure items, too.[53] [See also: **atmospheric deposition of anthropogenically derived acidic substances.**]

portable handheld communication inscriber. Pencil.[54]

A portable handheld communication inscriber.

post-health professional. An undertaker or crematorium operator.[55] [See also: **after-death care provider; bereavement care expert.**]

postmenopausal. Old.[56]

post-traumatic stress disorder (PTSD). A term for what used to be called "shell shock" that entered common usage during the Vietnam War. George Carlin, in a famous monologue about euphemisms, pointed out that, in the new coinage, "the pain is completely buried under jargon." "I'll bet you," he added ruefully, "if we'd of still been calling it 'shell shock,' some of those Viet Nam veterans might have gotten the attention they needed at the time. I'll betcha. I'll betcha. . . ."[57]

pre-born babies. Zygotes and embryos. The term is at the crux of the movement, on the part of anti-abortion rights advocates, to expand the legal definition of "personhood" to include—as the language of a proposed amendment to the Mississippi state constitution states it—"every human being from the moment of fertilization, cloning or the functional equivalent thereof." Doing so would, of course, win for the "pre-born" the same protections under the law currently enjoyed only by the post-born.[58] [See also: **personhood.**]

prebuttal. The dismissal of an unwelcome point of view before it is even raised.[59]

predawn vertical insertion. What the Reagan administration called the U.S. invasion of Grenada in 1983.[60]

preemptive. Unprovoked. For example, a "preemptive strike" is an "unprovoked attack" carried out, no doubt, for the purposes of "preemptive defense."[61]

preloved. A substitute for "used" or "secondhand" that, like "previously loved," is designed to be even more positive than "previously enjoyed."[62]

pre-owned. Used. Example: *David discovered that the* **pre-owned** *vehicle that he had purchased was a bit more degraded than he had expected.*[63] [See also: **new-to-you**; **preloved**; **previously enjoyed**; **previously loved**; **well-loved**.]

pre-reclined seats. What Spirit Airlines called the fixed upright seats it installed on some of its planes in 2010. Example: *Not only did my flight offer* **pre-reclined seats***, it also featured pre-sneezed-on pillows, pre-occupied toilets, and a pre-delayed departure and arrival.*[64]

pressure, a little. Pain. Doctors and dentists frequently warn patients that they might "feel a little pressure" just before doing something that promises to be truly agonizing.[65]

prestigious. An adjective that, according to writer John Leo, usually "heralds the arrival of a noun that nobody cares about," as in "the prestigious Jean Hersholt Humanitarian Award."[66]

presumably. Paul Dickson and Robert Skole, authors of *Journalese*, an invaluable dictionary of media jargon, identify this as a code word that guarantees "the writer is about to take a wild-assed guess."[67] [See also: **apparently**.]

pretailored. Off the rack and ready-to-wear.[68]

previously enjoyed. Used.[69] [See also: **previously loved**.]

previously loved. An even more effusive substitute for **"used"** than **"previously enjoyed."** Example: *After her tender uncou-*

pling from Nicholas, Sandra sold her **previously loved** *wedding gown for a tidy sum.*[70]

private. A less rapacious-sounding adjective than "corporate" to use when you're talking about funding or investments, particularly when the funding or investments you have in mind involve the corporate takeover of services, such as education or mail delivery, that are traditionally provided by the government.[71]

proactive pacifism. Greatly increased military spending. The phrase was coined by Japanese prime minster Shinzo Abe in 2013 to describe his country's newly robust five-year defense plan.[72]

proactivity expectations. Traffic ticket and arrest quotas. The term was used by two Arlington County, Virginia, police commanders in a memo, since rescinded, that also suggested that there would be disciplinary action for officers who didn't meet performance benchmarks.[73]

procedural safeguards. Red tape.[74]

pro-choice. Advocating legalized abortion.[75]

pro-death groups. Organizations that support abortion rights. The National Right to Life Committee used the term in a fundraising letter to describe Planned Parenthood and the National Organization for Women, among others.[76]

pro-growth tax policies. Tax cuts for corporations and the wealthy.[77]

pro-life. Opposed to legalized abortion.[78]

project. A term for a newly acquired athlete who, albeit possessing some innate athletic ability, doesn't seem to know a thing about how to play the game he's chosen as his life profession. The underlying assumption, writes Christina Hsu of Cracked

.com, is that "there's got to be *something* he can be trained to do, like maybe holding a clipboard."[79]

propaganda session. A press briefing held by a person, organization, or country with whom you disagree.[80]

property irregularity receipt. American Airlines' term for a voucher given to a passenger acknowledging the loss of his or her luggage.[81] [See also: **misconnect rate.**]

protective custody. Imprisonment without charge or trial.[82]

public assistance. Welfare.[83]

public diplomacy. Propaganda (waged by your side). The genius of the phrase "public diplomacy," opines Glenn Thompson on Cracked.com, is that it sounds "so dull that you don't even want to find out what it means."[84]

public option. An intentionally almost content-free term for "government-administered health insurance," coined by Democrats who supported it but, as author Ron Rosenbaum has pointed out, feared that voters would reject it if they knew what it actually meant.[85]

public safety unit. Former Ugandan dictator Idi Amin's name for his murder squad.[86]

Purell defense, the. Claiming that one's failure to pass a blood alcohol test was the result of recent, or frequent, use of hand sanitizer rather than of overzealous drinking. The term became popular after *Slate* columnist Nina Rastogi used it in an article inspired by Staten Island Republican congressman Vito Fossella's unsuccessful attempt to exonerate himself from DUI charges in 2008.[87]

pursuing gender diversity in marriages. Opposition to same-sex marriages. The phrase first came to light in an argument offered to the Supreme Court by the state of Utah in defense of its ban on same-sex marriages, which basically claimed that its statute did not really represent opposition to gay marriage per se but rather was an effort to ensure equal roles in wedlock for both men and women.[88]

push poll. A telemarketing call, disguised as an unbiased survey, made by a political campaign for the purpose of spreading negative information about the opposing candidate.[89]

putative offender. Former chief justice William Rehnquist's term for an individual accused of a crime and held without bail before his or her trial on the grounds of "dangerousness." As William Lutz, professor emeritus at Rutgers University, has pointed out, "putative offenders" are effectively "judged guilty until proven innocent."[90]

q

"Quiet Neighbors Across the Street." A phrase featured on a sign posted by upstate New York realtor Mary Shelsby at the entrance to a residential property located adjacent to a cemetery. As part of what proved to be a successful sales pitch for the house, she also made a second sign that stated, simply, "Good Bones."[1]

r

race-sensitive admissions policies. A new euphemism, offered by Supreme Court justice Sonia Sotomayor, for **affirmative action** (*itself* a euphemism for policies that give preferences to African-Americans and other minorities in employment and college admissions). Sotomayor unveiled her new coinage in the dissenting opinion she wrote in *Schuette v. Coalition to Defend Affirmative Action*, a 2014 case in which the court upheld the right of Michigan voters to ban the consideration of race as a criterion for admittance to the state's institutions of higher learning.[1]

radical. As Jerry Merchant and Mary Matthews point out on their website, ExtremelySmart.com, this is a convenient adjective to apply to anyone you strongly disagree with. As examples, they cite such usages as "radical feminists" and "radical environmentalists." Folks you strongly *agree* with, note Merchant and Matthews, are not "radical," they are "committed" and "focused."[2]

rainforest. Jungle.[3]

raising the bar on talent. A term used by Tesla Motors CEO Elon Musk to describe a series of layoffs at his company.[4]

rapid oxidation. A fire.[5]

raping the earth. An accusatory phrase that environmental activists find particularly useful because, as blogger Andrew K. Dart points out, it can be trotted out to condemn absolutely any activity, no matter how big (such as drilling for oil or strip-mining) or small (eating a steak or wearing leather shoes), that deviates from the path of sustainability.[6]

Mrs. O'Leary's cow accidentally kicks off the **Rapid Oxidation** of Chicago in 1871.

rarely appropriate. A new designation, recommended in 2013 by the American College of Cardiology, for a category of medical procedures that the college had previously labeled "inappropriate." Visual Thesaurus columnist Mark Peters notes that the new term doesn't seem to have been designed for the purpose of making malpractice suits against doctors easier to win.[7]

"reaching out to you." What telemarketers and spammers frequently tell you they're doing before assailing you with an unsolicited and unwelcome sales pitch.[8]

reality augmentation. Lying.[9]

rebalancing our workforce. A term used by AOL CEO Tim Armstrong in a memo announcing he was laying off nine hundred of his company's employees.[10]

rebate. Bribe.[11]

"recalculating route." The nonjudgmental message the soothing voice of your GPS system has been programmed to deliver

every time you fail to follow even the sim-
plest driving directions.[12]

receptacles for male semen. A term used by
Rush Limbaugh to describe unwed single
mothers.[13]

reclamation site. Toxic waste dump.[14]

reconnaissance in force. A Department of
Defense term for the military strategy
previously called "search-and-destroy."
General William C. Westmoreland, the
commander of U.S. forces in Vietnam,
writes that he changed the name himself

Saint Helena of
Constantinople, a
revered **semen
receptacle**.

after John Charles Daly, the noted news correspondent (and
What's My Line? panel show host), warned him that the public
had come to equate the phrase "search-and-destroy" with
"aimless searches in the jungle" and "the random destroying
of houses and other property."[15]

recreational eco-unit. Garden. Example: *When it comes to historical novels about Northern Italian Jews, you'd be hard
pressed to find a better one than Giorgio Bassani's The* **Recreational Eco-Unit** *of the Finzi-Continis.*[16]

redaction. Censorship.[17]

redeploying to the rear. Retreating.[18] [See also: **exfiltration**;
strategic withdrawal.]

redistribute assets. Embezzle.[19]

reduced state of awareness, in a. Asleep, drunk, or stoned, especially when the condition results in an accident. The term was
popularized in the early 1970s by two railroad engineers who
used it in the course of explaining how their train, which was
traveling seventy-two miles per hour through a twenty-five-

mile-per-hour speed zone at the time, managed to jump the tracks, causing $1.7 million in damage.[20]

reducing costs. Cutting salaries and/or firing people.[21]

reducing our footprint. What the Boeing Company said it was doing when it announced, in the spring of 2014, that it planned to lay off or transfer 1,300 of its research and engineering employees in Washington state and California.[22]

redundancy elimination. The laying off or firing of workers when a company or agency determines that it has too many employees (a condition often referred to as a "redundancy of human resources").[23]

referencing. An art connoisseur's term for referring to something. Example: *This definition references (even as it juxtaposes)* **"referencing"** *and "referring."*[24] [See also: **International Art English.**]

reform. According to British author John Lanchester, "This is something of a weasel word. In its modern economic usage it never, ever, not once, means 'hiring more people and giving your current workforce more generous pay and conditions.' Instead it usually means sacking people and making the ones who are in work do more for less."[25]

Noted neologists Sarah Palin and William Shakespeare.

refudiate. A verb coined, perhaps accidentally, by Sarah Palin, who demanded, on Sean Hannity's Fox News Channel show, that President Obama and the First Lady "refudiate" an NAACP charge that members of the Tea Party had engaged in racist behavior. When she was mocked for this neologism, Palin responded by comparing herself to Shakespeare, who, she tweeted proudly, "liked to coin new words, too. Got to celebrate it!"[26]

regeneration harvesting. A term loggers use to describe the removal of all trees from a previously forested area.[27]

regime change. A coinage, attributed to the neoconservative Project for the New American Century, that makes what authors John Stauber and Sheldon Rampton call "the imperial project of overthrowing a foreign government through a military invasion" seem "tidy, efficient, and rational." The phrase, Stauber and Rampton observe, made it possible for the George W. Bush administration "to talk about invading Iraq without even thinking about the human consequences: assassination, occupation, or the deaths of thousands of innocents."[28]

regrettable by-products. Civilians killed by mistake. The term gained currency within the U.S. military during the Vietnam War but was eventually replaced by the still more euphemistic **collateral damage.**[29]

relational capitalism. Nepotism.[30]

relay misinformation. To tell a lie.[31]

reliability enhancement. What computer software companies say they're offering you when they fix a bug or other flaw in one of their products.[32]

"reminiscent of Ellison and Baldwin." A publishing ad writers' phrase that can be, and often is, trotted out to promote any African-American novelist.[33]

remnants. Journalist Patrick Cockburn describes this as a word "that had been doing no harm until it was used in phrases like 'remnants of Saddam Hussein's regime' or 'Al-Qaeda remnants' to explain why people who Washington had claimed were dead and buried still seemed to be in business."[34]

remote tippees. A term coined by defense lawyers to describe a pair of hedge fund managers who, they argued, had been falsely accused of insider trading because the illegally obtained information they used to make millions of dollars had in fact been transmitted to them by *third parties* rather than by the actual Dell Computer and Nvidia employees who had been generously compensated by *someone else* in return for leaking their companies' secrets.[35]

rendition. The nonjudicial deportation of a terror suspect for purposes of torture. This practice was originally called **extraordinary rendition** but has apparently become so commonplace that the qualifying adjective "extraordinary" is now seldom used.[36] [See also: **black sites**.]

repeating your argument using different language. As Jerry Merchant and Mary Matthews of ExtremelySmart.com point out, this can be an extremely effective way of appearing to respond to a question while actually avoiding it all together. As an example, they offer the following Q&A: *You: If you don't agree with me that every word in the Scriptures is factual, you're going to Hell. Interviewer: Please explain why you say that. You: People who don't believe in literal biblical inerrancy are destined for eternal damnation.*[37]

repetitive administration of legitimate force. A term used by U.S. military lawyer Colonel David L. Hayden to explain the "accidental" beating to death of two detainees at the Bagram Air Force base in Afghanistan.[38] [See also: **enhanced interrogation techniques; pain compliance techniques; special methods of questioning; stress and duress tactics**.]

replacement workers. Strikebreakers; scabs (especially when referred to by those employing them).[39] [See also: **noncertified workers.**]

reportedly. Quite possibly not true.[40]

reporting guidelines. Censorship, particularly when you're the one doing the censoring.[41]

repositioning actions. Citigroup's term for the firing of eleven thousand employees worldwide in order to achieve "an optimized consumer footprint across geographies."[42]

reproductive health services. Clinics that provide contraception and/or perform abortions.[43]

reproductive health rights. A term that, as used by progressives, has become a synonym for the right to have an abortion. "The unwritten rule when the Left discusses abortion is that it shouldn't be called 'abortion,'" writes *National Review* editor Rick Lowry, "but always 'health' or, more specifically, 'reproductive health.' . . . You could be forgiven for thinking that the country is riven by a fierce dispute over whether women should be allowed to choose their own OB-GYNs."[44]

reprographics engineer. A photocopying clerk.[45]

research in retrospect. A term coined by convicted insider trader Dennis Levine for the creation of a false paper trail of altered or backdated documents to provide a plausible rationale for investments that were actually made on the basis of illegally obtained confidential information.[46]

researching a film. What actress Winona Ryder claimed she was doing after she was caught shoplifting in a Beverly Hills department store in 2001. "My director said I should try it out," she explained.[47]

reserve. An impressive-sounding marketing term used on wine labels, which, when applied to wines produced in the United States under regulation by the Alcohol and Tobacco Tax and Trade Bureau—the federal tax-collection agency with label-approval authority—means only that the label has the word "reserve" on it. (The agency has established no definition for the designation and has attached absolutely no legal requirements for its use.)[48]

resource development park. Dump. Example: *Who can forget Bette Davis's immortal expression of disgust in* Beyond the Forest—*"What a* **re-source development park***!"*[49]

A **resource development park**.

resource-intensive. Expensive.[50]

resources control program. A term used by the Pentagon to describe the use of Agent Orange to defoliate the Vietnamese countryside.[51]

Responsible Industry for a Sound Environment (RISE). An industry organization whose mission it is to defend the use of pesticides.[52]

restructuring. A corporate term for closing plants and firing workers.[53]

"results not typical." A qualifying phrase that, until recently, was frequently found in advertisements whose overall content conveyed the false impression that a consumer who used a particular product would actually be likely to obtain the benefits it claimed to provide. Under new rules enacted by the FTC in 2009, marketers are no longer permitted to describe unusual results in testimonials, even if they append this all-purpose disclaimer.[54]

reutilization marketing facility. Junkyard. Example: *Bad, bad Leroy Brown, the baddest man in the whole damn town, was meaner than a* **reutilization marketing facility** *dog.*[55]

revelers. See: **booze-fueled rampages.**

revenue deficiency. See: **net profits revenue deficiency.**

revenue enhancement. Tax increase.[56]

reverse engineering. Stealing a design by taking a product apart, seeing how it's made, and copying it.[57]

reverse infallibility. An impressive, and usefully impenetrable, term for the quality of being always wrong.[58] [See also: **acluistic.**]

reverse racism. A term that suggests that advocates of racial equality are taking things too far, and that, as RationalWiki phrases it, "in order to avoid the label, they must reduce their efforts."[59]

reversibility mechanism. A Pentagon term with no specific definition, except that any military exercise or operation that features one can be stopped or called off, even after it's begun.[60]

reversification. A word coined by British author John Lanchester in his book *How to Speak Money: What the Money People Say— And What It Really Means* to describe the way commonly used financial terms end up meaning pretty much the opposite of what they ought to mean. For example, Mr. Lanchester explains, a reasonable person might think "securitization" would have "something to do with security or reliability," but it doesn't. It actually describes "the process of turning something—and in the world of finance it can be pretty much anything—into a security."[61] [See also: **securitization.**]

revolution. Journalese for "any kind of change at all." Essayist John Leo offers, as an example, "the 'revolution' in meat packing."[62]

rewiring for growth. What Walgreens announced it was doing in 2009 when it eliminated approximately one thousand positions from its workforce.[63]

right to choose. The right to have an abortion, or (to borrow language popularized by Republican congressman Randy Neugebauer of Texas) to be a "baby killer."[64]

right-to-work laws. Union-busting legislation.[65]

rightsize. To lay off a significant percentage of one's employees.[66] [See also: **downsize**.]

risk management. Damage control.[67]

robust exchange of views. A shouting match.[68]

A robust exchange
of views.

robustifying learnability. Making a lesson easier to grasp. The term was used by economists Robert J. Tetlow and Peter von zur Muehlen in the title, and throughout the text, of a Federal Reserve Board paper urging that the language used in monetary policy rules should be simplified.[69]

rocket. A code word used by baseball player Alex Rodriguez and his drug supplier, Anthony P. Bosch, to describe a syringe containing banned performance-enhancing substances like human growth hormone and insulin growth factor.[70] [See also **food; gummies; liquid soap; pink cream**.]

Rocky Mountain oysters. A menu term for bull testicles.[71]

role-based pay. A British banking industry term for a bonus paid to a key employee that would be prohibited, if it were actually *called* a bonus, by new European Union regulations capping the size of large year-end cash payments tied to performance.[72]

role-player. A sports commentator's euphemism for an athlete who is less skilled than the majority of his teammates.[73]

Roses of the Prophet Mohammed. A new name for Danish pastries, adopted by the Iran Confectioners Union after a Danish newspaper published cartoons of Mohammed, a clear contravention of the Islamic proscription against the creation of representations of the Prophet.[74]

A **Rose of the Prophet Mohammed.**

round-nose shovel. A substitute descriptive name for the digging tool formerly called a spade, now widely used by hardware stores in an effort to avoid a word that was once a common racial epithet.[75]

rubber-hose cryptanalysis. Using violence, torture, or other forms of coercion to gain access to a computer password or other encrypted data. According to security guru Marcus J. Ranum, who coined this now widely used phrase, rubber-hose cryptanalysis "can take a surprisingly short time and is quite computationally inexpensive."[76]

Rubenesque. Fat.[77]

ruddy-faced. A journalists' euphemism for "drunk."[78] [See also: **impaired**; **over-refreshed**; **overserved**; **tired and emotional**.]

runway excursion. The Federal Aviation Administration's

A Caribbean Airlines Boeing 737 photographed at the Georgetown, Guyana, airport in July 2011, shortly after experiencing a **runway excursion.**

official term for a plane's accidentally, and perhaps cata-
strophically, veering off or overrunning the end of an airport
runway.[79]

rustic. According to Seattle realtor Conor MacEvilly, this means
"potentially no water or electricity."[80]

S

sacrificed. Medical jargon for what happened to laboratory animals that were unavoidably or deliberately killed in the course
of an experiment.[1]

"sacrificed by heartless terrorists." See: **human shields.**

SAD. See: **social anxiety disorder.**

"Sadly, we are publishing a book similar to this next spring." A
publisher's rejection letter staple that, according to literary
agent Jonny Geller, actually means, "It, too, has a beginning,
middle, and end."[2]

safety net as hammock. A Republican Party term for extended
unemployment benefits, which the GOP characterizes as a "nar-
cotic for the unemployed," who are, presumably, lulled away
from seeking work by handouts.[3]

sale. The words "sale" and "sale price" are used by advertisers or
store managers to make you think you're being given an opportunity to buy something at a discount, but these labels have no
enforceable legal definition. Therefore, unless the "regular

price" and/or the percentage by which it has been reduced are displayed, there's no reason to believe that the item you're interested in is selling for a penny less than it usually does.[4]

sanctified eggs. A term for deviled eggs that, like **angeled eggs** and **doubled eggs**, is preferred by those who feel that even mentioning the name of the devil could give him a foothold on this earth.[5]

Sanctified eggs.

Sandwich Artist®. The officially trademarked title given by Subway restaurants to the food preparers on what the organization modestly refers to as the "Greatest Team in Franchising History."[6]

sanitary landfill. A garbage dump. Example: *The "Global Sanitary Landfill" in Old Bridge, New Jersey, is just one of many **sanitary landfills** that the U.S. Environmental Protection Agency has closed because of dangerously unsanitary conditions.*[7]

sanitation engineer. Garbage collector.[8]

sanitize. A term used in a legal context to refer to the process of removing incriminating evidence—specifically, to the act of editing surreptitiously from a document any material that might subject its author to embarrassment or prosecution.[9]

A sanitation engineer.

Save Our Species Alliance. A coalition of American logging, timber, cattle, and mining interests dedicated to gutting the Endangered Species Act.[10]

"saving Social Security." The corporate lobbying group Fix the Debt uses this terminology to describe its proposal to slash benefits. The Koch Industries–funded **60 Plus Association**, a "non-partisan seniors advocacy group," prefers "saving Social Security for the young."[11]

savings. Spending cuts.[12]

scanning professional. A grocery store checkout clerk. [See also: **career associate scanning professional.**]

scrappy. A sports term that seems complimentary but actually means "hardworking but not good enough to win."[13]

screen test. Police terminology for an officer's deliberately slamming on the brakes of his patrol car in order to cause the suspect handcuffed in the backseat to be thrown forward, smashing his head against the thick wire-mesh partition mounted behind the driver's seat.[14]

sea kittens. Fish. The term was coined by People for the Ethical Treatment of Animals in hopes that giving denizens of the deep a cuter image might make children less likely to want to eat them. Ashley Byrne, PETA's sea kitten campaign coordinator, explains it this way: "Knowing that the fish sticks in the school cafeteria are really made out of tortured sea kittens makes most kids want to lose their lunch." Example (provided by Visual Thesaurus columnist Mark Peters): *Mom, you drink like a* **sea kitten.**[15]

seasonal employee. Migrant worker.[16]

secluded. A real-estate advertising term for an inconveniently located, or, perhaps, totally inaccessible, residential property.[17]

second-amendment. A verb for killing someone with a gun, favored by firearms-control advocates.[18] Example: *"American Sniper" Chris Kyle was* **second-amendmented** *by Eddie Ray Routh at a shooting range in Texas.*

sectarian conflict. A term that enabled the George W. Bush administration to discuss the civil war it ignited in Iraq without ever having to admit that it was occurring.[19]

securitization. A term that British financial writer John Lanchester explains has nothing to do with "security or reliability" but rather refers to "the process of turning something—and in the world of finance it can be pretty much anything—into a security, a financial instrument that can be traded as an asset." One example of securitization: the trillion dollars in "sub-prime" U.S. home mortgages that were packaged into multilayer collateralized debt obligations, many of which defaulted in 2008–2009, causing the greatest financial crisis since the Great Depression.[20]

security contractor. Mercenary.[21] [See also: **civilian contractor.**]

security directive. A secret law or regulation enacted by non-elected officials. The pace at which such laws are being made has "accelerated" since the 9/11 attacks, warns the Cato Institute's Timothy Lynch, and one of the consequences is "the possibility that Americans will now be held accountable for noncompliance with unknowable regulations."[22]

security fence. See: **Apartheid Wall.**

seemingly. See: **apparently.**

selected out. U.S. Department of State parlance for being fired.[23]

selective strike. A term for a bombing campaign designed to produce, in the words of lexicographer Hugh Rawson, "something less than total annihilation."[24]

self-deliverance. Suicide.[25]

self-determination. A term for what nationalist independence movements are advocating, favored by those who approve of their cause.[26] [See also: **separatist.**]

self-employed. Unemployed.[27]

self-injurious behavior incidents. A U.S. Department of Defense term for suicide attempts by prisoners at its Guantánamo detention facility.[28]

semantic violence. Shouting or yelling at someone.[29]

A man wearing a **semi-antique** rug.

semen receptacles. See: **receptacles for male semen.**

semi-antique. A term used by rug merchants to describe a carpet that's *kind of* old but not really *that* old. According to Rugs-Oriental.net, any rug that was made thirty years ago or more may properly be labeled "semi-antique."[30]

semi-boneless. Contains bones.[31]

semi-finalized. A business term useful for referring to any ongoing project that has progressed from being **in the early stages of finalization** to a point at which it is about 50 percent complete.[32]

semi-private. A widely used hospital term for a room that is not private at all, as a patient must share it with at least one, and possibly as many as three, other semi-healthy individuals.[33]

send someone on a trip to Belize. A euphemism for murder used by Saul "Better Call Saul" Goodman, lawyer

A bust of Franz Schubert, whose failure to fulfill his wellness potential prevented him from completing the last two movements of his **Semi-Finalized** Symphony in B Minor.

of chemistry-teacher-turned-meth-kingpin Walter White, in the TV series *Breaking Bad*.[34]

senior. An old person.[35]

Senior Sanitarian. A title bestowed by the township of Montclair, New Jersey, on the person in charge of waste disposal there.[36]

Sensible Food Policy Coalition. An industry group formed by soft drink bottlers, fast-food chains, and junk food manufacturers to lobby against what Mark Bittman of *The New York Times* calls "the government's pathetic attempt to nudge industry toward at least improving the nutritional profile of junk food advertising targeted at kids in the form of voluntary guidelines."[37]

sent into phased retirement. Fired.[38]

sentient property. A legal term for pets proposed by Davidson, North Carolina, attorney Carolyn B. Matlack. The designation would allow courts to recognize that household animals are a unique type of property, entitled—because they are thinking, feeling creatures—to more rights than tables and chairs (although not so many as people enjoy). In her book *We've Got Feelings Too!*, Matlack argues that the widely recognized legal "doctrine of substituted judgment" should be broadened to permit owners to speak on behalf of their animal companions in court.[39]

sentinel event. The Joint Commission, the nonprofit organization responsible for accrediting U.S. hospitals and medical care facilities, defines this as "an unexpected occurrence [in a health care setting] involving death or serious physical or psychological injury, or the risk thereof." If a surgeon cuts off the wrong leg or sews you up with a couple of needles inside, notes essayist John Leo, "the words 'malpractice' and 'gross negligence' may occur to you. But the medical world prefers 'sentinel event.'"[40]

separatist. An adjective used to describe nationalist independence movements, favored by those who disapprove of their cause.[41] [See also: **self-determination.**]

serious overdrive. Adulterous sex. South Carolina governor Mark Sanford used the phrase during a press conference to characterize his relationship with a woman in Argentina with whom, it turned out, he had been conducting an extramarital affair.[42] [See also: **hiking the Appalachian Trail; incredibly intense conversation.**]

service items. What airlines call the trash—used plastic cups and cellophane wrappers, for example—that flight attendants pick up from passengers before a landing.[43]

Hiroshima, August 6, 1945, shortly after being **serviced** by a force package.

servicing a target. Bombing enemy personnel, facilities, or territory. Example: *It's surprising that Hollywood has never thought of claiming that a big-budget movie that died at the box office had, in fact, been servicing the target audience.*[44] [See also: **visiting a site.**]

servicing the client. Having sex for money.[45]

severanced. Fired.[46]

sex addiction. A term for promiscuity that makes it sound like a difficult-to-treat affliction rather than a moral choice.[47]

sex care provider. A prostitute.[48] [See also: **morale welfare recreation; sex trade worker.**]

sex trade worker. A prostitute.[49] [See also: **morale welfare recreation; sex care provider.**]

sexual activity that is later deemed to have lacked consent.

Rape, especially of a woman who, at the time of the assault, was too inebriated to resist. The term originated in a "safety reminder" e-mailed to students by the University of Virginia.[50]

sexual preference. A phrase that, unlike "sexual orientation," implies that homosexuality is a moral choice rather than a natural condition. The term was used to great effect during a successful campaign in Colorado, in 1992, to pass a constitutional amendment barring laws designed to protect gays and lesbians against discrimination.[51]

sexually oriented business. A strip club, for example.[52]

shareholder activist. Corporate raider.[53] [See also: **takeover artist.**]

shedding weight. Firing people.[54]

shortening the dying process. Assisted suicide; euthanasia.[55]

"shot with lash inserts." A disclaimer—set in minuscule type and printed vertically for maximum unreadability—that appeared in a British television advertisement for Rimmel mascara, noting that Georgia May Jagger, the model shown in the spot, was actually wearing false eyelashes. The ad was ultimately banned as misleading by the British Advertising Standards Authority, despite protests from Rimmel that it had used the eyelash extenders only to ensure a "consistent and aesthetic" look, not to promise an exaggerated or unachievable result.[56]

signature strikes. The Obama administration's term for aerial drone attacks in Yemen targeting anyone who is suspected of "signing up" for al-Qaeda.[57]

significant originality issue. A term used by the scientific journal *Landslides* to explain what led it to retract a plagiarized paper.[58]

signifier. A term, increasingly fashionable in art criticism circles, for an image, form, color, tone, or anything else one might find in a painting, sculpture, or installation. Brian Ashbee cheered the ascendancy of the word in a famous article he wrote for *Art Review* in 1999. "Earlier critics," he observed, "had to battle with terms like symbol, icon, image, form, structure, colour, tone, drawing, composition (they do sound quaint, don't they!)—terms with a precise meaning. Happily today, for the busy critic, everything is a signifier!"[59] [See also: **International Art English.**]

simplifying and streamlining regulations to eliminate red tape. Weakening or repealing laws—particularly environmental ones—that impose limits on an industry's activities.[60]

simulation. The official international soccer term for "flopping"—or, as Visual Thesaurus's Mark Peters prefers to define it, "acting like a little boo-boo is a criminal assault to get the attention of the referee."[61]

single-use. A more responsible-sounding substitute for the word "disposable" that companies find convenient to use when they're trying to keep their products from attracting negative attention from environmentalists.[62]

60 Plus Association. An organization that advertises itself as "a non-partisan seniors advocacy group" and that seeks to make life easier for older Americans by working, among other things, for the repeal of the Affordable Care Act, for the replacement of the federal Social Security system by private investment accounts (it calls this "saving Social Security for the young"), for the defeat of gun control legislation proposals, and for the repeal of environmental regulations. According to the Center for Media and Democracy, the 60 Plus Association has received millions of dollars from organizations funded by billionaire industrialists Charles and David Koch.[63]

sleep management. A CIA euphemism for sleep deprivation, one of a group of **enhanced interrogation techniques** that President George W. Bush proudly referred to as "the tools necessary to protect the American people."[64]

slipping one's moorings. Having an illicit affair, for example. The phrase entered common usage after the former CIA director and commander of U.S. forces in Iraq, General David Petraeus, used it during a public apology to his family for having become sexually involved with his biographer. "[I will] try to move forward in a manner that is consistent with the values to which I subscribed before slipping my moorings," he promised.[65]

sluggish cognitive tempo (SCT). A mental health disorder that, according to Professor Russell A. Barkley, Ph.D., of the Medical University of South Carolina, is characterized by "daydreaming," "inattentiveness," and "lethargy." Because Barkley feels that the term "sluggish cognitive tempo" can be viewed by the public as "pejorative, derogatory, or frankly offensive," he has recently recommended that the name be changed to **concentration deficit disorder (CDD).**[66]

smart-sizing. Firing people.[67]

so-called. An adjective useful for describing something that you or your company just happens to have befouled or destroyed. For example, the Exxon Corporation, whose tanker the *Exxon Valdez* ran aground in Alaska's Prince William Sound in 1989, characterized the thirty-five miles of shoreline ravaged by the resulting spill as "so-called beaches, mainly piles of dark, volcanic rock."[68]

social anxiety disorder (SAD). One of the things the American

Psychiatric Association calls "shyness." They also call it **"avoidant personality disorder."** Luckily, the pharmaceutical giant GlaxoSmithKline has recently announced that its anti-depressant drug Paxil is a dandy treatment for social anxiety disorder, whose symptoms, according to the third edition of the "bible of modern psychiatry," *The Diagnostic and Statistical Manual of Mental Disorders (DSM)*, include a fear of public speaking, avoidance of communal rest-rooms, and being worried about saying the wrong thing.[69]

social expression product. Greeting card.[70]

social justice. According to Glenn Beck, the concept of "Christian social justice" is code for the redistribution of wealth, and can be compared to communism and Nazism. "I beg you, look for the words 'social justice' or 'economic justice' on

A **social expression product.**

your church website," Beck said during a March 2010 radio broadcast. "If you find it, run as fast as you can. Social justice and economic justice, they are code words. . . . Am I advising people to leave their church? Yes!"[71]

soft ordnance. A U.S. Department of Defense term for napalm.[72]

soft target. A human being who is bombed. (A "hard target" is a building that is bombed.)[73]

software anomaly. A bug.[74]

software architect. A computer programmer.[75]

"some assembly required." When this small-type disclaimer is used in connection with the marketing of a consumer item, you can be virtually certain you'll need skill, a considerable amount of time, and quite a few tools to turn it into a finished product.[76]

"Sorry for the inconvenience." "We regret that you elected to contact our Customer Service Department instead of engaging in a more productive activity, like banging your head against the wall."[77]

"sorry if . . ." Placing an "if" after any expression of regret turns an apology into a non-apology, not only by making it conditional, but also by shifting the blame to the victim for any perceived offense. For example, a simple "I'm sorry if something I might have said caused you distress" is a useful response to someone who is furious that you called them a stupid asshole.[78]

sparkling beverage. Wouldn't you rather buy one of these than a bottle of (flavored or unflavored) carbonated water?[79]

special investigation. British author Robert Hutton defines this as a journalistic account that's routine in every respect except that a photograph of the reporter appears next to his or her byline.[80]

special methods of questioning. Torture.[81] [See also: **enhanced interrogation techniques; stress and duress tactics.**]

special offer. See: **offer.**

spending more time with your family. You were fired, or dismissed for gross misbehavior, or forced out in a political power struggle, or quit in disgust, or were depicted naked in a Facebook posting, or are about to be indicted.[82]

spending spree. A phrase useful for characterizing a government-funded program enacted or proposed by an opposing party or group.[83]

Spring Egg Hunts. The New York Botanical Garden used to call these annual events "Easter Egg Rolls," until it rebranded them on the theory that a portion of their potential audience might be offended by the religious reference. Once "Easter" was changed to "spring," columnist John Leo points out, "hunt" had to be substituted for "roll" so that folks wouldn't "show up for a 'spring egg roll' expecting to be fed Chinese appetizers."[84]

spring water. A descriptive term that appeared next to images of a mountain and a lake on the labels of at least one brand of bottled water whose refreshing contents, it turns out, were actually obtained from a well contaminated with chemical solvents, including trichloroethylene, located in the middle of a warehouse facility next to a state-designated industrial waste site in Millis, Massachusetts. The FDA noted that, since no claim was made "to the effect that the location pictured in the vignette is the actual spring," the labels did not violate their regulations.[85]

stability maintenance. A term used by Chinese government censors and security forces to describe an aggressive campaign designed to suppress dissent during the twenty-fifth anniversary of the Tiananmen Square uprising. In addition to the widespread use of interrogations, detentions, and arrests of potential protestors, and the "scrubbing" of popular online messaging services, the Beijing authorities enlisted 850,000 civilian volunteers to patrol the city and an additional 100,000 citizens to act as informers, and instructed ordinary street vendors to report any suspicious activity to a "social service management authority."[86]

Stalinist redistribution of wealth program. Glenn Beck's definition of Social Security. "Do you know who created Social Security?" he asked viewers of his Fox News show in 2010, and then proceeded to answer his own question. "FDR and his progressive buddies started Social Security, not our Founding Fathers, that should be fairly obvious to people," he explained, adding that the actual idea for the program came from Roosevelt adviser Harry Hopkins, who "had a relationship with [Joseph] Stalin."[87]

stand by. As *Wordly Wisdom* blogger Lucy Fisher points out, "standing by" one's husband means to put up with his infidelities.[88]

states' rights. A phrase, famously used by Ronald Reagan while campaigning in Mississippi in 1980, that, in the lofty language of constitutional law, signals a belief that individual states have (or at least *should* have) the authority to ignore federal civil rights legislation.[89]

statesman. A politician you agree with.[90]

statist. A negative term favored by anarchists, capitalists, and libertarians to describe just about anybody who is not an anarchist, capitalist, or libertarian.[91]

statistically oriented projection of the significance of the findings. A term for "wild guess" favored by academic researchers.[92]

statuesque. A journalistic euphemism used to describe a woman whom the reporter considers to be overly large.[93]

stocky. Fat.[94]

"stone's throw from." A real-estate term that, according to *The Economist*, means "in reach of a powerful catapult."[95]

stop-loss program. The U.S. Department of Defense's term for its practice of involuntarily extending periods of voluntary military service. Many critics, including John Kerry when he was campaigning for president in 2004, have called this a **"backdoor draft."**[96]

"strapping young fellows using food stamps to buy T-bone steaks." See: strategic racism.

strategic misrepresentation. A Harvard Business School term for the tactic of hiding facts, bluffing, or lying during a business negotiation.[97]

strategic racism. A term used by University of California law professor Ian Haney López to describe politicians' conscious use of coded racial appeals to convince voters to support policies that, in the long run, are not in their interests. An example cited by Haney López is Ronald Reagan's references to "Cadillac-driving welfare queens" and "strapping young fellows using food stamps to buy T-bone steaks" to convince white voters that their tax dollars were being squandered on the undeserving and that, therefore, government spending, and tax rates, should be reduced. The resulting cuts, Haney López maintains, ultimately benefited corporations and the very rich "and hurt everyone else."[98]

strategic withdrawal. Retreat.[99] [See also: exfiltration; redeploying to the rear.]

"strengthening our alumni network." How EY (Ernst & Young), the London-headquartered financial services firm, characterized the mass layoffs it announced in 2013.[100]

stress and duress tactics. Interrogation techniques such as sleep deprivation, prolonged physical confinement in painful positions, and menacing encounters with attack dogs that the Bush-era Department of Justice insisted did not constitute the use of torture on targeted suspects.[101] [See also: abuse; enhanced interrogation techniques; pain compliance techniques; special methods of questioning.]

strip-search machines. See: enhanced screening procedures.

student outcomes. Grades.[102]

students. What the guards in Chinese "custody and education" forced-labor prison camps call their inmates.[103] [See also: **teacher.**]

"Studies show . . ." An all-purpose introductory phrase that permits advertisers to assert that scientific research supports their product claims without having to reveal anything about the nature of such research or who conducted and paid for it.[104]

subholocaust engagement. A military strategic planning term for a relatively benign nuclear conflict; a nuclear war on a scale insufficient to destroy all life on earth.[105]

suboptimal. Lousy. Example: *Her triumphal departure from Southampton notwithstanding, the* Titanic's *maiden voyage must be considered a* **suboptimal** *transatlantic crossing.*[106]

substance abuse. Drug addiction.[107] [See also: **chemical dependency; compulsive self-medication.**]

substandard housing. A slum.[108]

substantive negative outcome. A term used by a Canadian hospital for the accidental death of one of its patients.[109]

sunset. A verb that, as Steven Poole writes in *The Guardian*, "sounds more humane and poetic than 'cancel' or 'kill' or 'stop supporting.'" Poole adds, "Happily, sunsetting also sounds less smelly than the venerable old mothballing."[110]

sunshine unit. What the U.S. Department of Defense called the unit of measurement it used during the 1950s to specify the amount of radioactive strontium 90 detected in the fallout from atmospheric nuclear tests.[111]

super-prompt critical power excursion. A nuclear meltdown. The term "super-prompt" refers to the "runaway" nature of the event.[112] [See also: **above critical; core rearrangement.**]

"Support our troops." "Support our policy."[113]

supposedly. See: **apparently.**

surface coal. Manure that's burned for fuel.[114]

surge. When is a military escalation not a military escalation? When it's a "surge." The term was coined by the George W. Bush administration to describe the deployment, during the Iraq War, of twenty thousand additional troops to the Baghdad and Al Anbar areas. "The word has the benefit of seeming active, strong, and quick," an unidentified Republican strategist explained to *The New York Times.* "A surge is a lightning strike, over and done, the opposite of, say, a quagmire."[115]

surgical strike. Vizettes.com blogger Rich Coffey defines this as "Military jargon that makes a precision bombing sound like a beneficial medical procedure."[116]

surplused. Fired.[117]

Susan B. Anthony List. A powerful political group, named after the iconic women's rights advocate Susan B. Anthony, that spends millions of dollars annually to support political candidates opposed to a woman's right to choose.[118]

suspended campaign. The political campaign of a candidate who is no longer seeking an office but has not *officially* dropped out of the race. Why would candidates "suspend" rather than "end" their campaigns? Because, under federal law, doing so allows them to continue raising political funds as if they're still running, that's why.[119]

sustainable utilization. Essayist John Leo defines this as "a comforting term for despoiling the environment while claiming that there's really nothing to worry about." The phrase, he adds, has been used "to cover overzealous mining and foresting, as well as the trophy killing of big-game animals in

Africa. On safari, you might call out, 'Look, dear, you sustainably utilized that rhino!'"[120]

sweetbread. Menu term for the thymus gland of a calf.[121]

Swift Boat Veterans for Truth. A political group founded to spread lies about 2004 Democratic presidential candidate John Kerry, who they claimed had falsified stories about his heroic conduct as a swift-boat commander during the Vietnam War and had made misleading statements during his subsequent antiwar activities. As a consequence, the group maintained in a series of television ads and a bestselling book that Kerry was "unfit to be Commander in Chief." The term **swiftboating**, to describe an unfair and untrue political attack, owes its origin to this effort, which received significant funding from a group of wealthy Texas Republicans, and is widely credited with helping George W. Bush win his second term in office.[122]

swiftboating. See: **Swift Boat Veterans for Truth.**

synergy-related head count restructuring. A term used by Nokia Siemens in a 2008 press release to characterize its laying off nine thousand employees. The release went on to assure the public that the restructuring would occur only after the company's process of "sharing" its synergy-related plans with employees and "engaging constructively with employee representatives" had been completed.[123]

synthetic glass. Plastic.[124]

t

"**tailored shoulder darts specifically designed to accommodate the biodynamics of the shoulder.**" A feature included by designer David Blanch in the new soccer uniforms he designed for England's national side in 2009. "It's hard to tell from the official pictures," noted *The Guardian*'s Helen Pidd, "but this ever-so-clever touch appears to be a seam."[1]

takeover artist.[2] Corporate raider. [See also: **shareholder activist.**]

"**taking hold of a guy's Oregonian and snipping his Post-Dispatch right off.**" A euphemism for "circumcision," coined by Dave Barry after the Portland *Oregonian* and the *St. Louis Post-Dispatch* refused to print a column he had written about flatulence on the grounds that it was "tasteless and offensive."[3]

"**taking money from hardworking Americans.**" "If you talk about raising taxes on the rich," preaches Republican pollster and messaging guru Frank Luntz, the public responds favorably. But "if you talk about government *taking* the money from *hardworking Americans*, the public says no."[4]

talent acquisition manager. Recruiter.[5]

tall latte. The Starbucks Coffee Company's term for the smallest latte you can buy in its stores.[6]

tanker accident. The preferred petroleum-industry term for "oil spill."[7]

tax and spend. Journalist Norman Solomon defines these as "the inevitable fiscal activities of any government, made to sound diabolical."[8]

tax breaks. A term favored by Democrats to describe proposed reductions in tax rates.[9] [See also: **tax relief.**]

"tax-hiking, government-expanding, latte-drinking, sushi-eating, Volvo-driving, *New York Times*–reading, body-piercing, Hollywood-loving, left-wing freak show." A phrase used by the Club for Growth in a memorable 2004 television commercial to describe the presidential campaign being run by Howard Dean, the Democratic governor of Vermont, and his supporters during the run-up to that year's Iowa Caucuses. "Absurd or no," writes University of California, Berkeley, linguist Geoffrey Nunberg, this "clever ad" "neatly exemplified the pot-pourri of traits that conservatives have used to brand liberals as out-of-touch and pretentious weirdos—and by-the-by, the syntax that made the branding possible. The fact is that the right owns those **object + present participle compounds**, as surely as it owns *values, media bias,* [and] the lapel-pin flag. . . . In fact you could trace the whole history of the right's campaigns against liberals via those compounds—from *tree-hugging* and *NPR-listening* back through the Nixon era's *pot-smoking, bra-burning, draft-dodging,* and *America-hating,* until you finally excavate the crude origins of the trope in *nigger-loving,* the *ur*-denunciation of white liberal sentimentality."[10] [See also: **diversity.**]

tax incentive. Loophole.[11]

tax inversion. See: **inversion.**

tax on jobs. Mandated employee health insurance benefits. As British journalist and author Steven Poole points out, this terminology is more likely to be favored by "captains of industry" than by those who work for them.[12]

tax relief. A term favored by Republicans to describe proposed reductions in tax rates.[13] [See also: **tax breaks.**]

tax socialism. A more accurate name, according to the libertarian Cato Institute, for the progressive income tax. "In 1848 Marx and Engels proposed that progressive taxation be used 'to wrest, by degrees, all capital from the bourgeois, to centralize all instruments of production in the hands of the state,'" writes James A. Dorn, the institute's vice president for monetary studies. "Although communism has failed, the idea of progressive taxation, as a means of achieving 'social justice,' remains ingrained in the modern liberal psyche." He concludes: "We need to abolish progressive taxation, institute a fair flat tax and limit the size of government. Otherwise, class warfare and welfare will prevail."[14]

"taxation without respiration." What magazine magnate and former Republican presidential candidate Steve Forbes calls the estate tax, which, needless to say, he would like to see abolished.[15] [See also: **death tax; wealth tax.**]

taxpayers. Citizens (except for welfare beneficiaries, of course, or others too poor and unsuccessful to have to pay taxes or to benefit from "pro-growth" policies). This usage has become popular in the names of such advocacy groups as the National Taxpayers Union (whose mission is to "ensure that all Americans are able to pursue their dreams without the heavy hand of government holding them back") and the U.S. Taxpayers Party (dedicated to restoring "American jurisprudence to its Biblical foundations" and to limiting the federal government to its "Constitutional boundaries").[16]

teacher. A guard in a Chinese "custody and education" forced-labor prison camp.[17] [See also: **students.**]

team members. Term for workers at Domino's Pizza, including some disgruntled team members of the New York franchise, DPNY, who successfully sued their employer for $1.3 million over minimum wage and overtime violations.[18]

telephone intermediary. Receptionist.[19] [See also: **deceptionist; director of first impressions; welcoming agent.**]

"Tell your doctor if you experience . . ." An all-purpose liability-limiting catchphrase that accompanies ads for pharmaceutical products with a history of potentially life-threatening side effects. Translation: If you didn't tell your doctor, whatever our drug did to you is not our fault.[20]

temporarily displaced inventory. Stolen goods.[21]

temporarily geographically misplaced. A phrase used by the U.S. Air Force to describe a lost plane.[22]

temporary cessation of hostilities. Peace, as defined by the U.S. Department of Defense.[23]

"temporary indoor pool." Marketing expert Paul Stainton suggests that realtors might find this phrase useful while pitching a house with a flooded basement.[24]

temporary interruption of an economic expansion. Recession. The term was coined by President George H. W. Bush, who proclaimed in his 1991 State of the Union address that "the largest peacetime economic expansion in history has been temporarily interrupted."[25]

tender undoing. Not to be outdone by Gwyneth Paltrow, who famously called her divorce a "conscious uncoupling," singer Jewel termed *her* impending breakup a "tender undoing."[26]

terminal episode. A fatality, especially one that occurs in a hospital.[27]

terminate with extreme prejudice. To kill; assassinate. This phrase has become so well known, however, that it has lost its usefulness and is now seldom, if ever, employed.[28]

terminological inexactitude. Lying. The term was coined by Winston Churchill, then Under-Secretary of State for the Colonies, during the 1906 British parliamentary elections.[29]

terrain alteration. Saturation bombing.[30]

Texas funeral. Giving someone a "Texas funeral" means murdering, or attempting to murder, them by burying them alive. The term gained currency after Quentin Tarantino used it in his screenplay for *Kill Bill: Vol. 2*.[31]

thank you. According to novelist and screenwriter Richard Price, when someone in Hollywood says this to you, it means, "You're fired."[32]

"Thank you for your patience." See: **"We value your call. Thank you for your patience."**

"That said . . ." As the website Editorial Anonymous reminds us, this phrase always means, "Now that I've said something nice, here's the bad news . . ."[33]

"That's not recommended." A phrase that Apple Store employees are urged to use—instead of something like "That wasn't smart" or "That was really stupid!"—to avoid alienating customers who confess to a harebrained action, such as dropping their iPhone into a toilet, in the course of describing how the device they want repaired became disabled.[34]

"The narrative was right but the facts were wrong." An explanatory phrase used by *Newsweek* reporter Evan Thomas to

defend what he conceded was a biased account of an alleged
on-campus rape committed by members of the Duke lacrosse
team.[35]

"the occupied look." What the New York City Department of
Housing Preservation and Development said it was hoping to
achieve when it initiated a project to paste vinyl decals depicting shutters, curtains, and potted plants on the sheets of gal-
vanized metal that the city customarily nails over the windows
of abandoned buildings to keep out squatters and junkies. "It
looks much better than it did," a neighbor opined to reporters,
"but I feel they could spend the money better renovating the
houses."[36]

**"The ongoing challenging macro environment negatively
affected investor sentiment."** A statement made by Citibank
in a press release discussing the company's financial performance during the third quarter of 2011. Jeremy Hobson, on
Marketplace, explained that it means, "All that money we lost
wasn't our fault."[37]

"the true movement of diversity." A phrase used by the Tea Party
News Network's news director Scottie Hughes to describe the
overwhelmingly white and mostly middle-aged attendees at
the Western Conservative Conference held in Phoenix, Ari-
zona, in February 2014.[38]

therapeutic misadventure. A medical error during hospital
treatment that results in the death of a patient. (An error of
judgment during the initial examination process that leads to
a patient's demise is called a **diagnostic misadventure of high
magnitude.**)[39]

therapeutic segregation. Solitary confinement.[40]

"There is such excitement in-house!" A phrase frequently bandied about when editors report to their authors or to their company's sales force. Curtis Brown literary agent Jonny Geller translates it as "My assistant loved it."[41]

thermal incident. A term used by Bob Pearson, vice president for corporate group communications at Dell, to refer to the sudden spontaneous combustion of one of his company's computer notebooks in a boardroom in Osaka, Japan. Example: *Notwithstanding Justice Oliver Wendell Holmes Jr.'s noted caveat, the right to shout* **"Thermal incident!"** *in a crowded theater is probably constitutionally protected.*[42]

thermal therapy unit. An ice bag or hot water bottle. Also known as a "thermal therapy kit."[43]

A thermal therapy unit.

"things that didn't get accomplished." Failures. As language columnist Mark Peters notes, this "particularly useful, if not pithy, turn of phrase" was invoked to excellent advantage by Michigan governor Rick Snyder during a press conference about his first three years in office, and Peters offers several other examples of how it might be employed: *Mom, I didn't fail to get married and produce grandchildren; grandchildren just* **didn't get accomplished.** *Dad, I didn't fail math; a passing grade and numerical literacy were three things that* **didn't get accomplished.** *The NSA isn't spying on all Americans, and monitoring all e-mail and phone activity; privacy simply* **didn't get accomplished.**[44]

"This is the best first draft I've read all year." Novelist and screenwriter Tim Sandlin interprets this as "If they take it you'll be doing rewrites on your deathbed."[45]

"This is the time to put politics aside." Blogger Andrew K. Dart says this means, "*You* put *your* politics aside, while *we* politicize the crisis du jour."[46]

thought centers. What travel agency mogul, management guru, and self-styled "activist for the internal environment" Hal F. Rosenbluth named the meeting rooms at his company's Philadelphia headquarters.[47]

thrifty. Stingy; miserly; niggardly; parsimonious; Scrooge-like.[48]

tired and emotional. A libel-proof British journalists' term for someone who is drunk, typically used to describe a visibly inebriated politician. The phrase, coined by the satiric magazine *Private Eye*, soon migrated into general usage.[49] [See also: **impaired; overrefreshed; overserved; ruddy-faced.**]

"Tivo shot. FB hacked. Is my blender gonna attack me next? #TheToasterIsVeryLoyal." The text of a famous tweet posted in May 2011 by Representative Anthony Weiner (D-NY) in connection with his claim that his online accounts had been hacked and that he had played no part in "sexting" a picture of what was alleged to be his erect penis covered by boxer shorts to a young college student in Seattle. Less than a month later, as reports of other cybersex incidents involving Weiner swirled in the media, the Brooklyn congressman admitted that he had indeed taken and sent the photo, and a few days later, he resigned from the House of Representatives.[50]

toe-tapping. Soliciting gay sex. This term gained currency in 2007 after Idaho senator Larry Craig was apprehended in Minnesota for tapping his toe beneath the stall divider in an airport men's room as, to quote the arresting officer, "an invitation to engage in lewd conduct."[51]

tonsorial artist. Hairdresser.[52]

total and complete immobilization. Assassination. The term was coined by members of the Nixon administration in connection with a plan to "eliminate" Panamanian dictator Manuel Noriega.[53]

traffic study. A phrase used by aides in New Jersey governor Chris Christie's office in a failed attempt to cover up the real reason that they had ordered two lanes on the approach road to the George Washington Bridge closed for four days in September 2013. In fact, the closings—which turned the town of Fort Lee, New Jersey, into a "parking lot"—were motivated purely by a desire to punish Fort Lee's Democratic mayor, Mark Sokolich, for not endorsing Christie's reelection bid.[54]

tranquil. A real-estate advertising term that, according to San Francisco realtor Tara-Nicholle Nelson, means "not near anything you care about."[55]

A **tranquil**, cozy, and characterful property in the idyllic Montana woods, once owned, and meticulously cared for, by Unabomber Ted Kaczynski.

transitioning from home ownership. A euphemism for "foreclosure" used by Barbara Desoer, president of Bank of America's home loan and insurance unit, in prepared testimony before Congress in 2010.[56]

transparent-wall maintenance engineer. Window washer.[57]

transportation project enhancements. Flowers and shrubs planted along a highway.[58]

A **transparent-wall maintenance engineer.**

trans-species intimacy. Essayist John Leo offers this as a more positive synonym for "bestiality."[59] [See also: **zoosexuality.**]

tree-density reduction. A logging industry term for clear-cutting a forest. Example: *"I'm a* **tree-density** reduction *professional and I'm OK—I sleep all night and I work all day—that's what a savvy* **tree-density** reduction *professional should say," are suggested updated lyrics to Monty Python's famous song.*[60]

tree hugger. A term for "environmentalist," useful for pointing out how foolish or annoying advocates for the protection of trees, animals, and other parts of the natural world can be.[61]

trickle-down economics. The supply-side economic theory that holds that reducing regulations and lowering taxes will ultimately benefit poor, middle-class, and working-class Americans as well as the very rich.[62]

trimming the fat. Firing people.[63]

trouser cough. Fart.[64]

truthiness. A word coined by political satirist Stephen Colbert to characterize concepts that the proponent of an argument "knows in his gut are true" even if the facts don't support them. "That's where the truth comes from," Colbert "explained" on the pilot episode of his parody news show on Comedy Central, "the gut. Do you know you have more nerve endings in your stomach than your head? Look it up. Now, somebody's gonna say, 'I did look that up and it's wrong.' Well, Mister, that's because you looked it up in a book. Next time try looking it up in your gut."[65]

turf accountant. Bookie.[66]

turnkey. A real-estate advertising term for what Luke Mullins of *U.S News & World Report* describes as "a house filled with dated furniture that belongs in a dumpster."[67]

u

UAVs (unmanned aerial vehicles). A new name for "drones," a word that those who build them feel carries negative connotations because of the use of unpiloted aircraft in surveillance and interdiction missions.[1]

unacknowledged repetition. A term used by *The New York Times* instead of "plagiarism" to refer to historian Doris Kearns Goodwin's unattributed use of other writers' material in her books *The Fitzgeralds and the Kennedys* and *No Ordinary Time*.[2]

"unarmed teen." According to Fox News, the use of the term "unarmed teen" to describe any large African-American teenager shot by a policeman, even if he is not carrying a weapon, is an attempt by the liberal media to play the "race card," because, in effect, such teenagers are potentially dangerous— or, as Michael Lazzaro (aka "Hunter") of *Daily Kos* put it, they are "armed with themselves." After Michael Brown, an unarmed teenager, was gunned down by police in Ferguson, Missouri, in 2014, Linda Chavez appeared on Fox News' *Fox and Friends*, and as the text question "Is 'unarmed teen' description misleading?" flashed on the screen, she pointed out that Brown is "six-foot-four and weighs almost three hundred pounds." Apparently, wrote Lazzaro, "an unarmed American teen should not be declared 'unarmed' if Linda Chavez can't personally take him in a fight."[3]

unassigned. Fired, dismissed, laid off.[4]

unattributed overlap. Plagiarism. The *Journal of Biomedical Materials Research Part B: Applied Biomaterials* used this term in a notice explaining why it had retracted a scientific paper.[5]

unborn baby. A term for "fetus," favored by those opposed to abortion rights.[6]

unchanged change. A strategic concept articulated by Mark Timney, Merck's president of U.S. markets, in a 2011 memo discussing his company's plans to eliminate thirteen thousand jobs. "Our strategy," Timney explained, "which remains unchanged, reinforces the need for us to change our underlying operations."[7]

unclassified controlled information. Government information that is not legally classifiable but is withheld anyway.[8]

uncontained blade liberation. The breaking off of a helicopter rotor blade during flight. The term was coined by the Federal Aviation Administration to explain a fatal helicopter crash.[9] [See also: **uncontained failure.**]

uncontained failure. A phrase used to describe what might have once been called an "explosion" in the engine of a United Airlines plane in 1989. The plane crashed.[10] [See also: **uncontained blade liberation.**]

uncontrolled contact with the ground. A term for "airplane crash" favored by the U.S. National Transportation Safety Board.[11] [See also: **controlled flight into terrain; failure to maintain clearance from the ground.**]

under active consideration. Professor emeritus Paul Wasserman, of the University of Maryland's College of Information Studies, and his colleague, Don Hausrath, define this term as meaning your "application, manuscript or request has been stuffed in a file drawer, along with hundreds of others." Example: *The*

Dead Sea Scrolls were **under active consideration** *in a cave in Qumran for two thousand years.*[12]

underresourced. Poor.[13]

undocumented feature. See: feature.

undocumented workers. Illegal aliens who happen to be employed by you or your company.[14]

undue preferential treatment. Sex. According to Mary Roach, author of *Packing for Mars: The Curious Science of Life in the Void*, this phrase is the centerpiece of a delicately worded stricture against zero-gravity hookups that appears in NASA's "Code of Conduct for the International Space Station Crew."[15]

A couple engaging in **undue preferential treatment**.

unexpected life event. An unplanned or unwanted pregnancy, for example. AOL used the term in 2014 while breaking the news that reality TV star Kourtney Kardashian would soon be presenting her long-time partner Scott Disick with the couple's third child.[16]

unexpected non-powered tractor movement. In 2004, the John Deere company warned users of its farm vehicles that this might occur if they forgot to engage the hand brake.[17]

unhappy groups. A more compassionate term for "hate groups," preferred, for example, by the Board of Walworth County, Wisconsin, who passed a resolution directing that the Ku Klux Klan be referred to by this label. "The Klan is not a hate group," the citizen who proposed the resolution explained. "It's more or less people that are unhappy with what's going on and they don't necessarily hate."[18]

uni. Sea urchin gonads.[19]

unilaterally determined pre-emptive self-defense. Launching a surprise attack against a prospective adversary before that adversary has an opportunity to mount his own surprise attack; "getting your retaliation in first." President George W. Bush introduced the term and the concept in a speech at West Point in 2002 that radically redefined American national security policy, and provided the ideological underpinnings for the invasion of Iraq that was to come a year later.[20]

uninstalled. Fired, dismissed, laid off.[21]

unique. Weird.[22]

unique design. A real-estate advertiser's term for a house with a hopelessly eccentric floor plan.[23]

unique retail biosphere. Farmers' market.[24]

unlawful enemy combatants. See: **enemy combatants**.

unprivileged enemy belligerent. In October 2009, President Barack Obama signed into law the Military Commissions Act of 2009, which, among other things, scrapped the unpopular term "unlawful enemy combatants" that the Bush administration had used to classify War on Terror detainees, and replaced it with a new term, "unprivileged enemy belligerent." What the new law did *not* do, however, was grant the newly labeled detainees any of the protections and legal rights that they had previously been denied. "This is a cosmetic change," opined Human Rights Watch lawyer Joanne Mariner, "not a real improvement."[25] [See also: **enemy combatants**.]

unsavory character. A criminal (or suspected criminal).[26]

unsubstantiated. A relatively nonjudgmental adjective useful for characterizing baseless charges, bogus claims, crackpot theories, paranoid fantasies, and outright lies. Example: *The contention by "independent scientist" Leuren Moret that the March 11, 2011, Fukushima earthquake was intentionally "triggered" at the behest of "London bankers" by an "international racketeering war crimes network" with access to the U.S. Air Force's High Frequency Active Auroral Research Program (HAARP) facility in Gakona, Alaska, remains* **unsubstantiated.**[27]

unusual laboratory experience. A term coined by Kodak to help it describe what happened to customers' film that was destroyed or lost while Kodak was processing it.[28]

up-and-coming. A real-estate advertising term used to describe neighborhoods that are dangerously crime-ridden.[29]

uptitling. Giving a more impressive-sounding job name, like "senior associate executive assistant," to an employee instead of a raise.[30]

up to. A phrase that, when inserted before an otherwise impressive statistic, renders it meaningless. For example, as Robert Todd Carroll points out in *The Skeptic's Dictionary*, the advertising claim "This pen lasts *up to* 20 per cent longer" does not actually assert that the pen *will* last 20 percent longer. "But even if it did," Carroll continues, "it still wouldn't mean much since it doesn't say *longer than what.*"[31]

When Herb found out he'd been **uptitled** from Deputy Assistant Project Manager to Senior Associate Output Facilitator, he drank a virtual pint of beer to celebrate.

urban. Black; African-American.[32]

urban art. Graffiti.[33]

USA Patriot Act. See: **Patriot Act.**

using an expedited, court-supervised process to accelerate the reinvention of the company. Filing for bankruptcy. Troy A. Clarke, then president of General Motors North America, used this phrase in an upbeat letter designed to reassure customers after the company filed for Chapter 11 protection in federal bankruptcy court on June 1, 2009. The "b-word" was never mentioned once in Clarke's entire document.[34]

using one's credibility for accomplishing an objective. A more salutary term for "influence peddling" coined by former Reagan administration Secretary of the Interior James Watt to explain, during testimony before a House panel, the $300,000 fee he received for helping a builder secure federal funding for a Baltimore housing project.[35]

utensil maintenance professional. Dishwasher.[36]

V

vacancy management. The technique that Mark Timney, when he was Merck's president of U.S. markets, said his company was "increasing the use of" to facilitate the elimination of thousands of employee positions.[1]

values voters. "Social conservatives" who voice their opposition to gay rights and abortion at the ballot box.[2]

vegetation manipulation. A term used by the U.S. Department of the Interior to characterize the proposed clear-cutting of hundreds of acres of trees near Aspen, Colorado.[3]

vehicle appearance specialists. What Orinda Auto Detail, in Orinda, California (among many others), calls its car washers.[4]

vertical transportation condition audit. An elevator or escalator inspection.[5]

vertically deployed anti-personnel devices. A U.S. Department of Defense term for "bombs."[6]

very large, potentially disruptive, reentry system. A nuclear-armed intercontinental ballistic missile, as described by U.S. Air Force colonel Frank Horton.[7]

vibrant. An adjective that, when used by real-estate brokers to describe a neighborhood, means "deafeningly noisy."[8]

victim disarmament. Gun control. The coinage of this phrase is widely attributed to James Jay Baker, chief lobbyist for the National Rifle Association, who argued in 1993 that "gun control measures in the United States, if anything, contribute to increased criminal violence, because they deny guns to honest citizens but not to criminals. They might accurately be called victim disarmament laws."[9]

A **very large, potentially disruptive, reentry system.**

victimization encouragement. A theory advanced by Fox News Channel's Bill O'Reilly that many poor and unemployed people see their lot—which he seems convinced is not as difficult as they make it out to be—as an opportunity for financial advancement, and that the Obama administration is willfully incentivizing them to do so. Here's what O'Reilly said about all this on his February 25, 2013, broadcast: "There have always been people who see themselves as victims and want to be paid for their perceived suffering. . . . Now those people are in a comfort zone because their victimization isn't being challenged. It's being *encouraged*, by the Obama administration."[10]

victims of neo-liberalism. An ironic term for poor people favored by Israeli writer Tsafi Saar.[11]

victims of their gender. A phrase used by Mike Huckabee to describe how Democrats regard women. Huckabee elaborated on this idea by stating that "Democrats think that women are nothing more than helpless and hopeless creatures whose only goal in life is to have a government provide for them birth control medication."[12] [See also: **helpless creatures crawling around incapable of controlling their libidos.**]

vintage details. A real-estate term, typically used to tout a building that's hopelessly out of date.[13]

VIPR Squads. See: **Visible Intermodal Prevention and Response (VIPR) Squads.**

virgin vinyl. Imitation leather. (It's called "virgin" vinyl because no recycled plastic has been mixed in.)[14]

virtually. A widely used advertising **"weasel word"** that means "not actually," or "almost," or "up to a point."[15]

Visible Intermodal Prevention and Response (VIPR) Squads. What the U.S. Transportation Security Administration calls teams of TSA personnel assigned to provide airport-style screenings in "non-aviation environments" such as bus terminals, railway and subway stations, ports, and sports arenas. A 2012 report from the inspector general of the Department of Homeland Security raised serious questions about whether the VIPR squads—their intrepid-sounding name notwithstanding—possessed "the skills and information to perform successfully in the mass transit environment."[16]

visiting a site. Bombing something. (A U.S. Department of Defense term coined during the Gulf War.)[17] [See also: **servicing a target.**]

visuality. A sophisticated art criticism term for the act of really, really looking at something instead of just sort of happening to see it.[18] [See also: **International Art English.**]

volume-related production scheduling adjustment. A term used by General Motors to describe a factory closing.[19]

voluntary development opportunity. An unpaid job.[20]

voluntary interruption of pregnancy. What the UN calls abortion.[21]

W

"wake-up call for America." Novelist and critic Gary Krist says you can count on any book bearing this advertising copy line to be "a bad-tempered diatribe by a member of the previous administration."[1]

walk back from. A euphemism for attempting, after having been caught lying, to "clarify" or "justify" one's original statement. Politicians and public speakers typically do this—as frequent *Daily Kos* contributor SuzieQ4624 phrases it—by spouting "more bullshit."[2]

wallet biopsy. See: **negative wallet biopsy.**

walnut shampoo. See: **aluminum shampoo.**

war machine. The enemy's equivalent of our Army, Marines, Navy, and Air Force.[3]

War of Northern Aggression. A Confederate name for the Civil War, newly popularized by National Rifle Association president (and former Alabama assistant attorney general) Jim Porter, who used it during a 2013 speech to the New York State Rifle and Pistol Association.[4]

War on Terror. The George W. Bush administration's name for military and political operations undertaken to defeat al-Qaeda and other militant Islamist terrorist organizations in the wake of the September 11, 2001, attacks on the World Trade Center and the Pentagon. The term got off to a bad start when Bush introduced his new initiative as a "crusade," a reference to the Christian holy wars against Muslims in medieval times that greatly offended non-radical Muslims. But the phrase "War on Terror" (or **"Global War on Terror,"** as the initiative was also frequently called) was soon adapted uncritically by the media, a development that caused Jacob Levenson, writing in the *Columbia Journalism Review*, no end of distress. "If the war on terror had been called the war on Islamic extremism," Levenson inquired, "would the American public have supported the invasion of a country, like Iraq, with a secular government? Similarly, had it been called the war for global democracy, would the Patriot Act have become law? What if it hadn't been called a war at all?"[5]

wardrobe malfunction. Justin Timberlake coined this now legendary phrase to explain how Janet Jackson's right breast just happened to be become exposed when he ripped off her bodice

Janet Jackson's infamous **wardrobe malfunction** incident at Super Bowl XXXVIII.

during the Super Bowl XXXVIII half-time show.[6]

warfighter. Any member of the military or of the Department of Defense bureaucracy, regardless of whether he or she has ever seen or will ever see combat.[7]

watching badgers. Cruising for, or engaging in, outdoor sex. The term gained currency in 2003 after Ron Davies, the former secretary of state for Wales and a candidate for the Welsh Assembly, was photographed by the British tabloid *The Sun* emerging

Ron Davies, an eminent Welsh **badger-watcher**.

from the bushes near public picnic grounds north of Bath after allegedly having had sex there with a stranger. Davies denied the newspaper's charge, but eventually admitted that he had been to the area "two or three times . . . watching badgers."[8]

Water Environment Federation (WEF). A group organized and funded by the sewage sludge industry. Originally called the Federation of Sewage Works Associations, the WEF has as its self-stated mission, among other things, to increase public awareness of the fact that "biosolids, a natural by-product of wastewater treatment, are a renewable resource that is too valuable to waste given our growing needs for renewable energy and sustainability."[9]

water landing. An airplane crash into the ocean.[10]

A **water landing**.

waterboarding. A simulated-drowning technique that is clearly a form of torture, despite valiant attempts by lawyers in George W. Bush's Justice Department to find legal means to justify that it is not. According to Darius Rejali, a political science professor at Reed College and an expert on torture, the term "waterboarding" clearly originated as "a jailhouse joke." "They are attaching somebody to a board and helping them surf," he says. "Torturers create names that are funny to them."[11]

"We are currently experiencing a high volume of calls." An automated on-hold message that actually means, "We're so understaffed that any number of calls would be too many."[12]

"We don't doubt your word." A phrase used by banks, airlines, utilities, and retailers, which, roughly translated, means, "You're probably telling the truth, but so what?" *The New York Times'* Enid Nemy offers the following example: "**We don't doubt your word** *you reconfirmed your ticket, but it's not in the computer.*" "Don't bother asking," advises Nemy, "you're not on the flight."[13]

"We know your time is valuable . . ." But not valuable enough for us to stop wasting it."[14]

"We value your call. Thank you for your patience." British journalist Colin Randall translates this frequently encountered automated on-hold message as "We have better things to do than talk to you."[15]

wealth tax. A term for "estate tax," favored by those who oppose its repeal.[16] [See also: **death tax; "taxation without respiration."**]

weapons of mass destruction (WMD). As Spencer Ackerman wrote in *Wired,* "'Weapons of mass destruction' are a bitter punch line, thanks to the war that the United States launched, ostensibly to secure ones that weren't there. But the term endures, obscuring the fact that the holy trinity of weapons contained therein—nuclear, chemical and biological—are very different things." Indeed, although just about everyone remembers that the United States never found the WMD that the Bush administration assured us made preemptive war necessary, not enough attention has been paid to how cleverly localized, tactical weapons—albeit unpleasant ones—were conflated with nuclear ones to scare the public into believing that a possible global apocalypse was looming if America didn't act decisively and soon. "WMD implied nuclear for the untutored, demanding major military action," notes defense analyst James Holmes. "Lesser instruments of war may have warranted lesser countermeasures."[17]

weasel word. An adjective or adverb used for the purpose of undermining the meaning of the word or phrase it modifies. The coinage is generally attributed to the author Stewart Chaplin, who in 1900 wrote, "Weasel words are words that suck the life out of the words next to them, just as a weasel sucks the egg and leaves the shell."[18] [See, for example: **helps; like; virtually.**]

welcome. Warily acknowledge; grudgingly permit. Example: *We* **welcome** *comments from local residents.—The Nottingham (England) City Council.*[19]

welcoming agent. Receptionist.[20] [See also: **deceptionist; director of first impressions; telephone intermediary.**]

welfare queens. See: **strategic racism.**

well-endowed. A term used by journalists to describe a woman with large breasts.[21]

well-intentioned but naive. Socialist.[22]

well-loved. A real-estate advertising term roughly translatable as "previously owned and used *a lot*."[23] [See also: **new-to-you; preloved; pre-owned; previously enjoyed; previously loved.**]

wellness center. Hospital.[24]

"went to college in Boston." A euphemism frequently uttered by overbearing Harvard graduates who apparently worry, as Visual Thesaurus columnist Mark Peters puts it, that their "conversation partners will melt" at the mere mention of their alma mater, "like Nazis beholding the contents of the Ark of the Covenant."[25]

Western Hemisphere Institute for Security Cooperation (WHINSEC). A fresh new name bestowed, as of January 1, 2001, by the U.S. Congress on the notorious School of the Americas, a military training facility at Fort Benning, Georgia, that counted among its distinguished graduates the Nicaraguan dictator Manuel Noriega and Franck Romain, the former head of Haiti's Tontons Macoutes.[26]

wet work. Assassination.[27]

wetlands. Swamps. As Marcellus Drilling News ("Helping People & Businesses Profit from Northeast Shale Drilling") puts it, "Gotta love a good euphemism. We used to drain swamps. Now we make people get permits to walk across them, for fear of killing a mosquito (no doubt carrying West Nile Virus). Such is the *enlightened* age in which we live."[28]

"While it has not been possible to provide definite answers to the questions . . ." A phrase, commonly found in research reports, that basically means, "My experiment was unsuccessful, but I still hope to get additional funding."[29]

"while supplies last." A modifying phrase, frequently used in radio and television commercials, that TruthinAdvertising .org translates as "We're advertising this item at a ridiculously low price to get you into the store/showroom, but we're not likely to have any in stock by the time you get here, but that's alright because we'll just sell you something else."[30]

"White Like Me Tour." Rush Limbaugh's name for a campaign bus tour of the Midwest that Barack Obama took during the run-up to the 2012 presidential election.[31]

Larry Craig, a former senator with a **wide stance**.

wide stance. "Having a wide stance" became synonymous with "being a closeted homosexual" after Idaho senator Larry Craig, arrested during a sting operation at the Minneapolis–St. Paul Airport for soliciting sex by extending his toe into the men's room stall adjoining his, offered the excuse that, while he was "positioning his feet" to go to the bathroom, one of them had inadvertently strayed under the stall divider. "I'm a fairly wide guy," he added.[32]

wilderness. Lands not occupied by people like us.[33]

wildlife management. Killing, or permitting the hunting of, animals.[34]

willowy. Anorexic.[35]

"With all due respect." "Go fuck yourself."[36]

WMD. See: **weapons of mass destruction.**

wood-inspired. An adjective used by TrendsinFlooring.com to describe the 100 percent wood-free porcelain tiles that, according to the site, "the genius design gurus of several top tile manufacturing companies have daringly created . . . to evoke nostalgic feelings of natural hardwood."[37]

wooden interdental stimulator. Toothpick.[38]

work accident. A term used by Palestinian activists to describe a fatality resulting from the explosion of a missile during a failed attempt to fire it into Israel.[39]

work ethic. Lucy Fisher of the *Wordly Wisdom* blog defines this as "a willingness to be exploited."[40]

Wooden interdental stimulators.

work sandwich. Two batches of printed work material with a "filling" of personal documents in between them. Making a work sandwich is a dandy way to avoid getting caught while addressing personal issues at the office.[41]

workforce adjustment. A phrase used by SIG Sauer, Inc., to characterize a series of significant job cuts it carried out during 2014 at its Newington, New Hampshire, gun manufacturing plant. The use of this terminology did not sit well with the small-weapons-oriented blog *WeaponsMan.* "Hot tip for corporate PR dweebs," they wrote. "That kind of mealy-mouthed, nutless spin fools no one, and is why all productive workers hate you."[42]

workforce rebalancing. What IBM said it was "continuing its effort" to do when it instituted a program of mass layoffs in early 2014.[43]

workplace violence. The official U.S. Army term for the mass murder by Major Nidal Hasan of thirteen of his fellow soldiers and the wounding of thirty-two others, at Fort Hood, Texas, in November 2009. Because Hasan's act was not designated an act of terrorism, his victims and their families were denied combat benefits that they would otherwise have received, and the "workplace violence" designation also bolstered President

Obama's claim, at a National Defense University speech on May 23, 2013, that there had been no large-scale terror attacks on American soil since he took office.[44]

Y

"Your call is important to us." But not important enough to hire some more people to answer the phone.[1]

"Your Choice^SM." The official name given by American Airlines to its program of charging fees for slightly roomier seating, early boarding, avoiding luggage charges, and meals. The company insists its menu of Your Choice^SM products and services makes "the travel experience even more convenient, cost-effective, flexible and personalized." However, as *The New Yorker*'s Tim Wu points out, charging fees will only work if there are things worth paying to avoid, and the basic service provided without fees has to be horrible enough to make people desperate to escape. As a result, Wu writes, the major airlines are doing everything they can "to make flying basic economy, particularly on longer flights, an intolerable experience"—a strategy he characterizes as "calculated misery."[2]

"Your duties may vary." A phrase, frequently found in help-wanted ads, that Reid Kanaley of *The Philadelphia Inquirer* translates as "anyone in the office can boss you around."[3]

"Your results may vary." A fine-print disclaimer often used in "before and after" weight loss advertisements to indicate that the illustrated physical transformation depicted in the Photoshop-altered image of the featured model is an extreme outcome unlikely to be experienced by an actual consumer of the promoted product.[4]

Youth Development Campus. The official name for Augusta, Georgia's local juvenile jail.[5]

Z

zero latency. A corporate term for "without delay," adopted from the computer industry. Example: *Sandra was thrilled when Bill asked if he could take her home, but was deeply disappointed when he made a* **zero latency** *departure the next morning.*[1]

zero-tasking. An impressive-sounding business term to use instead of admitting that you're doing absolutely nothing.[2]

zero trans fat. Food-label language that indicates a particular product actually may contain up to half a gram of trans fat. That's because U.S. Food and Drug Administration regulations permit any number below 0.5 to be legally rounded down to zero.[3]

zipper problem. A euphemism commonly used to describe the congenital sexual misbehavior of, among others, President Bill Clinton.[4]

zoosexuality. A less judgmental synonym for "bestiality."[5] [See also: **trans-species initimacy.**]

zygote personhood. On Valentine's Day 2012, the Virginia House of Delegates became the first statewide governing body in the United States to pass legislation granting to zygotes "all the rights, privileges, and immunities available to other persons, citizens, and residents" of the territory under its jurisdiction. The Virginia Senate failed to approve the law, so, at least as of this writing, the zygotes will have to wait.[6]

en·glish–
spin·glish

a

abortion. Embryo reduction; induced miscarriage; planned termination; voluntary interruption of pregnancy.

accident. Anomaly.

acid rain. Atmospheric deposition of anthropogenically derived acidic substances; poorly buffered precipitation.

addiction. Dependency.

adultery. Hiking the Appalachian Trail.

affair. Inappropriate friendship.

affirmative action. Race-sensitive admission policies.

African-American. Inner-city; urban.

air sickness vomit sack. Motion discomfort receptacle.

aircraft engine explosion. Uncontained failure.

airplane collision (into another plane). Midair passenger exchange.

airplane crash (into the ground). Controlled flight into terrain; failure to maintain clearance from the ground.

airplane crash (into the ocean). Water landing.

amnesty (for illegal immigrants). Path to citizenship.

animal trainer. Interspecies communicator.

animals. Differentiated beings of startling variety and complexity.

anorexic. Willowy.

anti-abortion. Pro-life.

armholes (in a garment). Intelligent ventilation points.

art dealer. Gallerist.

assassination. Executive action; health alteration; termination with extreme prejudice; total and complete immobilization; wet work.

assisted suicide. Death with dignity; going to Switzerland; shortening the dying process.

attack ad (made by your side). Contrast ad.

b

bad behavior (by a child). Negative attention getting.

bad loan. Nonperforming asset (NPA).

bank fee (for bouncing a check). Courtesy overdraft protection fee.

bankruptcy. Negative net worth.

bartender. Beverage host; mixologist.

baseless. Unsubstantiated.

basement. Lower ground floor.

basement, flooded. Temporary indoor pool.

beauty shop. Cosmetorium.

beer. Adult beverage.

behind schedule. Ongoing.

benefits, slashing. Entitlement reform; modernizing Medicare and Social Security.

bestiality. Trans-species intimacy; zoosexuality.

bilingual education. English Plus.

black eye. Bilateral suborbital hematoma.

boiled pig intestines. Chitlins.

bomb. Vertically deployed anti-personnel device.

bomber. Force package.

bombing. Air support; armed reconnaissance; coercive diplomacy; servicing a target; terrain alteration; visiting a site.

bombing, pinpoint. Discriminate deterrence.

booing and hissing. Good-natured grunts.

bookie. Turf accountant.

borrowed money, use. Leverage.

bottled water. Affordable portable lifestyle beverage.

bouncer. Eviction technician.

box of tissues. Mucus recovery system.

bravery (exhibited by enemy troops). Fanaticism.

breakup (of a relationship). Conscious uncoupling; tender undoing.

bribe. After-sales service fee; campaign contribution; expediting fee; fee for product testing; incentive; rebate.

budget cuts. Savings.

bug (software). Software anomaly; undocumented feature.

bull testicles. Rocky Mountain oysters.

bullet wound. Ballistically induced aperture in the subcutaneous environment.

bum. Non-goal-oriented member of society.

burglar alarm. Intrusion detection system.

burglary. Inappropriate possession of the property of others.

butcher. Meat technologist.

C

cancel. Sunset.

cap-and-trade. Cap-and-tax; crap-and-trade.

cemetery. Garden of remembrance.

censorship. Redaction; reporting guidelines.

child molesting. Intergenerational intimacy.

Christmas tree. Holiday tree.

cigarette tax. Health impact fee.

civilian casualties. Collateral damage; regrettable by-products.

clarify. Disambiguate.

claustrophobic (in reference to real estate). Cozy; intimate.

clear-cutting. Regeneration harvesting; tree-density reduction.

clerk, grocery store check-out. Scanning professional.

clerk, photocopying. Reprographics engineer.

clueless. Acluistic.

cockroaches, flying. Palmetto bugs.

cocktail waiter. Beverage host.

committing adultery. Hiking the Appalachian Trail.

compensation payments. Goodwill payments.

constipation. Mild irregularity.

convenience store. Immediate consumption outlet.

copulation. Incredibly intense conversation; penile insertive behavior.

copywriter. Content strategist.

corporate raider. Shareholder activist; takeover artist.

corporate screwup. Contingent operating difficulty.

cow manure (burned as fuel). Surface coal.

cow manure (used as fertilizer). Dairy nutrients.

crappy. Suboptimal.

crash, stock market. Correction; equity retreat.

crematorium operator. Post-health professional.

customer service representatives. Happiness heroes.

customers, talking to. Client engagement; coterminous stakeholder engagement.

cuts, spending. Savings.

d

damage. Degrade.

damage control. Risk management.

dead. No longer a factor; nonviable.

dead soldiers. Nonoperative personnel.

death. Failure to fulfill one's wellness potential; immediate permanent incapacitation; negative patient care outcome; substantive negative outcome. [See also: **fatality.**]

death penalty. Capital punishment; our society's recognition of the sanctity of life.

debt collector. Customer assistance account manager.

debt-ridden. Highly leveraged.

defective. Suboptimal.

deficit reduction. Legacy protection.

deforestation. Regeneration harvesting.

demoted. Plutoed.

depression. Period of economic adjustment.

desk, classroom. Individual learning station.

destitute. At risk; culturally deprived; disadvantaged; under-resourced.

destroy. Degrade.

deviled eggs. Angeled eggs; doubled eggs; sanctified eggs.

diet. Nutritional avoidance therapy.

dilapidated house (in reference to real estate). Handyman's special.

discipline. Directive improvement.

dishwasher. Utensil maintenance professional.

disposable. Single-use.

divorce. Conscious uncoupling; downshifting into a platonic relationship; tender undoing.

doddering. Frail.

dogcatcher. Canine control officer.

doing nothing. Zero-tasking.

door. Entrance solution.

doublespeak. Creative ambiguity.

drones. UAVs (unmanned aerial vehicles).

drought. Deficit water situation.

drug addiction. Chemical dependency; compulsive self-medication; substance abuse.

drunk. Impaired; overrefreshed; overserved; ruddy-faced; tired and emotional.

dump, garbage. Resource development park; sanitary landfill.

e

Easter egg rolls. Spring egg hunts.

eavesdropping. Electronic intercepts.

editorial assistant. Content strategist.

electric toothbrush. Cordless rechargeable power plaque remover; home plaque removal instrument.

electrified fence. Energized fence.

embezzle. Redistribute assets.

embryo. Pre-born baby.

employee, low-level (and possibly exploited). Crew member; team member.

entitlements. Earned benefits.

estate tax. Death tax (favored by opponents); wealth tax (favored by proponents).

euthanasia. Death with dignity; shortening the dying process.

exam. Celebration of knowledge.

expensive. Resource-intensive.

explosion. Energetic disassembly.

extra-large. Generously cut.

f

face-lift. Aesthetic procedure.

factory closing. Volume-related production scheduling adjustment.

failing student. Emerging student.

failure. Deferred success; incomplete success; learning opportunity; something that "didn't get accomplished."

fake. Faux.

false teeth. Alternative dentation.

falsify documents. Clean up the historical record.

fan. High-velocity multipurpose air circulation device.

farmers' market. Unique retail biosphere.

fart. Gaseous intestinal by-product; trouser cough.

fat. Amply proportioned; big-boned; burly; curvy; fattractive; full-figured; Rubenesque; stocky.

fatality. Terminal episode. [See also: **death.**]

fatty (beef). Marbled.

Fedayeen, swarming. Pockets of resistance.

fellatio. Playing the bamboo flute.

fetus. Pre-born baby.

filing clerk. Data storage specialist.

final exam. Celebration of knowledge.

fire (combustion). Rapid oxidation.

fire (dismiss one employee). Attrition (verb); bangalore (if the job was outsourced to India); decruit; dehire; deinstall; deselect; excess; future endeavor; involuntarily leisure; let go; make available to the industry; make redundant; manage for value; nonrenew; offer a package to; outplace; present with an early retirement opportunity; select out; send into phased retirement; severance; surplus; unassign.

fire (dismiss many employees). Achieve one's synergy-related headcount restructuring goals; adhere more closely to a special forces philosophy; align cost, culture, and capabilities to enhance customer service and satisfaction levels for shoppers, patients, and payors; assign candidates to a mobility pool; carry out normal involuntary attrition; consolidate leadership; contain costs; degrow; delayer; demise human capital; destaff; downsize; effectuate a workforce adjustment; eliminate redundancies in the human resources area; engage in workforce imbalance rectification; enhance the customer experience; exercise negative employee retention; get lean and mean; implement a skills-mix adjustment; improve productivity; increase one's use of vacancy management; initiate a career alternative enforcement program; institute an involuntary reduction of force; make a modest reduction in near-term headcount; manage one's expense base; manage staff resources; maximize the use of the destaff process; meet the changing requirements of one's clients; optimize one's consumer footprint across geographies; outplace; raise the bar on talent; realign one's headcount; rebalance one's workforce; reduce expenses; require fewer people to wear more hats; restructure; rewire for growth; rightsize; shed weight; smart-size; streamline operations; strengthen one's alumni network; trim the fat.

fleas. Hematophagous arthropod vectors.

flip-flop. Modify one's position.

flooded basement. Temporary indoor pool.

flying cockroaches. Palmetto bugs.

fracking. Energy exploration.

fraud. Accounting irregularity; aggressive accounting; creative accounting; financial engineering; innovative accounting; miscertification.

fried squid testicles. Calamari.

frigidity. Female sexual interest/arousal disorder; hypoactive sexual desire disorder (HSDD).

front door, lockable. Controlled access entry.

fruit, spoiled. Distressed produce.

funeral director. After-death care provider; bereavement care expert; post-health professional.

furniture, newly purchased. Habitability improvements.

g

gambling. Gaming.

garbage collector. Sanitation engineer.

garbage dump. Resource development park; sanitary landfill.

garden. Recreational eco-unit.

gas station. Motor fuel dispensing facility. (Those that offer oil changes are also called **lubritoriums.**)

gay man. Confirmed bachelor.

genocide. Ethnic cleansing.

girdle. Outerwear enhancer.

global warming. Climate change.

global warming, efforts to curtail. Eco-evangelical hysteria.

global warming believer. Environmental hypochondriac.

god-awful. Suboptimal.

grades. Student outcomes.

graffiti. Urban art.

greeting card. Social expression product.

grocery bagger. Packaging agent.

grocery store check-out clerk. Scanning professional.

grouch. Disruptive mood dysregulation disorder (DMDD) sufferer.

gun control. Citizen disarmament; victim disarmament.

h

hairdresser. Tonsorial artist.

Halloween party. Harvest party.

hammer. Fastening device impact driver.

harebrained. Imprudent.

hate groups. Unhappy groups.

head-on plane collision. Midair passenger exchange.

hex nuts. Hexiform rotatable compression units.

hog-tie. Place in a four-point restraint.

home economics. Consumer sciences.

homeless person. Outdoor citizen.

homosexual. Confirmed bachelor.

hospital. Wellness center.

hospital accident. Diagnostic misadventure of high magnitude; sentinel event; therapeutic misadventure.

hot water bottle. Thermal therapy unit.

house, dilapidated (real-estate term). Handyman's special.

hunger. Food insecurity.

hungover. Jet-lagged.

hunting. Game management.

hurt. Negatively impact.

i

ice bag. Thermal therapy unit.

idiotic. Imprudent.

illegal. Imprudent.

illegal alien. Aspiring citizen; undocumented worker.

imitation leather. Virgin vinyl.

impotence. Erectile dysfunction disorder.

inattentive child. Concentration deficit disorder (CDD) sufferer.

income tax, progressive. Discriminatory taxation; tax socialism.

incontinence. OAB (overactive bladder syndrome).

incredibly stupid. Ill-advised.

indecent exposure. Wardrobe malfunction.

Indian summer. First Nations summer.

inheritance tax. Death tax (favored by opponents); wealth tax (favored by proponents).

insanity. Mental activity at the margins.

insolvent. Illiquid.

insurance salesperson. Family protection consultant; health care procurement specialist.

invader. Peacekeeper.

invasion. Incursion.

irritable child. Disruptive mood dysregulation disorder (DMDD) sufferer.

j

jail. Correctional facility; detention center.

job, unpaid. Voluntary development opportunity.

jungle. Rainforest.

junk mail. Direct mail.

junkyard. Reutilization marketing facility.

k

key. Controlled access entry module.

kick out. Escort from the premises.

kickbacks. After-sales service fees; fees for product testing.

kill. Alter the health of; de-life; dynamically address; neutralize; send on a trip to Belize; terminate with extreme prejudice; totally and completely immobilize.

l

lack of evidence. Evidentiary deficiency.

land mine. Area denial munition.

lay off. See: **fire.**

leather, imitation. Virgin vinyl.

lethargic child. Sluggish cognitive tempo sufferer.

liar. Fictitious disorder syndrome sufferer.

liberal. Elitist.

librarian. Information adviser.

lie. Carefully crafted, nuanced response; categorical inaccuracy; counterfactual proposition; factual shortcut; inadvertent disclosure of incorrect information; incorrect promise; inoperative statement; misstatement; now-disavowed claim; reality augmentation; terminological inexactitude.

lie-detector test. Credibility assessment.

life preserver. Flotation device.

lining-of-hog-belly soup. Pepperpot soup.

liquor. Adult beverage.

loan, bad. Nonperforming asset.

lobbyist. Government relations professional; legislative leadership advocate.

locker. Personal appurtenance storage unit.

logging, commercial. Forest thinning; regeneration harvesting.

loophole, tax. Tax incentive.

loss (financial). Deficit enhancement; degrowth; net profits revenue deficiency.

lost. Temporarily geographically misplaced.

loud. Extroverted.

lousy. Suboptimal.

lying. Reality augmentation; terminological inexactitude; being economical with the truth.

m

make the coffee. Leverage the drinkables infrastructure.

mall. Festival marketplace; lifestyle center.

manure, cow (burned as fuel). Surface coal.

manure, cow (used as fertilizer). Dairy nutrients.

masturbation. Partnerless sex.

medical thermometer. Digital fever computer.

meeting rooms. Thought centers.

meltdown, nuclear. Core rearrangement; super-prompt critical power excursion.

mental health. Behavioral health.

mental retardation. Intellectual disability.

mercenary. Security contractor.

migrant worker. Seasonal employee.

military power. Coercive potential.

military spending increases. Proactive pacifism.

miserly. Thrifty.

mistake. Learning opportunity.

mistress. Great and good friend.

morgue. ECU (eternal care unit).

mortician. After-death care provider; bereavement care expert; post-health professional.

movie, pornographic. Erotic film.

murder. Arbitrarily deprive of life; alter the health of; send on a trip to Belize.

mutiny. Collective indiscipline.

n

napalm. Soft ordnance.

nepotism. Relational capitalism.

neutron bomb. Enhanced radiation weapon.

niggardly. Thrifty.

nightmare. Extremely vivid nighttime hallucination.

nuclear meltdown. Core rearrangement; super-prompt critical power excursion.

nuclear war. All-out strategic exchange.

nudism. Clothing optional lifestyle.

o

obese. Amply proportioned; big-boned; burly; curvy; fattractive; full-figured; Rubenesque; stocky.

objections. Areas of concern.

off-the-rack. Pre-tailored.

oil drilling. Energy exploration.

oil spill. Tanker accident.

old. Experienced; postmenopausal; senior.

orphanage. Congregate care facility; group home.

overcrowding. Efficient use of space.

p

paint. Façade protectant.

parachute. Aerodynamic personnel decelerator.

parsimonious. Thrifty.

Patagonian toothfish. Chilean sea bass.

peace. Permanent pre-hostility; temporary cessation of hostilities.

peculiar. Eccentric.

pedophilia. Intergenerational intimacy.

pencil. Portable handheld communication inscriber.

personnel department. Human Resources Department.

phone call, unsolicited. Courtesy call.

phone sex operator. Discussion partner.

photocopying clerk. Reprographics engineer.

pick axe. Accreted morphological obstacle disruptor.

pig intestines, boiled. Chitlins.

pimp. Business manager; companionator.

plagiarism. Bad citation; duplication of a paper that has already been published; failure to use quotation marks around material written verbatim from another source; improper dependence; inappropriate copying; unacknowledged repetition; unattributed overlap.

plane collision, head-on. Midair passenger exchange.

plane crash (into the ground). Controlled flight into terrain; failure to maintain clearance from the ground.

plane crash (into the ocean). Water landing.

plastic. Synthetic glass.

plastic surgery. Aesthetic procedure.

plumber. Leak detection and repair specialist; piping technologist.

plunge, stock market. Correction; equity retreat.

plunger, toilet. Force cup.

poison gas. Inhalation hazard.

poor (person). At hope; at risk; culturally deprived; disadvantaged; underresourced.

poor (nation). Developing.

pork. Legislatively directed spending.

pornographic movie. Erotic film.

pornography. Adult entertainment.

prayer. Moment of silence.

prison. Correctional facility; detention center.

prison guard. Correction officer.

prisoner of war. Detainee; enemy combatant; illegal combatant; imperative security internee; unprivileged enemy belligerent. (All these terms are particularly useful when one wants to avoid granting the rights to which a prisoner of war is automatically entitled under the terms of the Geneva Conventions.)

privatization (of Social Security accounts, for example). Personalization.

pro-abortion rights. Pro-choice.

problem. Challenge; issue.

progressive. Elitist.

progressive income tax. Discriminatory taxation; tax socialism.

promiscuity. Sex addiction.

propaganda. Public diplomacy.

prostitute. Morale welfare recreation professional; sex care provider; sex trade worker.

prunes. Dried plums.

psychopath. Emotionally disturbed person (EDP); intense and driven individual.

public toilet. Comfort station.

publishing house. Laboratory for the written word.

punishment. Directive improvement; negative reinforcement.

q

quota. Pluralistic plan.

r

raising taxes. Budget reinforcement.

rape. Sexual activity that is later deemed to have lacked consent.

rapeseed oil. Canola oil.

rapist. Paraphilic coercive disorder sufferer.

reactor meltdown, nuclear. Core rearrangement; super-prompt critical power excursion.

ready-to-wear. Pre-tailored.

receptionist. Director of first impressions; telephone intermediary; welcoming agent.

recession. Period of economic adjustment; temporary interruption of an economic expansion.

reckless. Imprudent.

recruiter. Talent acquisition manager.

red tape. Procedural safeguards.

refugees. Ambient noncombatant personnel.

repression. Stability maintenance.

rerun (TV). Encore presentation.

retreat. Exfiltration; redeployment to the rear; strategic withdrawal.

revenue loss. Negative growth.

reverse discrimination. Affirmative action.

rich people. High-net-worth individuals; job creators.

riot. Collective indiscipline.

riot control. Confrontation management.

road signs. Ground-mounted confirmatory route markers.

rum-runner. Anti-prohibitionist.

S

salary cap. Cost certainty.

salesperson. Customer solution specialist; marketing representative.

saturation bombing. Terrain alteration.

scab. Noncertified worker; replacement worker.

school bus. Education transport module.

screwup, corporate. Contingent operating difficulty.

Scrooge-like. Thrifty.

sea urchin gonads. Uni.

secondhand. New-to-you; preloved; pre-owned; previously enjoyed; previously loved; well-loved.

secretary. Administrative professional; area associate; executive assistant; office manager; personal assistant.

senile. Confused; frail.

separation. Conscious uncoupling; downshifting into a platonic relationship; tender undoing.

sewage sludge. Biosolids; organic biomass.

sex, illicit, engaging in. Discussing Uganda; hiking the Appalachian Trail; slipping one's moorings.

sex, outdoor, engaging in. Watching badgers.

sex change operation. Gender reassignment surgery.

sexual predator, violent. Paraphilic coercive disorder sufferer.

sexual relations with a junior employee. Hands-on mentoring.

shelf stacker. Ambient replenishment assistant.

shell shock. Operational exhaustion; post-traumatic stress disorder (PTSD).

shock treatment. Aversion therapy.

shopping mall. Festival marketplace; lifestyle center.

shouting match. Robust exchange of views.

shovel. Combat emplacement evacuator.

shredding (paper evidence). Document management.

shyness. Avoidant personality disorder; social anxiety disorder (SAD).

skin flick. Erotic film.

slashing benefits. Entitlement reform; modernizing Medicare and Social Security.

slimehead (fish). Orange roughy.

slum. Culturally deprived environment; economically depressed neighborhood; substandard housing.

small latte (at Starbucks). Tall latte.

soft-drink vending machine. Immediate consumption channel.

soldiers, dead. Nonoperative personnel.

solitary confinement. Therapeutic segregation.

solitary confinement cell. Individual behavior adjustment unit.

spade. Round-nose shovel.

speeding. Inappropriate acceleration.

spending cuts. Savings.

spending money you don't have. Levering up.

spin doctor. Image adviser; media consultant.

spoiled fruits and/or vegetables. Distressed produce.

squid testicles, fried. Calamari.

stingy. Thrifty.

stink. Exceed the odor threshold.

stock market plunge. Correction; equity retreat.

stockbroker. Investment professional.

stolen goods. Temporarily displaced inventory.

stoned. In a reduced state of awareness.

street person. Non-goal-oriented member of society; outdoor citizen.

strike. Industrial action.

strike breakers. Replacement workers.

stripper. Exotic dancer.

stupid. Ill-advised.

subdue by force. Pacify.

sugar. Evaporated cane juice.

suicide. Planned termination; self-deliverance.

suicide, assisted. Death with dignity; shortening the dying process.

suicide attempts. Self-injurious behavior incidents.

suicide bomber. Homicide bomber.

surcharge. Convenience fee.

surprise attack. Unilaterally determined pre-emptive self-defense.

surveillance. Data collection.

suspect. Person of interest.

swamps. Wetlands.

swarming Fedayeen. Pockets of resistance.

t

talking to customers. Client engagement; coterminous stakeholder engagement.

talking to oneself. Audible verbal self-reinforcement.

tax avoidance. Income protection.

tax cuts. Pro-growth tax policies.

tax evasion. Creative accounting.

tax increase. Revenue enhancement.

tax loophole. Tax incentive.

taxing the rich. Taking money from hardworking Americans.

teacher. Learning facilitator.

terrorism. Man-caused disasters.

test. Celebration of knowledge.

theft. Inventory shrinkage.

thermometer, medical. Digital fever computer.

throw (a suspect) to the ground. Place in a prone position.

tissue (or box of tissues). Mucus recovery system.

toilet (public). Comfort station.

toilet paper. Bath tissue.

toilet plunger. Force cup.

toothbrush, electric. Cordless rechargeable power plaque remover; home plaque removal instrument.

toothfish, Patagonian. Chilean sea bass.

toothpick. Wooden interdental stimulator.

torture. Abuse; enhanced interrogation; human rights abuses; pain compliance techniques; repetitive administration of legitimate force; special methods of questioning; stress and duress tactics.

toxic waste dump. Reclamation site.

traffic ticket quotas. Proactivity expectations.

trailer. Mobile home.

trailer park. Mobile estate.

travel agent. Destination counselor.

troops (British). Lads.

troops (who oppose the British Army). Hordes.

u

unacceptable. Suboptimal.

undertaker. After-death care provider; bereavement care expert; post-health professional.

unemployed. Between jobs; economically inactive; embarking on a journey of self-discovery; in transition; self-employed; spending more time with one's family.

unemployed person. Consultant; freelancer; involuntary entrepreneur; job-market researcher; job seeker; normal involuntary attrition victim; payroll orphan.

unfinished. In the early stages of finalization.

"union-busting" legislation. Right-to-work laws.

unpaid job. Voluntary development opportunity.

unprovoked. Preemptive.

unsolicited phone call. Courtesy call.

used. New-to-you; preloved; pre-owned; previously enjoyed; previously loved; well-loved.

V

vacation. Annual leave.

vegetables, spoiled. Distressed produce.

vending machine, soft-drink. Immediate consumption channel.

vinyl. Genuine imitation leather.

W

---

war. Assertive disarmament; conflict (a term used to avoid having to adhere to the wartime rules set by the Geneva Conventions); kinetic military action; police action.

warplane. Force package.

water, bottled. Affordable portable lifestyle beverage.

waterboy. Hydration engineer.

weapons. Assets.

weird. Eccentric; unique.

welfare. Assistance for the poor; public assistance.

wheelchair bound. Living with mobility impairment.

wild guess. Statistically oriented projection of the significance of one's findings.

window cleaner. Transparent-wall maintenance engineer.

wine. Adult beverage.

worst. Least-best.

wounded soldiers. ICPs (impaired combat personnel).

wrinkles. Character lines; expression lines; laugh lines; maturity tracks.

Z

zygote. Pre-born baby.

acknowledgments

If I have seen further it is by standing on the shoulders of giants.
—Sir Isaac Newton

It's utterly beside the point that Sir Isaac actually engaged in a bit of plagiarism—or, as *The New York Times* would prefer to call it, "inappropriate copying"—when he borrowed this concept from twelfth-century scholar Bernard de Chartres. We love his quote anyway, because it applies to the role that four muses (and dozens of associate muses) played in making *Spinglish: The Definitive Dictionary of Deliberately Deceptive Language* possible.

If you look up "muse" in our Spinglish–English dictionary, you'll find it defined as "a word frequently used by authors to acknowledge another writer whose idea they've stolen, or whose words they've plagiarized." Of course, many—including us—prefer the traditional meaning of the word, which, according to the *Random House Dictionary*, is "the inspiration that motivates a poet, artist, thinker, and the like." Whichever definition you choose to honor, we believe you'll see why we've named two authors, and two consummate "spinmeisters," as the muses of our book.

The first author on our "muse" list is George Orwell—how could he not be? In his novel *1984*, published in 1949, Orwell introduced the concepts of Newspeak and Doublethink, using such phrases as "War is Peace," "Freedom is Slavery," and "Ignorance is Strength" to illustrate their meaning. Three years earlier, in his famous essay "Politics and the English Language," he had observed, "Political speech and writing are largely the defence of the indefensible. . . . Thus political language has to consist largely of euphemism, question-begging and sheer cloudy vagueness. . . . The great enemy of clear language is insincerity." Thank you, George, we couldn't have said it better ourselves.

The second author on our list is William Lutz, Ph.D.—an ardent champion of plain language, and perhaps the world's reigning expert on manipulative writing and speech. As chairman of the Committee on Public Doublespeak of the National Council of Teachers of English, and editor in chief of the council's *Quarterly Review of Doublespeak* from 1980 to 1994, Lutz indefatigably collected examples of deceptive language (many of which appear in our lexicon), wrote several books on the subject (most notably *Doublespeak: From "Revenue Enhancement" to "Terminal Living"*), and warned against the "use of language as a weapon or tool by those in power to achieve their ends at our expense." Our point exactly!

Our two spinmeister muses are Edward Bernays, the architect of modern public relations, and the acknowledged dean of present-day political strategists and language gurus, Frank Luntz. As Stewart Ewen relates in *PR! A Social History of Spin*, Bernays "fathered the link between corporate campaigns and popular social causes" in the 1920s, when, "while working for the American Tobacco Company, he persuaded women's rights marchers in New York City to hold up Lucky Strike cigarettes as symbolic 'Torches of Freedom.'" And Luntz is widely credited with helping countless Republican candidates to victory by advising them, for example, to say "energy exploration" instead of "oil drilling," "death tax" instead of "estate tax," and "free market economy" instead of "capitalism." Without these two towering figures, we'd have had far, far less to write about, and we are deeply indebted to them both.

As noted above, there are also many "associate muses" whose scholarship, writings, and/or creative employment of Spinglish terminology

have significantly aided our efforts. Prominent among them are Australian linguists Keith Allan and Kate Burridge, coauthors of *Euphemism &*
Dysphemism; philosopher Robert Todd Carroll of *The Skeptic's Dictionary*
fame; "journalese" experts Paul Dickson and Robert Skole; literary agent
Jonny Geller and novelist Janice Harayda, intrepid decoders of publishing buzzwords; Cracked.com's Christina Hsu, arguably the world's greatest authority on sports Spinglish; *Financial Times* management columnist
Lucy Kellaway, whose annual Golden Flannel Awards celebrate "the finest, freshest examples of corporate guff"; Ralph Keyes, author of *Euphe-*
mania: Our Love Affair with Euphemisms; the *Hartford Courant*'s "Word
Guy" columnist Rob Kyff; political framing theorist George P. Lakoff; our
friend John Leo, whose linguistic discoveries have enriched many of our
books, including this one; David Levine and Alix Rule, coauthors of the
brilliant, controversial, and hilarious essay "International Art English";
the National Rifle Association, "America's longest-standing civil rights
organization"; euphemism collectors Judith S. Neaman and Carole G. Silver;
Geoffrey Nunberg, author of *Talking Right: How Conservatives Turned*
Liberalism into a Tax-Raising, Latte-Drinking, Sushi-Eating, Volvo-Driving,
New York Times-*Reading, Body-Piercing, Hollywood-Loving, Left-Wing*
Freak Show, the title alone of which inspired a plethora of entries in our
book; TheOfficeLife.com, purveyors of the indispensable "Ridiculous
Business Jargon Dictionary"; VisualThesaurus.com's "euphemism colum-
nist" Mark Peters; artisanal toast connoisseur C. A. Pinkham; the Project
for the New American Century, which gave the world the term "regime
change," and, in the process, the Iraq War; the Plain English Campaign;
Steven Poole, who writes about politics and culture for *The Guardian* and
authored *Unspeak: How Words Become Weapons, How Weapons Become a*
Message, and How That Message Becomes Reality; the late lexicographer
Hugh Rawson, compiler of the seminal *Dictionary of Euphemisms and*

Other Doubletalk; Sheldon Rampton and John Stauber, editors of *PR Watch* (a publication of the Center for Media and Democracy, which Stauber founded in 1993); "winespeak" authority Marlene Rossman; Norman Solomon, author of *The Power of Babble* and founder of the Institute for Public Accuracy; CheesyCorporateLingo.com's Patrick Reinhart; the *Tampa Bay Times'* PolitiFact project; the United States Department of Defense; and, alphabetically last but hardly least, Don Watson, author of *Watson's Dictionary of Weasel Words, Contemporary Clichés, Cant, and Management Jargon.*

We are grateful, of course, to our colleagues on the Committee on Language Management of the Spinglish-Speaking Union—particularly Jane Aaron, Bill Effros, and Bruce Kluger—for their selfless and thoughtful contributions to our work, and to the Board of the American Hyphen Society for opening their archives to us. And heartfelt thanks, too, to Gwyneth Cravens, for sharing with our research staff her extensive library of information about the nuclear industry, on the one hand, and the purported connection between the United States Air Force's recently concluded High Frequency Active Auroral Research Program (HAARP) and the 2011 Fukushima earthquake, on the other. The inclusion of a significant number of entries in our dictionary, from "modernize" to "unsubstantiated," was made possible by her generosity.

Spinglish: The Definitive Dictionary of Deliberately Deceptive Language has also benefited greatly from the thoroughness and skill of our copy editor, Sharon Gonzalez, and from the literary evangelism skills of Blue Rider Press's crack team of communications professionals, Aileen Boyle, Brian Ulicky, and Frances Milliken. Thanks, Sharon, Aileen, Brian, and Frances!

Although we categorically deny any responsibility for Simon & Schuster's dismissal of our treasured colleague David Rosenthal just days after he signed up our last book, *Encyclopedia Paranoiaca*, for publication there, we apologize for any hard feelings he may have harbored as a result of the incident, and cannot overstate how profoundly appreciative we are that, despite all, he has welcomed us into his new Blue Rider family with open arms.

Finally, we would like to express our gratitude to our agent and dear friend, Ed Victor, and to Sarah Hochman, our editor, who has supervised the content of *Spinglish* with grace, insight, thoughtfulness, and patience. And above all, we offer our very special thanks to Katherine Vaz for selflessly agreeing to marry one of us (Christopher Cerf) within a week of our publication date and permitting us to include a brief blurb about our book in the official wedding announcement, thereby guaranteeing that *Spinglish* will be promoted in *The New York Times* at the most optimal moment possible.

notes

a

1. Shadee Ashtari, "Rush Limbaugh Slams Democrats for Turning Women 'into Abortion Machines,'" *The Huffington Post*, November 6, 2013, retrieved from http://www.huffingtonpost.com/2013/11/06/rush-limbaugh-abortion -machines_n_4228659.html, January 17, 2014.
2. Hugh Rawson, *A Dictionary of Euphemisms and Other Doubletalk* (New York: Crown, 1981), p. 12, cited in Henry Beard and Christopher Cerf, *The Official Politically Correct Dictionary and Handbook*, updated edition (New York: Villard Books, 1994), p. 131.
3. Rich Coffey, "Euphemisms Glossary," The American Empire, Vizettes.com, http://vizettes.com/kt/american_empire/pages/euphemisms-glossary.htm.
4. "Archives: Banished Words 2001," Lake Superior State University, retrieved from http://www.lssu.edu/banished/archive/2001.php, April 11, 2014.
5. "'Because' Is Chosen as Word of the Year," *The New York Times*, January 6, 2014, p. C3, http://artsbeat.blogs.nytimes.com/2014/01/05/american-dialect -society-chooses-because-as-word-of-the-year.
6. Paul Dickson, *Slang!* (New York: Pocket Books, 1990), p. 96, cited in Henry Beard and Christopher Cerf, *The Official Politically Correct Dictionary and Handbook*, updated edition (New York: Villard Books, 1994), p. 131.
7. Hugh Rawson, quoted in Rose De Wolf, "Sometimes a 'Cigar' Not Just a Smoke," *Philadelphia Daily News*, November 20, 1995, http://articles.philly.com/1995 -11-20/news/25680110_1_euphemisms-and-other-doubletalk-words-paddling.
8. *Quarterly Review of Doublespeak* (National Council of Teachers of English, Urbana, Illinois), July 1991, p. 2, cited in Henry Beard and Christopher Cerf, *The Official Politically Correct Dictionary and Handbook*, updated edition (New York: Villard Books, 1994), p. 131.
9. David Perdue, quoted in "Budget Vote Passes the Details to Two Panels," *The New York Times*, December 19, 2013, http://www.nytimes.com/2013/12/19/us/ politics/senate-64-36-sends-two-year-budget-to-obama.html.
10. Don Watson, *Watson's Dictionary of Weasel Words, Contemporary Clichés, Cant, and Management Jargon* (Sydney: Random House of Australia, 2004), p. 17.
11. "Superior Double-speak," Spellhold Studios, February 19, 2009, http://www .shsforums.net/topic/38925-superior-double-speak.
12. "Office Jargon for the 21st Century," DangerousLogic.com, retrieved from http://www.dangerouslogic.com/office_lexicon.html, January 26, 2014.

13. Robert Hutton, quoted in Michael Holtermann, "Romps, Tots and Boffins: Robert Hutton on Journalese," Holtermann Design LLC, September 21, 2013, http://holtermanndesign.com/romps-tots-and-boffins-book-on-journalese -by-robert-hutton.

14. Nick Heady, "8 Foods That Aren't What You Think They're Going to Be," *Food & Drink* (blog), InsureandGo.com, July 16, 2014, https://blog.insureandgo .com/food-and-drink/2014/07/8-foods-that-arent-what-you-think-they.are.

15. Oliver Burkeman, "Memo Exposes Bush's New Green Strategy," *The Guardian*, March 3, 2003, http://www.theguardian.com/environment/2003/ mar/04/usnews.climatechange.

16. Patrick Reinhart, CheesyCorporateLingo.com, http://www.cheesycorporate lingo.com/sections/a.

17. Edward Harrison, "Code Words and Dog Whistle Economics," CreditWrite downs.com, December 8, 2011, http://www.creditwritedowns.com/2011/12/ code-words-and-dog-whistle-economics.html.

18. David E. Sanger and Thom Shanker, "N.S.A. Devises Radio Pathway into Computers," *The New York Times*, January 15, 2014, http://www.nytimes.com/ 2014/01/15/us/nsa-effort-pries-open-computers-not-connected-to-internet .html.

19. Jerry Merchant and Mary Matthews, "Avoiding Difficult Questions," The Right-Wing Christian Dictionary, ExtremelySmart.com, http://www.extreme lysmart.com/humor/rightwingdictionary.php.

20. Jaime O'Neill, "A Glossary of Republican Doublespeak," *San Francisco Chronicle*, May 10, 2009, http://www.sfgate.com/politics/article/A-glossary-of -Republican-doublespeak-3242630.php.

21. "The Ridiculous Business Jargon Dictionary," *The Office Life* (blog), http:// www.theofficelife.com/business-jargon-dictionary-A.html.

22. Robert Sutton, "A Compilation of Euphemisms for Layoffs," *Work Matters* (blog), November 16, 2008, http://bobsutton.typepad.com/my_weblog/2008/ 11/a-compilation-of-euphemisms-for-layoffs.html.

23. Rachel L. Swarms, "Crowded Out of Ivory Tower, Adjuncts See a Life Less Lofty," *The New York Times*, January 20, 2014, http://www.nytimes.com/2014/ 01/20/nyregion/crowded-out-of-ivory-tower-adjuncts-see-a-life-less-lofty .html.

24. Vincent Fernando and Gus Lubin, "20 Examples of Corporate Doublespeak You Need to Know During Earnings Season," Business Insider, October 18, 2010, http://www.businessinsider.com/guide-to-earnings-season-2010?op=1.

25. "What Is an Office Manager Really?," *City-Data Forum: Work and Employment*, City-Data.com, http://www.city-data.com/forum/work -employment/2045187-what-office-manager-really.html.

26. Patrick Reinhart, CheesyCorporateLingo.com, http://www.cheesycorporate lingo.com/sections/a.

27. "Examples of Doublespeak," YourDictionary.com, http://examples.yourdictio nary.com/examples-of-doublespeak.html.

28. "Examples of Doublespeak," YourDictionary.com, http://examples.yourdictio nary.com/examples-of-doublespeak.html.

29. Patricia T. O'Conner, "Corporate-speak," *The Grammarphobia Blog*, October 9, 2008, http://www.grammarphobia.com/blog/2008/10/corporate-speak.html; and *Drug Safety Newsletter*, U.S. Federal Drug Administration, Spring 2008, http://www.fda.gov/downloads/Drugs/DrugSafety/DrugSafetyNewsletter/ ucm109174.pdf.

30. Thomas Kaplan and Suzanne Craig, "Defiant, Cuomo Denies Interfering with Ethics Commission," *The New York Times*, July 29, 2014, http://www.nytimes .com/2014/07/29/nyregion/cuomo-defends-his-handling-of-ethics-panel.html.

31. "Varieties of English: Gobbledygook," FunTrivia.com, http://www.funtrivia .com/en/subtopics/Gobbledygook-315836.html.

32. Rob Kyff, "Negative Patient Care Outcome? Yes, Euphemisms Are Alive and Well," *Hartford Courant*, April 4, 1997, http://articles.courant.com/1997-04- 04/features/9705230902_1_assisted-new-euphemism-nursing-home-care.

33. "Making Murder Respectable," *The Economist*, December 17, 2011, http:// www.economist.com/node/21541767.

34. John Fund, "Race-Based Preferences Forever," *National Review Online*, April 23, 2014, http://www.nationalreview.com/article/376358/raced-based-prefer ences-forever-john-fund; "Affirmative action," *The Economist Style Guide*, retrieved from http://www.economist.com/style-guide/affirmative-action, May 19, 2014; and Stanley Fish, "They Write the Songs," *The New York Times*, July 16, 2006, http://www.nytimes.com/2006/07/16/books/review/16fish.html.

35. John de Graaf, quoted in "The Affluenza Defense," *Here & Now*, WBUR.org, December 19, 2013, http://hereandnow.wbur.org/2013/12/19/the-affluenza -defense; and Maia Szalavitz, "The Value of 'Affluenza,' Addiction and Parental Neglect As Get Out of Jail Defenses," *The Fix*, January 6, 2014, http:// www.thefix.com/content/affluenza-Maia-Szalavitz-couch2101.

36. Shannon Bond, "Online Boom Proves an Abundant Source of Bottled Water," Food and Beverage, *Financial Times*, December 11, 2013, retrieved from http://www.ft.com/intl/cms/s/0/82eda31c-6260-11e3-bba5-00144feabdc0 .html#axzz2yuhLUYEf, April 14, 2014; and Lucy Kellaway, "The 2013 Golden Flannel Awards for Corporate Guff," *The Irish Times*, January 6, 2014, http://www.irishtimes.com/business/the-2013-golden-flannel-awards-for -corporate-guff-1.1644897.

37. "Honoring Our Own," Krause Funeral Homes and Cremation Services, March 11, 2014, http://www.krausefuneralhome.com/2014/03/11/honoring-our-own.

38. D. J. Kehl and Howard Livingston, "Doublespeak Detection for the English Classroom," *The English Journal*, July 1999, p. 79, retrieved from http://www .jstor.org/discover/10.2307/822191?uid=3739832&uid=2134&uid= 2479801677&uid=2&uid=70&uid=3&uid=2479801667&uid=3739256&uid=60& sid=21103823248907, April 8, 2014.

39. *Quarterly Review of Doublespeak* (National Council of Teachers of English, Urbana, Illinois), cited in "Strange Examples of 'Doublespeak,'" Strange

Cosmos.com, July 25, 2012, http://www.strangecosmos.com/archive/eletter_item
_828.html.

40. "Aggressive Accounting," *Investopedia Dictionary*, retrieved from http://www
.investopedia.com/terms/a/aggressiveaccounting.asp, May 11, 2014.

41. William Davis, "Interfacing with Biz Speak," *The New York Times Magazine*,
June 8, 1986, http://www.nytimes.com/1986/06/08/magazine/interfacing
-with-biz-speak.html.

42. William Lutz, *Doublespeak* (New York: Harper Perennial, 1990), p. 176, cited
in Henry Beard and Christopher Cerf, *The Official Politically Correct
Dictionary and Handbook*, updated edition (New York: Villard Books, 1994),
p. 131.

43. Julie Bertagna, quoted in Janice Harayda, "23 British Publishing Euphemisms
Decoded by Industry Experts," *One-Minute Book Reviews* (blog), February 24,
2012, http://oneminutebookreviews.wordpress.com/2012/02/24/23-british
-publishing-euphemisms-decoded-by-industry-experts.

44. U.S. Department of Defense term, cited in Judith S. Neaman and Carole G.
Silver, *Kind Words* (New York: Avon Books, 1991), p. 351.

45. Mark Peters, "Non-Thinking-Type Think Pieces," Visual Thesaurus, May 2,
2012, https://www.visualthesaurus.com/cm/evasive/non-thinking-type-think
-pieces; and "Gonna miss Gungnir and PlicketyCat for a while," *Chris
Martenson's Peak Prosperity*, July 25, 2009, http://www.peakprosperity.com/
forum/gonna-miss-gungnir-and-plicketycat-while/22641?page=1.

46. "Walgreens Announces Reduction in Corporate and Field Management
Positions," news release, Walgreens, January 8, 2009, http://news.walgreens
.com/article_print.cfm?article_id=5133.

47. Penny Tristram, "Arty Bollocks Decoder: What They Say vs What They Mean,"
Le Art Corner, October 19, 2013, http://pennytristram.co.uk/tag/artspeak.

48. "Doublespeak," Center for Media and Democracy, updated August 30, 2009,
retrieved from http://www.sourcewatch.org/index.php/Doublespeak, April 9,
2014.

49. Stephanie Strom, "Kellogg Agrees to Alter Labeling on Kashi Line," *The New
York Times*, May 9, 2014, p. B7, http://www.nytimes.com/2014/05/09/busi
ness/kellogg-agrees-to-change-labeling-on-kashi-line.html.

50. Alain C. Enthoven and K. Wayne Smith, *How Much Is Enough?: Shaping the
Defense Program, 1961–1969* (New York: Harper & Row, 1971), p. 190.

51. "Doublespeak," Center for Media and Democracy, updated August 30, 2009,
retrieved from http://www.sourcewatch.org/index.php/Doublespeak, April 9,
2014.

52. "The Rule of Verbal Packaging—The Leverage of Language," chap. 8 of *The
Rules of Persuasion* (Westside Toastmasters, Los Angeles), retrieved from
http://westsidetoastmasters.com/resources/laws_persuasion/chap8.html,
April 18, 2014.

53. Kate Cocuzzo, "Real Estate Euphemisms: An Agent's Literary Loophole," *Geo
Properties, Inc.* (blog), May 21, 2013, http://www.geopropertiesinc.com/word
press/real-estate-euphemisms-an-agents-literary-loophole.

54. Steve Rubin, "Uses and Abuses of Language," Santa Rosa Junior College, November 27, 2013, http://online.santarosa.edu/presentation/page/?30609.

55. Lee Lofland, "The Language of Police: Cop Slang," *The Graveyard Shift* (blog), retrieved from http://www.leelofland.com/wordpress/the-language-of-police -cop-slang, July 2, 2014.

56. Ralph Keyes, *Euphemania: Our Love Affair with Euphemisms* (New York: Little, Brown, 2010), p. 199.

57. Nigel Rees, "In Other Words . . . ," *The Guardian*, October 13, 2006, http:// www.theguardian.com/money/2006/oct/14/careers.work.

58. Paula Span, "Escape from the Hospital Bed," *The New York Times*, July 8, 2011, https://www.peppercenter.org/docs/hotfind/UTMB_Fisher_NYTimesHot Topics.pdf.

59. The National Rifle Association, home page, NRA.org, retrieved from http:// home.nra.org, July 13, 2014.

60. Andy Kroll and Jeremy Schulman, "Leaked Documents Reveal the Secret Finances of a Pro-Industry Science Group," *Mother Jones*, October 28, 2013, http://www.motherjones.com/politics/2013/10/american-council-science -health-leaked-documents-fundraising; and Martin Donohue, "Corporate Front Groups and the Abuse of Science: The American Council on Science and Health (ACSH)," June 25, 2010, http://www.spinwatch.org/index.php/issues/ more/item/12-corporate-front-groups-and-the-abuse-of-science-the -american-council-on-science-and-health-acsh.

61. Ronald D. Smith, *Becoming a Public Relations Writer: A Writing Workbook for the Profession* (Oxford, UK: Taylor and Francis, 2003), p. 29.

62. John Leo, "Journalese as a Second Tongue," *Time*, March 18, 1985, http://bhs .cc/journalism/pdf/pw/journalese.pdf.

63. Julie Hollar, "In Immigration Debate, Time to 'Drop and Leave' Loaded Language," *Extra!*, March 16, 2011, retrieved from http://www .commondreams.org/view/2011/03/16-1, April 11, 2014.

64. Patrick Cockburn, "Weasel Words That Politicians Use to Obscure Terrible Truths," *The Independent*, October 14, 2012, http://www.independent.co.uk/ voices/comment/weasel-words-that-politicians-use-to-obscure-terrible -truths-8210302.html.

65. Oladele Ogunseitan, ed., *Green Health: An A-to-Z Guide* (Los Angeles: Sage Publications, 2011), p. 6; and Copley, "What Is It: Angel Dusting," *Truth in Aging*, March 26, 2009, https://www.truthinaging.com/review/what-is-it -angel-dusting.

66. "Doubled Eggs," *Dictionary of Christianese*, April 22, 2012, http://www .dictionaryofchristianese.com/doubled-eggs.

67. Mark Peters, "Quench Your Thirst! (Within the Defect Action Levels, of Course)," Visual Thesaurus, October 6, 2010, http://www.visualthesaurus.com/ cm/evasive/quench-your-thirst-within-the-defect-action-levels-of-course.

68. "'Because' Is Chosen as Word of the Year," *The New York Times*, January 6, 2014, p. C3, http://artsbeat.blogs.nytimes.com/2014/01/05/american-dialect -society-chooses-because-as-word-of-the-year.

69. William Lutz, "The World of Doublespeak," anthologized in Christopher Ricks and Leonard Michaels, eds., *The State of the Language* (Berkeley: University of California Press, 1990), p. 260; and "Virgin Galactic Spacecraft Crash Kills Pilot," BBC News US & Canada, October 31, 2014, http://www.bbc.com/news/world-us-canada-29857182.

70. Christopher Klein, "10 Things You May Not Know About the Berlin Wall," History.com, November 7, 2014, http://www.history.com/news/10-things-you-may-not-know-about-the-berlin-wall.

71. "Advocating," Susan B. Anthony List, 2012, retrieved from http://www.sba-list.org/about-sba-list/our-mission/advocating, April 23, 2014.

72. Christopher Fountain, "A New Low in Euphemisms," *For What It's Worth* (blog), July 28, 2008, https://christopherfountain.wordpress.com/2008/07/28/a-new-low-in-euphemism.

73. "Subject Guides: Israel and the Palestinians," BBC, updated February 2013, http://www.bbc.co.uk/academy/journalism/article/art20130702112133696; John Dugard, "An Illegal Annexation: Tear Down Israel's Wall," *The New York Times*, August 2, 2003, http://www.nytimes.com/2003/08/02/opinion/02iht-eddugard_ed3_.html; and "Under the Guise of Security: Routing the Separation Barrier to Enable Israeli Settlement Expansion in the West Bank," B'Tselem—The Israeli Information Center for Human Rights in the Occupied Territories, December 2005, http://www.btselem.org/publications/summaries/200512_under_the_guise_of_security.

74. Mark Peters, "Hiking the Euphemistic Trail," Visual Thesaurus, July 2, 2009, https://www.visualthesaurus.com/cm/evasive/hiking-the-euphemistic-trail.

75. Troy Simpson, "Writing Skills: Hedge Words," English-Language-Skills.com, July 14, 2011, http://english-language-skills.com/item/177-writing-skills-hedge-words.html.

76. Adam Nossiter, "New Orleans Probing Alleged Police Looting," Associated Press, September 30, 2005, retrieved from http://www.washingtonpost.com/wp-dyn/content/article/2005/09/29/AR2005092901975.html, August 21, 2014.

77. "Rights Survey Stops Using Word 'Killing,'" *The New York Times*, February 11, 1984, http://www.nytimes.com/1984/02/11/world/rights-survey-stops-using-word-killing.html.

78. "Job Description: Area Associate, Part Time," Kohler Company, retrieved from https://kohler.taleo.net/careersection/kohlercom/jobdetail.ftl?job=122945&src=JB-10021, January 29, 2014.

79. "M67 / M72 Area Denial Anti-personnel Mine (ADAM)," GlobalSecurity.org, retrieved from http://www.globalsecurity.org/military/systems/munitions/adam.htm, January 29, 2014.

80. "The Rule of Verbal Packaging—The Leverage of Language," chap. 8 of *The Rules of Persuasion* (Westside Toastmasters, Los Angeles), retrieved from http://westsidetoastmasters.com/resources/laws_persuasion/chap8.html, April 18, 2014.

81. Richard Nordquist, "What Are Weasel Words?," About.com, retrieved from http://grammar.about.com/od/words/a/What-Are-Weasel-Words.htm, January 29, 2014.

82. Hugh Rawson, *A Dictionary of Euphemisms and Other Doubletalk* (New York: Crown, 1981), p. 20.

83. Robert Todd Carroll, *Becoming a Critical Thinker*, chap. 2, p. 28, retrieved from http://www.skepdic.com/refuge/ctlessons/ch2.pdf, August 14, 2014.

84. C. A. Pinkham, "Artisanal Toast Is Apparently a Fucking Thing Now," *Kitchenette*, June 1, 2014, http://kitchenette.jezebel.com/artisanal -toast-is-apparently-a-fucking-thing-now-1584472659; and David Rees, "How to Sharpen Pencils," video documentary about Rees's artisanal pencil sharpening business, retrieved from http://vimeo.com/60718161, July 20, 2014.

85. Robert Todd Carroll, *Becoming a Critical Thinker*, chap. 2, p. 41, retrieved from http://www.skepdic.com/refuge/ctlessons/ch2.pdf, August 14, 2014.

86. Robert Todd Carroll, *Becoming a Critical Thinker*, chap. 2, p. 41, retrieved from http://www.skepdic.com/refuge/ctlessons/ch2.pdf, August 14, 2014.

87. Tom Albrighton, "How to Use Weasel Words to Bend the Truth," *ABC Copywriting*, January 25, 2010, http://www.abccopywriting.com/blog/2010/01/25/ weasel-words-bend-the-truth.

88. "Past Recipients of the NCTE Doublespeak Award: 2008," National Council of Teachers of English, retrieved from http://www.ncte.org/library/NCTEFiles/ Involved/Volunteer/Appointed%20Groups/Past_Recipients_Doublespeak _Award.pdf, January 29, 2014.

89. "TINA's Glossary," TruthinAdvertising.org, retrieved from https://www .truthinadvertising.org/tinas-glossary/#gs_index. February 15, 2014.

90. Anat Shenker-Osorio, "Stop Saying 'Undocumented Workers,'" *Salon*, July 17, 2013, http://www.salon.com/2013/07/17/stop_saying_undocumented _workers.

91. John Algeo, *American Speech*, quoted in Adele Wilson, "Military Terminology in the English Language," University of Toronto Graduate Department of English, 2008, retrieved from http://homes.chass.utoronto.ca/~cpercy/cours es/6362-WilsonAdele.htm, April 11, 2014.

92. Ryan Tate, "The Hyperlocal Web Bleeds as AOL Pushes Patch to the Curb," *Wired*, December 16, 2013, http://www.wired.com/2013/12/local-media-death; and David Carr, "AOL Chief's White Whale Finally Slips His Grasp," *The New York Times*, December 14, 2013, http://www.nytimes.com/2013/12/16/busi ness/media/aol-chiefs-white-whale-finally-slips-his-grasp.html.

93. Rich Coffey, "Euphemisms Glossary," The American Empire, Vizettes.com, http://vizettes.com/kt/american_empire/pages/euphemisms-glossary.htm.

94. Caroline Waxler, "Corporate Speak Glossary," *Upstart Business Journal*, April 16, 2007, http://upstart.bizjournals.com/resources/business-intelligence/ 2007/04/16/corporate-speak.html?page=all.

95. Ralph Keyes, *Euphemania: Our Love Affair with Euphemisms* (New York: Little, Brown, 2010), p. 213.

96. Rob Kyff, "Negative Patient Care Outcome? Yes, Euphemisms Are Alive and Well," *Hartford Courant*, April 4, 1997, http://articles.courant.com/ 1997-04-04/features/9705230902_1_assisted-new-euphemism-nursing -home-care.

97. "TINA's Glossary," TruthinAdvertising.org, https://www.truthinadvertising .org/tinas-glossary/#gs_index.

98. "Astroturf," Center for Media and Democracy, October 22, 2005, retrieved from http://www.sourcewatch.org/index.php/Astroturf, January 19, 2014.

99. "Astrotweeting," Taegan Goddard's Political Dictionary, retrieved from http://politicaldictionary.com, May 18, 2014.

100. Steven Poole, *Unspeak* (New York: Grove Press, 2006), p. 162.

101. Scott Akire, "Introducing Euphemisms to Language Learners," *The Internet TESL Journal,* retrieved from http://iteslj.org/Lessons/Alkire-Euphemisms .html, January 13, 2014; and Donna Gordon Blankinship, "Wash. Lawmaker Wants Euphemism for Poor: 'At Hope,'" *The Seattle Times,* January 12, 2010, http://seattletimes.com/html/nationworld/2010769806_apuschildrenathope .html.

102. Judith S. Neaman and Carole G. Silver, *Kind Words* (New York: Avon Books, 1991), p. 161, cited in Henry Beard and Christopher Cerf, *The Official Politically Correct Dictionary and Handbook*, updated edition (New York: Villard Books, 1994), p. 132.

103. Norman Lebrecht, "Katherine Jenkins's US Hit Show Replaces Live Musicians with Dead Tracks," *Slipped Disc* (blog), February 2, 2014, retrieved from http://slippedisc.com/2014/02/katherine-jenkinss-us-hit -show-replaces-live-musicians-with-dead-tracks/, February 2, 2014.

104. Ralph Keyes, *Euphemania: Our Love Affair with Euphemisms* (New York: Little, Brown, 2010), p. 203.

105. Hal DeKeyser, "Replace Stilted Bureaucratese with Words People Actually Use," *AZWritingCoach* (blog), May 4, 2010, http://azwritingcoach.blogspot .com/2010/05/replace-stilted-bureaucratese-with.html.

106. William Lutz, *Doublespeak* (New York: HarperCollins, 1990), p. 61.

107. Steven Poole, "Austerity Measures," *Unspeak* (blog), January 31, 2011, http:// unspeak.net/austerity-measures.

108. Mark Peters, "One Man's Trash Is Another Man's Service Item," Visual Thesaurus, July 7, 2014, http://www.visualthesaurus.com/cm/evasive/one -mans-trash-is-another-mans-service-item.

109. Hugh Rawson, *A Dictionary of Euphemisms and Other Doubletalk* (New York: Crown, 1981), p. 27, cited in Henry Beard and Christopher Cerf, *The Official Politically Correct Dictionary and Handbook*, updated edition (New York: Villard Books, 1994), p. 132.

110. Christopher Lane, "Shy? Or Something More Serious?," *The Washington Post*, November 6, 2007, http://www.washingtonpost.com/wp-dyn/content/article/ 2007/11/02/AR2007110201767.html.

b

1. Jessica Belasco and Ellery Jividen, "Would You Eat Slimehead? With Food, Names Make All the Difference," *San Antonio Express-News*, July 15, 2014, http://www.expressnews.com/news/local/article/Would-you-eat-slimehead -With-food-names-make-5623959.php.

2. Steven Poole, "An A–Z of Modern Office Jargon," *The Guardian*, October 22, 2013, http://www.theguardian.com/money/2013/oct/22/a-z-modern-office -jargon.

3. Ray Horak, "backhoe fade," *Webster's New World Telecom Dictionary* (Indianapolis: Wiley, 2010), retrieved from http://www.yourdictionary .com/backhoe-fade#computer, November 3, 2014.

4. "Geekspeak Glossary," *The Compleat Winegeek*, retrieved from http://www .compleatwinegeek.com/glossary.html, July 3, 2014.

5. James Kroll, "Excerpts from the Plagiarism Hall of Excuses," lecture slide, reproduced in Ivan Oransky, *Retraction Watch* (blog), May 14, 2013, http:// retractionwatch.com/2013/05/14/bird-vocalizations-and-other-best-ever -plagiarism-excuses-a-wrap-up-of-the-3rd-world-conference-on-research -integrity.

6. "Superior Double-Speak," Spellhold Studios, February 19, 2009, http://www .shsforums.net/topic/38925-superior-double-speak.

7. Michael Delahunt, ArtLex Art Dictionary, retrieved from http://artlex.com, February 18, 2014.

8. "The Ridiculous Business Jargon Dictionary," *The Office Life* (blog), retrieved from http://www.theofficelife.com/business-jargon-dictionary-B.html, January 27, 2014.

9. Christina Hsu, "The Seven Most Condescending Sports Euphemisms," Cracked.com, May 17, 2011, http://www.cracked.com/blog/the-7-most -condescending-sports-euphemisms.

10. Alex Hern, "Top Five Racist Republican Dog-Whistles," *New Statesman*, July 27, 2012, http://www.newstatesman.com/politics/2012/07/top-five -racist-republican-dog-whistles.

11. Lacey Sheppy, "This Wordsmith Has Had Enough of Phoney Titles," *Moose Jaw Times Herald* (Moose Jaw, Saskatchewan), February 29, 2008, http:// www.mjtimes.sk.ca/Business/Employment/2008-02-29/article-15006/This wordsmith-has-had-enough-of-phoney-titles.

12. Marlene Rossman, "'Winespeak' and Other Obscenities," *The Huffington Post*, August 15, 2008, http://www.huffingtonpost.com/marlene-rossman/wine speak-and-other-obsce_b_118508.html.

13. Gary C. Woodward and Robert E. Denton, Jr., *Persuasion and Influence in American Life*, 7th edition (Long Grove, IL: Waveland Press, 2014), p. 71.

14. Matt McMillan, "'Bath Salts' Drug Trend—Expert Q&A," WebMD, February 26, 2013, http://www.webmd.com/mental-health/addiction/features/bath-salts -drug-dangers; and "Synthetic/Designer Drugs Fact Sheet," Drug Free Marion County, Marion County, Indiana, retrieved from http://www.drugfreemc.org/

Portals/0/Flyers%20and%20Fact%20Sheets/Designer%20Drugs%20Fact%20Sheet%20Updated%20January%202012.pdf, September 1, 2014.

15. Ralph Keyes, *Euphemania: Our Love Affair with Euphemisms* (New York: Little, Brown, 2010), p. 175.

16. Elana Premack Sandler, MSW, MPH, "Behavioral Health versus Mental Health," *Promoting Health and Preventing Suicide* (blog), *PsychologyToday*, October 28, 2009, http://www.psychologytoday.com/blog/promoting-hope-preventing-suicide/200910/behavioral-health-versus-mental-health.

17. Steven Roger Fischer, *A History of Language* (London: Reaktion Books, 2004), p. 193.

18. Shira Ovide, "Perfect Fit: To Some Outfits, Nothing Speaks Like 'Bespoke,'" *The Wall Street Journal*, May 3, 2012, http://online.wsj.com/news/articles/SB10001424052702303877604577381951110399674; and "About Us," Bespoke Cleaning Contractors, retrieved from http://bespokecc.co.uk/about_us_10.html, May 3, 2014.

19. Patrick Reinhart, CheesyCorporateLingo.com, retrieved from http://www.cheesycorporatelingo.com/sections/a, January 26, 2014.

20. Clare Whitmell, "English Euphemisms," English-at-home.com, http://www.english-at-home.com/vocabulary/english-euphemisms.

21. Hugh Rawson, *A Dictionary of Euphemisms and Other Doubletalk* (New York: Crown, 1981), p. 32.

22. Daniel Okrent, "The War of the Words: A Dispatch from the Front Lines," *The New York Times*, March 6, 2005, http://www.nytimes.com/2005/03/06/week inreview/06bott.html?pagewanted=1&_r=0&oref=login.

23. William Lambdin, *Doublespeak Dictionary* (Los Angeles: Pinnacle Books, 1981), p. 10.

24. "Big Pharma," RationalWiki, updated May 17, 2014, http://rationalwiki.org/wiki/Big_Pharma.

25. "Common Core Standards: Double Double Speak Speak," Southern Nevada Regional Professional Development Program, p. 2, retrieved from http://rpdp.net/files/ccss/ELA/ELA_9-10_Curr_Res/Language%209-10/Language%20Standard%206%20(9-10).pdf, April 9, 2014.

26. Glenn Thompson, "The 12 Most Horrifically Misleading Euphemisms," Cracked.com, December 16, 2008, www.cracked.com/article_16884_the-12-most-horrifically-misleading-euphemisms.html.

27. Glossary, *Spy & Counterspy*, October 9, 1998, retrieved from http://webcache.googleusercontent.com/search?q=cache:iZfflXvtX4QJ:www.ncmilitia.org/spycounterspy/fs012.html, July 2, 2014.

28. "Evolution on the Mind in Georgia," *Geotimes*, American Geosciences Institute, February 10, 2004, retrieved from http://www.geotimes.org/feb04/WebExtra021004.html, July 19, 2014.

29. "Suicide Mission to Chernobyl," *Nova*, PBS Television, 1991, cited in Henry Beard and Christopher Cerf, *The Official Politically Correct Dictionary and Handbook*, updated edition (New York: Villard Books, 1994), p. 132.

30. "Sewage Sludge," SourceWatch, Center for Media and Democracy, last modified on January 25, 2014, http://www.sourcewatch.org/index.php/ Sewage_sludge.

31. David Bromwich, "Euphemism and American Violence," *The New York Review of Books,* April 3, 2008, http://www.nybooks.com/articles/archives/2008/apr/ 03/euphemism-and-american-violence; and "Middle East Crisis: Facts and Figures," BBC News, August 31, 2006, http://news.bbc.co.uk/2/hi/middle _east/5257128.stm.

32. Jon Henley, "A Glossary of US Military Torture Euphemisms," *The Guardian,* December 13, 2007, http://www.theguardian.com/world/2007/dec/13/usa .humanrights.

33. Marjorie Wolfe, "Euphemisms for the New Office," *National Business Employment Weekly,* October 16, 1999, p. 50.

34. "Unequal Naming: The Gulf War 1991," *Guardian Weekly,* February 3, 1991, retrieved from http://www.myread.org/images/cloze/unequal_print.pdf, May 24, 2014.

35. Keith Allan and Kate Burridge, *Euphemism & Dysphemism: Language Used as Shield and Weapon* (New York: Oxford University Press, 1991), p. 27.

36. Nick Heady, "8 Foods That Aren't What You Think They're Going to Be," *Food & Drink* (blog), InsureandGo.com, July 16, 2014, https://blog.insureandgo .com/food-and-drink/2014/07/8-foods-that-arent-what-you-think-they.are.

37. Crissie Brown, "Midday Matinee—Boots on the Ground," Blogistan Polytechnic Institute, April 18, 2011, retrieved from http://bpicampus.com/ 2011/04/18/midday-matinee-boots-on-the-ground/, January 23, 2014.

38. Robert Hutton, quoted in Michael Holtermann, "Romps, Tots and Boffins: Robert Hutton on Journalese," Holtermann Design LLC, September 21, 2013, http://holtermanndesign.com/romps-tots-and-boffins-book-on-journalese -by-robert-hutton.

39. JR post to "Favorite Euphemisms," SportsJournalists.com, September 28, 2006, http://www.sportsjournalists.com/forum/index.php/topic,32365.0/ nowap.html; and "ITC Hotels: Responsible Luxury," website home page, http://www.itcportal.com/businesses/hotels.aspx.

40. Luke Mullins, "The Real Estate Euphemism Pocket Translator," *U.S. News & World Report*: Money, September 9, 2008, http://money.usnews.com/money/ blogs/the-home-front/2008/09/09/the-real-estate-euphemism-pocket -translator.

41. James Meader, quoted in Janice Harayda, "40 Publishing Buzzwords, Clichés and Euphemisms Decoded," *One-Minute Book Reviews* (blog), August 21, 2011, http://oneminutebookreviews.wordpress.com/2011/08/21/40-publishing -buzzwords-cliches-and-euphemisms-decoded.

42. Glenn Thompson, "The 12 Most Horrifically Misleading Euphemisms," Cracked.com, December 16, 2008, www.cracked.com/article_16884_the-12 -most-horrifically-misleading-euphemisms.html; and "Sweden's Convergence Programme, 2013," European Commission, retrieved from http://ec.europa.eu/ europe2020/pdf/nd/cp2013_sweden_en.pdf, January 25, 2014.

43. Ralph Keyes, *Euphemania: Our Love Affair with Euphemisms* (New York: Little, Brown, 2010), p. 79.

44. Amanda Hess, "'I Don't Believe in the Word Pimp': Sex-Work Bosses Attempt to Rebrand." *Slate*, March 23, 2014, http://www.slate.com/blogs/xx_factor/2014/03/13/urban_institute_sex_work_study_pimps_sex_workers_child _pornographers_and.html.

45. Philip Howard, quoted in Colin Randall, "'Let's Do Lunch': Putting a Name to an Insincere Phrase," *The National*, July 26, 2014, http://www.thenational.ae/opinion/comment/lets-do-lunch-putting-a-name-to-an-insincere-phrase.

46. Bob Woodward and Carl Bernstein, "Nixon Debated Paying Blackmail, Clemency," *The Washington Post*, May 1, 1974, http://www.washingtonpost .com/wp-srv/national/longterm/watergate/articles/050174-2.htm; and Dennis Lythgoe, "Tapes Show Nixon Weighed Pros and Cons of Hush Money," *Deseret News*, June 22, 1992, http://www.deseretnews.com/article/233222/TAPES -SHOW-NIXON-WEIGHED-PROS-AND-CONS-OF-HUSH-MONEY.html?pg=all.

47. Robert Hutton, "Why I Believe Everyone Should Learn Journalese," *The Day*, October 16, 2013, http://theday.co.uk/opinion/why-i-believe-everyone-should -learn-journalese.html.

C

1. Page H. Onorato, "Talk of the Table Uses Euphemisms," *The Dispatch* (Lexington, North Carolina), February 28, 2012, http://www.the-dispatch .com/article/20120228/COLUMNISTS/302289969?p=2&tc=pg#gsc.tab=0.

2. Jack Abramoff, cited in Stacy Curtin, "Ex-Lobbyist Jack Abramoff: Money and Elections Do Mix, Except When Bribery Is Involved," *The Daily Ticker*, Yahoo! Finance, http://finance.yahoo.com/blogs/daily-ticker/ex-lobbyist-jack -abramoff-money-elections-mix-except-200440657.html.

3. Ronda Bowen, "Marketing 101: Don't Call It Ungood When You Want to Say It's Bad," BrightHub.com, March 11, 2013, http://www.brighthub.com/office/entrepreneurs/articles/123518.aspx.

4. Nigel Rees, "In Other Words . . . ," *The Guardian*, October 13, 2006, http:// www.theguardian.com/money/2006/oct/14/careers.work.

5. Rob Kyff, "Book Strives to Make Journalese Crystal Clear," *Trib Live— Lifestyles*, August 30, 2013, http://triblive.com/lifestyles/morelifestyles/4608436-74/journalese-kyff-rob#axzz331IbP47e.

6. "Euphemisms and Jargon in American English," University of Tampere (Finland), April 3, 2013, http://www15.uta.fi/FAST/US1/REF/euphemsm.html.

7. Coral Davenport, "Obama Said to Be Planning to Use Executive Authority on Carbon Rule," *The New York Times*, May 29, 2014, p. A20, http://www.nytimes .com/2014/05/29/us/politics/obama-to-offer-rules-to-sharply-curb-power -plants-carbon-emissions.html; and Brad Johnson, "Teabaggers Protest Clean Energy Summit: 'Say No to Crap and Trade,'" ThinkProgress.org, August 11, 2009, http://thinkprogress.org/climate/2009/08/11/174400/crap-and-trade.

8. "Doublespeak," Center for Media and Democracy, updated August 30, 2009, http://www.sourcewatch.org/index.php/Doublespeak.

9. Patrick Reinhart, CheesyCorporateLingo.com, http://www.cheesycorporate lingo.com/dictionary/carbon-based-error.

10. Paul Dickson and Robert Skole, *Journalese: A Dictionary for Deciphering the News* (Portland, OR: Marion Street Press, 2012), retrieved from http://books .google.com/books?id=mLkbSCeGPcgC&pg=PT6&source=gbs_toc_r&cad= 4#v=onepage&q&f=false, April 21, 2014.

11. Ron Grossman, "It's the Jargon, Stupid—and It Doesn't Belong in Business," *Chicago Tribune*, February 11, 2007, http://articles.chicagotribune.com/ 2007-02-11/news/0702110185_1_jargon-long-term-strength-vocabulary.

12. William Lutz, *Doublespeak* (New York: HarperCollins, 1990), pp. 24–25.

13. Leah Garchick, "Personals," *San Francisco Chronicle*, October 18, 1990, cited in "Career-change opportunity," *Academic Dictionaries and Encyclopedias*, retrieved from http://new_words.enacademic.com/719/career-change_oppor tunity, August 24, 2014.

14. "The Rule of Verbal Packaging—The Leverage of Language," chap. 8 of *The Rules of Persuasion* (Westside Toastmasters, Los Angeles), retrieved from http://westsidetoastmasters.com/resources/laws_persuasion/chap8.html, April 18, 2014.

15. James Rowley, "Prosecutor Says Many Statements Made to Congress Can Be Used in Court," Associated Press, May 19, 1988, http://www.apnewsarchive .com/1988/Prosecutor-Says-Many-Statements-Made-To-Congress -Can-Be-Used-in-Court/id-08697fb190c57bcad014c1ea0e3d6d3d.

16. Rob Kyff, "Modern-Day Euphemisms Can Leave Head in a Spin," *Hartford Courant*, January 18, 2010, http://articles.courant.com/2010-01-18/news/hc -words0118.artjan18_1_euphemisms-negative-patient-care-outcome-motion -discomfort.

17 Frances Denmark, "The Rising Challenge of Measuring and Managing Longevity Risk," *Institutional Investor*, August 25, 2014, http://www .institutionalinvestor.com/article/3373646/investors-pensions/the-rising -challenge-of-measuring-and-managing-longevity-risk.html.

18. EuphemismList.com, retrieved from http://www.euphemismlist.com/Categor ical-Inaccuracy, January 23, 2014.

19. Kurt Mortensen, "Doublespeak: Words Evoke Emotions," ArticlesBase.com, October 27, 2006, http://www.articlesbase.com/affiliate-programs-articles/ doublespeak-words-invoke-emotions-67728.html.

20. Patrick Reinhart, CheesyCorporateLingo.com, http://www.cheesycorporate lingo.com/?s=center+of+excellence.

21. John Humphrys, "Lost for Words," *The Independent*, November 8, 2004, http://www.independent.co.uk/arts-entertainment/books/features/john -humphrys-lost-for-words-532430.html.

22. Ralph Keyes, *Euphemania: Our Love Affair with Euphemisms* (New York: Little, Brown, 2010), p. 78.

23. "Making Murder Respectable," *The Economist*, December 17, 2011, http://
    www.economist.com/node/21541767.
24. Norman Solomon, *The Power of Babble* (New York: Dell, 1992), p. 46.
25. Perry Romanowski, "The 10 Most Misleading Cosmetic Claims," Chemists
    Corner, January 23, 2012, http://chemistscorner.com/the-10-most-misleading
    -cosmetic-claims; and Lorraine Dallmeier, "The Myth of Chemical-Free
    Cosmetics," *Herb & Hedgerow* (blog), http://www.herbhedgerow.co.uk/the
    -myth-of-chemical-free-cosmetics, retrieved October 22, 2014.
26. Glenn Grothman, "Wisconsin Senator, Proposes Law That Declares Single
    Parenthood Child Abuse," *The Huffington Post*: Black Voices, March 2, 2012,
    http://www.huffingtonpost.com/2012/03/02/glenn-grothman-wisconsin-law
    -single-parenthood-child-abuse_n_1316834.html.
27. "Chasing the Perfect Fish," *The Wall Street Journal*, May 4, 2006, http://online
    .wsj.com/news/articles/SB114670694136643399; and "Eat No Sea Bass Campaign
    a Hit in Nation's Capital," European Cetacean Bycatch Campaign, May 8, 2002,
    retrieved from http://www.eurocbc.org/page51.html, January 30, 2014.
28. Page H. Onorato,"Talk of the Table Uses Euphemisms," *The Dispatch*
    (Lexington, North Carolina), February 8, 2012, http://www.the-dispatch.com/
    article/20120228/COLUMNISTS/302289969?p=2&tc=pg.
29. "Demand a Real Plan," a video by Alex Jones, InfoWars.com, retrieved from
    http://www.infowars.com/demand-a-real-plan, January 17, 2014.
30. "Organizing Astroturf: Evidence Shows Bogus Grassroots Groups Hijack
    the Political Debate," *Public Citizen*, January 2007, http://www.citizen.org/
    documents/Organizing-Astroturf.pdf.
31. "COPE Files Legal Complaint: "COPE, Inc., et al., v. Kansas State Board of
    Education, et al., in the Federal District Court of Kansas," press release,
    Citizens for Objective Public Education, September 26, 2013, http://www
    .copeinc.org/legal-complaint.html.
32. The National Rifle Association, home page, NRA.org, retrieved from http://
    home.nra.org, July 13, 2014.
33. "At Least 300 Civilian Contractor Deaths in 2012: We Are the Best Kept Secret
    of the Wars," *The Defense Base Act Compensation* (blog), dba.com, January
    3, 2013, http://dbacomp.com/defensebaseactcomp/2013/01/03/at-least-300
    -civilian-contractor-deaths-in-2012.
34. Paul Dickson and Robert Skole, *Journalese: A Dictionary for Deciphering the
    News* (Portland, OR: Marion Street Press, 2012), cited in Bill Lucey, "Finally, a
    Dictionary for Deciphering the News," *Newspaper Alum* (blog), March 4, 2013,
    http://www.newspaperalum.com/2013/03/finally-a-dictionary-for
    -deciphering-the-news.html.
35. "Clarify," EuphemismList.com, retrieved from http://www.euphemismlist
    .com/Clarify, November 16, 2014.
36. Jaime O'Neill, "A Glossary of Republican Doublespeak," *San Francisco
    Chronicle*, May 10, 2009, http://www.sfgate.com/politics/article/A-glossary-of
    -Republican-doublespeak-3242630.php.
37. Dave Barry, *Dave Barry Turns 40* (New York: Ballantine Books, 1991), p. 59.

38. Amanda Little, "Bush Administration Isn't Putting Its Money Where Its Mouth Is on 'Clean Coal,'" *Grist*, December 4, 2004, http://grist.org/article/little-coal.

39. Lee H. Hamilton and Daniel K. Inouye, *Report of the Congressional Committees Investigating the Iran/Contra Affair* (Darby, PA: DIANE Publishing, 1995), p. 126, accessed at http://books.google.com/books?id=ew_K3auTwEgC, January 25, 2014.

40. Rich Coffey, "Euphemisms Glossary," The American Empire, Vizettes.com, retrieved from http://vizettes.com/kt/american_empire/pages/euphemisms-glossary.htm, April 13, 2014.

41. "Clear Skies R.I.P.," editorial, *The New York Times*, March 7, 2005, http://www.nytimes.com/2005/03/07/opinion/07mon3.html.

42. "Lawyer: Port Authority Chairman's Vote Misrecorded," Associated Press, February 20, 2014, retrieved from http://www.washingtontimes.com/news/2014/feb/20/lawyer-port-authority-chairs-vote-misrecorded, April 13, 2014.

43. University of Oregon School of Journalism and Communication, "Euphemism—Definition and List," retrieved from http://journalism.uoregon.edu/~tbivins/J496/readings/LANGUAGE/euphemism_defandlist.pdf, February 16, 2014.

44. Patrick Reinhart, CheesyCorporateLingo.com, http://www.cheesycorporatelingo.com/?s=client+engagement.

45. Frank Luntz, "A Cleaner, Safer, Healthier America," excerpt from a memorandum to the George W. Bush White House, 2002, retrieved from https://www2.bc.edu/~plater/Newpublicsite06/suppmats/02.6.pdf, November 4, 2014.

46. Richard Pauli, comment on *ClimateProgress* (blog), December 1, 2011, retrieved from http://thinkprogress.org/climate/2011/12/01/380121/luntz-gop-occupy-wall-street-capitalism-is-immoral, April 21, 2014.

47. John Leo, "Euphemism, Double-Speak Marginalize the Language," *The Seattle Times*, August 15, 1995, http://community.seattletimes.nwsource.com/archive/?date=19950815&slug=2136517.

48. Will Evans, "Profile: Coalition for a Democratic Workplace," NPR, September 8, 2008, http://www.npr.org/templates/story/story.php?storyId=94399074.

49. Ivo H. Daalder, "The Coalition That Isn't," *Brookings Daily War Report*, Brookings Institution, March 24, 2003; Glenn Kessler, "United States Puts Its Spin on Coalition Numbers," *The Washington Post*, March 21, 2003, p. A29; Ian MacLeod, "The 'Coalition of the Willing': 3 of 45 Have Sent Combat Troops to War; Many of the Others Will Expect Payback," *Ottawa Citizen*, March 26, 2003, p. A04; all cited in Christopher Cerf and Victor S. Navasky, *Mission Accomplished! or How We Won the War in Iraq* (New York: Simon & Schuster, 2008), p. 66.

50. Jeff Shesol, "Obama's Coalition of the Willing and Unable," *The New Yorker*, September 11, 2014, http://www.newyorker.com/news/news-desk/obamas-new-war-isis.

51. Steve Rubin, "Uses and Abuses of Language," Santa Rosa Junior College, November 27, 2013, retrieved from http://online.santarosa.edu/presentation/page/?30609, January 11, 2014.

52. Mona Charen, "Coercive Humanitarians," *National Review Online*, April 12, 2011, http://www.nationalreview.com/corner/264463/coercive-humanitarians -mona-charen.

53. *USAF Targeting Guide*, United States Air Force Pamphlet 14-210 Intelligence, February 1, 1998, Attachment 7, p. 180, retrieved from http://www.fas.org/ irp/doddir/usaf/afpam14-210/part20.htm#page180, May 24, 2014.

54. "The Government's Word Games When Talking About NSA Domestic Spying," Electronic Frontier Foundation, collected from https://www.eff.org/nsa -spying/Wordgames, October 31, 2014.

55. Ian Haney López, *Dog Whistle Politics: How Coded Racial Appeals Have Reinvented Racism and Wrecked the Middle Class* (New York: Oxford University Press, 2014), cited in John Scott, "Getting in Touch with Your Inner Racist: Book Review of 'Dog Whistle Politics,'" *Publishers Newswire*, April 25, 2014, http://publishersnewswire.com/2014/04/25/PNW3213_123124.php/ getting-touch-inner-racist-book-review-dog-whistle-politics/.

56. "Varieties of English: Gobbledygook," FunTrivia.com, http://www.funtrivia .com/en/subtopics/Gobbledygook-315836.html.

57. Rocky Smith, "Gobbledygook," *Mr. Write's Page* (blog), March 12, 2013, http:// rockysmith.wordpress.com/2013/03/12/gobbledygook.

58. Sally Bedell, "3 Major TV Networks Asking Syndication Rights on Shows," *The New York Times*, January 23, 1983, http://www.nytimes.com/1983/01/23/ nyregion/3-major-tv-networks-asking-syndication-rights-on-shows.html.

59. Robert Todd Carroll, *Becoming a Critical Thinker*, chap. 2, p. 41, retrieved from http://www.skepdic.com/refuge/ctlessons/ch2.pdf, August 14, 2014.

60. Mark Peters, "Bald-Faced Factual Shortcuts," Visual Thesaurus, October 3, 2012, https://www.visualthesaurus.com/cm/evasive/bald-faced-factual-shortcuts.

61. Glenn Thompson, "The 12 Most Horrifically Misleading Euphemisms," Cracked.com, December 16, 2008, www.cracked.com/article_16884_the-12 -most-horrifically-misleading-euphemisms.html.

62. Amy Sullivan, "Is Compassionate Conservatism Dead," *USA Today*, January 29, 2012, http://usatoday30.usatoday.com/news/opinion/forum/story/ 2012-01-29/compassionate-conservatism-bush-santorum-republican/ 52873150/1; and Geoffrey Nunberg, *Talking Right: How Conservatives Turned Liberalism into a Tax-Raising, Latte-Drinking, Sushi-Eating, Volvo-Driving,* New York Times–*Reading, Body-Piercing, Hollywood-Loving, Left-Wing Freak Show* (New York: Public Affairs, 2006), p. 11.

63. Adam Nagourney, "Honolulu Shores Up Tourism with Crackdown on Homeless," *The New York Times*, June 23, 2014, p. A13, http://www.nytimes.com/2014/06/ 23/us/honolulu-shores-up-tourism-with-crackdown-on-homeless.html.

64. Albert Bandura, "Impeding Ecological Sustainability Through Selective Moral Disengagement," *International Journal of Innovation and Sustainable Development* 2, no. 1 (2007), p. 18, retrieved from http://www.uky .edu/~eushe2/Bandura/Bandura2007MDEcology.pdf, August 16, 2014.

65. Dr. Andrew J. Byrne, "Addict in the Family: Finding Out: What Terms to Use and Who to Tell?," retrieved from http://www.addictinthefamily.org/chapone .html, November 23, 2014.

66. Michael Delahunt, ArtLex Art Dictionary, retrieved from http://artlex.com, February 18, 2014.

67. Melissa Burden and David Shepardson, "NHTSA: GM's Word Choices Hampered Problem-Solving," *The Detroit News*, May 16, 2014, http://www.detroitnews.com/article/20140516/AUTO0103/305160108.

68. "Making Murder Respectable," *The Economist*, December 17, 2011, http://www.economist.com/node/21541767.

69. Emily Steel, "Brian Williams, Under Scrutiny, Will Take Leave from 'NBC Nightly News,'" *The New York Times*, February 8, 2015, http://www.nytimes.com/2015/02/08/business/brian-williams-to-take-leave-from-nbc-nightly-news.html.

70. Steven Poole, *Unspeak* (New York: Grove Press, 2006), p. 162.

71. "Members of the 435th Tactical Air Wing Confrontation Management Team, equipped with body armor and riot control helmets, prepare to protect the base," photo caption, Department of Defense, American Forces Information Service, December 12, 1982, retrieved from http://dp.la/item/67a064426743983d9c81fbcfafbd679d, February 2, 2014.

72. Ralph Keyes, *Euphemania: Our Love Affair with Euphemisms* (New York: Little, Brown, 2010), p. 242.

73. Michael Delahunt, "ArtLex Art Dictionary," retrieved from http://artlex.com, February 18, 2014.

74. "'O' Word by Any Other Euphemism," *Sun-Sentinel* (Broward County, Florida), January 29, 1995, http://articles.sun-sentinel.com/1995-01-29/features/9501270447_1_welfare-reform-farm-bill-clinton-welfare.

75. Katherine Woodward Thomas, MA, MFT, "Conscious Uncoupling: A 5-Week Program to Release the Trauma of a Breakup, Reclaim Your Power & Reinvent Your Life," digital psychotherapy course available at http://evolvingwisdom.com/consciousuncoupling/enroll-now/, accessed April 8, 2014; and Gwyneth Paltrow and Chris Martin, "Conscious Uncoupling," Goop, March 25, 2014.

76. Oliver Burkeman, "Memo Exposes Bush's New Green Strategy," *The Guardian*, March 3, 2003, http://www.theguardian.com/environment/2003/mar/04/usnews.climatechange.

77. Lucy Kellaway, "The First Word in Mangled Meanings," *Financial Times*, January 6, 2013, http://www.bradreese.com/blog/john-chambers-coc.pdf, April 14, 2014.

78. John Stauber and Sheldon Rampton, "The Fog of War Talk," AlterNet, July 27, 2003, http://www.alternet.org/story/16497/the_fog_of_war_talk.

79. Michael Spiro, "'In Transition' and Other Awkward Euphemisms," *Recruiter Musings* (blog), March 30, 2010, http://michaelspiro.wordpress.com/2010/03/30/in-transition-and-other-awkward-euphemisms.

80. "Politically Incorrect Dictionary," NewspeakDictionary.com, retrieved from http://www.newspeakdictionary.com/ns-pi.html, May 7, 2014.

81. Tom Chatfield, "10 Worst Digital Words," *The Good Web Guide*, October 2013, http://www.thegoodwebguide.co.uk/article/10-worst-digital-words-by-tom -chatfield/16124.

82. "Job Title Stuffing 101: 12 Buzzwords to Inflate a Job's Importance," Online Masters Degree, July 25, 2010, retrieved from http://onlinemastersdegree .org/job-title-stuffing-101-12-buzzwords-to-inflate-a-job%E2%80%99s -importance, January 17, 2014.

83. Bob Weinstein, "Business Buzzwords Survive the Test of Time," Troy Media Corporation, retrieved from http://www.reliableplant.com/Read/26846/ business-buzzwords-survive-time, April 13, 2014.

84. Tony Watson, *Organizing and Managing Work*, quoted in Sarah Halls, "Few Are Fooled by Business Babble," *Business Because*, http://www.business because.com/news/mba-faculty/220/few-are-fooled-by-business-babble.

85. Jason Pinter, quoted in Janice Harayda, "40 Publishing Buzzwords, Clichés and Euphemisms Decoded," August 21, 2011, http://oneminutebookreviews .wordpress.com/2011/08/21/40-publishing-buzzwords-cliches-and -euphemisms-decoded.

86. Ralph Keyes, *Euphemania: Our Love Affair with Euphemisms* (New York: Little, Brown, 2010), p. 212.

87. Mark Peters, "Tender Undoing and Other Surface Coal," Visual Thesaurus, August 6, 2014, http://www.visualthesaurus.com/cm/evasive/tender-undoing -and-other-surface-coal.

88. The U.S. National Transportation Safety Board, quoted in William Lutz, *Doublespeak* (New York: HarperCollins, 1990), p. 214.

89. John Leo, "Journalese as a Second Tongue," *Time*, March 18, 1985, retrieved from http://bhs.cc/journalism/pdf/pw/journalese.pdf, June 1, 2014.

90. Tamara E. Holmes, "Convenience Fees: When Is It OK to Charge Extra to Use a Credit Card?," CreditCards.com, December 20, 2012.

91. Patrick Cockburn, "Weasel Words That Politicians Use to Obscure Terrible Truths," *The Independent*, October 14, 2012, http://www.independent.co.uk/ voices/comment/weasel-words-that-politicians-use-to-obscure-terrible -truths-8210302.html.

92. Margalit Fox, "Hugh Massingberd, 60, Laureate of the Departed, Dies," *The New York Times*, December 30, 2007, http://www.nytimes.com/2007/12/30/ nyregion/30massingberd.html.

93. "OptiClean™ Cordless Rechargeable Power Plaque Remover," InterPlak by ConAir, 2014, retrieved from http://www.interplak.com/catalog.php?pcID= 109&product_id=369, May 26, 2014.

94. Leo Buscaglia, "Euphemisms Sometimes Are Just 'Residual Effluents,'" *Spokane Chronicle*, August 19, 1985, p. 7, retrieved from http://news.google .com/newspapers?nid=1345&dat=19850819&id=_vlLAAAAIBAJ&sjid=qfk DAAAAIBAJ&pg=1631,497057, August 24, 2014; and Henry Beard and Christopher Cerf, *The Official Politically Correct Dictionary and Handbook*, updated edition (New York: Villard Books, 1994), p. 133.

95. Robin Stummer, "Who Are You Calling Pilchard? It's 'Cornish Sardine' to You . . . ," *The Independent,* August 17, 2003, http://www.independent.co.uk/ news/uk/home-news/who-are-you-calling-pilchard-its-cornish-sardine-to -you-536136.html.

96. James A. Martin, Ph.D., CMA, "The Language of Politics: Political Euphemisms, Abstractions, and Weasel Words," *Management and Accounting Web,* retrieved from http://maaw.info/PoliticalLanguage.htm, February 22, 2014.

97. Rob Kyff, "Negative Patient Care Outcome? Yes, Euphemisms Are Alive and Well," *Hartford Courant,* April 4, 1997, http://articles.courant.com/1997-04 -04/features/9705230902_1_assisted-new-euphemism-nursing-home-care.

98. Geoffrey Norman, "Retreat to Euphemism," *The Blog, The Weekly Standard,* September 25, 2013, http://www.weeklystandard.com/blogs/retreat -euphemism_757143.html.

99. Rob Kyff, "Negative Patient Care Outcome? Yes, Euphemisms Are Alive and Well," *Hartford Courant,* April 4, 1997, http://articles.courant.com/1997-04 -04/features/9705230902_1_assisted-new-euphemism-nursing-home-care.

100. William Lambdin, *Doublespeak Dictionary* (Los Angeles: Pinnacle Books, 1981), p. 139.

101. University of Oregon School of Journalism and Communication, "Euphemism—Definition and List," retrieved from http://journalism .uoregon.edu/~tbivins/J496/readings/LANGUAGE/euphemism_defandlist .pdf, February 16, 2014; and "Rodent's Real Defense," HockeyRodent.com, February 6, 2005, http://hockeyrodent.com/r1162.htm3.

102. Dictionary of Management Jargon, retrieved from http://dictionaryofman agementjargon.yolasite.com, January 27, 2014.

103. Patricia T. O'Conner, "Corporate-speak," *The Grammarphobia Blog,* October 9, 2008, http://www.grammarphobia.com/blog/2008/10/corporate-speak.html.

104. "Shall We Do Coterminous Stakeholder Engagement?," *Northampton Chronicle* (UK), March 18, 2009, http://www.northamptonchron.co.uk/news/ local/shall-we-do-coterminous-stakeholder-engagement-1-887413.

105. "Doublespeak," Center for Media and Democracy, updated August 30, 2009, http://www.sourcewatch.org/index.php/Doublespeak.

106. Paul Dickson, *Slang!* (New York: Pocket Books, 1990), p. 47, cited in Henry Beard and Christopher Cerf, *The Official Politically Correct Dictionary and Handbook,* updated edition (New York: Villard Books, 1994), p. 134.

107. Paul Dickson and Robert Skole, *Journalese: A Dictionary for Deciphering the News* (Portland, OR: Marion Street Press, 2012), retrieved from http://books .google.com/books?id=mLkbSCeGPcgC&pg=PT6&source=gbs_toc_r&cad= 4#v=onepage&q&f=false, April 21, 2014.

108. Lynn Schneider, "20 Examples of Great Euphemisms," December 23, 2011, http://lynnschneiderbooks.com/2011/12/23/20-examples-of-great-euphemisms.

109. Patricia Cohen, "Need Help From the I.R.S.? It May Take More Patience This Year," *The New York Times,* January 14, 2015, http://www.nytimes.com/ 2015/01/15/business/irs-taxpayer-advocate-service-report.html; and "IRS Phone Help Wait Times Double in Two Years," Allgov.com, October 10, 2009,

http://www.allgov.com/news/controversies/irs-phone-help-wait-times
-double-in-two-years?news=839678.

110. Ralph Keyes, *Euphemania: Our Love Affair with Euphemisms* (New York:
      Little, Brown, 2010), p. 177.

111. Robert Todd Carroll, "Language and Critical Thinking," *Becoming a Critical
      Thinker* (New York: Pearson, 2004), pp. 30–31, retrieved from http://www
      .skepdic.com/refuge/ctlessons/ch2.pdf, April 11, 2014.

112. Ross Kaplan, "Homes with 'Great Personalities' and Other White Lies," *City
      Lakes Real Estate Blog* (Minneapolis), March 15, 2013, http://rosskaplan
      .com/2013/03/real-estate-euphemisms.

113. Mark Peters, "Hiking the Euphemistic Trail," Visual Thesaurus, July 2,
      2009, http://www.visualthesaurus.com/cm/evasive/
      hiking-the-euphemistic-trail.

114. Laura Beil, "Opponents of Evolution Adopting a New Strategy," *The New York
      Times*, June 4, 2008, http://www.nytimes.com/2008/06/04/us/04evolution
      .html.

115. "Government Double-speak," *Operation Maple*, retrieved from www.opera
      tionmaple.ca/for-your-information/government-double-speak.html, April
      19, 2014.

116. Robin Marantz Henig, "Looking for the Lie," *The New York Times Magazine*,
      February 5, 2006, http://www.nytimes.com/2006/02/05/magazine/05lying
      .html?pagewanted=all.

117. Steve Rubin, "Uses and Abuses of Language," Santa Rosa Junior College,
      retrieved from http://online.santarosa.edu/presentation/page/?30609,
      January 11, 2014.

118. William Lutz, *Doublespeak* (New York: Harper Perennial, 1990), p. 223, cited in
      Henry Beard and Christopher Cerf, *The Official Politically Correct Dictionary
      and Handbook*, updated edition (New York: Villard Books, 1994), p. 134.

119. Rich Coffey, "Euphemisms Glossary," The American Empire, Vizettes.com, re-
      trieved from http://vizettes.com/kt/american_empire/pages/euphemisms
      -glossary.htm, April 13, 2014.

120. Peter Ginna, cited in Janice Harayda, "40 Publishing Buzzwords, Clichés
      and Euphemisms Decoded," *One-Minute Book Reviews* (blog), August 21,
      2011, http://oneminutebookreviews.wordpress.com/2011/08/21/
      40-publishing-buzzwords-cliches-and-euphemisms-decoded.

121. Joe Messerli, "The Media's 'How-To' Guide for Manipulating the Truth,"
      BalancedPolitics.org, July 14, 2011, http://www.balancedpolitics.org/
      editorials/media_manipulation.htm.

122. David Sedaris, "Standing By," *The New Yorker*, August 9, 2012, http://www
      .newyorker.com/magazine/2010/08/09/standing-by.

123. Lynn Schneider, "20 Examples of Great Euphemisms," December 23, 2011,
      retrieved from http://lynnschneiderbooks.com/2011/12/23/20-examples-of
      -great-euphemisms, January 16, 2014.

124. Grace Hechinger, *The Wall Street Journal*, October 27, 1971, quoted in Hugh
      Rawson, *A Dictionary of Euphemisms and Other Doubletalk* (New York:
      Crown, 1981), p. 78.

125. Kate Cocuzzo, "Real Estate Euphemisms: An Agent's Literary Loophole," *Geo Properties, Inc.* (blog), May 21, 2013, http://www.geopropertiesinc.com/word press/real-estate-euphemisms-an-agents-literary-loophole.

126. Paul Dickson and Robert Skole, *Journalese: A Dictionary for Deciphering the News* (Portland, OR: Marion Street Press, 2012), retrieved from http://books .google.com/books?id=mLkbSCeGPcgC&pg=PT6&source=gbs_toc_r&cad= 4#v=onepage&q&f=false, April 21, 2014.

127. "Euphemisms I Hate," Straight Dope Message Board, May 6. 2013, http:// boards.straightdope.com/sdmb/showthread.php?t=690163.

128. Alex Zorach, "Euphemisms," retrieved from http://cazort.net/topic/ euphemisms, January 22, 2014.

129. "Customer Solutions Specialist," job description, TechSmith Corporation, Glass Door.com, http://www.glassdoor.com/job-listing/customer-solutions -specialist-JV_IC1134935_KO0,29_IE329815.htm?jl=1219284979.

d

1. Steve Rubin, "Uses and Abuses of Language," Santa Rosa Junior College, November 27, 2013, retrieved from http://online.santarosa.edu/ presentation/page/?30609, January 11, 2014.

2. Luke Mullins, "The Real Estate Euphemism Pocket Translator," *U.S. News & World Report*: Money, September 9, 2008, http://money.usnews.com/money/ blogs/the-home-front/2008/09/09/the-real-estate-euphemism-pocket -translator.

3. Edward J. Snowden, quoted in Simon Romero, "Snowden Offers Help to Brazil in Spy Case," *The New York Times*, December 17, 2013, http://www .nytimes.com/2013/12/18/world/americas/snowden-offers-to-help-brazil-in -nsa-inquiry.html.

4. Lacey Sheppy, "This Wordsmith Has Had Enough of Phoney Titles," *Moose Jaw Times Herald* (Moose Jaw, Saskatchewan), February 29, 2008, http:// www.mjtimes.sk.ca/Business/Employment/2008-02-29/article-15006/ This-wordsmith-has-had-enough-of-phoney-titles.

5. James B. Stewart, "With Art, Investing In Genius," *The New York Times*, November 29, 2014, http://www.nytimes.com/2014/11/29/business/with-art -investing-in-genius.html.

6. Rich Coffey, "Euphemisms Glossary," The American Empire, Vizettes.com, retrieved from http://vizettes.com/kt/american_empire/pages/euphemisms- glossary.htm, April 13, 2014; and Neta C. Crawford, *Accountability for Killing: Moral Responsibility for Collateral Damage in America's Post-9/11 Wars* (New York: Oxford University Press, 2013), p. 50.

7. William R. Tracey, *The Human Resources Glossary*, 3rd edition (Boca Raton, FL: CRC Press, 2003), p. 167, retrieved from http://books.google.com/books ?id=E3ZIC-uo6xkC&pg=PA167&ots=R9NG5qjhYl&dq=dead-tree-edition&sig =esA6I7CDmcjGSJDuVxLkDpfi3jA#v=onepage&q=dead-tree-edition&f= false, April 19, 2014.

8. Brendan Nyhan, "Why the 'Death Panel' Myth Wouldn't Die: Misinformation in the Health Care Reform Debate," *The Forum*, p. 9, The Berkeley Electronic Press, 2010, retrieved from http://www.dartmouth.edu/~nyhan/health-care -misinformation.pdf, July 21, 2014; and Angie Drobnic Holan, "PolitiFact's Lie of the Year: Death Panels," PolitiFact.com, December 18, 2009, http://www .politifact.com/truth-o-meter/article/2009/dec/18/politifact-lie-year -death-panels.

9. Rush Limbaugh, *The Rush Limbaugh Show*, Premiere Radio Networks, August 8, 2012, retrieved from http://mediamatters.org/video/2012/08/08/limbaugh-on -planned-parenthood-and-naral-pro-ch/189197, January 17, 2014.

10. Deborah Solomon, "The Wordsmith, Questions for Frank Luntz," *The New York Times Magazine*, May 21, 2009, http://www.nytimes.com/2009/05/24/maga zine/24wwln-q4-t.html; and Joshua Green, "Meet Mr. Death," *The American Prospect*, December 19, 2001, http://prospect.org/article/meet-mr-death.

11. Wesley J. Smith, "Euphemisms as Political Manipulation," *First Things*, May 17, 2013, http://www.firstthings.com/onthesquare/2013/05/euphemisms-as -political-manipulation.

12. "Doublespeak," Center for Media and Democracy, updated August 30, 2009, retrieved from http://www.sourcewatch.org/index.php/Doublespeak, April 9, 2014.

13. "The Ridiculous Business Jargon Dictionary," *The Office Life* (blog), retrieved from http://www.theofficelife.com/business-jargon-dictionary-D.html, January 27, 2014.

14. William Lutz, *The New Doublespeak: Why No One Knows What Anyone's Saying Anymore* (New York: HarperCollins, 1996), cited by Frank Grazian, "On Euphemisms, Gobbledygook and Doublespeak," *Public Relations Quarterly*, Summer 1997, retrieved from http://users.manchester.edu/FacStaff/MPLah man/Homepage/BerkebileMyWebsite/euphemisms.pdf, February 17, 2014.

15. "The Ridiculous Business Jargon Dictionary," *The Office Life* (blog), retrieved from http://www.theofficelife.com/business-jargon-dictionary-D.html, April 14, 2014.

16. Mat Johnson, quoted in Janice Harayda, "More Publishing Buzzwords Decoded with Wit on Twitter," *One-Minute Book Reviews* (blog), August 31, 2011, http://oneminutebookreviews.wordpress.com/2011/08/31.

17. William Lutz, "Doublespeak in Education," *Education Week*, 1989, cited in Henry Beard and Christopher Cerf, *The Official Politically Correct Dictionary and Handbook*, updated edition (New York: Villard Books, 1994), p. 134.

18. "The Ridiculous Business Jargon Dictionary," *The Office Life* (blog), re-trieved from http://www.theofficelife.com/business-jargon-dictionary-D.html, November 15, 2014.

19. William Lutz, "Life Under the Chief Doublespeak Officer," accessed at www.dt .org/html/Doublespeak.html.

20. George Carlin, cited by Frank Grazian, "On Euphemisms, Gobbledygook and Doublespeak," *Public Relations Quarterly*, Summer 1997, retrieved from http://users.manchester.edu/FacStaff/MPLahman/Homepage/ BerkebileMyWebsite/euphemisms.pdf, February 17, 2014.

21. Ralph Keyes, *Euphemania: Our Love Affair with Euphemisms* (New York: Little, Brown, 2010), p. 203.

22. Lucy Kellaway, "The First Word in Mangled Meanings," *Financial Times*, January 6, 2013, http://www.ft.com/intl/cms/s/0/86f0383a-54f6-11e2-89e0 -00144feab49a.html#axzz2yWb3XRR3.

23. "The Ridiculous Business Jargon Dictionary," *The Office Life* (blog), retrieved from http://www.theofficelife.com/business-jargon-dictionary-D.html, April 14, 2014.

24. Dan McCarthy, "Office Jargon," *HR People*, March 27, 2009, http://hrpeople .monster.com/news/articles/2035-office-jargon?page=3&utm_content=art mini&utm_source=hrpeople.com.

25. Carol Hymowitz, "Mind Your Language: To Do Business Today, Consider Delayering," *The Wall Street Journal*, March 27, 2006, http://online.wsj.com/ news/articles/SB114341219645208528m.

26. Kevin L. Hoover, *The Arcata Eye* (Arcata, California), April 20, 2010, cited in Mark Peters, "Quench Your Thirst! (Within the Defect Action Levels, Of Course)," October 6, 2010, http://www.visualthesaurus.com/cm/evasive/ quench-your-thirst-within-the-defect-action-levels-of-course.

27. Lucy Kellaway, "And the Golden Flannel of the Year Award Goes to . . . ," *Financial Times*, January 4, 2015, http://www.ft.com/intl/cms/s/0/8438a3ee -926a-11e4-b213-00144feabdc0.html#axzz3SRhpTKWQ.

28. Michael Delahunt, ArtLex Art Dictionary, retrieved from http://artlex.com, February 18, 2014.

29. "'Demising' Judged Worst Word of 2013," Plain English Foundation, December 19, 2013, retrieved from https://www.plainenglishfoundation.com/docu ments/10179/54323/Plain%20English%20-%20Worst%20words%20of% 202013%20-%20PEF%20media%20release., July 20, 2014; and Julia Stroots, "Management-speak: Double Take on the Double Talk," *Financial Management*, July 15, 2013, http://www.fm-magazine.com/feature/depth/ management-speak-double-take-double-talk#.

30. Norman Solomon, *The Power of Babble* (New York: Dell, 1992), p. 46.

31. William Lutz, *Doublespeak* (New York: Harper Perennial, 1990), p. 213, cited in Henry Beard and Christopher Cerf, *The Official Politically Correct Dictionary and Handbook*, updated edition (New York: Villard Books, 1994), p. 118.

32. "The Ridiculous Business Jargon Dictionary," *The Office Life* (blog), retrieved from http://www.theofficelife.com/business-jargon-dictionary-D.html, April 14, 2014.

33. "The Ridiculous Business Jargon Dictionary," *The Office Life* (blog), retrieved from http://www.theofficelife.com/business-jargon-dictionary-D.html, January 27, 2014.

34. "Department of Human Resources Supports Schools and Departments During Budget Process," Fairfax County Public Schools, press release, January 23, 2014, http://www.fcps.edu/cco/pubs/myfcps/employees/2014_01_22/destaff.shtml.

35. Paul Wasserman and Don Hausrath, *Weasel Words: The Dictionary of American Doublespeak* (Herndon, VA: Capital Books, 2006), p. 48.

36. Jen Hayden, "Ferguson Police Beat a Man and Then Charged Him with 'Destruction of Property' for Bloody Uniforms," *Daily Kos*, August 15, 2014, http://www.dailykos.com/story/2014/08/15/1321904/-Ferguson-police-beat-a -man-and-then-charged-him-with-destruction-of-property-for-bloody -uniforms.

37. "What Is an Example of 'Slanted Words,'" *Wiki Answers*, retrieved from http://wiki.answers.com/Q/What_is_an_example_of_slanted_words.

38. "Examples of Doublespeak," YourDictionary.com, http://examples.yourdictio nary.com/examples-of-doublespeak.html; Caroline V. Hamilton, "Let's Ditch 'Detainee' and 'Enhanced Interrogation Techniques' and Use the Right Words: 'Prisoner' and 'Torture,'" History News Network, January 16, 2012, http://his torynewsnetwork.org/article/143907; and "Legal Arguments for Avoiding the Jurisdiction of the Geneva Conventions," Center for Media and Democracy, updated August 11, 2008, retrieved from http://www.sourcewatch.org/index .php?title=Legal_Arguments_for_Avoiding_the_Jurisdiction_of_the_Geneva _Conventions, November 15, 2014.

39. Wilson Follett, "Euphemisms," *Modern American Usage: A Guide* (New York: Hill & Wang, 1998), p. 123; Daniel Trilling, "Short Cuts," *London Review of Books*, March 5, 2015, http://www.lrb.co.uk/v37/n05/daniel-trilling/short-cuts.

40. "Euphemisms," *The Economist Style Guide*, retrieved from http://www .economist.com/style-guide/euphemisms. January 19, 2014.

41. William Lutz, *Doublespeak* (New York: Harper Perennial, 1990), p. 67, cited in Henry Beard and Christopher Cerf, *The Official Politically Correct Dictionary and Handbook*, updated edition (New York: Villard Books, 1994), p. 134; and "Therapeutic Misadventure," National Association of Personal Injury Lawyers, August 25, 2011, http://www.napil.net/2011/08/therapeutic-misadventure .html.

42. Margalit Fox, "Hugh Massingberd, 60, Laureate of the Departed, Dies," *The New York Times*, December 30, 2007, http://www.nytimes.com/2007/12/30/ nyregion/30massingberd.html.

43. Kevin Horrigan, "Animal Instincts," *St. Louis Post-Dispatch*, May 8, 2011, http://www.stltoday.com/news/opinion/columns/kevin-horrigan/animal -instincts/article_dd27a6ee-2493-536c-9636-70a5fb76453e.html.

44. Deborah Noyes, *Captivity* (Lakewood, CO: Unbridled Books, 2011), p 33.

45. Jon Barron, "Debunking the Detox Debunkers," Baseline of Health Foundation, January 19, 2009, retrieved from http://jonbarron.org/article/ debunking-detox-debunkers#.U0Q0YMdRGUM, April 8, 2014.

46. William Lutz, *Doublespeak* (New York: HarperCollins, 1990), p. 22.

47. "Examples of Euphemism," *Examples 10*, January 11, 2011, http://www .examples10.com/e/euphemism.

48. "The Ridiculous Business Jargon Dictionary," *The Office Life* (blog), retrieved from http://www.theofficelife.com/business-jargon-dictionary-D.html, April 14, 2014.

49. Arthur H. Hawkins, *Self-Discipline in Labor-Management Relations*, quoted in Mario Pei, *Double-Speak in America* (New York: Hawthorn Books, 1973),

p. 137, cited in Henry Beard and Christopher Cerf, *The Official Politically Correct Dictionary and Handbook*, updated edition (New York: Villard Books, 1994), p. 134.

50. A job title discovered on a desk plaque in the waiting room of a New York City law office by Justine Kaye, as reported in "25 of Readers' Inflated Job Titles," *BBC News Magazine,* July 31, 2012. http://www.bbc.co.uk/news/magazine -18983009.

51. Hugh Rawson, *A Dictionary of Euphemisms and Other Doubletalk* (New York: Crown, 1981), p. 78.

52. "The Ridiculous Business Jargon Dictionary," *The Office Life* (blog), retrieved from http://www.theofficelife.com/business-jargon-dictionary-D.html, January 27, 2014.

53. Tamara E. Holmes, "Convenience Fees: When Is It OK to Charge Extra to Use a Credit Card?," CreditCards.com, December 20, 2012.

54. Rich Coffey, "Euphemisms Glossary," The American Empire, Vizettes.com, retrieved from http://vizettes.com/kt/american_empire/pages/euphemisms-glossary.htm, April 13, 2014.

55. James A. Dorn, "Ending Tax Socialism," Cato Institute, September 13, 1996, http://www.cato.org/publications/commentary/ending-tax-socialism.

56. Jon Kelly, "The 10 Most Scandalous Euphemisms," *BBC News Magazine*, May 15, 2013, http://www.bbc.co.uk/news/magazine-22470691.

57. William Lutz, cited in Gareth Branwyn, "This Shit Doesn't Stink. It Exceeds the Odor Threshold," *Stim* 8, no. 2 (January 24, 1997), http://www.stim.com/ Stim-x/8.2/doublespeak/doublespeak.html.

58. Norman Solomon, *The Power of Babble* (New York: Dell, 1992), p. 71.

59. Ian Cobain, "Obama's Secret Kill List—The Disposition Matrix," *The Guardian*, July 14, 2013, http://www.theguardian.com/world/2013/jul/14/ obama-secret-kill-list-disposition-matrix.

60. "Disputed Territories: Forgotten Facts About the West Bank and Gaza Strip," Israel Ministry of Foreign Affairs, February 1, 2003, retrieved from http:// mfa.gov.il/MFA/MFA-Archive/2003/Pages/DISPUTED%20TERRITORIES-% 20Forgotten%20Facts%20About%20the%20We.aspx, September 18, 2014; and "They Say, We Say: Why Does the Left Insist on Referring to 'Occupied Territories'?" Americans for Peace Now, retrieved from http://peacenow.org/ page.php?name=tsws-judea-samaria-and-gaza-cannot-be-occupied, November 15, 2014.

61. Joe Wegman, PD, LCSW, "Disruptive Mood Dysregulation Disorder: Yet Another Setback for Child Psychiatry," *The PharmaTherapist*, retrieved from http://www.pharmatherapist.com/articles/disruptive-mood-dysregulation -disorder-yet-another-setback-for-child-psychiatry, May 27, 2014.

62. William Lutz, *Doublespeak* (New York: Harper Perennial, 1990), p. 42.

63. Dave Barry, "An Off-Color Rift," *The Washington Post*, December 19, 2004, http://www.washingtonpost.com/wp-dyn/articles/A218-2004Dec14.html.

64. Marilyn Colaninno, "Today's Hot Topic: The White-Coat Rule," *AdLaw By Request,* Reed Smith LLC, May 2, 2013, http://www.adlawbyrequest.com/

tags/white-coat-rule; and "What Disclaimer Text Should Be Included in a TV Commercial," *Just Answer Business Law,* retrieved from http://www.justanswer.com/business-law/7f8v2-disclaimer-text-included-tv-commercial.html, October 26, 2014.

65. "Euphemisms: Say Less with More," *Johnson* (blog), *The Economist,* July 7, 2010, http://www.economist.com/blogs/johnson/2010/07/euphemisms.

66. Dan Amira, "Puerto Rican Lawmaker Gives the Best Excuse Ever for Naked Photos," News & Politics, *New York,* August 26, 2011, http://nymag.com/daily/intelligencer/2011/08/puerto_rican_lawmaker_gives_th.html.

67. WebMD, http://www.webmd.com, accessed November 20, 2014.

68. Robert Todd Carroll, *Becoming a Critical Thinker,* chap. 2, p. 27, retrieved from http://www.skepdic.com/refuge/ctlessons/ch2.pdf, August 14, 2014.

69. Gabe Bokor, "Would You Eat This? Euphemisms in Business and Politics," *Translation Journal,* January 2015, http://www.translationjournal.net/January-2015/would-you-eat-this-euphemisms-in-business-and-politics.html.

70. John Leo, "Euphemism, Double-Speak Marginalize the Language," *The Seattle Times,* August 15, 1995, http://community.seattletimes.nwsource.com/archive/?date=19950815&slug=2136517; and John Hiscock, "Hugh Grant on Prostitute Charge," June 28, 1995, http://www.telegraph.co.uk/news/1471976/Hugh-Grant-on-prostitute-charge.html.

71. "The Government's Word Games When Talking About NSA Domestic Spying," Electronic Frontier Foundation, https://www.eff.org/nsa-spying/Wordgames.

72. Steve Rubenstein, *San Francisco Chronicle,* March 10, 2001, http://www.sfgate.com/business/article/Plain-Speaking-Also-Falls-Victim-to-Cisco-s-Ax-2943774.php.

73. Robert Hutton, quoted in Michael Holtermann, "Romps, Tots and Boffins: Robert Hutton on Journalese," Holtermann Design LLC, September 21, 2013, http://holtermanndesign.com/romps-tots-and-boffins-book-on-journalese-by-robert-hutton.

74. "Are Dried Plums the Same as Prunes?," California Dried Plum Board, 2014, http://www.californiadriedplums.org/about-prunes-and-dried-plums/faq#question-1.

75. Jason Brockert, "Artspeak or, Art Words and Phrases We Use All the Time and Might Wish We Didn't," *Colored Mud* (blog), January 23, 2008, retrieved from http://jasonbrockert.com/ayearinart/?p=55, April 9, 2014.

76. *International Journal of Cardiology,* cited in Adam Marcus and Ivan Oransky, "The Euphemism Parade: What's Behind Paper Retractions?," *Lab Times,* July 2013, http://www.labtimes.org/labtimes/ranking/dont/2013_07.lasso.

77. J. J. Sutherland, "Battle Against IEDs Spreads from Iraq to Afghanistan," NPR, October 28, 2009, http://www.npr.org/templates/story/story.php?storyId=114221171&from=mobile; and Colonel A. T. Ball and Lieutenant Colonel Berrien T. McCutchen, "Task Force ODIN Using Innovative Technology to Support Ground Forces," Defense Video and Imagery Information System, September 20, 2007, http://www.dvidshub.net/news/12463/task-force-odin-using-innovative-technology-support-ground-forces#.U1bki8cozSA#ixzz2zeeS9Hsh.

e

1. Lynn Schneider, "20 Examples of Great Euphemisms," December 23, 2011, http://lynnschneiderbooks.com/2011/12/23/20-examples-of-great -euphemisms.

2. Jill W. Klausen, "How to Talk Like a Republican," The Winning Words Project, March 12, 2012, http://www.winningwordsproject.com/five _words_and_phrases_democrats_should_never_say_again#sthash .1rVaBKW0.dpuf.

3. Luke Mullins, "The Real Estate Euphemism Pocket Translator," *U.S. News & World Report*: Money, September 9, 2008, http://money.usnews.com/money/ blogs/the-home-front/2008/09/09/the-real-estate-euphemism-pocket- translator.

4. "The Rule of Verbal Packaging—The Leverage of Language," chap. 8 of *The Rules of Persuasion* (Westside Toastmasters, Los Angeles), retrieved from http://westsidetoastmasters.com/resources/laws_persuasion/chap8.html, April 18, 2014.

5. Lee Fang, "Lobbyist Dick Armey's Pollution Gospel: 'As an Article of Faith,' It Is 'Pretentious' to Believe in Global Warming," ThinkProgress.org, July 31, 2009, http://thinkprogress.org/politics/2009/07/31/53658/armey-pollution- gospel.

6. "The Ridiculous Business Jargon Dictionary," *The Office Life* (blog), retrieved from http://www.theofficelife.com/business-jargon-dictionary-E.html.

7. Mike Konczal, "Frank Luntz and the Battle Over Economic Freedom," *The National Memo*, December 5, 2011, http://www.nationalmemo.com/frank -luntz-and-battle-over-economic-freedom.

8. Lynn Schneider, "20 Examples of Great Euphemisms," December 23, 2011, retrieved from http://lynnschneiderbooks.com/2011/12/23/20-examples-of -great-euphemisms, January 16, 2014.

9. "E Euphemisms," EuphemismList.com, retrieved from http://www.euphe mismlist.com/Economically-Depressed-Neighbourhood, July 20, 2014.

10. Paul Wasserman and Don Hausrath, *Weasel Words: The Dictionary of American Doublespeak* (Herndon, VA: Capital Books, 2006), p. 55.

11. "Topic Guide to: Economic Inactivity," Gateway to UK National Statistics, http://webarchive.nationalarchives.gov.uk/20140721132900/http://www.sta tistics.gov.uk/hub/labour-market/people-not-in-work/economic-inactivity/ index.html.

12. Leonard R. N. Ashley, "Right on the Money," *Word Ways: The Journal of Recreational Linguistics*, 1991, retrieved from http://digitalcommons.butler .edu/wordways/vol24/iss4/5, May 12, 2014.

13. "Funny List of Medical Slang and Acronyms: The Definitive Resource," *The Happy Hospitalist* (blog), retrieved from http://thehappyhospitalist.blogspot .com/2011/05/medical-slang-vocabulary-in-icu.html, July 3, 2014.

14. William Davis, "Interfacing with Biz Speak," *The New York Times Magazine*, June 8, 1986, http://www.nytimes.com/1986/06/08/magazine/interfacing -with-biz-speak.html.

15. Kerry Redshaw, "Plain English Alternatives for Jargon Words," 2003, retrieved from http://www.kerryr.net/webwriting/plain_english.htm, May 5, 2014.

16. Matt Farmer, "Of Rich Dads and iPads . . . ," *The Huffington Post* (Chicago), April 11, 2013, http://www.huffingtonpost.com/matt-farmer/chicago-school -closings_b_3057430.html.

17. Timothy Lange (aka "Meteor Blades"), "Torture Gets Further Mush-Mouthed in John Brennan's Massage . . . er. . . . Questioning by the Press," *Daily Kos*, December 11, 2014, http://www.dailykos.com/story/2014/12/11/1351075/ -Torture-gets-further-mush-mouthed-in-John-Brennan-s-massage-er -questioning-by-the-press; and John Cassidy, "America's Shame: What's in the Senate Torture Report?," *The New Yorker*, December 9, 2014, http://www .newyorker.com/news/john-cassidy/americas-shame-whats-senate-torture -report.

18. Deborah Solomon, "The Wordsmith, Questions for Frank Luntz," *The New York Times Magazine*, May 21, 2009, http://www.nytimes.com/2009/05/24/ magazine/24wwln-q4-t.html.

19. William Lutz, "Life Under the Chief Doublespeak Officer," accessed at www.dt .org/html/Doublespeak.html, April 13, 2014.

20. Nancy Pelosi, interviewed by Maria Bartiromo on *Closing Bell*, CNBC, October 21, 2009, cited in Mac Slavo, "Pelosi Doublespeak: It's Not a Tax Increase; We're Eliminating a Tax Decrease," SHTFplan.com, October 23, 2009, http:// www.shtfplan.com/headline-news/pelosi-doublespeak-its-not-a-tax-increase -were-eliminating-a-tax-decrease_10232009.

21. Geoffrey Nunberg, *Talking Right: How Conservatives Turned Liberalism into a Tax-Raising, Latte-Drinking, Sushi-Eating, Volvo-Driving,* New York Times– *Reading, Body-Piercing, Hollywood-Loving, Left-Wing Freak Show* (New York: Public Affairs, 2006), p. 88.

22. Dr. Cynthia Boaz, "Fourteen Propaganda Techniques Fox 'News' Uses to Brainwash Americans," Truthout, July 2, 2011, http://www.truth-out.org/ news/item/1964:fourteen-propaganda-techniques-fox-news-uses-to -brainwash-americans.

23. Michael Spiro, "'In Transition' and Other Awkward Euphemisms," *Recruiter Musings* (blog), March 30, 2010, http://michaelspiro.wordpress.com/2010/03/ 30/in-transition-and-other-awkward-euphemisms.

24. Paul Krugman, "Health Care Horror Hooey," *The New York Times*, February 24, 2014, p. A19.

25. *Encyclopedia of Medical Concepts*, Reference.MD, retrieved from http://www .reference.md/files/D018/mD018607.html, February 22, 2014.

26. U.S. Air Force Spare Parts Microfiche, accessed at Travis Air Force Base by the Project on Military Procurement, as cited in Henry Beard and Christopher Cerf, *The Pentagon Catalog* (New York: Workman, 1986), p. 18.

27. *Quarterly Review of Doublespeak* (National Council of Teachers of English, Urbana, Illinois), cited in Gareth Branwyn, "This Shit Doesn't Stink. It Exceeds the Odor Threshold," retrieved from http://www.stim.com/Stim-x/ 8.2/doublespeak/doublespeak.html, April 10, 2014.

28. Al Baker, "City Room: Police Parlance 'Packaged' (10-4)," *The New York Times,* March 4, 2010, http://cityroom.blogs.nytimes.com/2010/03/04/police -parlance-packaged-10-4.

29. Jason Brockert, "Artspeak or, Art Words and Phrases We Use All the Time and Might Wish We Didn't," *Colored Mud* (blog), January 23, 2008, retrieved from http://jasonbrockert.com/ayearinart/?p=55, November 15, 2014.

30. "ABC Family 25 Days of Christmas December 23, 2010," DisneyDreaming.com, December 23, 2010, http://www.disneydreaming.com/2010/12/23/abc-family -25-days-of-christmas-december-23-2010.

31. "Doublespeak," Center for Media and Democracy, updated August 30, 2009, retrieved from http://www.sourcewatch.org/index.php/Doublespeak, April 9, 2014; and Mona Charen, "What the Euphemisms Tell Us," Real Clear Politics, April 10, 2010, http://www.realclearpolitics.com/articles/2010/04/10/what_the _euphemisms_tell_us_105104.html.

32. Judith S. Neaman and Carole G. Silver, *Kind Words* (New York: Avon Books, 1991), p. 337, cited in Henry Beard and Christopher Cerf, *The Official Politically Correct Dictionary and Handbook,* updated edition (New York: Villard Books, 1994), p. 135.

33. Don Watson, *Watson's Dictionary of Weasel Words, Contemporary Clichés, Cant, and Management Jargon* (Sydney: Random House of Australia, 2004), p. 122.

34. Deborah Solomon, "The Wordsmith, Questions for Frank Luntz," *The New York Times Magazine,* May 21, 2009, http://www.nytimes.com/2009/05/24/ magazine/24wwln-q4-t.html.

35. William Lutz, *Doublespeak* (New York: Harper Perennial, 1990), p. 176, cited in Henry Beard and Christopher Cerf, *The Official Politically Correct Dictionary and Handbook,* updated edition (New York: Villard Books, 1994), p. 136.

36. Geoffrey Nunberg, "Simpler Terms; If It's 'Orwellian,' It's Probably Not," *The New York Times,* June 22, 2003, http://www.nytimes.com/2003/06/22/weekin review/simpler-terms-if-it-s-orwellian-it-s-probably-not.html, April 17, 2014; and Mary Carol Combs, "English Plus: Responding to English Only," essay in James Crawford, *Language Loyalties: A Source Book on the Official English Controversy* (Chicago: University of Chicago Press, 1992), retrieved from http://www.languagepolicy.net/archives/combs.htm, April 19, 2014.

37. Jon Henley, "A Glossary of US Military Torture Euphemisms," *The Guardian,* December 12, 2007, http://www.theguardian.com/world/2007/dec/ 13/usa.humanrights.

38. John Leo, "Reality Gets a Makeover with Words That Buff and Polish," Town hall.com, August 18, 2003, http://townhall.com/columnists/johnleo/2003/08/ 18/reality_gets_a_makeover_with_words_that_buff_and_polish/page/full.

39. Hugh Rawson, *A Dictionary of Euphemisms and Other Doubletalk* (New York: Crown, 1981), p. 87.

40. Erin McKean, "Frisky: The TSA Spawns Anger—and a New Lexicon," *The Boston Globe,* November 28, 2010, http://www.boston.com/bostonglobe/ideas/ articles/2010/11/28/frisky.

41. David Oxenford, "FCC Underwriting Rules for Noncommercial Radio and TV—A Seminar on the Issues," *Broadcast Law Blog*, February 11, 2011, http://www.broadcastlawblog.com/2011/02/articles/fcc-underwriting-rules -for-noncommercial-radio-and-tv-a-seminar-on-the-issues.

42. "ABN Amro to Cut Up to 1,000 Retail Bank Jobs," *Financial Times*, November 14, 2014, http://www.ft.com/intl/fastft/236612/abn-amro-cut-up-1000-retail -bank-jobs.

43. "Lv64 Livingston Peak Road, Livingston, Montana 59047," Prudential Montana Real Estate, retrieved from http://www.prumt.com/property/ details/Residential/198601/LV64-Livingston-Peak-Road-Livingston -Montana-, November 13, 2014.

44. David Dodge, "Sperm Donation Is Full of Euphemisms, and an 11-Year-Old Is Full of Questions," *The New York Times*, June 3, 2014, http://parenting.blogs .nytimes.com/2014/06/03/sperm-donation-is-full-of-euphemisms-and-an-11 -year-old-is-full-of-questions/?_php=true&_type=blogs&.

45. Richard Eskow, "'Entitlement Reform' Is a Euphemism for Letting Old People Get Sick and Die," *The Blog, The Huffington Post*: Politics, February 25, 2011, http://www.huffingtonpost.com/rj-eskow/entitlement-reform-is-a-e_b _828544.html.

46. Justin Berrier, "Fox Regularly Uses the 'Racial Code Words' Denounced by Fox's Juan Williams," Media Matters, January 31, 2012, http://mediamatters .org/research/2012/01/31/fox-regularly-uses-the-racial-code-words-denoun/ 184184.

47. Lee Fang, "Lobbyist Dick Armey's Pollution Gospel: 'As an Article of Faith,' It Is 'Pretentious' to Believe in Global Warming," ThinkProgress.org, July 31, 2009, http://thinkprogress.org/politics/2009/07/31/53658/armey-pollution-gospel.

48. Jonny Geller, tweet to #publishingeuphemisms, February 23, 2012, https:// twitter.com/search?q=%23publishingeuphemisms.

49. William Lutz, *Doublespeak* (New York: Harper Perennial, 1990), p. 105, cited in Henry Beard and Christopher Cerf, *The Official Politically Correct Dictionary and Handbook*, updated edition (New York: Villard Books, 1994), p. 136.

50. "What's in a Name? Medical Jargon Sounds Scary," CBC News, February 26, 2009, http://www.cbc.ca/news/technology/what-s-in-a-name-medical-jargon -sounds-scary-1.808880; and Jonathan Richman, "Medical Jargon Makes You Sicker (Sort Of)," DoseofDigital.com, December 12-16, 2008, http://www .doseofdigital.com/2008/12/medical-jargon-makes-you-sicker-sort-of.

51. Robert Todd Carroll, *Becoming a Critical Thinker*, chap. 2, p. 27, retrieved from http://www.skepdic.com/refuge/ctlessons/ch2.pdf, August 14, 2014.

52. "Prostitute Euphemisms," EuphemismList.com, January 29, 2013, http://www .euphemismlist.com/category/prostitute-euphemisms.

53. University of Oregon School of Journalism and Communication, "Euphemism—Definition and List," retrieved from http://journalism.uoregon .edu/~tbivins/J496/readings/LANGUAGE/euphemism_defandlist.pdf, February 16, 2014.

54. Sangita Iyer, "How Doublespeak is Ruining Our Environment," *The Huffington Post* (Canada), February 25, 2013, http://www.huffingtonpost.ca/sangita-iyer/ethical-oil-canada_b_2750333.html.

55. Mostafa Heddaya, "When Artspeak Masks Oppression," Hyperallergic .com, March 6, 2013, http://hyperallergic.com/66348/when-artspeak-masks -oppression.

56. "Sununu Solicits Free Trips Aboard Corporate Aircraft," *Los Angeles Times*, June 18, 1991, cited in Norman Solomon, *The Power of Babble* (New York: Dell, 1992), p. 84.

57. "Doublespeak," SourceWatch, Center for Media and Democracy, updated August 30, 2009, http://www.sourcewatch.org/index.php/Doublespeak.

58. Richard Mooney, "If This Sounds Slippery . . . How to Apologize and Admit Nothing," *The New York Times*, November 30, 1992, http://www.nytimes.com/1992/11/30/opinion/editorial-notebook-if-this-sounds-slippery-how-to -apologize-and-admit-nothing.html; and "President Ronald Reagan's Polish Italian Mafia Duck Joke," *Mitchell's Ramblings* (blog), September 9, 2010, http://kentmitchellsramblings.blogspot.com/2010/09/president-ronald-reagans -polish-italian.html. (For history buffs curious about the "insensitive" joke Reagan told, here 'tis: "How do you tell the Polish guy at a cockfight? He's the guy who brings a duck. How do you tell the Italian guy? He's the guy who bets on the duck. How do you tell that the Mafia's running the cockfight? The duck wins.")

59. David Schultz, "Evaporated Cane Juice: Sugar in Disguise?," NPR, October 18, 2012, http://www.npr.org/blogs/thesalt/2012/10/18/163098211/evaporated -cane-juice-sugar-in-disguise.

60. "25 of Readers' Inflated Job Titles," *BBC News Magazine*, July 31, 2012. http://www.bbc.co.uk/news/magazine-18983009.

61. "Euphemisms," *The Economist Style Guide*, retrieved from http://www .economist.com/style-guide/euphemisms, January 19, 2014.

62. William Lutz, cited in Gareth Branwyn, "This Shit Doesn't Stink. It Exceeds the Odor Threshold," *Stim* 8, no. 2 (January 24, 1997), http://www.stim.com/Stim-x/8.2/doublespeak/doublespeak.html.

63. Soni Sangha, "Viral Post Draws Attention to Plight at a Brooklyn School," *The New York Times*, March 5, 2014, p. A22.

64. "Executary," *Collins English Dictionary*, http://www.collinsdictionary.com/dictionary/english/executary.

65. Hugh Rawson, *A Dictionary of Euphemisms and Other Doubletalk* (New York: Crown, 1981), p. 91, cited in Henry Beard and Christopher Cerf, *The Official Politically Correct Dictionary and Handbook*, updated edition (New York: Villard Books, 1994), p. 136.

66. Joanne B. Ciulla, *The Working Life: The Promise and Betrayal of Modern Work* (New York: Crown Business, 2001), p. 24.

67. John Leo, "Euphemisms," Townhall.com, February 23, 2004, http://townhall .com/columnists/johnleo/2004/02/23/euphemisms/page/full.

68. Geoffrey Norman, "Retreat to Euphemism," *The Blog, The Weekly Standard*, September 25, 2013, http://www.weeklystandard.com/blogs/retreat -euphemism_757143.html.

69. "Glossary of Some of the Words Used During the Vietnam War," 1st Cav Medic, http://www.1stcavmedic.com/glossary.html.

70. Prospero, "Johnson: Dear Flacks . . . Love Hack," *The Economist*, January 20, 2014, retrieved from http://www.economist.com/blogs/prospero/2014/01/public-relations-and-journalism?page=1&spc=scode&spv=xm&ah=9d7f7ab945510a56fa6d37c30b6f1709, July 7, 2014.

71. Jim Edwards, "A Layoff by Any Other Name: Merck Memo Uses 12 Euphemisms for Job Cuts," *CBS Money Watch*, September 19, 2011, http://www.cbsnews.com/news/a-layoff-by-any-other-name-merck-memo-uses-12-euphemisms-for-job-cuts.

72. Alix Rule and David Levine, "International Art English," *Triple Canopy*, July 30, 2012, http://canopycanopycanopy.com/issues/16/contents/international_art_english.

73. "Examples of Doublespeak," YourDictionary.com, http://examples.yourdictionary.com/examples-of-doublespeak.html.

74. Ronni Bennett, "The Danger of Euphemism," *Time Goes By* (blog), October 7, 2005, retrieved from http://www.timegoesby.net/weblog/2005/10/the_danger_of_e.html, January 17, 2014.

75. *Quarterly Review of Doublespeak* (National Council of Teachers of English, Urbana, Illinois), cited in "Strange Examples of 'Doublespeak,'" StrangeCosmos.com, July 25, 2012, retrieved from http://www.strangecosmos.com/archive/eletter_item_828.html, April 8, 2014.

76. Steven Poole, *Unspeak* (New York: Grove Press, 2006), pp. 64–65.

77. Paul Whitfield, "Eight Stocks That Might Not Be Too High to Buy," *Investor's Business Daily*, June 19, 2014, http://news.investors.com/061914-705432-stocks-still-in-buy-areas.htm.

78. Jonny Geller, tweet to #publishingeuphemisms, February 23, 2012, https://twitter.com/search?q=%23publishingeuphemisms.

79. Rich Coffey, "Euphemisms Glossary," The American Empire, Vizettes.com, retrieved from http://vizettes.com/kt/american_empire/pages/euphemisms-glossary.htm, April 13, 2014; and Neta C. Crawford, *Accountability for Killing: Moral Responsibility for Collateral Damage in America's Post-9/11 Wars* (New York: Oxford University Press, 2013), p. 50.

80. Ronda Bowen, "Marketing 101: Don't Call It Ungood When You Want to Say It's Bad," BrightHub.com, March 11, 2013, http://www.brighthub.com/office/entrepreneurs/articles/123518.aspx.

81. "The Rule of Verbal Packaging—The Leverage of Language," chap. 8 of *The Rules of Persuasion* (Westside Toastmasters, Los Angeles), retrieved from http://westsidetoastmasters.com/resources/laws_persuasion/chap8.html, April 18, 2014.

f

1. "Varieties of English: Gobbledygook," FunTrivia.com, http://www.funtrivia.com/en/subtopics/Gobbledygook-315836.html.

2. R. W. Holder, *Oxford Dictionary of Euphemisms* (New York: Oxford University Press, 2008), p. 173.

3. Arthur J. Martin, "Deceptive Billing Practices Mislead Individuals into Paying Fabricated 'Facility Fees,'" *Modern Journal* (blog), May 2, 2012, https://arthurjmartin.wordpress.com/2012/05/02/deceptive-billing-practices-mislead-individuals-into-paying-fabricated-facility-fees.

4. William Lambdin, *Doublespeak Dictionary* (Los Angeles: Pinnacle Books, 1981), p. 74.

5. "The Media Coverage of Paul Ryan's Speech: 15 Euphemisms for 'Lying,'" *The Week*, August 30, 2012, http://theweek.com/article/index/232670/the-media-coverage-of-paul-ryans-speech-15-euphemisms-for-lying.

6. Notation on a deceased patient's hospital chart, cited in William Lutz, *Doublespeak* (New York: Harper Perennial, 1990), p. 66.

7. The U. S. National Transportation Safety Board, quoted in William Lutz, *Doublespeak* (New York: HarperCollins, 1990), p. 214.

8. *Polyvocia: The SOAS Journal of Graduate Research* (University of London), cited in "Mistaken Punctuation, Misreferencing, and Other Euphemisms for Plagiarism," *Retraction Watch* (blog), retrieved from http://retractionwatch.com/2014/08/14/mistaken-punctuation-misreferencing-and-other-euphemisms-for-plagiarism, November 18, 2014.

9. Fox News Channel, corporate logo, retrieved from http://www.foxnews.com, December 24, 2014; "On Air Personalities," Fox News Channel, retrieved from http://www.foxnews.com/on-air/personalities, December 24, 2014; and Katherine Fung, "Fox News: Glenn Beck Left Network 'To Save His Ass,'" *The Huffington Post*, April 29, 2013, http://www.huffingtonpost.com/2013/04/29/fox-news-glenn-beck_n_3177932.html.

10. Hugh Rawson, *A Dictionary of Euphemisms and Other Doubletalk* (New York: Crown, 1981), p. 98.

11. Eric Cummings and Michael Cummings, "Our Politically Correct Communist Milblogs," OnViolence.com, retrieved from http://onviolence.com/?e=634, July 17, 2014.

12. *BBC News Magazine,* http://news.bbc.co.uk/2/hi/uk_news/magazine/8570244.stm.

13. Joanne B. Ciulla, *The Working Life: The Promise and Betrayal of Modern Work* (New York: Crown Business, 2001), p. 25.

14. "Family Values," RationalWiki, http://rationalwiki.org/wiki/Family_values.

15. "Unequal Naming: The Gulf War 1991," *Guardian Weekly*, February 3, 1991, retrieved from http://www.myread.org/images/cloze/unequal_print.pdf, May 24, 2014; and "Der Waffen SS—Brutal Fanatics or Brave Fighters?," Heaven Games.com, June 25–26, 2003, http://www.heavengames.com/cgi-bin/forums/display.cgi?action=ct&f=10,5383,1800,all.

16. "Varieties of English: Gobbledygook," FunTrivia.com, http://www.funtrivia.com/en/subtopics/Gobbledygook-315836.html.

17. Fattractive.com, website home page, retrieved from http://www.fattractive.com/, May 25, 2014.

18. Arthur Phillips, tweet to #pubcode, August 22, 2011, https://twitter.com/search?f=realtime&q=%23pubcode, cited in Janice Harayda, "40 Publishing Buzzwords, Clichés and Euphemisms Decoded," *One-Minute Book Reviews*

(blog), August 21, 2011, http://oneminutebookreviews.wordpress.com/2011/
08/21/40-publishing-buzzwords-cliches-and-euphemisms-decoded.

19. Jeanne Cavelos, quoted in Lewis Burke Frumkes, *Favorite Words of Famous
People* (Portland, OR: Marion Street Press, 2011), cited in Richard Nordquist,
"Weasel Word," About.com, retrieved from http://grammar.about.com/od/tz/
g/weaselwordterm.htm, November 16, 2014.

20. Dan Amira, "The Six Worst Excuses by Anti-Gay Public Figures Caught Doing
(Allegedly) Gay Things," *New York*, August 29, 2011, http://nymag.com/daily/
intelligencer/2011/08/worst_excuses_gay_politicians.html.

21. Melody Johnson, "Federal Family Reunion: Obama Admin's Use of Phrase
Isn't New," Media Matters, August 31, 2011, http://mediamatters.org/research/
2011/08/31/federal-family-reunion-obama-admins-use-of-phra/182686.

22. William Lutz, "Life Under the Chief Doublespeak Officer," accessed at www.dt
.org/html/Doublespeak.html.

23. Gordon Pritchard, "Marketing 101—'Weasel' Words," *The Print Guide* (blog),
May 3, 2012, http://the-print-guide.blogspot.com/2012/05/marketing-101
-weasel-words.html

24. Waguih William IsHak and Gabriel Tobia, "DSM-5 Changes in Diagnostic
Criteria of Sexual Dysfunctions," *Reproductive System & Sexual Disorders*,
August 2, 2013, http://omicsonline.org/dsm-5-changes-in-diagnostic-criteria
-of-sexual-dysfunctions-2161-038X.1000122.php?aid=18508.

25. Linda Lowen, "What Is a Feminazi?," About.com, retrieved from http://women
sissues.about.com/od/feminismequalrights/f/What-Is-A-Feminazi
-Definition-Of-Feminazi.htm, November 16, 2014.

26. Andrew Blum, "The Mall Goes Undercover," *Slate,* April 6, 2005, http://www
.slate.com/articles/arts/culturebox/2005/04/the_mall_goes_undercover.html.

27. "Crowd Management: Report of the Task Force on Crowd Control and Safety,"
Cincinnati City Manager's Office, Cincinnati, Ohio, 1980, chap. 2, retrieved
from http://www.crowdsafe.com/taskrpt/chpt2.html. September 1, 2014; and
Hugh Rawson, *A Dictionary of Euphemisms and Other Doubletalk* (New York:
Crown, 1981), p. 103.

28. Peer Lawther, "25 Euphemisms for 'You've Been Made Redundant,'"
StepChange MoneyAware (blog), November 11, 2011, http://moneyaware
.co.uk/2011/11/25-euphemisms-for-youve-been-made-redundant.

29. "The Rule of Verbal Packaging—The Leverage of Language," chap. 8 of *The
Rules of Persuasion* (Westside Toastmasters, Los Angeles), retrieved from
http://westsidetoastmasters.com/resources/laws_persuasion/chap8.html,
April 18, 2014.

30. Andrew K. Dart, "Why Don't Liberals Just Say What They Mean?," akdart
.com, http://www.akdart.com/libspeak.html.

31. D. J. Kehl and Howard Livingston, "Doublespeak Detection for the English
Classroom," *The English Journal,* July 1999, p. 80, retrieved from http://www
.jstor.org/discover/10.2307/822191?uid=3739832&uid=2134&uid=
24798016776&uid=2&uid=706&uid=3&uid=24798016676&uid=3739256&uid=60&
sid=21103823248907, April 8, 2014.

32. Stan Carey, "The Unreality of Real Estate Language," *Macmillan Dictionary Blog,* May 1, 2012, http://www.macmillandictionaryblog.com/the-unreality -of-real-estate-language.

33. Joseph Lambert, "Why Bad People Do Bad Things: The Power of Names, Frames and Personality Factors," *STOP Framing Us* (blog), September 12, 2012, http://stopframingus.com/tag/deceptive-language.

34. Jackie Jura, "Doublespeak Words," Orwell Today, http://www.orwelltoday .com/doublespeak.shtml.

35. "The Doublespeak Dictionary for 2008," DemocraticUnderground.com, retrieved from http://www.democraticunderground.com/discuss/duboard.php ?az=view_all&address=389x3624498, April 12, 2014.

36. Paul Wasserman and Don Hausrath, *Weasel Words: The Dictionary of American Doublespeak* (Herndon, VA: Capital Books, 2006), p. 66.

37. Paul Begala, "Paul Begala on Washington's Euphemistic Deceptions," *Newsweek,* December 10, 2012, http://www.newsweek.com/paul-begala -washingtons-euphemistic-deceptions-63441.

38. Michael Suede, "Euphemisms for the New Corporate Berlin Wall," *Libertarian News,* August 26, 2014 http://www.libertariannews.org/2014/08/26/euphe misms-for-the-new-corporate-berlin-wall.

39. "'Plutoed' Voted Word of the Year by American Dialect Society," press release, American Dialect Society, January 5, 2007, http://www.americandialect.org/ Word-of-the-Year_2006.pdf.

40. George Carlin, "Euphemistic Washington," speech before the National Press Club, May 25, 1999, archived by the Federation of American Scientists, and retrieved from http://fas.org/news/usa/1999/05/990525-carlin.htm, November 2, 2014.

41. Rob Kyff, "Modern-Day Euphemisms Can Leave Head in a Spin," *Hartford Courant,* January 18, 2010, http://articles.courant.com/2010-01-18/news/hc -words0118.artjan18_1_euphemisms-negative-patient-care-outcome-motion -discomfort.

42. Randy Parker, "Euphemism Can Lead to Copywriting Sin," *Wordnut* (blog), February 19, 2009, http://wordnut.com/2009/02/19/euphemism-can-lead-to -copywriting-sin.

43. John Rudoren, "In Gaza, Epithets Are Fired and Euphemisms Give Shelter," *The New York Times,* July 20, 2014, http://www.nytimes.com/2014/07/21/world/ middleeast/in-a-clash-between-israel-and-gaza-both-sides-use-social-media -to-fire-epithets-and-hide-behind-euphemisms.html.

44. Steve Eder, "Rodriguez's 'Gummies': Files Detail Doping, Down to Milligram," *The New York Times,* January 14, 2014, p. A1.

45. Bill Poser, "Doublespeak and the War on Terror," *Language Log* (blog), November 26, 2006, retrieved from http://itre.cis.upenn.edu/~myl/ languagelog/archives/003826.html, April 10, 2014.

46. Rhian Davis, quoted in Janice Harayda, "23 British Publishing Euphemisms Decoded by Industry Experts," *One-Minute Book Reviews* (blog), February 24, 2012, http://oneminutebookreviews.wordpress.com/2012/02/24/23-british -publishing-euphemisms-decoded-by-industry-experts.

47. Paul Wasserman and Don Hausrath, *Weasel Words: The Dictionary of American Doublespeak* (Herndon, VA: Capital Books, 2006), p. 66.

48. Barbara Von Diether, "Language Evolution Affects Business Writing," Ezine Articles, August 30, 2007, http://ezinearticles.com/?Language -Evolution-Affects-Business-Writing&id=709980.

49. U.S. Department of Defense term, cited in *Quarterly Review of Doublespeak* (National Council of Teachers of English, Urbana, Illinois), July 1991, p. 2.

50. Mark Thompson, "U.S. Boots Stepping Closer to Iraq," *Time*, August 13, 2014, http://time.com/3108778/iraq-isis-obama-troops.

51. "Rewriting the Rules. Year-end Report 2002: The Bush Administration's Assault on the Environment," Natural Resources Defense Fund, p. 30, retrieved from http://www.nrdc.org/legislation/rollbacks/rr2002.pdf, January 22, 2014.

52. Mona Charen, "What the Euphemisms Tell Us," Real Clear Politics, April 10, 2010, retrieved from http://www.realclearpolitics.com/articles/2010/04/10/ what_the_euphemisms_tell_us_105104.html, November 16, 2014.

53. Jonathan Wolfman, "Print Euphemism: The Most Absurd I've Ever Seen. Yours?," *Our Salon* (blog), October 18, 2013, http://oursalon.ning.com/profiles/ blogs/print-euphemism-the-most-absurd-i-ve-seen-yours.

54. "Teachers List Year's Worst Doublespeak," *The Register-Guard* (Eugene, Oregon), November 19, 1988, retrieved from http://news.google.com/ newspapers?nid=1310&dat=19881119&id=beZVAAAAIBAJ&sjid= 0eEDAAAAIBAJ&pg=6725,4637604, April 27, 2014.

55. Mike Apsey, "Weasel Words," *Musings, Memories, and the Occasional Rant* (blog), October 30, 2011, http://mikeapsey.wordpress.com/2011/10/30/1739.

56. "Making Murder Respectable," *The Economist*, December 17, 2011, http://www .economist.com/node/21541767.

57. "In Brief: Disengagement, Frankenscience, Nanosoft." *World Wide Words*, Issue #167, November 20, 1999, http://listserv.linguistlist.org/pipermail/ worldwidewords/1999-November.txt.

58. Gordon Pritchard, "Marketing 101—'Weasel' Words," *The Print Guide* (blog), May 3, 2012, http://the-print-guide.blogspot.com/2012/05/marketing-101 -weasel-words.html.

59. Geoffrey Nunberg. interviewed in Lauren Feeney, "Decoding the Political Buzzwords of Election 2012," *Moyers & Company*, February 17, 2012, http:// billmoyers.com/2012/02/17/decoding-the-political-buzzwords-of-2012.

60. Frank Luntz, 2005, quoted in Joe Romm, "Luntz Warns GOP on Occupy Wall Street, 'Don't Say *Capitalism*' Because Americans 'Think Capitalism Is Immoral.'" *ClimateProgress* (blog), December 1, 2011, retrieved from http:// thinkprogress.org/climate/2011/12/01/380121/luntz-gop-occupy-wall-street -capitalism-is-immoral, April 21, 2014.

61. Walter Wiekes, "Free Seminar," Dictionary of Management Jargon, http:// dictionaryofmanagementjargon.yolasite.com.

62. "Doublespeak and the New World Order," *New Dawn Magazine*, March–April 1996, http://www.newdawnmagazine.com/Articles/Doublespeak%20and% 20the%20New%20World%20Order.html.

63. "US Congress Opts for 'Freedom Fries,'" BBC News, March 12, 2003, http:// news.bbc.co.uk/2/hi/americas/2842493.stm.

64. "US Congress Opts for 'Freedom Fries,'" BBC News, March 12, 2003, http:// news.bbc.co.uk/2/hi/americas/2842493.stm.

65. Michael Spiro, "'In Transition' and Other Awkward Euphemisms," *Recruiter Musings* (blog), March 30, 2010, retrieved from http://michaelspiro.word press.com/2010/03/30/in-transition-and-other-awkward-euphemisms, July 19, 2014.

66. Rhonda Abrams, "Strategies: These Buzzwords Make You Sound Cutting Edge," *USA Today*, October 7, 2012, http://www.usatoday.com/story/money/ columnist/abrams/2012/10/05/strategies-nine-buzzwords/1612071.

67. Henry Steele Commager, "The Defeat of America," *The New York Review of Books*, October 5, 1972, cited in Henry Beard and Christopher Cerf, *The Official Politically Correct Dictionary and Handbook*, updated edition (New York: Villard Books, 1994), p. 137.

68. Patrick Reinhart, CheesyCorporateLingo.com, retrieved from http://www .cheesycorporatelingo.com/sections/f, January 26, 2014.

69. Ewing, Jack, "Draghi Sees No Risk of Eurozone Bubbles," *The New York Times*, July 15, 2014, p. B2, retrieved from http://www.nytimes.com/2014/07/15/busi ness/central-bank-chief-sees-no-risk-of-eurozone-bubbles.html, July 21, 2014.

70. Mark Jason, "Eco Euphemisms Confuse Our Understanding of Environmental Destruction," *Earth Island Journal*, March 28, 2014, http://www.earthisland .org/journal/index.php/elist/eListRead/eco_euphemisms_confuse_our_under standing_of_environmental_destruction.

71. Colin Randall, "'Let's Do Lunch': Putting a Name to an Insincere Phrase," *The National*, July 26, 2014, http://www.thenational.ae/opinion/comment/lets-do -lunch-putting-a-name-to-an-insincere-phrase.

72. John Leo, "Journalese as a Second Tongue," *Time*, March 18, 1985, http://bhs .cc/journalism/pdf/pw/journalese.pdf.

73. Jim Hightower, "5 Signs That America Has Gone Bonkers—And a Glimmer of Hope," Moyers & Company, May 30, 2014, http://billmoyers.com/2014/05/30/ 5-signs-that-america-has-gone-bonkers-—-and-a-glimmer-of-hope.

74. Reid Dickie, "Obituary Euphemisms," *ReadReidRead* (blog), April 8, 2011, http://readreidread.wordpress.com/2011/04/08/obituary-euphemisms.

75. Robert Hutton, quoted in Michael Holtermann, "Romps, Tots and Boffins: Robert Hutton on Journalese," Holtermann Design LLC, September 21, 2013, http://holtermanndesign.com/romps-tots-and-boffins-book-on-journalese -by-robert-hutton.

76. Robert Hutton, "Why I Believe Everyone Should Learn Journalese," *The Day*, October 16, 2013, http://theday.co.uk/opinion/why-i-believe-everyone-should -learn-journalese.html.

77. John Leo, "Reality Gets a Makeover with Words that Buff and Polish," Town hall.com, August 18, 2003, http://townhall.com/columnists/johnleo/2003/08/ 18/reality_gets_a_makeover_with_words_that_buff_and_polish/page/full.

78. Brad Jones, "WWE: 8 Wrestlers Set to Be 'Future Endeavored' in 2014, WhatCulture.com, December 23, 2013, http://whatculture.com/wwe/wwe-8 -wrestlers-set-future-endeavored-2014.php.

g

1. Grace Glueck, "Old Business, New Name: Behold the Gallerist," *The New York Times*, December 24, 2005, http://www.nytimes.com/2005/12/24/arts/design/ 24gall.html.
2. Carl Hiaasen, *The Downhill Lie* (New York: Alfred A. Knopf, 2008), p. 26.
3. Hugh Rawson, *A Dictionary of Euphemisms and Other Doubletalk* (New York: Crown, 1981), p. 119, cited in Henry Beard and Christopher Cerf, *The Official Politically Correct Dictionary and Handbook*, updated edition (New York: Villard Books, 1994), p. 137.
4. "Euphemisms," *CliffsNotes*, Houghton Mifflin Harcourt, retrieved from http:// www.cliffsnotes.com/writing/grammar/idioms-cliches-jargon-slang -euphemisms-and-wordiness/euphemisms, January 15, 2014.
5. George Carlin, "Euphemistic Washington," speech before the National Press Club, May 25, 1999, archived by the Federation of American Scientists, and retrieved from http://fas.org/news/usa/1999/05/990525-carlin.htm. November 2, 2014.
6. *Eupehmism List*, retrieved from www.euphemismlist.com, April 20, 2104.
7. Ross Toro, "How Gender Reassignment Surgery Works," *LiveScience*, August 26, 2013, http://www.livescience.com/39170-how-gender-reassignment-surgery -works-infographic.html.
8. Peter Bart, "Hold That Euphemism," *Variety*, February 10, 1991, http://variety .com/1991/film/features/hold-that-euphemism-99125609.
9. "Stripper Euphemisms," EuphemismList.com, January 19, 2013, http://www .euphemismlist.com/category/stripper-euphemisms.
10. Kathy Kellerman, "Doublespeak," retrieved from http://www.kkcomcon.com/ doc/KDoublespeak.pdf, October 19, 2014.
11. "The New Costa Brown by Amble Footwear," *VotreArt* (blog), April 14, 2014, http://votreart.blogspot.com/2014/04/the-new-costa-brown-by-amble -footwear.html.
12. "Euphemism Used in Dismissal," Baidu.com, retrieved from http://wenku .baidu.com/view/1c84df82e53a580216fcfe98.html, May 25, 2014.
13. "The Funders of Climate Disinformation," The Campaign Against Climate Change, retrieved from http://www.campaigncc.org/climate_change/ sceptics/funders, April 11, 2014.
14. Julie Beck, "'Going to Switzerland' Is a Euphemism for Assisted Suicide," *The Atlantic*, August 27, 2014, http://www.theatlantic.com/health/archive/2014/ 08/going-to-switzerland-is-a-euphemism-for-assisted-suicide/379182.
15. David Beckwith, quoted in "Academy Hisses Greet Quayle," United Press International, May 25, 1989, retrieved from http://news.google.com/ newspapers?nid=860&dat=19890525&id=5sw0AAAAIBAJ&sjid=

DI8DAAAAIBAJ&pg=5734,3385215, August 24, 2014, cited in Henry Beard and Christopher Cerf, *The Official Politically Correct Dictionary and Handbook*, updated edition (New York: Villard Books, 1994), p. 137.

16. *Quarterly Review of Doublespeak* (National Council of Teachers of English, Urbana, Illinois), April 1990, p. 2, cited in Henry Beard and Christopher Cerf, *The Official Politically Correct Dictionary and Handbook*, updated edition (New York: Villard Books, 1994), p. 137.

17. Vincent Fernando and Gus Lubin, "20 Examples of Corporate Doublespeak You Need to Know During Earnings Season," Business Insider, October 18, 2010, http://www.businessinsider.com/guide-to-earnings-season-2010?op=1.

18. Patrick Collinson, "Peverel's 'Goodwill' Payments Are Compensation by Any Other Name," *The Guardian*, December 13, 2013, http://www.theguardian .com/money/blog/2013/dec/14/peverel-goodwill-payments-oft-report.

19. Ben Dimiero, "Leaked Email: Fox Boss Caught Slanting News Reporting," *Media Matters* (blog), December 9, 2010, http://mediamatters.org/blog/2010/ 12/09/leaked-email-fox-boss-caught-slanting-news-repo/174090.

20. Megan R. Wilson, "Group Founded to Defend K Street Considers Dropping 'Lobbyist' from Name," *The Hill*, September 9, 1913, http://thehill.com/ business-a-lobbying/321121-association-founded-to-defend-k-street -considers-dropping-lobbyist-from-its-name.

21. John Leo, "Journalese as a Second Tongue," *Time*, March 18, 1985, retrieved from http://bhs.cc/journalism/pdf/pw/journalese.pdf, July 7, 2014.

22. Kate Cocuzzo, "Real Estate Euphemisms: An Agent's Literary Loophole," *Geo Properties, Inc.* (blog), May 21, 2013, http://www.geopropertiesinc.com/word press/real-estate-euphemisms-an-agents-literary-loophole.

23. Keith Allan and Kate Burridge, *Euphemism & Dysphemism: Language Used as Shield and Weapon* (New York: Oxford University Press, 1991), p. 169, cited in Henry Beard and Christopher Cerf, *The Official Politically Correct Dictionary and Handbook*, updated edition (New York: Villard Books, 1994), p. 137.

24. Tom Engelhardt, "The Rise of 'Green-on-Blue' Violence in Afghanistan," *Mother Jones,* August 1, 2012, http://www.motherjones.com/politics/2012/07/ rise-green-blue-violent-attacks-afghanistan-tom-dispatch.

25. Rich Coffey, "Euphemisms Glossary," The American Empire, Vizettes.com, http://vizettes.com/kt/american_empire/pages/euphemisms-glossary.htm.

26. Michael Manekin, interview with John Stauber in the *Valley Advocate, PR Nation*, August 16, 2001, retrieved from http://www.ratical.org/ratville/PRna tion.html, April 11, 2014.

27. "The Ridiculous Business Jargon Dictionary," *The Office Life* (blog), retrieved from http://www.theofficelife.com/business-jargon-dictionary-G.html, January 27, 2014.

28. "*Post* Questions Spitzer's Gremlins Excuse," *Gothamist*, April 7, 2009, http:// gothamist.com/2009/04/07/post_questions_spitzers_gremlins_ex.php.

29. *Quarterly Review of Doublespeak* (National Council of Teachers of English, Urbana, Illinois), cited in "Strange Examples of 'Doublespeak,'" Strange

Cosmos.com, July 25, 2012, retrieved from http://www.strangecosmos
.com/archive/eletter_item_828.html, April 8, 2014.

30. "'O' Word by Any Other Euphemism," *Sun-Sentinel* (Broward County, Florida),
January 29, 1995, http://articles.sun-sentinel.com/1995-01-29/features/
9501270447_1_welfare-reform-farm-bill-clinton-welfare.

31. Seth Lee Abrams, comment posted to Mark Peters, "Evasive Maneuvers,
Euphemisms Old and New," Visual Thesaurus, March 4, 2009, http://www
.visualthesaurus.com/cm/evasive/shooting-sea-kittens-in-a-barrel.

32. Adrian Wooldridge, "Too Many Chiefs: Inflation in Job Titles Is Approaching
Weimar Levels," Schumpeter column, *The Economist*, June 24, 2010, http://
www.economist.com/node/16423358; and "Kim Jong-Il Honored as a Deity,
Has More Than 1,200 Titles," WorldNews.com, December 1, 2003, http://www
.worldtribune.com/worldtribune/WTARC/2003/ea_nkorea_12_01.html.

33. Steve Eder, "Rodriguez's 'Gummies': Files Detail Doping, Down to Milligram,"
The New York Times, January 14, 2014, p. A1.

34. Liberty Rogue, "Deception by Language: Creating Stereotypes and Destroying
Meaning," PrisonPlanet.com, http://www.prisonplanet.com/analysis_liberty
_011703_doublethink.html.

h

1. William Lutz, *Doublespeak* (New York: HarperCollins, 1990), p. 171.

2. "Fastskin3 Hair Management System," product featured on the Speedo
International Ltd. online store, retrieved from http://www.speedousa.com/
fastskin3-hair-management-system.shtml, April 14, 2014.

3. Emily Dotson Biggs, Claudia L Reinhardt, and Jean Eggenschwiler,
CliffsNotes Writing: Grammar, Usage, and Style Quick Review, 3rd edition
(Hoboken, NJ: Wiley, 2011), p. 140.

4. "Translations from the Journalese," *The Washington Post* article reprinted in
Quarterly Review of Doublespeak (National Council of Teachers of English,
Urbana, Illinois), January 1991, p. 11, cited in Henry Beard and Christopher
Cerf, *The Official Politically Correct Dictionary and Handbook*, updated
edition (New York: Villard Books, 1994), p. 138.

5. "Making Murder Respectable," *The Economist*, December 17, 2011, http://www
.economist.com/node/21541767.

6. Rob Kyff, "Modern-Day Euphemisms Can Leave Head in a Spin," *Hartford
Courant*, January 18, 2010, http://articles.courant.com/2010-01-18/news/hc
-words0118.artjan18_1_euphemisms-negative-patient-care-outcome-motion
-discomfort.

7. "Meet the Team," Buffer, https://bufferapp.com/about/team#carolyn, retrieved
October 15, 2014.

8. Lucy Fisher, "Euphemisms II," *Wordly Wisdom* (blog), retrieved from http://
wordlywisdom.net/Euphemisms-II.php, April 11, 2014.

9. Chris Moody, "How Republicans Are Being Taught to Talk About Occupy Wall
Street," Yahoo! News, December 1, 2011, http://news.yahoo.com/blogs/ticket/
republicans-being-taught-talk-occupy-wall-street-133707949.html.

10. Paul Wasserman and Don Hausrath, *Weasel Words: The Dictionary of American Doublespeak* (Herndon, VA: Capital Books, 2006), p. 78; and Hugh Rawson, *A Dictionary of Euphemisms and Other Doubletalk* (New York: Crown, 1981), p. 132.

11. Randy Parker, "Euphemism Can Lead to Copywriting Sin," *Wordnut* (blog), February 19, 2009, http://wordnut.com/2009/02/19/euphemism-can-lead-to -copywriting-sin.

12. Peer Lawther, "25 Euphemisms for 'You've Been Made Redundant,'" *StepChange MoneyAware* (blog), November 11, 2011, http://moneyaware. co.uk/2011/11/25-euphemisms-for-youve-been-made-redundant; and William Lutz, "Life Under the Chief Doublespeak Officer," retrieved from www.dt.org/ html/Doublespeak.html, May 31, 2014.

13. Anand Sanwal, "Jargon Word of Early 2008: Headwind," Toolbox.com, February 12, 2008, http://it.toolbox.com/blogs/brilliontblog/jargon-word -of-early-2008-headwind-22433.

14. Ralph Keyes, *Euphemania: Our Love Affair with Euphemisms* (Little, Brown, 2010), p. 204.

15. "Forty Per Cent of Canadians Facing Financial Hardship After Serious Health Event," news release, Sun Life Financial Canada, September 30, 2013, http:// www.sunlife.ca/Canada/sunlifeCA/About+us/Newsroom/News+releases/ 2013/Forty+per+cent+of+Canadians+facing+financial+hardship+after+ serious+health+event; and JR post to "Favorite Euphemisms," SportsJournal ists.com, September 28, 2006, http://www.sportsjournalists.com/forum/ index.php/topic,32365.0/nowap.html.

16. A term used by Simply Hired, Inc., "the next generation of online recruiting solutions." Retrieved from http://www.simplyhired.com/salaries-k-health -care-procurement-specialist-jobs.html, January 15, 2014.

17. "Healthy Forests Initiative," Sierra Forest Legacy, 2012, http://www.sierra forestlegacy.org/FC_LawsPolicyRegulations/KFSP_HealthyForests.php; and George Lakoff, *Don't Think of an Elephant!* (White River Junction, VT: Chelsea Green, 2004), p. 119.

18. Katha Pollitt, tweet to #pubcode in response to a question from novelist Janice Harayda about publishing clichés, buzzwords, and euphemisms, August 22, 2012, https://twitter.com/search?f=realtime&q=%23pubcode.

19. Hugh Rawson, *A Dictionary of Euphemisms and Other Doubletalk* (New York: Crown, 1981), p. 133; and Walter Martin, *The Kingdom of the Cults* (Bloomington, MN: Bethany House, 2003), p. 377.

20. R. W. Holder, *Oxford Dictionary of Euphemisms* (New York: Oxford University Press, 2008), p. 212.

21. "Heck of a Job," Taegan Goddard's Political Dictionary, retrieved from http:// politicaldictionary.com, May 18, 2014.

22. R. W. Holder, *Oxford Dictionary of Euphemisms* (New York: Oxford University Press, 2008), p. 212.

23. Mike Huckabee, speech at the 2014 Winter Meeting of the Republican National Committee, Washington, DC, January 23, 2014, quoted in Alexandra Petri, "Mike Huckabee and Women's Uncontrolled Libido," *The Washington*

Post, January 23, 2014, http://www.washingtonpost.com/blogs/compost/wp/2014/01/23/mike-huckabee-and-womens-uncontrolled-libido-or-uncle-sugar.

24. Jeffrey Schrank, "The Language of Advertising Claims," *Teaching About Doublespeak,* ed. Daniel Dieterich (Urbana, IL: National Council of Teachers of English, 1976), retrieved from http://users.drew.edu/sminegar/English_1_FA08_Sect_003/The%20Language%20of%20Advertising%20Claims.htm, April 19, 2014.

25. Stephen K. Wikel., "Immunological Control of Hematophagous Arthropod Vectors: Utilization of Novel Antigens," *Veterinary Parasitology* 29, nos. 2–3, September 1988, pp. 235–264, http://www.sciencedirect.com/science/article/pii/0304401788901276.

26. Arthur Phillips, tweet to #pubcode, August 22, 2011, https://twitter.com/search?f=realtime&q=%23pubcode, cited in Janice Harayda, "40 Publishing Buzzwords, Clichés and Euphemisms Decoded," *One-Minute Book Reviews* (blog), August 21, 2011, http://oneminutebookreviews.wordpress.com/2011/08/21/40-publishing-buzzwords-cliches-and-euphemisms-decoded.

27. John Leo, "Euphemism, Double-Speak Marginalize the Language," *The Seattle Times,* August 15, 1995, http://community.seattletimes.nwsource.com/archive/?date=19950815&slug=2136517.

28. Lori Comeau, *Nuts and Bolts at the Pentagon,* U.S. Senate Committee on Governmental Affairs, staff investigation, 1984, cited in Henry Beard and Christopher Cerf, *The Pentagon Catalog* (New York: Workman, 1986), p. 23.

29. Patrick Reinhart, CheesyCorporateLingo.com, retrieved from http://www.cheesycorporatelingo.com/sections/h, January 26, 2014.

30. Rocky Smith, "Gobbledygook," *Mr. Write's Page* (blog), March 12, 2013, http://rockysmith.wordpress.com/2013/03/12/gobbledygook.

31. Based on information provided in Rob Kyff, "Negative Patient Care Outcome? Yes, Euphemisms Are Alive and Well," *Hartford Courant,* April 4, 1997, http://articles.courant.com/1997-04-04/features/9705230902_1_assisted-new-euphemism-nursing-home-care.

32. Kate Phillips, "Sanford Resurfaces—From Argentina," *The New York Times,* June 24, 2009, http://thecaucus.blogs.nytimes.com/2009/06/24/sanford-resur faces-from-argentina.

33. John M. Oldham, M.D., M.S., Andrew E. Skodol, M.D., and Donna S. Bender, Ph.D., FIPA, eds., *The American Psychiatric Publishing Textbook of Personality Disorders,* 2nd edition (Arlington, VA: American Psychiatric Association, 2014), p. 202.

34. Amanda Busse, "Liberal Fascism Explained," *Accuracy in Media,* January 16, 2008, http://www.aim.org/briefing/liberal-fascism-explained.

35. Randy Parker, "Euphemism Can Lead to Copywriting Sin," *Wordnut* (blog), February 19, 2009, http://wordnut.com/2009/02/19/euphemism-can-lead-to-copywriting-sin.

36. "Interplak Home Plaque Removal Instrument: Technical Description," retrieved from https://www.tu-chemnitz.de/phil/english/chairs/linguist/

independent/kursmaterialien/TechComm/acchtml/descx2.html, May 26, 2014; and "OptiClean™ Cordless Rechargeable Power Plaque Remover," InterPlak by ConAir, 2014, retrieved from http://www.interplak.com/catalog .php?pcID=109&product_id=369, May 26, 2014.

37. Jeff Bercovici, "Fox News Can't Keep Its Made-Up Propaganda Words Straight," *Forbes*, January 26, 2011, www.forbes.com/sites/jeffbercovici/2011/ 01/26/fox-news-cant-keep-its-made-up-propaganda-words-straight; and "Homicide Bombing," RationalWiki, updated December 13, 2013, http:// rationalwiki.org/wiki/Homicide_bombing.

38. "Unequal Naming: The Gulf War 1991," *Guardian Weekly*, February 3, 1991, retrieved from http://www.myread.org/images/cloze/unequal_print.pdf, May 24, 2014.

39. Alix Rule and David Levine, "International Art English," *Triple Canopy*, July 30, 2012, http://canopycanopycanopy.com/issues/16/contents/international_art _english.

40. Oracle 2007, "Unclear and Misleading Language," *The Weekly Gripe*, retrieved from http://www.weeklygripe.co.uk/a481.asp, April 19, 2014; and Metropolitan Nashville Public Schools, http://www.hr.mnps.org/Page32361.aspx.

41. "Euphemisms," *The Economist Style Guide*, retrieved from http://www.econo mist.com/style-guide/euphemisms. January 19, 2014.

42. John Rudoren, "In Gaza, Epithets Are Fired and Euphemisms Give Shelter," *The New York Times*, July 20, 2014, http://www.nytimes.com/2014/07/21/ world/middleeast/in-a-clash-between-israel-and-gaza-both-sides-use-social -media-to-fire-epithets-and-hide-behind-euphemisms.html.

43. Rob Hutton, "My 'Shameful Secret': I've Learnt to Love Clichéd Journalese," *The Telegraph*, September 8, 2013, http://www.telegraph.co.uk/culture/ 10288967/My-shameful-secret-Ive-learnt-to-love-cliched-journalese.html.

44. Steven Rosburg, review of *The Waterboy*, IMDb, August 30, 1999, http://www .imdb.com/title/tt0120484/reviews-155.

45. Waguih William IsHak and Gabriel Tobia, "DSM-5 Changes in Diagnostic Criteria of Sexual Dysfunctions," *Reproductive System & Sexual Disorders*, August 2, 2013, http://omicsonline.org/dsm-5-changes-in-diagnostic-criteria -of-sexual-dysfunctions-2161-038X.1000122.php?aid=18508.

i

1. Bob Lewis, *Keep the Joint Running*, quoted in Celeste and Peter Stokely, "Management Speak Translation Guide," Stokely Consulting, Cotopaxi, Colorado, 2013, retrieved from http://www.stokely.com/lighter.side/mgmt .spk.html, April 11, 2014.

2. Enid Nemy, "What's Said Isn't Always What's Meant," a 1998 article in *The New York Times*, reprinted in *Quarterly Review of Doublespeak* (National Council of Teachers of English, Urbana, Illinois), July 1990, p, 12, cited in Henry Beard and Christopher Cerf, *The Official Politically Correct Dictionary and Handbook*, updated edition (New York: Villard Books, 1994), p. 138.

3. R. W. Holder, *Oxford Dictionary of Euphemisms* (New York: Oxford University
    Press, 2008), p. 221.
4. Guy Winch, "The 10 Most Annoying Customer Service Practices" (blog
    post), GuyWinch.com, September 17, 2011, http://www.guywinch.com/10
    -most-annoying-customer-service-practices.
5. Stacey Colino, "A Decoder for Common Medical Terms," *Real Simple*, retrieved
    from http://www.realsimple.com/health/common-medical-terms/page2,
    November 18, 2014.
6. Joel Postman, "10 Business Buzzwords We Can Do Without," *Social Media
    Today*, April 7, 2011, http://socialmediatoday.com/socialized/284713/10-busi
    ness-buzz-words-we-can-do-without.
7. Kenny Lin, "Decoding Doctor-Speak: Translations of Common Medical
    Terms," *U.S. News & World Report*, Health, July 25, 2011, http://health
    .usnews.com/health-news/blogs/healthcare-headaches/2011/07/25/decoding
    -doctor-speak-translations-of-common-medical-terms.
8. Page H. Onorato, "Talk of the Table Uses Euphemisms," *The Dispatch*
    (Lexington, North Carolina), February 28, 2012, http://www.the-dispatch
    .com/article/20120228/COLUMNISTS/302289969?p=2&tc=pg#gsc.tab=0,
    January 30, 2014.
9. "Doublespeak in Everyday Language," YourDictionary.com, http://examples
    .yourdictionary.com/examples-of-doublespeak.html.
10. Lynn Schneider, "20 Examples of Great Euphemisms," December 23, 2011,
    http://lynnschneiderbooks.com/2011/12/23/20-examples-of-great-euphemisms.
11. "Doublespeak," Center for Media and Democracy, updated August 30, 2009,
    http://www.sourcewatch.org/index.php/Doublespeak.
12. *Quarterly Review of Doublespeak* (National Council of Teachers of English,
    Urbana, Illinois), July 1989, p. 10, cited in Henry Beard and Christopher Cerf,
    The Official Politically Correct Dictionary and Handbook, updated edition
    (New York: Villard Books, 1994), p. 138.
13. "15 Reasons Why Estate Agents Are Idiots," *Landlord Blog*, Property
    Investment Project, January 20, 2007, http://www.propertyinvestmentproject
    .co.uk/blog/15-reasons-why-estate-agents-are-idiots.
14. Kenneth A. Osgood, "Propaganda," *Encyclopedia of the New American Nation*,
    retrieved from http://www.americanforeignrelations.com/O-W/Propaganda
    .html#b, July 21, 2014.
15. R. W. Holder, *Oxford Dictionary of Euphemisms* (New York: Oxford University
    Press, 2008), p. 222.
16. D. J. Kehl and Howard Livingston, "Doublespeak Detection for the English
    Classroom," *The English Journal,* July 1999, p. 79, retrieved from http://www
    .jstor.org/discover/10.2307/822191?uid=3739832&uid=2134&uid=
    2479801677&uid=2&uid=70&uid=3&uid=2479801667&uid=3739256&uid=60&
    sid=21103823248907, April 8, 2014.
17. Councillor David Dean, submission to the Licensing Subcommittee of the
    Merton Council concerning Snoggy's application to open an outlet on the
    lower concourse of the Wimbledon train station, June 21, 2010, http://

democracy.merton.gov.uk/Data/Licensing%20sub-committee/20100621/
Agenda/524.pdf.

18. Jorma K. Miettinen, "Enhanced Radiation Warfare," *Bulletin of the Atomic Scientists*, September 1977, p. 35.

19. Charles M. Phipps, "Immigration Reform—Euphemism for Vote Buying," *OK Politechs: The Right Assessment* (blog), November 26, 2012, http://www .charlesmphipps.net/immigration-reform-euphemism-for-vote-buying.

20. Rob Kyff, "Modern-Day Euphemisms Can Leave Head in a Spin," *Hartford Courant*, January 18, 2010, http://articles.courant.com/2010-01-18/news/hc -words0118.artjan18_1_euphemisms-negative-patient-care-outcome-motion -discomfort.

21. Steven Roger Fischer, *A History of Language* (London: Reaktion Books, 2004), p. 193.

22. Timothy Lynch, "Doublespeak and the War on Terrorism," Cato Institute Briefing Paper #98, September 6, 2006, http://object.cato.org/sites/cato.org/ files/pubs/pdf/bp98.pdf.

23. William Lutz, "Life Under the Chief Doublespeak Officer," accessed at www .dt.org/html/Doublespeak.html.

24. Mark Peters, "Malarkey-Inspired Euphemisms," Visual Thesaurus, August 7, 2013, http://www.visualthesaurus.com/cm/evasive/malarkey-inspired -euphemisms.

25. "Spotting Spin: The Lies Before Your Eyes," *Truth, Lies, Deception, and Coverups* (blog), May 2013, http://www.truthliesdeceptioncoverups.info/ 2013/05/spotting-spin-some-tricks-of-trade.html.

26. Norman Solomon, *The Power of Babble* (New York: Dell, 1992), p. 130.

27. Robert Todd Carroll, *Becoming a Critical Thinker*, chap. 2, p. 28, retrieved from http://www.skepdic.com/refuge/ctlessons/ch2.pdf, August 14, 2014.

28. Christine Hsu, "The 7 Most Condescending Sports Euphemisms," Cracked .com, May 17, 2011, http://www.cracked.com/blog/the-7-most-condescending -sports-euphemisms_p2.

29. Charles W. Bryant, "When Do TV Commercials Need to Use Disclaimers?," HowStuffWorks, http://entertainment.howstuffworks.com/tv-commercial -disclaimer.htm, retrieved October 26, 2014.

30. Patrick Cockburn, "Weasel Words That Politicians Use to Obscure Terrible Truths," *The Independent*, October 14, 2012, http://www.independent.co.uk/ voices/comment/weasel-words-that-politicians-use-to-obscure-terrible -truths-8210302.html.

31. Judith S. Neaman and Carole G. Silver, *Kind Words* (New York: Avon Books, 1991), p. 321, cited in Henry Beard and Christopher Cerf, *The Official Politically Correct Dictionary and Handbook*, updated edition (New York: Villard Books, 1994), p. 135.

32. Michael Spiro, "'In Transition' and Other Awkward Euphemisms," *Recruiter Musings* (blog), March 30, 2010, http://michaelspiro.wordpress.com/2010/03/ 30/in-transition-and-other-awkward-euphemisms.

33. Joseph H. Boyett, Ph.D., "When Does Rhetoric Become Propaganda?," Guru GuideBooks.com, 2009, http://www.guruguidebooks.com/files/When_Does _Rhetoric_Become_Propaganda.pdf.

34. Peter Donnelly, "Weasel Words," *Skookum*, http://skookumpete.com/euphe mism.htm.

35. B. G. Milligan, letter to the editor, *The New York Times*, February 27, 2002, http://www.nytimes.com/2002/02/27/opinion/l-tales-twice-told-a -historian-s-story-825859.html.

36. David D. Kirkpatrick, "Historian Says Borrowing Was Wider Than Known," *The New York Times*, February 23, 2002, http://www.nytimes.com/2002/02/ 23/books/23BOOK.html.

37. Lisa Kerr, "Healing Place Pastor Founder Resigns; Affair Cover Up Suspected," *My Cult Life* (blog), September 18, 2012, http://www.mycultlife.com/dino -rizzo/dinno-rizzo-resigns; and Lisa Kerr, "Here's What People Are Saying About Dino Rizzo's Affair Cover-Up," *My Cult Life* (blog), August 10, 2013, http://www.mycultlife.com/dino-rizzo/heres-what-people-are-saying-about -dino-rizzos-affair-cover-up.

38. B. G. Milligan, letter to the editor, *The New York Times*, February 27, 2002, http://www.nytimes.com/2002/02/27/opinion/l-tales-twice-told -a-historian-s-story-825859.html.

39. R. W. Holder, *Oxford Dictionary of Euphemisms* (New York: Oxford University Press, 2008), p. 225.

40. Rich Coffey, "Euphemisms Glossary," The American Empire, Vizettes.com, retrieved from http://vizettes.com/kt/american_empire/pages/euphemisms- glossary.htm, April 13, 2014; and Chet Richards, "The Ghosts of Orientation," *Slightly East of New* (blog), November 18, 2013, http://slightlyeastofnew.com/ 2013/11/18/the-ghosts-of-orientation.

41. "Making Murder Respectable," *The Economist*, December 17, 2011, retrieved from http://www.economist.com/node/21541767, January 22, 2014.

42. Lucy Moore, "Backwards or Brainwashed," *b92 Blog*, May 14, 2007, http://blog .b92.net/arhiva/node/5728.html.

43. R. W. Holder, *Oxford Dictionary of Euphemisms* (New York: Oxford University Press, 2008), p. 225.

44. Robert Todd Carroll, *Becoming a Critical Thinker*, chap. 2, p. 28, retrieved from http://www.skepdic.com/refuge/ctlessons/ch2.pdf, August 14, 2014.

45. "Military Doublespeak: How Jargon Turns Gore into Glory," Center for Media Literacy, retrieved from http://www.medialit.org/reading-room/mili tary-doublespeak-how-jargon-turns-gore-glory, August 17, 2014.

46. Michael D. Shear and Robert Pear, "Obama in Bind Trying to Keep Health Law Vow," *The New York Times*, November 12, 2014, http://www.nytimes.com/ 2013/11/13/us/bill-clinton-urges-obama-to-yield-on-health-law.html.

47. Mark Peters, "Hiking the Euphemistic Trail," Visual Thesaurus, July 2, 2009, retrieved from http://www.visualthesaurus.com/cm/evasive/hiking-the -euphemistic-trail, June 1, 2014.

48. Rob Kyff, "Modern-Day Euphemisms Can Leave Head in a Spin," *Hartford Courant*, January 18, 2010, http://articles.courant.com/2010-01-18/news/hc -words0118.artjan18_1_euphemisms-negative-patient-care-outcome -motion-discomfort.
49. Carol Lehman and Debbie DuFrene, *BCOM5* (Boston: Cengage Learning, 2005), p. 64.
50. William Lutz, *Doublespeak* (New York: Harper Perennial, 1990), p. 230.
51. "Varieties of English: Gobbledygook," FunTrivia.com, retrieved from http://www .funtrivia.com/en/subtopics/Gobbledygook-315836.html, January 25, 2014.
52. Paul Hsieh, "Why the Federal Government Wants to Redefine the Word 'Cancer,'" *Forbes*, September 28, 2013, http://www.forbes.com/sites/ paulhsieh/2013/09/29/why-the-federal-government-wants-to-redefine -the-word-cancer.
53. Mark Peters, "Quench Your Thirst! (Within the Defect Action Levels, Of Course)," October 6, 2010, http://www.visualthesaurus.com/cm/evasive/ quench-your-thirst-within-the-defect-action-levels-of-course; and "Now Your Pet Can Go When He Needs To," PottyPatch.com, https://www .pottypatch.com.
54. Janet, comment published in Dr. Gerard M. Nadal, "How Many Pro-Choice Euphemisms Can You List?," *Coming Home* (blog), GerardNadal.com, June 1, 2010, http://gerardnadal.com/2010/05/31/how-many-pro-choice-euphemisms -can-you-list.
55. Rob Kyff, "Modern-Day Euphemisms Can Leave Head in a Spin," *Hartford Courant*, January 18, 2010, http://articles.courant.com/2010-01-18/news/hc -words0118.artjan18_1_euphemisms-negative-patient-care-outcome-motion -discomfort.
56. "The Ridiculous Business Jargon Dictionary," *The Office Life* (blog), retrieved from http://www.theofficelife.com/business-jargon-dictionary-I.html, January 27, 2014.
57. "Your Silliest Job Titles," *BBC News Magazine*, March 17, 2010. http://news .bbc.co.uk/2/hi/uk_news/magazine/8570244.stm.
58. Bruce Hilton, "Doublespeak Again Comes to the Rescue," *San Francisco Examiner*, December 10, 1989, syndicated in the *Chicago Tribune*, http:// articles.chicagotribune.com/1989-12-10/features/8903160824_1_doublespeak -awards-hospital-report-negative-patient-care-outcome.
59. George Carlin, "Euphemistic Washington," speech before the National Press Club, May 25, 1999, archived by the Federation of American Scientists, and retrieved from http://fas.org/news/usa/1999/05/990525-carlin.htm, November 2, 2014.
60. Ian Haney López, *Dog Whistle Politics: How Coded Racial Appeals Have Reinvented Racism and Wrecked the Middle Class* (New York: Oxford University Press, 2014), cited in Jenée Desmond-Harris, "8 Sneaky Code Words and Why Politicians Love Them," *The Root*, March 15, 2014, http://www .theroot.com/articles/politics/2014/03/_racial_code_words_8_term _politicians_love.3.html.

61. Norman Solomon, *The Power of Babble* (New York: Dell, 1992), p. 133.

62. Sam Biddle, "The Biggest Bullshit Job Titles in Tech," *Gawker*, February 12, 2014, http://valleywag.gawker.com/the-biggest-bullshit-job-titles-in-tech-1521536472; and "William Bunce: Background Summary," LinkedIn, retrieved from https://www.linkedin.com/in/billbunce, November 13, 2014.

63. Todd S. Purdum, "The Nation: The Nondenial Denier," *The New York Times*, February 16, 2003, http://www.nytimes.com/2003/02/16/weekinreview/the-nation-the-nondenial-denier.html.

64. Steven Davidoff Solomon, "Battle Over Darden Restaurants Leaves Little Room for Compromise," *The New York Times*, May 5, 2014, p. B8, http://dealbook.nytimes.com/2014/05/20/battle-over-darden-leaves-little-room-for-compromise.

65. Dan David, "Doublespeak: Recognize It When You Hear It Medium Rare," *Windspeaker* 21, no. 2 (2003), p. 15, retrieved from http://www.ammsa.com/publications/windspeaker/doublespeak-recognize-it-when-you-hear-it-medium-rare, April 9, 2014.

66. William Lutz, "Doublespeak in Education," *Education Week*, November 29, 1989, cited in Henry Beard and Christopher Cerf, *The Official Politically Correct Dictionary and Handbook*, updated edition (New York: Villard Books, 1994), p. 139.

67. William Lutz, "Doublespeak in Education," *Education Week*, November 29, 1989, cited in Henry Beard and Christopher Cerf, *The Official Politically Correct Dictionary and Handbook*, updated edition (New York: Villard Books, 1994), p. 139.

68. Vincent Fernando and Gus Lubin, "20 Examples of Corporate Doublespeak You Need to Know During Earnings Season," Business Insider, October 18, 2010, http://www.businessinsider.com/guide-to-earnings-season-2010?op=1.

69. Joseph Goldstein, "Forbidden Zone for the Police: Places Ready-Made for a Nap," *The New York Times*, p. A1, January 17, 2014.

70. "Intellectual disability," *Medline Plus*, retrieved from http://www.nlm.nih.gov/medlineplus/ency/article/001523.htm, February 18, 2014.

71. Helen Pidd, "New All-White England Kit Could Highlight Stains of Defeat," *The Guardian,* March 29, 2009, http://www.theguardian.com/football/2009/mar/29/new-england-kit-white.

72. John Leo, "Journalese as a Second Tongue," *Time*, March 18, 1985, retrieved from http://bhs.cc/journalism/pdf/pw/journalese.pdf, June 1, 2014.

73. *Quarterly Review of Doublespeak* (National Council of Teachers of English, Urbana, Illinois), July 1991, p. 1, cited in Henry Beard and Christopher Cerf, *The Official Politically Correct Dictionary and Handbook*, updated edition (New York: Villard Books, 1994), p. 139.

74. Washington ethics lawyer Kenneth A. Gross, quoted in Erik Lipton, "Tangled Role in G.O.P. War Over Tea Party," *The New York Times,* January 4, 2014, http://www.nytimes.com/2014/01/04/us/politics/tangled-role-in-gop-war-over-tea-party.html.

75. John Leo, "Reality Gets a Makeover with Words That Buff and Polish," Town hall.com, August 18, 2003, http://townhall.com/columnists/johnleo/2003/08/18/reality_gets_a_makeover_with_words_that_buff_and_polish/page/full.

76. "Johnson Controls Announces New Power Solutions and Interior Experience Leadership Appointments," online press release, Johnson Controls, July 29, 2006, retrieved from http://www.prnewswire.com/news-releases/johnson-controls-announces-new-power-solutions-and-interior-experience-leadership-appointments-56129902.html, October 31, 2014; and William Lutz, interviewed by Jamie Eckle, "CareerWatch: Combatting Doublespeak," *Computer World*, October 24, 2011, http://www.computerworld.com/article/2550212/it-management/career-watch—combatting-doublespeak.html.

77. Alix Rule and David Levine, "International Art English," *Triple Canopy*, July 30, 2012, http://canopycanopycanopy.com/issues/16/contents/international_art_english; and Andy Beckett, "A User's Guide to Artspeak," *The Guardian*, January 27, 2013, http://www.evanstonartcenter.org/sites/default/files/images/Beckett_Art%20Speak%20Guardian.pdf.

78. ("Aspiring scientist and security researcher") Taylor Hornsby, tweet, October 9, 2013, https://twitter.com/DefuseSec/status/387939415776964609.

79. Lorraine J. Smith, "Heal 2 Heal: Training and Beyond: A Little Background. . . . ," web page, retrieved from http://www.heal2heal.net/Heel2HealAboutUs.html, October 16, 2014.

80. Kevin Grolig, "Rockvillian's Guide to Real Estate AdSpeak," October 18, 2012, http://www.kevingrolig.com/rockvillian%E2%80%99s-guide-to-real-estate-adspeak.

81. Ruth Harris, tweet to #pubcode, August 22, 2011, retrieved from https://twitter.com/search?f=realtime&q=%23pubcode, October 20, 2014.

82. William Lutz, *Doublespeak* (New York: HarperCollins, 1990), p. 172.

83. Scott Akire, "Introducing Euphemisms to Language Learners," *The Internet TESL Journal*, http://iteslj.org/Lessons/Alkire-Euphemisms.html.

84. Zachary R. Mider, "Tax Inversion: How U.S. Companies Buy Tax Breaks," Bloomberg.com, July 18, 2014, http://www.bloomberg.com/quicktake/tax-inversion.

85. "Spend/invest," "Doublespeak," NewspeakDictionary.com, http://www.newspeakdictionary.com/ns-same.html.

86. Patrick Reinhart, CheesyCorporateLingo.com, retrieved from http://www.cheesycorporatelingo.com/sections/i, January 26, 2014.

87. "The 5 Most Common Service Desk Euphemisms," Samanage.com, August 9, 2013, http://www.samanage.com/blog/2013/08/the-5-most-common-service-desk-euphemisms.

88. William Davis, "Interfacing with Biz Speak," *The New York Times Magazine*, June 8, 1986, http://www.nytimes.com/1986/06/08/magazine/interfacing-with-biz-speak.html.

89. Don Watson, *Watson's Dictionary of Weasel Words, Contemporary Clichés, Cant, and Management Jargon* (Sydney: Random House of Australia, 2004), p. 181.

90. William Lutz, *Doublespeak* (New York: Harper Perennial, 1990), p. 4, cited in Henry Beard and Christopher Cerf, *The Official Politically Correct Dictionary and Handbook*, updated edition (New York: Villard Books, 1994), p. 139.

91. Geoffrey Nunberg, quoted in David Gillen and Will Storey, "'You're Fired,' in Terms Only a Boss Could Love," *The New York Times*, October 24, 2013, http://www.nytimes.com/2013/10/25/business/youre-fired-in-terms-only-a-boss-could-love.html.

92. "The New Corporate-Speak Hotness: 'Employee Voluntary Separation Programs,'" *Gawker*, April 23, 2007, http://gawker.com/254632/the-new-corporate-speak-hotness-employee-voluntary-separation-programs.

93. "The Ridiculous Business Jargon Dictionary," *The Office Life* (blog), retrieved from http://www.theofficelife.com/business-jargon-dictionary-I.html, January 27, 2014.

94. "Doublespeak," SourceWatch, Center for Media and Democracy, updated August 30, 2009, http://www.sourcewatch.org/index.php/Doublespeak.

95. Timothy Noah, "Bill Clinton and the Meaning of 'Is,'" *Slate*, September 13, 1998, http://www.slate.com/articles/news_and_politics/chatterbox/1998/09/bill_clinton_and_the_meaning_of_is.html.

96. "The Ten Worst Euphemisms," *Man in the Woods* (blog), March 25, 2012, http://woodsydude-gkcrocks.blogspot.com/2012/03/10-worst-euphemisms.html.

97. Carl Hulse, "Ads Attacking Health Law Stagger Outspent Democrats," *The New York Times*, January 15, 2014, http://www.nytimes.com/2014/01/15/us/politics/ads-attacking-on-health-law-stagger-outspent-democrats.html.

98. Steven Poole, "Misspeak," *Unspeak* (blog), March 25, 2008, http://unspeak.net/misspeak.

99. Peter Jones, comment published in Alexander Cockburn, *Guillotined, Being a Summary Broadside Against the Corruption of the English Language* (Petrolia, CA: CounterPunch, 2012), p. 19.

100. Lois Beckwith, "The Dictionary of Corporate Bullshit," video trailer for book *The Dictionary of Corporate Bullshit*, YouTube, uploaded November 6, 2008, http://www.youtube.com/watch?v=KBhcEymNQq0.

101. Duncan Rhodes, "Bluffer's Guide to Wine Tasting," *Catavino* (blog), February 27, 2013, http://catavino.net/bluffers-guide-to-wine-tasting.

102. Dale Bumpers, quoted in Mark Steyn, "Statist Delusions," *National Review Online*, December 10, 2011, http://www.nationalreview.com/articles/285409/statist-delusions-mark-steyn.

j

1. Wayne LaPierre, fund-raising letter for the National Rifle Association, 1995, quoted in "NRA Defends Vitriol Toward Federal Agents / Letter Calls Them 'Jack-booted Thugs,'" Associated Press, May 1, 1995, retrieved from http://www.sfgate.com/news/article/NRA-Defends-Vitriol-Toward-Federal-Agents-3034757.php, July 20, 2014.

2. "Jet lag," Online Slang Dictionary, retrieved from http://slangwordsdictio
nary.com/jet%20lag, May 16, 2014.
3. Matt McMillan, "'Bath Salts' Drug Trend—Expert Q&A," WebMD, February
26, 2013, http://www.webmd.com/mental-health/addiction/features/bath-salts
-drug-dangers; and "Synthetic/Designer Drugs Fact Sheet," Drug Free Marion
County, Marion County, Indiana, retrieved from http://www.drugfreemc.org/
Portals/0/Flyers%20and%20Fact%20Sheets/Designer%20Drugs%20Fact%
20Sheet%20Updated%20January%202012.pdf, September 1, 2014.
4. Jamie Malanowski, "Job Creator: The Republican Euphemism du Jour," *Ten
Mile Square* (a *Washington Monthly* blog), September 20, 2011, http://www
.washingtonmonthly.com/ten-miles-square/2011/09/job_creator_the_repub
lican_eup032318.php.
5. John Perr, "The Republican 'Job-Killing Myth' Gets Demolished," *Daily Kos*,
November 15, 2011, http://www.dailykos.com/story/2011/11/15/1036757/-The
-Republican-Job-Killing-Regulations-Myth-Gets-Demolished; and Michael A.
Livermore, "Use of Phrase 'Job Killing Regulations' Increases 17,550% in
Newspapers Since 2007," *Daily Kos*, April 24, 2013, http://thinkprogress.org/
climate/2012/04/24/469582/phrase-job-killing-regulations-increases
-17000-in-newspapers-since-2007.
6. Michael Spiro, "'In Transition' and Other Awkward Euphemisms," *Recruiter
Musings* (blog), March 30, 2010, retrieved from http://michaelspiro.wordpress
.com/2010/03/30/in-transition-and-other-awkward-euphemisms, July 19,
2014.
7. Michael Spiro, "'In Transition' and Other Awkward Euphemisms," *Recruiter
Musings* (blog), March 30, 2010, retrieved from http://michaelspiro.wordpress
.com/2010/03/30/in-transition-and-other-awkward-euphemisms, July 19, 2014.
8. Georgina Gustin, "F as in Fatter or Food Industry?," *St. Louis Post-Dispatch*,
July 8, 2011, http://www.stltoday.com/business/columns/georgina-gustin/
article_46264936-a9a6-11e0-bacd-001a4bcf6878.html#ixzz1RpHxbBBi.
9. Steven Poole, "An A–Z of Modern Office Jargon," *The Guardian*, October
22, 2013, http://www.theguardian.com/money/2013/oct/22/a-z-modern-office
-jargon.
10. Jerry Merchant and Mary Matthews, "Avoiding Difficult Questions," *The
Right-Wing Christian Dictionary*, ExtremelySmart.com, http://www
.extremelysmart.com/humor/rightwingdictionary.php.
11. *Quarterly Review of Doublespeak* (National Council of Teachers of English,
Urbana, Illinois), July 1991, p. 2, cited in Henry Beard and Christopher Cerf,
The Official Politically Correct Dictionary and Handbook, updated edition
(New York: Villard Books, 1994), p. 139.
12. Michael D. Shear, "G.O.P. Turns to the Courts to Aid Agenda," *The New York
Times*, January 4, 2015, http://www.nytimes.com/2015/01/04/us/politics/gop
-turns-to-the-courts-to-aid-agenda.html.
13. "Junk science," Urban Dictionary, retrieved from http://www.urbandictionary
.com/define.php?term=junk+science, April 19, 2014.

14. Ross Kaplan, "Homes with 'Great Personalities' and Other White Lies," *City Lakes Real Estate Blog* (Minneapolis), March 15, 2013, http://rosskaplan.com/2013/03/real-estate-euphemisms.
15. Penny Tristram, "Arty Bollocks Decoder: What They Say vs What They Mean," *Le Art Corner*, October 19, 2013, http://pennytristram.co.uk/tag/artspeak.
16. David Remnick, "Going the Distance—On and Off the Road with Barack Obama," *The New Yorker*, January 27, 2014, http://www.newyorker.com/magazine/2014/01/27/going-the-distance-2; and Steve Contorno, "What Obama Said About Islamic State as a 'JV Team,'" *Tampa Bay Times*, PolitiFact.com, September 7, 2014, http://www.politifact.com/truth-o-meter/statements/2014/sep/07/barack-obama/what-obama-said-about-islamic-state-jv-team.

k

1. Jonathan Allen, "'Kinetic Military Action' or 'War'?," Politico, March 24, 2011, http://www.politico.com/news/stories/0311/51893.html.

l

1. Blue Rider Press, Facebook page, accessed at https://www.facebook.com/BlueRiderPress, November 7, 2014.
2. "Unequal Naming: The Gulf War 1991," *Guardian Weekly*, February 3, 1991, retrieved from http://www.myread.org/images/cloze/unequal_print.pdf, May 24, 2014.
3. "North Carolina's Hog Waste Lagoons: A Public Health Time Bomb," Environmental Defense Fund, June 10, 1999, cited in Jason Mark, "Eco Euphemisms Confuse Our Understanding of Environmental Destruction," *Earth Island Journal*, March 28, 2014, http://www.earthisland.org/journal/index.php/elist/eListRead/eco_euphemisms_confuse_our_understanding_of_environmental_destruction.
4. Herbert Buchsbaum, "Centreville Journal, Alligators Turn a Couple's Dream into a Court Fight," *The New York Times*, March 20, 2014, http://www.nytimes.com/2014/03/20/us/alligators-turn-mississippi-couples-dream-into-a-court-fight.html.
5. *Critical Reviews in Environmental Science and Technology*, cited in Ivan Oransky (with a "hat tip" to Jaime A. Teixeira da Silva), "A New Plagiarism Euphemism: 'Language from Already Published Sources Without Using Proper Citation Methods,'" *Retraction Watch* (blog), August 23, 2013, http://retractionwatch.com/2013/08/23/a-new-plagiarism-euphemism-language-from-already-published-sources-without-using-proper-citation-methods.
6. Leo F. Buscaglia, "Euphemisms Provide Us Ways to Say What We'd Rather Not," *Milwaukee Sentinel*, August 19, 1985, retrieved from http://news.google.com/newspapers?nid=1368&dat=19850819&id=V4hQAAAAIBAJ&sjid=ahIEAAAAIBAJ&pg=4089,5008215, July 17, 2015.

7. R. W. Holder, *Oxford Dictionary of Euphemisms* (New York: Oxford University Press, 2008), p. 41.

8. Edith Felber, "Long Island Opinion: Euphemism Strikes Again," *The New York Times*, May 26, 1985, http://www.nytimes.com/1985/05/26/nyregion/long -island-opinion-euphemism-strikes-again.html.

9. R. W. Holder, *Oxford Dictionary of Euphemisms* (New York: Oxford University Press, 2008), p. 243.

10. "You Deserve More Than a Plumber!," online advertisement, American Leak Detection, San Bernardino, California, retrieved from www.americanleak detection.com/sanbernardino/residential-service, February 2, 2014.

11. "Euphemism Used in Dismissal," Baidu.com, retrieved from http://wenku .baidu.com/view/1c84df82e53a580216fcfe98.html, May 25, 2014.

12. "What Is Lean Finely Textured Beef?," *Beef* magazine (America's "leading cattle publication"), March 29, 2012, http://beefmagazine.com/beef-quality/ what-lean-finely-textured-beef.

13. Timothy C. Clapper, Ph.D., "Moving Away from Teaching and Becoming a Facilitator of Learning," *PAILAL Newsletter* 2, no. 2, 2009, retrieved from https://www.academia.edu/1180001/Moving_away_from_teaching_and _becoming_a_facilitator_of_learning, October 19, 2014.

14. Patrick Reinhart, CheesyCorporateLingo.com, retrieved from http://www .cheesycorporatelingo.com/sections/1, January 27, 2014.

15. Joel Postman, "10 Business Buzzwords We Can Do Without," *Social Media Today*, April 7, 2011, http://socialmediatoday.com/socialized/284713/10 -business-buzz-words-we-can-do-without.

16. William Lutz, *Doublespeak* (New York: Harper Perennial, 1980), p. 106, cited in Henry Beard and Christopher Cerf, *The Official Politically Correct Dictionary and Handbook*, updated edition (New York: Villard Books, 1994), p. 35.

17. James Warren, "A Nifty Addition to Washington Doublespeak: 'The Least Untruthful' Response," *Daily News* (New York), June 13, 2013, http://www.ny dailynews.com/blogs/dc/nifty-addition-washington-doublespeak-untruthful -response-blog-entry-1.1698143.

18. Sue Horner, "Corporatespeak for Axed," *Get It Write*, November 19, 2010, http://getitwrite.ca/2010/11/19/axed.

19. John Leo, "Journalese as a Second Tongue," *Time*, March 18, 1985, retrieved from http://bhs.cc/journalism/pdf/pw/journalese.pdf, June 1, 2014.

20. Rob Kyff, "Obfuscation Clearly Pervasive," *Hartford Courant*, March 22, 2010, http://articles.courant.com/2005-03-22/features/0503220194_1_tax -cuts-social-security-tax-relief.

21. Judith S. Neaman and Carole G. Silver, *Kind Words* (New York: Avon Books, 1991), p. 334, cited in Henry Beard and Christopher Cerf, *The Official Politically Correct Dictionary and Handbook*, updated edition (New York: Villard Books, 1994), p. 140.

22. Sethuraman Subramanian, "Notes from North Carolina: Political Euphemisms Galore," Chennaionline.com, February 27, 2010,

http://chennaionline.com/Columns/Notes-From-North-Carolina/Political
-Euphemisms-Galore/20104027104050.col.

23. John Eligon and Michael Schwirtz, "Senate Candidate Provokes Ire with
'Legitimate Rape' Comment," *The New York Times*, August 19, 2012, p. A13,
http://www.nytimes.com/2012/08/20/us/politics/todd-akin-provokes-ire
-with-legitimate-rape-comment.html.

24. Ted Scott, "Self-Deceiving Euphemisms," July 14, 2012, http://tedscott
.aampersanda.com/2012/07/14/self-deceiving-euphemisms.

25. Rob Kyff, "Negative Patient Care Outcome? Yes, Euphemisms Are Alive and
Well," *Hartford Courant*, April 4, 1997, http://articles.courant.com/1997-04
-04/features/9705230902_1_assisted-new-euphemism-nursing-home-care.

26. Steven Poole, "An A–Z of Modern Office Jargon," *The Guardian*, October 22,
2013, http://www.theguardian.com/money/2013/oct/22/a-z-modern-office
-jargon.

27. Lynn Schneider, "20 Examples of Great Euphemisms," December 23, 2011,
http://lynnschneiderbooks.com/2011/12/23/20-examples-of-great
-euphemisms.

28. Norman Solomon, *The Power of Babble* (New York: Dell, 1992), p. 152.

29. Ron Torossian, "There Is No Such Thing as 'Occupied Territory' in Israel,"
The Algemeiner, July 3, 2014, http://www.algemeiner.com/2014/07/03/there-is
-no-such-thing-as-occupied-territory.

30. Joe Crubaugh, "How to Speak Pentagonese," JoeCrubaugh.com, November 24,
2006, http://joecrubaugh.com/blog/2006/11/24/how-to-speak-pentagonese.

31. Andrew Blum, "The Mall Goes Undercover," *Slate*, April 6, 2005, http://www
.slate.com/articles/arts/culturebox/2005/04/the_mall_goes_undercover
.html.

32. Gordon Pritchard, "Marketing 101—'Weasel' Words," *The Print Guide* (blog),
May 3, 2012, http://the-print-guide.blogspot.com/2012/05/marketing-101
-weasel-words.html.

33. Steve Eder, "Rodriguez's 'Gummies': Files Detail Doping, Down to Milligram,"
The New York Times, January 14, 2014, p. A1.

34. "Euphemisms," *The Economist Style Guide*, retrieved from http://www
.economist.com/style-guide/euphemisms.

35. Adrian Wooldridge, "Too Many Chiefs: Inflation in Job Titles Is Approaching
Weimar Levels," Schumpeter column, *The Economist,* June 24, 2010, http://
www.economist.com/node/16423358.

36. Carol Rosenberg, "U.S. Now Calls Guantánamo Hunger Strike 'Long Term
Non-Religious Fasting,'" *The Miami Herald*, March 11, 2013; and
"Guantanamo Detainees' Hunger Strikes Will No Longer Be Disclosed by U.S.
Military," Associated Press, December 4, 2013, retrieved from http://www
.washingtonpost.com/world/national-security/guantanamo-detainees-hunger
-strikes-will-no-longer-be-disclosed-by-us-military/2013/12/04/f6b1aa96-
5d24-11e3-bc56-c6ca94801fac_story.html, October 24, 2014.

37. Jack Shafer, "Shut Your Loophole," *Slate*, July 24, 2007, http://www.slate.com/
articles/news_and_politics/press_box/2007/07/shut_your_loophole.html.

38. Luke Mullins, "The Real Estate Euphemism Pocket Translator," *U.S. News & World Report*: Money, September 9, 2008, http://money.usnews.com/money/blogs/the-home-front/2008/09/09/the-real-estate-euphemism-pocket-translator.

39. Conor MacEvilly, "Real Estate Lingo and Euphemisms," *My North Seattle Home,* http://www.mynorthseattlehome.com/finding-the-right-home-for-me/real-estate-lingo-and-euphemisms-nw-style.

40. Milica Radulović, "Expressing Values in Positive and Negative Euphemisms," *Facta Universitatis: Series Linguistics and Literature* 10, no. 1, 2012, p. 20, retrieved from http://facta.junis.ni.ac.rs/lal/lal201201/lal201201-03.pdf, August 17, 2014.

41. "More Than Just a 'Gas' Station," *Electrical Contractor*, April 2003, http://www.ecmag.com/section/codes-standards/more-just-gas-station.

42. Jon Pareles, "ABC Avoids a Lyric Malfunction but Allows Mick's Midriff," *The New York Times*, February 6, 2006, http://www.nytimes.com/2006/02/06/sports/football/06half.html.

m

1. James Hohmann, "George Allen Apologizes for 'Macaca' Moment," *Politico*, June 3, 2011, http://www.politico.com/news/stories/0611/56212.html.

2. Paul Dickson and Robert Skole, *Journalese: A Dictionary for Deciphering the News* (Portland, OR: Marion Street Press, 2012), cited in Bill Lucey, "Finally, a Dictionary for Deciphering the News," *Newspaper Alum* (blog), March 4, 2013, retrieved from http://www.newspaperalum.com/2013/03/finally-a-dictionary-for-deciphering-the-news.html, July 7, 2014.

3. Steve Rubenstein, "Plain Speaking Also Falls Victim to Cisco's Ax," *San Francisco Chronicle*, March 10, 2001, http://www.sfgate.com/business/article/Plain-Speaking-Also-Falls-Victim-to-Cisco-s-Ax-2943774.php.

4. Peer Lawther, "25 Euphemisms for 'You've Been Made Redundant,'" *StepChange MoneyAware* (blog), November 11, 2011, http://moneyaware.co.uk/2011/11/25-euphemisms-for-youve-been-made-redundant.

5. "Fooled by Food Labels: 9 Deceptive Claims to Watch Out For," CNCA Health, retrieved from http://www.cncahealth.com/explore/learn/nutrition-food/fooled-by-food-labels-9-deceptive-claims-to-watch-out-for#.U1LL0McozSB, April 19, 2014; and Tara Parker-Pope, "Six Meaningless Claims on Food Labels," *The New York Times*, January 28, 2010, http://well.blogs.nytimes.com/2010/01/28/six-meaningless-claims-on-food-labels.

6. Eric Bolling, remarks on *Bulls & Bears*, Fox Business Channel, July 24, 2010, retrieved from http://mediamatters.org/video/2010/07/24/bolling-is-glad-the-young-will-have-to-work-rat/168211.

7. Ben Evans, "'Major Malfunction': The Final Launch of Challenger, 28 Years Ago Today," AmericaSpace, January 28, 2014, http://www.americaspace.com/?p=50764.

8. Chase.com, https://www.chase.com, 2012.

9. Frank Luntz, "A Cleaner, Safer, Healthier America," excerpt from a memorandum to the Bush White House, 2002, retrieved from https://www2 .bc.edu/~plater/Newpublicsite06/suppmats/02.6.pdf, November 4, 2014.

10. Bari'ah Naqshabandi, "Women's Changing Participation in Jordan," doctoral thesis, University of Durham (England), August 29, 1995, http://etheses.dur.ac .uk/998/1/998.pdf.

11. "Napolitano Tells It Like It Isn't," editorial, *The Washington Times*, March 29, 2009, www.washingtontimes.com/news/2009/mar/29/tell-it-like-it-is-man -caused-disasters-is-napolit.

12. "Business Cliches and Phrases," *Said What?* (blog), retrieved from http://www .saidwhat.co.uk/bizphrases.php, October 21, 2014.

13. William Lutz, "Life Under the Chief Doublespeak Officer," accessed at www.dt .org/html/Doublespeak.html, November 20, 2014.

14. "Nokia Siemens Networks Puts Mobile Broadband and Services at the Heart of Its Strategy; Initiates Restructuring to Maintain Long-Term Competitiveness and Improve Profitability," press release, Nokia Siemens Networks, November 23, 2011, http://company.nokia.com/en/news/press -releases/2011/11/23/nokia-siemens-networks-puts-mobile-broadband-and -services-at-the-heart-of-its-strategy-initiates-restructuring-to-maintain -long-term-competitiveness-and-improve-profitability.

15. John Leo, "On Society: Evasive Language Results in Suboptimal Outcomes," *The Porterville Reporter*, February 27, 2006, retrieved from http://www .recorderonline.com/on-society-evasive-language-results-in-suboptimal -outcomes/article_91862650-3314-558c-a0f8-c1c0a627beee.html, August 21, 2014.

16. Richard Lederer, "Oxymoronology," *Word Ways: The Journal of Recreational Linguistics*, 1990, retrieved from http://www.fun-with-words.com/oxym _oxymoronology.html, February 16, 2014.

17. Kurt Mortensen, "Doublespeak: Words Evoke Emotions," ArticlesBase.com, October 27, 2006, http://www.articlesbase.com/affiliate-programs-articles/ doublespeak-words-invoke-emotions-67728.html.

18. Johann Hari, "Lies, Damned Lies . . . and the Double-Speak I Would Expunge," *The Independent,* September 2, 2009, http://www.independent.co.uk/voices/ commentators/johann-hari/johann-hari-lies-damned-lies-and-the -doublespeak-i-would-expunge-1780241.html.

19. Rob Kyff, "Modern-Day Euphemisms Can Leave Head in a Spin," *Hartford Courant*, January 18, 2010, http://articles.courant.com/2010-01-18/news/hc -words0118.artjan18_1_euphemisms-negative-patient-care-outcome-motion -discomfort.

20. Lisa Duggan, "Beyond Marriage: Democracy, Equality, and Kinship for a New Century," *The Scholar and Feminist Online*, Fall 2011/Spring 2012, retrieved from http://sfonline.barnard.edu/a-new-queer-agenda/beyond -marriage-democracy-equality-and-kinship-for-a-new-century, April 25, 2014.

21. J. P. Grace, "Euphemisms Mask Realities of Sexual Politics," *Huntington Herald-Dispatch* (Huntington, West Virginia), July 8, 2013, http://www.herald -dispatch.com/opinions/x1489433633/JP-Grace-Euphemisms-mask -realities-of-sexual-politics.

22. Patrick Reinhart, CheesyCorporateLingo.com, http://www.cheesycorporate lingo.com/sections/m.

23. Ronni Bennett, "The Danger of Euphemism," *Time Goes By* (blog), October 7, 2005, http://www.timegoesby.net/weblog/2005/10/the_danger_of_e.html.

24. Robert Todd Carroll, "Weasel Words," *The Skeptic's Dictionary*, updated December 24, 2013, http://www.skepdic.com/weaselwords.html.

25. "On Euphemism," CCJK.com, June 29, 2012, http://www.ccjk.com/on -euphemism.

26. Kenneth A. Osgood, "Propaganda," *Encyclopedia of the New American Nation*, retrieved from http://www.americanforeignrelations.com/O-W/Propaganda .html#b, July 21, 2014.

27. Daniel Okrent, "The War of the Words: A Dispatch from the Front Lines," *The New York Times*, March 6, 2005, http://www.nytimes.com/2005/03/06/week inreview/06bott.html?pagewanted=1&_r=0&oref=login.

28. Carolyn McClanahan, "What Is a Medical Loss Ratio? The Check Will Be in the Mail," *Forbes*, May 15, 2012, http://www.forbes.com/sites/carolyn mcclanahan/2012/05/15/what-is-a-medical-loss-ratio-the-check-will-be-in -the-mail/.

29. Darryl K. Taft, "IBM Layoffs Begin in Workforce Rebalancing Effort," eWeek, March 1, 2014, http://www.eweek.com/it-management/ibm-layoffs-begin-in -workforce-rebalancing-effort.html.

30. "Doublespeak Examples," *Damron Planet* (blog), retrieved from http://www .damronplanet.com/doublespeak/examples.htm, February 18, 2014.

31. Ross Kaplan, "Homes with 'Great Personalities' and Other White Lies," *City Lakes Real Estate Blog* (Minneapolis), March 15, 2013, http://rosskaplan.com/ 2013/03/real-estate-euphemisms.

32. Dan McCarthy, "Office Jargon," *HR People*, March 27, 2009, http://hrpeople .monster.com/news/articles/2035-office-jargon?page=3&utm_content=art mini&utm_source=hrpeople.com.

33. "Office Jargon for the 21st Century," DangerousLogic.com, retrieved from http://www.dangerouslogic.com/office_lexicon.html, January 26, 2014.

34. Paul Wasserman and Don Hausrath, *Weasel Words: The Dictionary of American Doublespeak* (Herndon, VA: Capital Books, 2006), quoted in "The Art of Deceptive Language," Advance Healthcare Network for Speech and Hearing, January 9, 2006, http://speech-language-pathology-audiology .advanceweb.com/Article/The-Art-of-Deceptive-Language.aspx.

35. "Residential Milieu Coordinator," job posting, Cunningham Children's Home, SocialService.com, December 23, 2013, http://www.socialservice.com/job details.cfm/62215/Residential-Milieu-Coordinator.

36. Stephen M. Walt, "What's in a Name?," *Foreign Policy*, July 7, 2010, http://www .foreignpolicy.com/posts/2010/07/07/whats_in_a_name.

37. Mark Peters, "One Man's Trash Is Another Man's Service Item," Visual Thesaurus, July 7, 2014, http://www.visualthesaurus.com/cm/evasive/one -mans-trash-is-another-mans-service-item.

38. William Lutz, "Doublespeak," *Public Relations Quarterly*, Winter 1988–1989, http://users.manchester.edu/FacStaff/MPLahman/Homepage/BerkebileMy Website/doublespeak.pdf.

39. Richard H. Polsky, Ph.D., "The Case of Diane Whipple," *Dog Behavior & the Law*, reprinted in "The San Francisco Dog Mauling," retrieved from http:// www.sfdogmauling.com/CaseofWhipple.html, July 7, 2014.

40. Philip S. Gutis, "On Land and in Air, Kennedy Delays Persist," *The New York Times*, January 19, 1990, http://www.nytimes.com/1990/01/19/nyregion/on -land-and-in-air-kennedy-delays-persist.html.

41. "Euphemisms: Say Less with More" (*Johnson* blog), *The Economist*, July 7, 2010, http://www.economist.com/blogs/johnson/2010/07/euphemisms.

42. Steve Rubin, "Uses and Abuses of Language," Santa Rosa Junior College, November 27, 2013, http://online.santarosa.edu/presentation/page/?30609.

43. "Figures of Speech: Euphemism Examples," retrieved from http://fos.ilove india.com/euphemism-examples.html, January 13, 2014.

44. University of Oregon School of Journalism and Communication, "Euphemism— Definition and List," retrieved from http://journalism.uoregon.edu/~tbivins/ J496/readings/LANGUAGE/euphemism_defandlist.pdf, February 16, 2014.

45. Steve Rubin, "Uses and Abuses of Language," Santa Rosa Junior College, November 27, 2013, http://online.santarosa.edu/presentation/page/?30609.

46. Hugh Rawson, *A Dictionary of Euphemisms and Other Doubletalk* (New York: Crown, 1981), p. 184.

47. Jonathan Denn, "Is Ending 'Too Big to Fail' Banking a GREATER Idea," Independent Voter Network, April 24, 2013, http://ivn.us/2013/04/24/is -ending-too-big-to-fail-banking-a-greater-idea; and Rod Adams, "Don't Allow EPA to Use 'Modernize' as Euphemism for 'Tighten,'" *Atomic Insights* (blog), February 4, 2014, http://atomicinsights.com/dont-allow-epa-use-modernize -euphemism-tighten.

48. Sarah Anderson, "Understanding Corporate Doublespeak on Social Security," *Athens Banner-Herald* (Athens, Georgia), November 23, 2013, http://online athens.com/opinion/2013-11-23/anderson-understanding-corporate -doublespeak-social-security.

49. Robert Sutton, "A Compilation of Euphemisms for Layoffs," *Work Matters* (blog), November 16, 2008, http://bobsutton.typepad.com/my_weblog/2008/ 11/a-compilation-of-euphemisms-for-layoffs.html.

50. Norman Solomon, *The Power of Babble* (New York: Dell, 1992), p. 169.

51. Wayne Biddle, "Mr. $600 Toilet Seat: On the Death of Lawrence Kitchen," WayneBiddle.com, December 24, 2013, http://waynebiddle.com/on-the-death -of-lawrence-kitchen.

52. Randy Parker, "Euphemism Can Lead to Copywriting Sin," *Wordnut* (blog), February 19, 2009, http://wordnut.com/2009/02/19/euphemism-can-lead-to -copywriting-sin.

53. Mark Peters, "A Bad Case of the Peedoodles," Visual Thesaurus, March 5, 2010, http://www.visualthesaurus.com/cm/evasive/a-bad-case-of-the -peedoodles.

54. "Beheading of Convicted Drug Dealers Discussed by Bennett," *Los Angeles Times*, June 16, 1989, http://articles.latimes.com/1989-06-16/news/mn-2008 _1_drug-dealers-beheading-fight-against-illegal-drugs.

55. "The Rule of Verbal Packaging—The Leverage of Language," chap. 8 of *The Rules of Persuasion* (Westside Toastmasters, Los Angeles), retrieved from http://westsidetoastmasters.com/resources/laws_persuasion/chap8.html, April 18, 2014.

56. "Euphemisms and Jargon in American English," University of Tampere (Finland), April 3, 2013, http://www15.uta.fi/FAST/US1/REF/euphemism .html.

57. "More Than Just a 'Gas' Station," *Electrical Contractor*, April 2003, http:// www.ecmag.com/section/codes-standards/more-just-gas-station.

58. Steven Poole, "Royal Mail: The Rhetoric of Privatisation," *The Guardian*, September 20, 2013, http://www.theguardian.com/books/2013/sep/20/answer -unspeak-is-more-unspeak.

59. Hugh Delehanty, editor of *Modern Maturity*, interview with Charles Gibson, *Good Morning America*, April 12, 2001, http://abcnews.go.com/GMA/story ?id=127077.

60. "Islamic State Urges Attacks on US, Calls Obama 'Mule of the Jews,'" *The Jerusalem Post*, September 22, 2014, http://www.jpost.com/Middle-East/ Islamic-State-urges-attacks-on-US-calls-Obama-mule-of-the-Jews-376035.

61. Jonny Geller, tweet to #publishingeuphemisms, February 23, 2012, https:// twitter.com/search?q=%23publishingeuphemisms.

62. Tweet to #publishingeuphemisms, cited in R. Garcia, "Some Reflections on Publishing Euphemisms," *Phantomimic* (blog), February 25, 2012, http:// phantomimic.weebly.com/blog-the-eclectic-life/publishing-euphemisms.

63. Michael Delahunt, ArtLex Art Dictionary, retrieved from http://artlex.com, February 18, 2014.

64. "The Ridiculous Business Jargon Dictionary," *The Office Life* (blog), retrieved from http://www.theofficelife.com/business-jargon-dictionary-M.html, January 27, 2014.

n

1. "Fooled by Food Labels: 9 Deceptive Claims to Watch Out For," CNCA Health, retrieved from http://www.cncahealth.com/explore/learn/nutrition-food/ fooled-by-food-labels-9-deceptive-claims-to-watch-out-for#.U1LL0McozSB, April 19, 2014.

2. Michelle Cottle, "What Is 'Natural Marriage,'" *The Daily Beast*, March 27, 2014, http://www.thedailybeast.com/articles/2014/03/27/the-family-research -council-s-natural-marriage-fight.html.

3. Steven Poole, *Unspeak* (New York: Grove Press, 2006), pp. 64–65.

4. William Lutz, *Doublespeak* (New York: Harper Perennial, 1980), p. 61, cited in
    Henry Beard and Christopher Cerf, *The Official Politically Correct Dictionary
    and Handbook*, updated edition (New York: Villard Books, 1994), p. 41.

5. Jack Smith, "Clearly It's a Plastic Language with Devious Overtones," *Los
    Angeles Times*, October 24, 1990, http://articles.latimes.com/1990-10-24/
    news/vw-2724_1_clear-language.

6. William Lutz, *Doublespeak* (New York: Harper Perennial, 1990), p. 63, cited in
    Henry Beard and Christopher Cerf, *The Official Politically Correct Dictionary
    and Handbook*, updated edition (New York: Villard Books, 1994), p. 140.

7. Gary C. Woodward and Robert E. Denton, Jr., *Persuasion and Influence in
    American Life,* 7th edition (Long Grove, IL: Waveland Press, 2014), p. 70.

8. D. J. Kehl and Howard Livingston, "Doublespeak Detection for the English
    Classroom," *The English Journal,* July 1999, p. 79, retrieved from
    http://www.jstor.org/discover/10.2307/822191?uid=3739832&uid=2134&uid
    =2479801677&uid=2&uid=70&uid=3&uid=2479801667&uid=3739256&uid
    =60&sid=21103823248907, April 8, 2014.

9. "Archives: Banished Words 2001," Lake Superior State University, 2001, re-
    trieved from http://www.lssu.edu/banished/archive/2001.php, April 20, 2014.

10. Ralph Keyes, *Euphemania: Our Love Affair with Euphemisms* (New York:
    Little, Brown, 2010), p. 167.

11. Stephen Law, "Pseudo-profundity—from *Believing Bullshit*," June 15, 2011,
    http://stephenlaw.blogspot.com/2011/06/pseudo-profundity-from-believing
    .html.

12. Rob Kyff, "Negative Patient Care Outcome? Yes, Euphemisms Are Alive and
    Well," *Hartford Courant*, April 4, 1997, http://articles.courant.com/1997-04
    -04/features/9705230902_1_assisted-new-euphemism-nursing-home-care.

13. Hugh Rawson, *A Dictionary of Euphemisms and Other Doubletalk* (New York:
    Crown, 1981), p. 190.

14. "Business Jargon," *The Skibbereen Eagle*, August 6, 2007, http://www.skibber
    eeneagle.ie/?p=796.

15. "Hospital Defends Decision Not to Treat Man with Knife in Back," Associated
    Press, October 27, 1980, quoted in Paul, McFedries, "Wallet Biopsy," *Word
    Spy*, retrieved from http://wordspy.com/words/walletbiopsy.asp, July 3,
    2014.

16. Michael Sebastian, "The 10 Most Useless Buzzwords," *PR Daily*, December 20,
    2012, http://www.entrepreneur.com/article/225310.

17. Tsafi Saar, "We Have Lied," *Haaretz*, October 7, 2011, http://www.haaretz
    .com/weekend/week-s-end/we-have-lied-1.388695.

18. William Safire, "On Language: Euphemisms and Other Upgradings," *The New
    York Times* (syndicated), August 14, 1983, retrieved from http://news.google
    .com/newspapers?nid=1346&dat=19830814&id=LVlRAAAAIBAJ&sjid=hfs
    DAAAAIBAJ&pg=3936,4767835, November 2, 2014.

19. *The Free Dictionary,* retrieved from http://www.thefreedictionary.com/
    neutralization, January 14, 2014.

20. Ross Kaplan, "Homes with 'Great Personalities' and Other White Lies," *City Lakes Real Estate Blog* (Minneapolis), March 15, 2013, http://rosskaplan.com/2013/03/real-estate-euphemisms.

21. Evan Osnos, "Will the Middle Class Shake China?" *The New Yorker,* March 8, 2013, http://www.newyorker.com/news/daily-comment/will-the-middle-class-shake-china.

22. Bill Allen, comment published in Alexander Cockburn, *Guillotined, Being a Summary Broadside Against the Corruption of the English Language* (Petrolia, CA: CounterPunch, 2012), pp. 25–26.

23. Randy Parker, "Euphemism Can Lead to Copywriting Sin," *Wordnut* (blog), February 19, 2009, http://wordnut.com/2009/02/19/euphemism-can-lead-to-copywriting-sin; http://www.newtouauto.com; and http://www.nu2ucars.biz/TN/nu2ucars.

24. Iain Paton, quoted in Janice Harayda, "23 British Publishing Euphemisms Decoded by Industry Experts," *One-Minute Book Reviews* (blog), February 24, 2012, http://oneminutebookreviews.wordpress.com/2012/02/24/23-british-publishing-euphemisms-decoded-by-industry-experts.

25. Bryon Quertermous, quoted in Janice Harayda, "40 Publishing Buzzwords, Clichés and Euphemisms Decoded," August 21, 2011, http://oneminutebookreviews.wordpress.com/2011/08/21/40-publishing-buzzwords-cliches-and-euphemisms-decoded.

26. George Black, "Briefing Speak," anthologized in Micah Sifry and Christopher Cerf, *The Gulf War Reader* (New York: Times Books/Random House, 1991), cited in Henry Beard and Christopher Cerf, *The Official Politically Correct Dictionary and Handbook*, updated edition (New York: Villard Books, 1994), p. 141.

27. Mat Johnson, quoted in Janice Harayda, "More Publishing Buzzwords Decoded with Wit on Twitter," *One-Minute Book Reviews* (blog), August 31, 2011, http://oneminutebookreviews.wordpress.com/2011/08/31.

28. Arthur H. Hawkins, *Self-Discipline in Labor-Management Relations,* quoted in Mario Pei, *Double-Speak in America* (New York: Hawthorn Books, 1973), p. 137, cited in Henry Beard and Christopher Cerf, *The Official Politically Correct Dictionary and Handbook*, updated edition (New York: Villard Books, 1994), p. 124.

29. John Lanchester, "Annals of Argot—Money Talks," *The New Yorker,* August 4, 2014, http://www.newyorker.com/magazine/2014/08/04/money-talks-6.

30. Ross McMullin, "The Great Deceiver Is in a Class of His Own," *The Age* (Melbourne, Australia), November 13, 2007, http://www.theage.com.au/news/opinion/the-great-deceiver-is-in-a-class-of-his-own/2007/11/12/1194766588117.html?page=fullpage.

31. *Quarterly Review of Doublespeak* (National Council of Teachers of English, Urbana, Illinois), April 1991, p. 9, cited in Henry Beard and Christopher Cerf, *The Official Politically Correct Dictionary and Handbook*, updated edition (New York: Villard Books, 1994), p. 141.

32. Robert Harris, "Semantics 2: Denotation and Connotation," *Virtual Salt* (blog), June 8, 2000, http://www.virtualsalt.com/think/semant2.htm.

33. Rona Fried, "Heartland Releases More Hogwash Ahead of IPCC Climate Change Report," SustainableBusiness.com, March 24, 2014, http://www.sustainablebusiness.com/index.cfm/go/news.display/id/25601.

34. Rob Kyff, "Negative Patient Care Outcome? Yes, Euphemisms Are Alive and Well," *Hartford Courant*, April 4, 1997, http://articles.courant.com/1997-04-04/features/9705230902_1_assisted-new-euphemism-nursing-home-care.

35. "Business Regulations: Adult-Oriented Businesses," Dana Point Municipal Code, Dana Point, California, July 2014, retrieved from http://www.qcode.us/codes/danapoint/view.php?topic=5-5_32-5_32_050&frames=on, September 6, 2014.

36. *Quarterly Review of Doublespeak* (National Council of Teachers of English, Urbana, Illinois), April 1990, p. 7, cited in Henry Beard and Christopher Cerf, *The Official Politically Correct Dictionary and Handbook*, updated edition (New York: Villard Books, 1994), p. 141.

37. Glenn Thompson, "The 12 Most Horrifically Misleading Euphemisms," Cracked.com, December 16, 2008, http://www.cracked.com/article_16884_the-12-most-horrifically-misleading-euphemisms_p2.html.

38. S. Murlidharan, "For Banks, ALM as Big a Problem as NPA," *Business Standard*, March 23, 2014, http://www.business-standard.com/article/opinion/for-banks-alm-as-big-a-problem-as-npa-114032300747_1.html.

39. School Board in Cleveland, Ohio, 1982, cited in William Lutz, "Doublespeak in Education," *Education Week*, November 29, 1989, cited in Henry Beard and Christopher Cerf, *The Official Politically Correct Dictionary and Handbook*, updated edition (New York: Villard Books, 1994), p. 141.

40. Stephen M. Perle, D.C., M.S., "Euphemisms or Lies?," American Chiropractic Association, December 2010, https://www.acatoday.org/content_css.cfm?CID=4203.

41. Janet Allon, "From the Mean-Spirited to the Asinine: 7 Prime Examples of Right-Wing Lunacy This Week," AlterNet, September 28, 2013, http://www.alternet.org/tea-party-and-right/mean-spirited-asinine-7-prime-examples-right-wing-lunacy-week?page=0%2C2.

42. John Leo, "Reality Gets a Makeover with Words That Buff and Polish," Town hall.com, August 18, 2003, http://townhall.com/columnists/johnleo/2003/08/18/reality_gets_a_makeover_with_words_that_buff_and_polish/page/full.

43. Sheryl Gay Stolberg. "Gingrich Set to Run, with Wife in Central Role," *The New York Times*, May 9, 2011, http://www.nytimes.com/2011/05/10/us/politics/10gingrich.html.

44. John Leo, "Euphemism, Double-Speak Marginalize the Language," *The Seattle Times*, August 15, 1995, http://community.seattletimes.nwsource.com/archive/?date=19950815&slug=2136517; and Myriam Marquez, "Hey, President Wishy-washy: Lani Guinier Is No Sister Souljah, *Orlando Sentinel*,

June 4, 1993, http://articles.orlandosentinel.com/1993-06-04/news/ 9306041106_1_lani-guinier-bork-distorted.

45. William Lutz, *Doublespeak* (New York: Harper Perennial, 1990), p. 145, cited in Henry Beard and Christopher Cerf, *The Official Politically Correct Dictionary and Handbook*, updated edition (New York: Villard Books, 1994), p. 141.

46. Steve Rubenstein, "Plain Speaking Also Falls Victim to Cisco's Ax," *San Francisco Chronicle*, March 10, 2001, http://www.sfgate.com/business/ article/Plain-Speaking-Also-Falls-Victim-to-Cisco-s-Ax-2943774.php.

47. Marianne DiNapoli, "Rantings and Conspiracy Theories on Medical Jargon," *Times Union* (Albany, New York), October 7, 2010, http://blog.timesunion.com/ mdtobe/rantings-and-conspiracy-theories-on-medical-jargon/255.

48. Penn Bullock and Brandon K. Thorp, "Christian Right Leader George Rekers Takes Vacation with 'Rent Boy,'" *Miami New Times*, May 6, 2010, http://www .miaminewtimes.com/2010-05-06/news/christian-right-leader-george -rekers-takes-vacation-with-rent-boy; and Dan Amira, "The Six Worst Excuses by Anti-Gay Public Figures Caught Doing (Allegedly) Gay Things," *New York*, August 29, 2011, http://nymag.com/daily/intelligencer/2011/08/ worst_excuses_gay_politicians.html.

49. William Lutz, *Doublespeak* (New York: HarperCollins, 1990), p. 14.

50. Evan Peter Smith, "A Drug Called Molly—The Rest of the Story," *The Athens News* (Athens, Ohio), January 12, 2014, http://www.athensnews.com/ohio/ article-41478-a-drug-called-molly-the-rest-of-the-story.html; and Matt McMillan, "'Bath Salts' Drug Trend—Expert Q&A," WebMD, February 26, 2013, http://www.webmd.com/mental-health/addiction/features/bath-salts -drug-dangers.

51. Paul Dickson and Robert Skole, *Journalese: A Dictionary for Deciphering the News* (Portland, OR: Marion Street Press, 2012), cited in Bill Lucey, "Finally, a Dictionary for Deciphering the News," *Newspaper Alum* (blog), March 4, 2013, http://www.newspaperalum.com/2013/03/finally-a-dictionary-for -deciphering-the-news.html.

52. Norman Solomon, *The Power of Babble* (New York: Dell, 1992), p. 184.

53. Larry Hughes, cited in Janice Harayda, "40 Publishing Buzzwords, Clichés and Euphemisms Decoded," *One-Minute Book Reviews* (blog), August 21, 2011, http://oneminutebookreviews.wordpress.com/2011/08/21/40-publishing -buzzwords-cliches-and-euphemisms-decoded.

54. Mike Walsh, "The Bush Euphemism Game: When Lies Cannot be Called 'Lies,'" 2003, *Mouth Wash* (blog), retrieved from http://www.missioncreep.com/mw/ bushlie.htm, November 18, 2014.

55. John Stauber and Sheldon Rampton, "The Fog of War Talk," AlterNet, July 27, 2003, http://www.alternet.org/story/16497/the_fog_of_war_talk.

56. Steve Rubin, "Uses and Abuses of Language," Santa Rosa Junior College, November 27, 2013, retrieved from http://online.santarosa.edu/presentation/ page/?30609, January 11, 2014.

O

1. "Incontinence and OAB Overview," WebMD, retrieved from http://www
   .webmd.com/urinary-incontinence-oab, June 3, 2014.
2. "Steven Poole, "From Facebook to Twitter: Why Advertisers Love
   Euphemism," *The Guardian*, November 21, 2013, http://www.theguardian
   .com/books/2013/nov/21/facebook-twitter-advertisers-love-euphemism.
3. Michael Spiro, "'In Transition' and Other Awkward Euphemisms," *Recruiter
   Musings* (blog), March 30, 2010, http://michaelspiro.wordpress.com/2010/03/
   30/in-transition-and-other-awkward-euphemisms.
4. "What Is an Office Manager Really?," City-Data Forum: Work and
   Employment, retrieved from http://www.city-data.com/forum/work
   -employment/2045187-what-office-manager-really.html, April 14, 2014.
5. Freeland, "Why #RussiaInvadedUkraine Matters," *The New York Times,*
   September 6, 2014, p. A21.
6. Kate Cocuzzo, "Real Estate Euphemisms: An Agent's Literary Loophole," *Geo
   Properties, Inc.* (blog), May 21, 2013, http://www.geopropertiesinc.com/word
   press/real-estate-euphemisms-an-agents-literary-loophole.
7. Gini Dietrich, "Top 20 Buzzwords PR Pros Use," ragan.com, January 16, 2013,
   http://www.ragan.com/Main/Articles/Top_20_buzzwords_PR_pros_use
   _46071.aspx#.
8. Dick Cheney, interviewed by Wolf Blitzer on *The Situation Room*, January 25,
   2007, transcript, CNN.com, retrieved from http://i.a.cnn.net/cnn/2007/
   images/01/24/cheney.transcript.pdf, July 14, 2014; and Barbara Morrill, "Dick
   Cheney on Iraq," *Daily Kos*, January 25, 2007, http://www.dailykos.com/story/
   2007/01/25/294631/-Dick-Cheney-On-Iraq.
9. Robert Todd Carroll, "Weasel Words," *The Skeptic's Dictionary*, updated
   December 30, 2013, http://www.skepdic.com/weaselwords.html.
10. Elizabeth Becker, "A Nation Challenged; Renaming an Operation to Fit the
    Mood," *The New York Times*, September 26, 2001, http://www.nytimes.com/
    2001/09/26/us/a-nation-challenged-renaming-an-operation-to-fit-the-mood
    .html.
11. Spencer Ackerman, "A Glossary of Iraq Euphemisms," *The American Prospect*,
    August 6, 2008, http://prospect.org/article/glossary-iraq-euphemisms.
12. John B. Oakes, "Bush in Panama: A Tragicomedy," *The New York Times,*
    January 28, 1990, http://www.nytimes.com/1990/01/26/opinion/bush-in
    -panama-a-tragicomedy.html; and John M. McClintock, "Panama Leader's
    Bank Is Linked to Drug Money," *The Baltimore Sun*, October 23, 1990, http://
    articles.baltimoresun.com/1990-10-23/news/1990296066_1_general
    -noriega-endara-panama.
13. Tsafi Saar, "We Have Lied," *Haaretz*, October 7, 2011, http://www.haaretz
    .com/weekend/week-s-end/we-have-lied-1.388695.
14. Paul Abercrombie, "The 25 Least Inspiring Military Operation Names,"
    Cracked.com, April 27, 2008, http://www.cracked.com/article_16213_the-25
    -least-inspiring-military-operation-names_p2.html.

15. Geoffrey Nunberg, "A Name Too Far," *San Jose Mercury News*, September 30, 2001, retrieved from http://people.ischool.berkeley.edu/~nunberg/operations .html, October 5, 2014.

16. Geoffrey Nunberg, "A Name Too Far," *San Jose Mercury News*, September 30, 2001, retrieved from http://people.ischool.berkeley.edu/~nunberg/operations .html, October 5, 2014; and "Operation Masher (White Wing)," *History Wars Weapons*, August 26, 2010, http://historywarsweapons.com/operation-masher -white-wing.

17. George Carlin, "Euphemistic Washington," speech before the National Press Club, May 25, 1999, archived by the Federation of American Scientists, and retrieved from http://fas.org/news/usa/1999/05/990525-carlin.htm, November 2, 2014.

18. Rich Coffey, "Euphemisms Glossary," The American Empire, Vizettes.com, http://vizettes.com/kt/american_empire/pages/euphemisms-glossary.htm.

19. Ralph Keyes, *Euphemania: Our Love Affair with Euphemisms* (New York: Little, Brown, 2010), p. 213.

20. "Citigroup Announces Repositioning Actions to Further Reduce Expenses and Improve Efficiency," press release, Citigroup, Inc., December 5, 2012, http:// www.citigroup.com/citi/news/2012/121205a.htm.

21. John Leo, "Euphemisms," Townhall.com, February 23, 2004, http://townhall .com/columnists/johnleo/2004/02/23/euphemisms/page/full.

22. "'Pilchards' and 'Slimehead' Fish Renamed to Boost Popularity," *Daily Mail*, September 24, 2007, http://www.dailymail.co.uk/news/article-483457/Pil chards-slimehead-fish-renamed-boost-popularity.html#ixzz2rx29wD2P; and "Australia Adds Orange Roughy to Threatened Species List," TerraNature.org, November 9, 2006, http://terranature.org/orangeRoughyEndangered.htm.

23. Todd Gregory, "Rush Limbaugh's Or-bam-eo Slur," *Media Matters* (blog), August 17, 2011, http://mediamatters.org/blog/2011/08/17/rush-limbaughs-or -bam-eo-slur/182956; and "Kraft Launches the Triple Double Oreo," *Chicago Tribune,* August 17, 2011, http://articles.chicagotribune.com/2011-08-17/ business/chi-kraft-launches-the-triple-double-oreo-20110817_1_oreo-sales -kraft-foods-ceo-irene-rosenfeld.

24. *Quarterly Review of Doublespeak* (National Council of Teachers of English, Urbana, Illinois), April 1990, p. 1, cited in Henry Beard and Christopher Cerf, *The Official Politically Correct Dictionary and Handbook*, updated edition (New York: Villard Books, 1994), p. 141.

25. Paul Wasserman and Don Hausrath, *Weasel Words: The Dictionary of American Doublespeak* (Herndon, VA: Capital Books, 2006), p. 126.

26. Wendy Dickstein, "What Do Real Estate Descriptions Mean?," Realtor.com, retrieved from http://www.realtor.com/home-finance/homebuyer-information/ what-do-real-estate-descriptions-mean.aspx?source=web, January 30, 2014.

27. "Silgan Holdings: Rationalization Charges," Wikinvest, retrieved from http:// www.wikinvest.com/stock/Silgan_Holdings_%28SLGN%29/Ationalization% 20Harges, May 25, 2014.

28. Lloyd H. Steffen, *Executing Justice: The Moral Meaning of the Death Penalty* (Eugene, OR: Wipf and Stock, 2006), p. 103.
29. Patrick Reinhart, CheesyCorporateLingo.com, retrieved from http://www .cheesycorporatelingo.com/sections/o, January 27, 2014.
30. Harry Bruce, "Rancid Publicity over Tuna Shows How Critical Words Can Be," *Montreal Gazette*, September 28, 1985, retrieved from http://news.google .com/newspapers?nid=1946&dat=19850928&id=qIoxAAAAIBAJ&sjid =3aUFAAAAIBAJ&pg=5665,4071403, November 20, 2014.
31. Michael V. Miller and Cherylon Robinson, "Managing the Disappointment of Job Termination: Outplacement as a Cooling-Out Device," *The Journal of Applied Behavioral Science* 40, no. 1 (January 2004), abstract, http://jab.sage pub.com/content/40/1/49.abstract.
32. Dina Rasor, "The Pentagon Continues to Overpay for Everything; Let's Fix It," *Truthout*, December 8, 2010, http://truth-out.org/news/item/462-the -pentagon-continues-to-overpay-for-everything-lets-fix-it.
33. "Overserved," The Drunktionary, retrieved from http://freaky_freya.tripod .com/Drunktionary/I-O.html, July 7, 2014.
34. Scott Wilson and Al Kamen, "'Global War on Terror' Is Given New Name," *The Washington Post*, March 25, 2009, http://www.washingtonpost.com/wp-dyn/ content/article/2009/03/24/AR2009032402818.html.
35. "Overserved," The Drunktionary, retrieved from http://freaky_freya.tripod .com/Drunktionary/I-O.html, July 7, 2014.

p

1. John Stauber and Sheldon Rampton, "The Fog of War Talk," AlterNet, July 27, 2003, http://www.alternet.org/story/16497/the_fog_of_war_talk; and Frances FitzGerald, *Fire in the Lake: The Vietnamese and the Americans in Vietnam* (Boston: Little, Brown, 1972), quoted in Hugh Rawson, *A Dictionary of Euphemisms and Other Doubletalk* (New York: Crown, 1981), p. 202.
2. Marsha Rakestraw, "The Art of Circumlocution and Verbal Evasion: Exploring Euphemisms," *Institute for Humane Education* (blog), March 13, 2014, http://humaneeducation.org/blog/2014/03/13/art-circumlocution -verbal-evasion-exploring-euphemisms.
3. Caroline Thurlow, "Lost in Translation 5—Euphemisms," Altitude Public Relations, September 2, 2013, http://www.altitudepr.com.au/lost-in -translation-6-euphemisms.
4. Larry Welborn and Vik Jolly, "Kelly Thomas Case: Police Used 'Pain Compliance' Techniques," *Orange County Register*, December 9, 2013, http:// www.ocregister.com/articles/thomas-540873-wilson-police.html.
5. Mark Peters, "Shooting Sea Kittens in a Barrel," Visual Thesaurus, March 4, 2009, http://www.visualthesaurus.com/cm/evasive/shooting-sea-kittens-in -a-barrel.
6. Jonathan Salem Baskin, "Code Words & Secret Meanings," *Futurelab*, January 26, 2009, http://www.futurelab.net/blog/2009/01/code-words-secret-meanings.

7. William Neuman, "Sale of Paper in Venezuela Raises Fears on Freedom," *The New York Times*, July 15, 2014, p. A4, retrieved from http://www.nytimes .com/2014/07/15/world/americas/sale-of-paper-in-venezuela-raises-fears -on-freedom.html.

8. Jeremy Laurance, "Lonely? Shy? Sad? Well Now You're 'Mentally Ill,' Too," *The Independent*, http://www.independent.co.uk/life-style/health-and-families/ health-news/lonely-shy-sad-well-now-youre-mentally-ill-too-6699884.html.

9. Lynn Schneider, "20 Examples of Great Euphemisms," December 23, 2011, http://lynnschneiderbooks.com/2011/12/23/20-examples-of-great -euphemisms; and Gregory J. Cizek, *Setting Performance Standards: Theory and Applications* (London: Routledge, 2001), retrieved from http://books .google.com/books?id=uTy9Ncfd-1wC&pg=PT70&lpg=PT70&dq=% 22partially+proficient%22+unqualified&source=bl&ots=5LWx0GHgLJ&sig =KLuMNcWNXUjnr6Q8ZqToEgZkKLo&hl=en&sa=X&ei= EolnU5D9MJHQsQTmz4GADQ&ved=0CEQQ6AEwAw#v=onepage&q =%22partially%20proficient%22%20unqualified&f=false, May 4, 2014.

10. Russell R. Standish and Colin D. Standish, *Half a Century of Apostasy* (Rapidan, VA: Hartland Publications, 2006), p. 106.

11. Mark Krikorian, "Wanted: New Euphemisms," *National Review Online*, March 19, 2013, http://www.nationalreview.com/corner/343400/wanted-new-euphe misms-mark-krikorian.

12. Alex Zorach, "Euphemisms," October 30, 2011, http://cazort.net/topic/euphe misms; and "USA Patriot Act," *Investopedia*, http://www.investopedia.com/ terms/p/patriotact.asp.

13. Dave Reber, "It's MY Money—A Teacher's Response to Deceptive Anti-Union Ads," *Ed Voices* (blog), March 18, 2011, http://www.edvoices.com/blog/2011/ 03/18/teacher-responds-union-ads.

14. "The Ridiculous Business Jargon Dictionary," *The Office Life* (blog), http:// www.theofficelife.com/business-jargon-dictionary-P.html.

15. Wade Boese, "United States Retires MX Missile," Arms Control Association, October 10, 2005, http://www.armscontrol.org/act/2005_10/OCT-MX; and "Past Recipients of the Doublespeak Award," National Council of Teachers of English, 2014, http://www.ncte.org/library/NCTEFiles/Involved/Volunteer/ Appointed%20Groups/Past_Recipients_Doublespeak_Award.pdf.

16. William Lutz, cited in Gareth Branwyn, "This Shit Doesn't Stink. It Exceeds the Odor Threshold," *Stim* 8, no. 2 (January 24, 1997), http://www.stim.com/ Stim-x/8.2/doublespeak/doublespeak.html.

17. Page H. Onorato, "Talk of the Table Uses Euphemisms," *The Dispatch* (Lexington, North Carolina), February 28, 2012, http://www.the-dispatch .com/article/20120228/COLUMNISTS/302289969?p=2&tc=pg#gsc.tab=0.

18. "The Ridiculous Business Jargon Dictionary," *The Office Life* (blog), retrieved from http://www.theofficelife.com/business-jargon-dictionary-P.html, January 27, 2014.

19. Judith S. Neaman and Carole G. Silver, *Kind Words* (New York: Avon Books, 1991), p. 324, cited in Henry Beard and Christopher Cerf, *The Official*

Politically Correct Dictionary and Handbook, updated edition (New York: Villard Books, 1994), p. 141.

20. Patrick Reinhart, CheesyCorporateLingo.com, retrieved from http://www .cheesycorporatelingo.com/sections/p, January 27, 2014.

21. "Doublespeak: How to Say Killing Without Saying It," Associated Press, November 17, 1984, http://news.google.com/newspapers?nid=110&dat=1984 1117&id=FhRQAAAAIBAJ&sjid=31UDAAAAIBAJ&pg=6677,5528362.

22. Edward Lazarus, "Why Police and the FBI Should Be Wary to Use the 'Person of Interest' Designation," FindLaw.com, May 26, 2005, http://writ.news.find law.com/lazarus/20050526.html.

23. "Varieties of English: Gobbledygook," FunTrivia.com, http://www.funtrivia .com/en/subtopics/Gobbledygook-315836.html.

24. "Figures of Speech: Euphemism Examples," retrieved from http://fos.ilove india.com/euphemism-examples.html, January 14, 2014.

25. Frank Luntz, quoted in Matthew Gentzkow and Jesse M. Shapiro, "What Drives Media Slant? Evidence from U.S. Daily Newspapers," *Econometrica* 78, no. 1 (January 2010), pp. 44–45, retrieved from http://faculty.chicagobooth .edu/matthew.gentzkow/research/biasmeas.pdf, July 9, 2014.

26. Eric Eckholm, "Push for 'Personhood' Amendment Represents New Tack in Abortion Fight," *The New York Times*, October 25, 2011, p. A16, retrieved from http://www.nytimes.com/2011/10/26/us/politics/personhood-amendments -would-ban-nearly-all-abortions.html?pagewanted=all, July 20, 2014.

27. "7 Misleading Words Used in Real Estate Ads," *Today*, NBC, April 24, 2012, http://www.today.com/video/today/47158279.

28. Matt McMillan, "'Bath Salts' Drug Trend—Expert Q&A," WebMD, February 26, 2013, http://www.webmd.com/mental-health/addiction/features/bath-salts -drug-dangers; and "Synthetic/Designer Drugs Fact Sheet," Drug Free Marion County, Marion County, Indiana, updated January 20, 2012, http://www.drug freemc.org/Portals/0/Flyers%20and%20Fact%20Sheets/Designer%20Drugs% 20Fact%20Sheet%20Updated%20January%202012.pdf.

29. Christina Hsu, "The Seven Most Condescending Sports Euphemisms," Cracked.com, May 17, 2011, http://www.cracked.com/blog/the-7-most -condescending-sports-euphemisms.

30. Peter Campbell, "Dogberry 2013 Awards: Burberry Boss Angela Ahrendts Wins Meaningless Jargon Contest," *This Is Money*, January 3, 2014, http:// www.thisismoney.co.uk/money/news/article-2533526/Dogberry-2013-awards -Burberry-boss-Angela-Ahrendts-wins-meaningless-jargon-contest.html.

31. Elisabeth Rosenthal, "Patients' Costs Skyrocket; Specialists' Incomes Soar," *The New York Times*, January 19, 2014, p. A1.

32. Steve Eder, "Rodriguez's 'Gummies': Files Detail Doping, Down to Milligram," *The New York Times*, January 14, 2014, p. A1.

33. "Before You Buy Pink," *Think Before You Pink*, Breast Cancer Action, retrieved from http://thinkbeforeyoupink.org/?page_id=13, November 21, 2014.

34. "Uptitling: Who Pays the Piping Technologist?," *e-cyclopedia*, BBC News, March 7, 2002, http://news.bbc.co.uk/2/hi/uk_news/1859965.stm.

35. Rhonda Abrams, "Strategies: These Buzzwords Make You Sound Cutting Edge," *USA Today*, October 7, 2012, http://www.usatoday.com/story/money/columnist/abrams/2012/10/05/strategies-nine-buzzwords/1612071.

36. Lynda Sue Cooper, "How to Talk Like a Cop," 1996, reprinted in a blog post on *Caissa's Web*, http://www.caissa.com/ext/bulletin/ms/java020/post-fms12228 27415001679000001.

37. Lynda Sue Cooper, cited in Ryan Haggerty, "Cops Say It Their Own Way," *Pittsburgh Post-Gazette*, July 3, 2006, http://www.post-gazette.com/news/portfolio/2006/07/03/Cops-say-it-their-own-way/stories/200607030115.

38. Heidi Chapman, "The 10 Worst Euphemisms," *Man in the Woods* (blog), March 25, 2012, http://woodsydude-gkcrocks.blogspot.com/2012/03/10-worst -euphemisms.html.

39. R. W. Holder, *Oxford Dictionary of Euphemisms* (New York: Oxford University Press, 2008), p. 309.

40. Matt McMillan, "'Bath Salts' Drug Trend—Expert Q&A," WebMD, February 26, 2013, http://www.webmd.com/mental-health/addiction/features/bath-salts -drug-dangers; and "Synthetic/Designer Drugs Fact Sheet," Drug Free Marion County, Marion County, Indiana, retrieved from http://www.drugfreemc.org/Portals/0/Flyers%20and%20Fact%20Sheets/Designer%20Drugs%20Fact%20Sheet%20Updated%20January%202012.pdf, September 1, 2014.

41. Michael Delahunt, ArtLex Art Dictionary, retrieved from http://artlex.com, February 18, 2014.

42. "Plausible deniability," Taegan Goddard's Political Dictionary, retrieved from http://politicaldictionary.com, May 18, 2014.

43. "Making Murder Respectable," *The Economist*, December 17, 2011, http://www .economist.com/node/21541767.

44. "Doublespeak," SourceWatch, Center for Media and Democracy, updated August 30, 2009, retrieved from http://www.sourcewatch.org/index.php/Doublespeak, April 9, 2014.

45. "Doublespeak," SourceWatch, Center for Media and Democracy, updated August 30, 2009, retrieved from http://www.sourcewatch.org/index.php/Doublespeak, April 9, 2014.

46. John Leo, "Awash in Euphemisms," Townhall.com, February 27, 2006, http://townhall.com/columnists/johnleo/2006/02/27/awash_in_euphemisms.

47. "'Plutoed' Voted 2006 Word of the Year," American Dialect Society, January 5, 2007, http://www.americandialect.org/plutoed_voted_2006_word_of_the_year.

48. Rich Coffey, "Euphemisms Glossary," The American Empire, Vizettes.com, http://vizettes.com/kt/american_empire/pages/euphemisms-glossary.htm.

49. Daniel Dunaief, *Times Beacon Record* (Setauket, New York), September 5, 2012, http://www.northshoreoflongisland.com/Articles-Opinion-i-2012-09 -06-93592.112114-sub-The-spinmasters-of-corporate-speak.html.

50. Louis Fisher, "The Korean War: On What Legal Basis Did Truman Act?," *The American Journal of International Law* 89, no. 21 (January 1995), p. 21, retrieved from http://www.constitutionproject.org/wp-content/uploads/2012/09/425.pdf, January 9, 2015.

51. "The Ridiculous Business Jargon Dictionary," *The Office Life* (blog), retrieved from http://www.theofficelife.com/business-jargon-dictionary-P.html, January 27, 2014.

52. Dr. Ari Kohen, "Potentially the Worst Apology of All Time," *Terrible Apologies*, August 9, 2013, http://terribleapologies.com/post/57806117877/dot -official-likens-illegal-immigrants-to-satan-then.

53. William Lutz, "Doubts About Doublespeak," anthologized in Cheryl Glenn, *The Harbrace Guide to Writing*, concise 2nd edition (Boston: Wadsworth, Cengage Learning, 2012), p. 399.

54. "Superior Double-Speak," Spellhold Studios, February 19, 2009, http://www .shsforums.net/topic/38925-superior-double-speak.

55. Scott Simon, Twitter message cited in Brian Stelter, "Goodbyes and Grief in Real Time," *The New York Times*, July 31, 2013, http://www.nytimes.com/ 2013/08/01/business/media/goodbyes-and-grief-in-real-time.html.

56. Lynn Schneider, "20 Examples of Great Euphemisms," December 23, 2011, http://lynnschneiderbooks.com/2011/12/23/20-examples-of-great -euphemisms.

57. George Carlin, "Euphemisms," monologue featured on *Parental Advisory: Explicit Lyrics*, CD (Eardrum Records, 1990), recorded at the State Theater, New Brunswick, New Jersey, January 12–13, 1990, transcription retrieved from http://www.iceboxman.com/carlin/pael.php#track15, October 19, 2014.

58. "Mississippi Pro-Life Group Affirms Preborn Personhood Rights; Exceeds State Signature Requirements," press release, Personhood USA, February 17, 2011, http://www.personhoodusa.com/press-release/mississippi-pro-life -group-affirms-preborn-personhood-rights-exceeds-state-signature-r.

59. "The Ridiculous Business Jargon Dictionary," *The Office Life* (blog), retrieved from http://www.theofficelife.com/business-jargon-dictionary-P.html, January 27, 2014.

60. Francis X. Clines, "At Reagan Press Office, It's Avoid the Negative," *The New York Times*, October 28, 1983, http://www.nytimes.com/1983/10/28/world/at -reagan-press-office-it-s-avoid-the-negative.html.

61. John Stauber and Sheldon Rampton, "The Fog of War Talk," AlterNet, July 27, 2003, http://www.alternet.org/story/16497/the_fog_of_war_talk.

62. "Pre-Loved Wedding Dresses," EasyWeddings.com.au, http://www.easy weddings.com.au/preloved.

63. "Certified Pre-Owned: Now with Unlimited Peace of Mind," online advertisement, Mercedes-Benz, mbusa.com, retrieved from http://www .mbusa.com/mercedes/cpo, October 30, 2014.

64. Steve Inskeep, "Spirit Airlines Installs 'Pre-Reclined' Seats," *Morning Edition*, NPR, April 21, 2010, http://www.npr.org/templates/story/story.php?storyId= 126155461.

65. "The Rule of Verbal Packaging—The Leverage of Language," chap. 8 of *The Rules of Persuasion* (Westside Toastmasters, Los Angeles), retrieved from http://westsidetoastmasters.com/resources/laws_persuasion/chap8.html, April 18, 2014.

66. John Leo, "Journalese as a Second Tongue," *Time*, March 18, 1985, retrieved from http://bhs.cc/journalism/pdf/pw/journalese.pdf, June 1, 2014.

67. Paul Dickson and Robert Skole, *Journalese: A Dictionary for Deciphering the News* (Portland, OR: Marion Street Press, 2012), cited in Bill Lucey, "Finally, a Dictionary for Deciphering the News," *Newspaper Alum* (blog), March 4, 2013, http://www.newspaperalum.com/2013/03/finally-a-dictionary-for -deciphering-the-news.html.

68. William Lutz, interviewed by Jamie Eckle, "CareerWatch: Combatting Doublespeak," *Computer World*, October 24, 2011, http://www.computerworld .com/article/2550212/it-management/career-watch—combatting -doublespeak.html.

69. "Previously Enjoyed Necklaces," online advertisement, The Jewelry Box of Lake Forest, Lake Forest, California, 2014, http://thejewelryboxlf.com/ previously-enjoyed-necklaces.

70. "Previously Loved Art Sale," online advertisement, Edmonds Art Festival Foundation, Edmonds, Washington, 2014, http://www.eaffoundation.org/ how-can-you-help/plas.

71. Steven Poole, "Royal Mail: The Rhetoric of Privatisation," *The Guardian*, September 20, 2013, http://www.theguardian.com/books/2013/sep/20/answer -unspeak-is-more-unspeak.

72. Martin Fackler, "Amid Chinese Rivalry, Japan Seeks More Muscle," *The New York Times*, December 17, 2013, http://www.nytimes.com/2013/12/18/world/ asia/japan-moves-to-strengthen-military-amid-rivalry-with-china.html.

73. "Arlington Police Chief Rescinds 'Quota' Memo," ARLNow.com, March 26, 2012, http://www.arlnow.com/2012/03/20/arlington-police-chief-rescinds -quota-memo.

74. Don Ethan Miller, *The Book of Jargon* (New York: Macmillan, 1982), cited in Paul Dickson, *Slang!* (New York: Pocket Books, 1990), p. 51.

75. Alicia C. Shepard, "In the Abortion Debate, Words Matter," NPR.org, March 18, 2010, http://www.npr.org/blogs/ombudsman/2010/03/in_the_abortion _debate_words_m_1.html.

76. Robert Todd Carroll, *The Skeptic's Dictionary*, chap. 2, p. 28, retrieved from http://www.skepdic.com/refuge/ctlessons/ch2.pdf, August 14, 2014.

77. J. Santana, "Collateral Language," *L.I.E.S. (Language in Extreme Situations)*, retrieved from http://www.ugr.es/~jsantana/lies/doublespeak.htm, January 13, 2014.

78. Alicia C. Shepard, "In the Abortion Debate, Words Matter," NPR.org, March 18, 2010, http://www.npr.org/blogs/ombudsman/2010/03/in_the_abortion _debate_words_m_1.html.

79. Christina Hsu, "The Seven Most Condescending Sports Euphemisms," Cracked.com, May 17, 2011, http://www.cracked.com/blog/the-7-most -condescending-sports-euphemisms.

80. "Unequal Naming: The Gulf War 1991," *Guardian Weekly*, February 3, 1991, retrieved from http://www.myread.org/images/cloze/unequal_print.pdf, May 24, 2014.

81. Nermin Oomer, "Jargon Busters: The Worst Examples of 'Gobbledegook' and the Campaign That Seeks to Restore Plain English," Yahoo! News, http://uk.news.yahoo.com/jargon-busters--the-worst-examples-of--gobbledegook--and-the-campaign-that-seeks-to-protect-plain-english-171557674.html#2GVqIz8.

82. Rich Coffey, "Euphemisms Glossary," The American Empire, Vizettes.com, retrieved from http://vizettes.com/kt/american_empire/pages/euphemisms-glossary.htm, April 13, 2014.

83. Rob Kyff, "Modern-Day Euphemisms Can Leave Head in a Spin," *Hartford Courant*, January 18, 2010, http://articles.courant.com/2010-01-18/news/hc-words0118.artjan18_1_euphemisms-negative-patient-care-outcome-motion-discomfort.

84. Glenn Thompson, "The 12 Most Horrifically Misleading Euphemisms," Cracked.com, December 16, 2008, http://www.cracked.com/article_16884_the-12-most-horrifically-misleading-euphemisms_p2.html.

85. Ron Rosenbaum, "Worst Framing Device Ever: How the Misbegotten Phrase Public Option Has Undermined Health Care Reform," *Slate*, October 13, 2009, http://www.slate.com/articles/life/the_spectator/2009/10/worst_framing_device_ever.html.

86. Robert Todd Carroll, "Language and Critical Thinking," *Becoming a Critical Thinker* (New York: Pearson, 2004), p. 31, retrieved from http://www.skepdic.com/refuge/ctlessons/ch2.pdf, April 11, 2014.

87. Nina Rastogi, "The Purell Defense: Can Hand Sanitizers Really Affect Your Blood-Alcohol Level?," *Slate*, October 20, 2008, http://www.slate.com/articles/news_and_politics/explainer/2008/10/the_purell_defense.html; and Daniel Libit, "The Lamest Excuses Ever," *Politico*, May 9, 2009, http://www.politico.com/news/stories/0509/22264_Page2.html.

88. Adam Liptak, "Utah, in Opposing Gay Marriage, Finds Three Arguments Are Better Than One," *The New York Times*, January 14, 2014, p. A16.

89. "Push Poll," Taegan Goddard's Political Dictionary, retrieved from http://politicaldictionary.com, May 18, 2014.

90. William Lutz, *Doublespeak* (New York: Harper Perennial, 1990), p. 219, cited in Henry Beard and Christopher Cerf, *The Official Politically Correct Dictionary and Handbook*, updated edition (New York: Villard Books, 1994), p. 142.

q

1. Rebecca Thompson, "Awesome Real Estate Signs—NY Realtor's Funny Sign Goes Viral," *The Condoist* (blog), April 30, 2014, http://www.chicagonow.com/the-condoist/2014/04/awesome-real-estate-signs-funny-sign.

r

1. George F. Will, "In a Tangle over Euphemisms for Affirmative Action," *The Washington Post*, April 25, 2014, http://www.washingtonpost.com/opinions/ george-f-will-the-supreme-court-tangles-over-euphemisms-for-affirmative -action/2014/04/25/9bed399c-cbd1-11e3-95f7-7ecdde72d2ea_story.html? wpisrc=nl_opnsat.

2. Jerry Merchant and Mary Matthews, "Avoiding Difficult Questions," *The Right-Wing Christian Dictionary*, ExtremelySmart.com, retrieved from http://www.extremelysmart.com/humor/rightwingdictionary.php, May 17, 2014.

3. Andrew K. Dart, "Why Don't Liberals Just Say What They Mean?" akdart .com, http://www.akdart.com/libspeak.html.

4. Daniel Lyons, "Tesla's Electric Car Loses Its Juice," *Newsweek*, November 14, 2008, http://www.newsweek.com/daniel-lyons-teslas-electric-car-loses-its -juice-85403.

5. Judith S. Neaman and Carole G. Silver, *Kind Words* (New York: Avon Books, 1991), p. 337, cited in Henry Beard and Christopher Cerf, *The Official Politically Correct Dictionary and Handbook*, updated edition (New York: Villard Books, 1994), p. 143.

6. Andrew K. Dart, "Why Don't Liberals Just Say What They Mean," akdart.com, retrieved from http://www.akdart.com/libspeak.html, November 25, 2014.

7. Mark Peters, "Inappropriate and Uncertain Difficulties with Personal Deportment," Visual Thesaurus, August 6, 2014, retrieved from http://www .visualthesaurus.com/cm/evasive/inappropriate-and-uncertain-difficulties -with-personal-deportment, August 30, 2014.

8. Kevin Rath, comment published in Alexander Cockburn, *Guillotined, Being a Summary Broadside Against the Corruption of the English Language* (Petrolia, CA: CounterPunch, 2012), pp. 8–9.

9. Cheryl Glenn, *The Harbrace Guide to Writing,* concise 2nd edition (Boston: Wadsworth, Cengage Learning, 2012), p. 400.

10. Nicholas Carlson, "The Gory Details: Tim Armstrong's Layoffs Memo," Business Insider, March 10, 2011, http://www.businessinsider.com/tim -armstrongs-were-firing-hundreds-memo-2011-3?op=1, April 11, 2014.

11. William Lutz, "Life Under the Chief Doublespeak Officer," accessed at www.dt .org/html/Doublespeak.html, February 1, 2014.

12. "Tech Euphemisms: What Those Error Messages Really Mean," *PC World*, http://www.pcworld.com/article/193270/sssss.html.

13. "Cuccinelli Won the Wholesome in Droves," transcript of *The Rush Limbaugh Show*, November 8, 2013, http://www.rushlimbaugh.com/daily/2013/11/08/ cuccinelli_won_the_wholesome_in_droves.

14. Ray Grigg, "Shades of Green: The Devious Language of Doublespeak," Common Sense Canadian, March 2, 2011, http://commonsensecanadian.ca/ shades-of-green-the-devious-language-of-doublespeak.

15. Hugh Rawson, *A Dictionary of Euphemisms and Other Doubletalk* (New York: Crown, 1981), p. 233.

16. William Davis, "Interfacing with Biz Speak," *The New York Times Magazine*, June 8, 1986, http://www.nytimes.com/1986/06/08/magazine/interfacing -with-biz-speak.html.

17. Ralph Keyes, *Euphemania: Our Love Affair with Euphemisms* (New York: Little, Brown, 2010), p. 207.

18. AlleyAllen, post to "Favorite Euphemisms," SportsJournalists.com, September 28, 2006, http://www.sportsjournalists.com/forum/index.php/topic,32365.0/ nowap.html.

19. Rob Kyff, "Negative Patient Care Outcome? Yes, Euphemisms Are Alive and Well," *Hartford Courant*, April 4, 1997, http://articles.courant.com/ 1997-04-04/features/9705230902_1_assisted-new-euphemism-nursing -home-care.

20. Jack Smith, "Clearly It's a Plastic Language with Devious Overtones," *Los Angeles Times*, October 24, 1990, p. E6, cited in Henry Beard and Christopher Cerf, *The Official Politically Correct Dictionary and Handbook*, updated edition (New York: Villard Books, 1994), p. 143.

21. "Examples of Doublespeak," YourDictionary.com, http://examples .yourdictionary.com/examples-of-doublespeak.html.

22. Dominic Gates, "Boeing Plans Layoffs, Transfer of Research Jobs," *Wichita Eagle*, April 30, 2014, http://www.kansas.com/news/business/aviation/ article1141657.html.

23. *Executive Recruiter News* (Fitzwilliam, New Hampshire), November 1990; and Paul Dickson, *Slang!* (New York: Pocket Books, 1990), p. 51, cited in Henry Beard and Christopher Cerf, *The Official Politically Correct Dictionary and Handbook*, updated edition (New York: Villard Books, 1994), p. 127.

24. Roberta Smith, "What We Talk About When We Talk About Art," *The New York Times*, December 23, 2007, http://www.nytimes.com/2007/12/23/arts/ design/23smit.html.

25. Larry Elliott, "*How to Speak Money* by John Lanchester—review," *The Guardian*, September 4, 2014, http://www.theguardian.com/books/2014/sep/ 04/how-to-speak-money-john-lanchester-review.

26. Matt DeLong, "Palin Invents Word 'Refudiate,' Compares Herself to Shakespeare," *The Washington Post*, July 19, 2010, http://voices .washingtonpost.com/44/2010/07/palin-invents-word-compares-he.html.

27. "Earth Island Institute Says Not So Fast with Moonlight Emergency Logging," *Westwood Pine Press* (Westwood, California), August 18, 2009, http://smalltownnews.com/article.php?catname=Regional%20Government& pub=Westwood%20PinePress&aid=26393.

28. John Stauber and Sheldon Rampton, "The Fog of War Talk," AlterNet, July 27, 2003, http://www.alternet.org/story/16497/the_fog_of_war_talk.

29. Ralph Keyes, *Euphemania: Our Love Affair with Euphemisms* (New York: Little, Brown, 2010), p. 205.

30. "Euphemisms," *The Economist Style Guide*, retrieved from http://www .economist.com/style-guide/euphemisms, January 19, 2014.

31. Lynn Schneider, "20 Examples of Great Euphemisms," December 23, 2011, http://lynnschneiderbooks.com/2011/12/23/20-examples-of-great -euphemisms.

32. University of Oregon School of Journalism and Communication, "Euphemism—Definition and List," from http://journalism.uoregon .edu/~tbivins/J496/readings/LANGUAGE/euphemism_defandlist.pdf.

33. Mat Johnson, quoted in Janice Harayda, "More Publishing Buzzwords Decoded with Wit on Twitter," *One-Minute Book Reviews* (blog), August 31, 2011, http://oneminutebookreviews.wordpress.com/2011/08/31.

34. Patrick Cockburn, cited in Alexander Cockburn, *Guillotined, Being a Summary Broadside Against the Corruption of the English Language* (Petrolia, CA: CounterPunch, 2012), pp. 8–9.

35. Floyd Norris, "Loosening the Rules on Insider Trading," *The New York Times*, April 25, 2014, p. B1, http://www.nytimes.com/2014/04/25/business/loosen ing-the-rules-on-insider-trading.html.

36. "Doublespeak," Center for Media and Democracy, updated August 30, 2009, http://www.sourcewatch.org/index.php/Doublespeak.

37. Jerry Merchant and Mary Matthews, "Avoiding Difficult Questions," *The Right-Wing Christian Dictionary*, ExtremelySmart.com, http://www .extremelysmart.com/humor/rightwingdictionary.php.

38. Steven Poole, "Repetitive Administration," *Unspeak* (blog), May 22, 2005, http://unspeak.net/repetitive-administration.

39. "Replacement Workers," EuphemismList.com, January 19, 2013, http://www .euphemismlist.com/replacement-workers.

40. John Gregory Dunne, "Your Time Is My Time," *The New York Review of Books*, April 23, 1992, quoted in Richard Nordquist, "Weasel Word" definition, About .com, retrieved from http://grammar.about.com/od/tz/g/weaselwordterm .htm, July 20, 2014.

41. "Unequal Naming: The Gulf War 1991," *Guardian Weekly,* February 3, 1991, retrieved from http://www.myread.org/images/cloze/unequal_print.pdf, May 24, 2014.

42. Derek Thompson, "Citigroup Eliminates 11,000 Jobs in History's Most Corporate-Jargony Paragraph Ever," *The Atlantic*, December 5, 2012, http://www.theatlantic.com/business/archive/2012/12/citigroup-eliminates -11-000-jobs-in-historys-most-corporate-jargony-paragraph-ever/265925.

43. Geoffrey Nunberg, "Simpler Terms; If It's 'Orwellian,' It's Probably Not," *The New York Times*, June 22, 2003, http://www.nytimes.com/2003/06/22/weekin review/simpler-terms-if-it-s-orwellian-it-s-probably-not.html.

44. Rick Lowry, "The Euphemism Imperative," *National Review Online,* May 3, 2013, http://www.nationalreview.com/article/347268/euphemism-imperative.

45. Lech Mintowt-Czyz, "How That Humble Filing Clerk Became a Specialist in Data Storage," *Daily Mail*, April 18, 2000, http://www.highbeam.com/doc/1G1 -109696099.html.

46. Dennis Levine, as quoted by Floyd Norris, "Market Watch," *The New York Times,* September 22, 1991, cited in Henry Beard and Christopher Cerf, *The*

Official Politically Correct Dictionary and Handbook, updated edition (New York: Villard Books, 1994), p. 144.

47. "Winona 'Claimed Shoplifting Was for Movie Role,'" *Daily Mail*, October 31, 2002, http://www.dailymail.co.uk/tvshowbiz/article-145349/Winona-claimed -shoplifting-movie-role.html.

48. Dan Berger, "Regulatory Agencies Leave a Lot to Be Desired with Wine-Speak," *Herald-Tribune* (Sarasota, Florida), February 9, 2011, http://www .heraldtribune.com/article/20110209/columnist/102091001?p=1&tc=pg.

49. William Lutz, *The New Doublespeak: Why No One Knows What Anyone's Saying Anymore* (New York: HarperCollins, 1996), cited by Frank Grazian, "On Euphemisms, Gobbledygook and Doublespeak," *Public Relations Quarterly*, Summer 1997, retrieved from http://users.manchester.edu/ FacStaff/MPLahman/Homepage/BerkebileMyWebsite/euphemisms.pdf, February 16, 2014.

50. "The Ridiculous Business Jargon Dictionary," *The Office Life* (blog), retrieved from http://www.theofficelife.com/business-jargon-dictionary-R.html, April 14, 2014.

51. William Brasch, *The Joy of Sax: America During the Bill Clinton Era* (Deerfield Beach, FL: Lighthouse Editions, 2001), p. 99.

52. "Responsible Industry for a Sound Environment," SourceWatch, January 10, 2008, http://www.sourcewatch.org/index.php?title=Responsible_Industry _for_a_Sound_Environment.

53. Paul Wasserman and Don Hausrath, *Weasel Words: The Dictionary of American Doublespeak* (Herndon, VA: Capital Books, 2006), p. 147.

54. "FTC Publishes Final Guides Governing Endorsements, Testimonials," U.S. Federal Trade Commission, FTC.gov, October 5, 2009, http://www.ftc.gov/ news-events/press-releases/2009/10/ftc-publishes-final-guides-governing -endorsements-testimonials.

55. "Doublespeak Examples," *Damron Planet* (blog), retrieved from http://www .damronplanet.com/doublespeak/examples.htm, February 18, 2014.

56. "Doublespeak," Center for Media and Democracy, updated August 30, 2009, http://www.sourcewatch.org/index.php/Doublespeak.

57. Hugh Rawson, *A Dictionary of Euphemisms and Other Doubletalk* (New York: Crown, 1981), p. 97, cited in Henry Beard and Christopher Cerf, *The Official Politically Correct Dictionary and Handbook*, updated edition (New York: Villard Books, 1994), p. 144.

58. "The Ridiculous Business Jargon Dictionary," *The Office Life* (blog), http://www.theofficelife.com/business-jargon-dictionary-R.html.

59. "Reverse Racism," RationalWiki, updated February 1, 2014, http://rationalwiki.org/wiki/Reverse_racism.

60. Edwin Newman, lecture at Allentown College of St. Francis de Sales, February 3, 1984, quoted in Dan Pearson, "Misuse of Language Called Damaging to America," *The Morning Call* (Allentown, Pennsylvania), February 4, 1984, http://articles.mcall.com/1984-02-04/news/2407229_1_officers -report-misuse-language.

61. Sarah Lyall, "A Decoder for Financial Illiterates," *The New York Times,* October 23, 2014, http://www.nytimes.com/2014/10/23/arts/john-lanchesters -how-to-speak-money.html.

62. John Leo, "Journalese as a Second Tongue," *Time,* March 18, 1985, retrieved from http://bhs.cc/journalism/pdf/pw/journalese.pdf, June 1, 2014.

63. "Walgreens Announces Reduction in Corporate and Field Management Positions," news release, Walgreens, January 8, 2009, http://news.walgreens .com/article_print.cfm?article_id=5133.

64. Wesley J. Smith, "Euphemisms as Political Manipulation," *First Things,* May 17, 2013, http://www.firstthings.com/onthesquare/2013/05/euphemisms-as -political-manipulation, January 17, 2014; and Michael Falcone, "Randy Neugebauer Revealed As 'Baby Killer' Shouter: Texas Republican Apologizes," *The Huffington Post,* May 22, 2010, http://www.huffingtonpost.com/2010/03/ 22/randy-neugebauer-revealed_n_508525.html.

65. Paul Wasserman and Don Hausrath, *Weasel Words: The Dictionary of American Doublespeak* (Herndon, VA: Capital Books, 2006), p. 148.

66. Steve Rubenstein, "Plain Speaking Also Falls Victim to Cisco's Ax," *San Francisco Chronicle,* March 10, 2001, http://www.sfgate.com/business/ article/Plain-Speaking-Also-Falls-Victim-to-Cisco-s-Ax-2943774.php.

67. John Leo, "Reality Gets a Makeover with Words That Buff and Polish," Town hall.com, August 18, 2003, http://townhall.com/columnists/johnleo/2003/08/ 18/reality_gets_a_makeover_with_words_that_buff_and_polish/page/full.

68. "Making Murder Respectable," *The Economist,* December 17, 2011, http://www .economist.com/node/21541767.

69. Robert J. Tetlow and Peter von zur Muehlen, "Robustifying Learnability," Divisions of Research & Statistics and Monetary Affairs, Federal Reserve Board, Washington, DC, 2005, http://www.federalreserve.gov/pubs/feds/2005/ 200558/200558pap.pdf, cited in Ron Grossman, "It's the Jargon, Stupid—and It Doesn't Belong in Business," *Chicago Tribune,* February 11, 2007, http:// articles.chicagotribune.com/2007-02-11/news/0702110185_1_jargon-long -term-strength-vocabulary.

70. Steve Eder, "Rodriguez's 'Gummies': Files Detail Doping, Down to Milligram," *The New York Times,* January 14, 2014, p. A1.

71. Ralph Keyes, *Euphemania: Our Love Affair with Euphemisms* (New York: Little, Brown, 2010), pp. 148–149.

72. Jenny Anderson and Peter Eavis, "Banks in London Devise Way Around Europe's Bonus Rules," *The New York Times,* February 14, 2014, p. B1.

73. Christina Hsu, "The Seven Most Condescending Sports Euphemisms," Cracked.com, May 17, 2011, http://www.cracked.com/blog/the-7-most -condescending-sports-euphemisms.

74. "Iran Targets Danish Pastries," Al-Jazeera.net, March 2, 2006, http://web .archive.org/web/20061208031400/http://english.aljazeera.net/news/archive/ archive?ArchiveId=18788.

75. Peter Donnelly, "Weasel Words," *Skookum,* http://skookumpete.com/euphe mism.htm, July 18, 2014.

76. Eric Lee Green, "The Origin of the Term 'Rubber Hose Cryptanalysis,'" post to Google newsgroup *sci.crypt*, January 17, 2002, https://groups.google.com/forum/#!msg/sci.crypt/RjpbAJNfLd0/DSZ5EJTzDsUJ.

77. Steve Rubin, "Uses and Abuses of Language," Santa Rosa Junior College, November 27, 2013, http://online.santarosa.edu/presentation/page/?30609.

78. John Leo, "Journalese as a Second Tongue," *Time*, March 18, 1985, retrieved from http://bhs.cc/journalism/pdf/pw/journalese.pdf, June 1, 2014.

79. "Runway Safety—Runway Excursions," Federal Aviation Administration, retrieved from http://www.faa.gov/airports/runway_safety/excursion, August 30, 2014.

80. Conor MacEvilly, "Real Estate Lingo and Euphemisms," My North Seattle Home, retrieved from http://www.mynorthseattlehome.com/finding-the-right -home-for-me/real-estate-lingo-and-euphemisms-nw-style, January 15, 2014.

S

1. Alfred D. Berger, "Medical Jargon: Lesions on the Language," Rethinking Cancer.org, retrieved from http://www.rethinkingcancer.org/resources/magazine-articles/18_1-2/medical-jargon.php, June 22, 1014.

2. Jonny Geller, "What Publishers Actually Mean in Their Rejection Letters," *Shortcuts Blog, The Guardian*, February 26, 2012, http://www.theguardian .com/books/shortcuts/2012/feb/26/what-publishers-rejection-letters-mean ?CMP=twt_gu.

3. Jonathan Weisman, "Vote in Senate Starts Talks on Extending Unemployment Benefits," *The New York Times*, January 8, 2014, p. A11, http://www.nytimes .com/2014/01/08/us/politics/unemployment-benefits.html.

4. Gordon Pritchard, "Marketing 101—'Weasel' Words," *The Print Guide* (blog), May 3, 2012, http://the-print-guide.blogspot.com/2012/05/marketing-101 -weasel-words.html.

5. "Doubled Eggs," *Dictionary of Christianese*, April 22, 2012, http://www .dictionaryofchristianese.com/doubled-eggs.

6. Subway.com, official SUBWAY® website, accessed at http://www.subway .com/subwayroot/careers/default.aspx#, January 15, 2014.

7. "Region 2 Superfund: Global Sanitary Landfill," Environmental Protection Agency, October 5, 2010, http://www.epa.gov/region02/superfund/npl/global sanitary.

8. Geoffrey Norman, "Retreat to Euphemism," *The Blog, The Weekly Standard*, September 25, 2013, http://www.weeklystandard.com/blogs/retreat-euphemism_757143.html.

9. Hugh Rawson, *A Dictionary of Euphemisms and Other Doubletalk* (New York: Crown, 1981), p. 245, cited in Henry Beard and Christopher Cerf, *The Official Politically Correct Dictionary and Handbook*, updated edition (New York: Villard Books, 1994), p. 144.

10. "Organizing Astroturf: Evidence Shows Bogus Grassroots Groups Hijack the Political Debate," *Public Citizen*, January 2007, http://www.citizen.org/documents/Organizing-Astroturf.pdf.

11. Sam Pizzigati, "How to Fix Social Security Without Cutting a Penny," *The Washington Spectator*, November 26, 2013, http://washingtonspectator.org/index.php/Economics/how-to-fix-social-security-without-cutting-a-penny.html#.Uu5byPappOE.

12. "Making Murder Respectable," *The Economist*, December 17, 2011, http://www.economist.com/node/21541767.

13. Peter Pietrangelo, "Raiders, Bulldogs Reach Volleyball District Final," *Sault Ste. Marie Evening News*, November 2, 2012, http://www.sooeveningnews.com/article/20121102/SPORTS/121109892.

14. Lee Lofland, "The Language of Police: Cop Slang," *The Graveyard Shift* (blog), retrieved from http://www.leelofland.com/wordpress/the-language-of-police-cop-slang, July 2, 2014.

15. "Save the Sea Kittens!," PETA, http://features.peta.org/PETASeaKittens/about.asp, February 24, 2014; "PETA Wants to Rename Fish 'Sea Kittens,'" *The Huffington Post*, February 4, 2009, http://www.huffingtonpost.com/2009/01/14/peta-wants-to-rename-fish_n_157836.html; and Mark Peters, "Shooting Sea Kittens in a Barrel," Visual Thesaurus, March 4, 2009, http://www.visualthesaurus.com/cm/evasive/shooting-sea-kittens-in-a-barrel.

16. Judith S. Neaman and Carole G. Silver, *Kind Words* (New York: Avon Books, 1991), p. 300, cited in Henry Beard and Christopher Cerf, *The Official Politically Correct Dictionary and Handbook*, updated edition (New York: Villard Books, 1994), p. 54.

17. Paul Wasserman and Don Hausrath, *Weasel Words: The Dictionary of American Doublespeak* (Herndon, VA: Capital Books, 2006), p. 153.

18. "2014 Word of the Year Is '#blacklivesmatter,'" press release, American Dialect Society, January 9, 2015, http://www.americandialect.org/2014-word-of-the-year-is-blacklivesmatter.

19. Jonathan Matusitz, *Terrorism and Communication: A Critical Introduction* (Thousand Oaks, CA: SAGE Publications, 2012), p. 220.

20. John Lanchester, "Annals of Argot—Money Talks," *The New Yorker*, August 4, 2014, http://www.newyorker.com/magazine/2014/08/04/money-talks-6; and Vikas Bajaj, "Mechanism for Credit Is Still Stuck," *The New York Times*, August 12, 2008, http://www.nytimes.com/2008/08/13/business/world business/13credit.html?em=&pagewanted=all.

21. "Government Doublespeak," Motley News and Photos, June 23, 2012, http://motleynews.net/2012/06/23/government-doublespeak-to-deceive-and-confuse.

22. Timothy Lynch, "Doublespeak and the War on Terrorism," Cato Institute Briefing Paper #98, September 6, 2006, http://object.cato.org/sites/cato.org/files/pubs/pdf/bp98.pdf.

23. Philip Shenon, *A Cruel and Shocking Act: The Secret History of the Kennedy Assassination* (New York: Henry Holt, 2013), p. 1.

24. Hugh Rawson, *A Dictionary of Euphemisms and Other Doubletalk* (New York: Crown, 1981), p. 248, cited in Henry Beard and Christopher Cerf, *The Official Politically Correct Dictionary and Handbook*, updated edition (New York: Villard Books, 1994), p. 144.

25. Rob Kyff, "Modern-Day Euphemisms Can Leave Head in a Spin," *Hartford Courant*, January 18, 2010, http://articles.courant.com/2010-01-18/news/hc -words0118.artjan18_1_euphemisms-negative-patient-care-outcome-motion -discomfort.

26. "Loaded Language," RationalWiki, updated May 11, 2014, http://rationalwiki .org/wiki/Loaded_language.

27. Michael Spiro, "'In Transition' and Other Awkward Euphemisms," *Recruiter Musings* (blog), March 30, 2010, http://michaelspiro.wordpress.com/2010/03/ 30/in-transition-and-other-awkward-euphemisms.

28. U.S. Southern Command, statement cited in Jackie Northam, "Guantanamo [*sic*] Detainees Attempted Mass Suicide in 2003," *All Things Considered*, NPR, January 24, 2005, broadcast transcript, http://www.npr.org/templates/story/ story.php?storyId=4464452.

29. John Leo, "Awash in Euphemisms," Townhall.com, February 27, 2006, http:// townhall.com/columnists/johnleo/2006/02/27/awash_in_euphemisms.

30. "Antique Oriental Rug: How to Evaluate Quality," Rugs-Oriental.net, 2008, retrieved from http://www.rugs-oriental.net/antique-oriental-rug.html, May 25, 2014.

31. Richard Lederer, "Oxymoronology," *Word Ways: The Journal of Recreational Linguistics*, 1990, retrieved from http://www.fun-with-words.com/oxym_oxy moronology.html, February 16, 2014.

32. Judith S. Neaman and Carole G. Silver, *Kind Words* (New York: Avon Books, 1991), p. 321, cited in Henry Beard and Christopher Cerf, *The Official Politically Correct Dictionary and Handbook*, updated edition (New York: Villard Books, 1994), p. 144.

33. "Semi-private," *The American Heritage Dictionary of the English Language* (Boston: Houghton Mifflin, 2009), quoted in The Free Dictionary, http://www .thefreedictionary.com/semiprivate, retrieved October 23, 2014.

34. Margaret Eby, "'Breaking Bad' Cast Invited to Belize Thanks to Show's Euphemism for Murder," *Daily News* (New York), August 22, 2013, www .nydailynews.com/entertainment/tv-movies/breaking-bad-cast-invited -belize-thanks-show-euphemism-murder-article-1.1433984.

35. Patricia T. O'Conner and Stewart Kellerman, "A Senior Moment," *The Grammarphobia Blog*, January 29, 2014, http://www.grammarphobia.com/ blog/2014/01/senior.html.

36. William Safire, "Prettification Patrol," *The New York Times*, January 16, 1994, http://www.nytimes.com/1994/01/16/magazine/on-language-prettification- patrol.html.

37. Mark Bittman, "The Right to Sell Kids Junk," *The New York Times*, March 27, 2012, http://opinionator.blogs.nytimes.com/2012/03/27/the-right-to-sell-kids -junk.

38. Steve Rubenstein, "Plain Speaking Also Falls Victim to Cisco's Ax," *San Francisco Chronicle*, March 10, 2001, http://www.sfgate.com/business/ article/Plain-Speaking-Also-Falls-Victim-to-Cisco-s-Ax-2943774.php.

39. Mark Peters, "Euphemisms of Interest," Visual Thesaurus, April 7, 2010, http://www.visualthesaurus.com/cm/evasive/euphemisms-of-interest; and Kelly Wilson, "Catching the Unique Rabbit: Why Pets Should Be Reclassified as Inimitable Property under the Law," Cleveland State University, 2009, retrieved from https://www.animallaw.info/article/catching-unique-rabbit -why-pets-should-be-reclassified-inimitable-property-under-law, September 1, 2014.

40. "Sentinel Event Policy and Procedures," The Joint Commission, June 10, 2013, http://www.jointcommission.org/Sentinel_Event_Policy_and_Procedures; and John Leo, "Reality Gets a Makeover with Words That Buff and Polish," Townhall.com, August 18, 2003, http://townhall.com/columnists/johnleo/ 2003/08/18/reality_gets_a_makeover_with_words_that_buff_and_polish/ page/full.

41. "Loaded Language," RationalWiki, updated May 11, 2014, http://rationalwiki .org/wiki/Loaded_language.

42. Mark Peters, "Hiking the Euphemistic Trail," Visual Thesaurus, July 2, 2009, http://www.visualthesaurus.com/cm/evasive/hiking-the-euphemistic-trail.

43. Rob Kyff, "The Word Guy: Avoid 'Trash Talk' When Employing Euphemism," *Pittsburgh Tribune-Review*, May 23, 2014, http://triblive.com/aande/ moreaande/6153366-74/euphemisms-trash-kyff#ixzz3GDIvNBHa.

44. Cheryl Glenn, *The Harbrace Guide to Writing*, concise 2nd edition (Boston: Wadsworth, Cengage Learning, 2012), p. 400.

45. Glenn Thompson, "The 12 Most Horrifically Misleading Euphemisms," Cracked.com, December 16, 2008, www.cracked.com/article_16884_the-12 -most-horrifically-misleading-euphemisms.html.

46. Michael Spiro, "'In Transition' and Other Awkward Euphemisms," *Recruiter Musings* (blog), March 30, 2010, http://michaelspiro.wordpress.com/2010/03/ 30/in-transition-and-other-awkward-euphemisms.

47. Ralph Keyes, *Euphemania: Our Love Affair with Euphemisms* (New York: Little, Brown, 2010), p. 79.

48. *Quarterly Review of Doublespeak* (National Council of Teachers of English, Urbana, Illinois), April 1990, p. 4, cited in Henry Beard and Christopher Cerf, *The Official Politically Correct Dictionary and Handbook*, updated edition (New York: Villard Books, 1994), p. 55.

49. Phil Andrews, "A Weighty Lesson on the Power of Words Used by Media," Guelph Mercury.com, February 15, 2014, http://www.guelphmercury.com/opinion -story/4369428-a-weighty-lesson-on-the-power-of-words-used-by-media.

50. Amanda Hess, "The University of Virginia Excels in Rape Euphemism," *Washington City Paper*, April 26, 2010, http://www.washingtoncitypaper.com/ blogs/sexist/2010/04/26/the-university-of-virginia-excels-in-rape-euphemism.

51. Robert Todd Carroll, "Language and Critical Thinking," *Becoming a Critical Thinker* (New York: Pearson, 2004), p. 42, retrieved from http://www.skepdic .com/refuge/ctlessons/ch2.pdf, April 11, 2014.

52. Manny Fernandez, "Strip Clubs and Their City Call a Truce," *The New York Times*, January 3, 2014, p. A11.

53. Gideon Rosenblatt, "Corporate Raider Carl Icahn Is Not Entitled to Apple's Cash," *The Vital Edge*, February 10, 2014, http://www.the-vital-edge.com/corporate-raider.

54. "Euphemism Used in Dismissal," Baidu.com, retrieved from http://wenku.baidu.com/view/1c84df82e53a580216fcfe98.html, May 25, 2014.

55. Wesley J. Smith, "Euphemisms as Political Manipulation," *First Things*, May 17, 2013, http://www.firstthings.com/onthesquare/2013/05/euphemisms-as-political-manipulation.

56. "Georgia Jagger's Advert for Rimmel Mascara Is Banned," *The Telegraph*, November 24, 2010, http://fashion.telegraph.co.uk/news-features/TMG8153833/Georgia-Jaggers-advert-for-Rimmel-mascara-is-banned.html.

57. Shikha Dalmia, "Obama's Orwellian Doublespeak on the Drone Program," Reason.com, May 28, 2013, http://reason.com/archives/2013/05/28/obamas-orwellian-doublespeak-on-the-dron.

58. From *Landslides,* cited in Adam Marcus and Ivan Oransky, "The Euphemism Parade: What's Behind Paper Retractions?," *Lab Times*, July 2013, http://www.labtimes.org/labtimes/ranking/dont/2013_07.lasso.

59. Brian Ashbee, "Art Bollocks," *Art Review*, April 1999, retrieved from http://www.ipod.org.uk/reality/art_bollocks.asp, February 18, 2014.

60. "Environmental Doublespeak—Environmental Ethics, Anti-Environmental Propaganda, and Greenwashing Language," GrinningPlanet.com, updated September 20, 2008, http://www.grinningplanet.com/2004/10-19/environmental-doublespeak-ethics-article.htm.

61. Mark Peters, "Tender Undoing and Other Surface Coal," Visual Thesaurus, August 6, 2014, http://www.visualthesaurus.com/cm/evasive/tender-undoing-and-other-surface-coal.

62. Jack Smith, "Clearly It's a Plastic Language with Devious Overtones," *Los Angeles Times*, October 24, 1990, http://articles.latimes.com/1990-10-24/news/vw-2724_1_clear-language.

63. Paul Abowd, "60 Plus Association," Center for Public Integrity, June 21, 2012, http://www.publicintegrity.org/2012/06/21/9171/nonprofit-profile-60-plus-association; and "60 Plus Association," updated July 8, 2014, http://www.sourcewatch.org/index.php/60_Plus_Association#Ties_to_the_Koch_Brothers.

64. Jon Henley, "A Glossary of US Military Torture Euphemisms," *The Guardian*, December 13, 2007, http://www.theguardian.com/world/2007/dec/13/usa.humanrights.

65. Peter Foster, "David Petraeus Apologises Publicly for Affair," *The Telegraph*, March 26, 2013, http://www.telegraph.co.uk/news/worldnews/northamerica/usa/9954845/David-Petraeus-apologises-publicly-for-affair.html.

66. Russell A. Barkley, Ph.D., "Concentration Deficit Disorder (Sluggish Cognitive Tempo)," in *Attention Deficit Hyperactivity Disorder: A Handbook for Diagnosis and Treatment*, 4th edition (New York: Guilford Press, 2015), retrieved, before book publication, from http://www.russellbarkley.org/factsheets/SluggishCognitiveTempo.pdf, May 28, 2014.

67. Peer Lawther, "25 Euphemisms for 'You've Been Made Redundant,'" *StepChange MoneyAware* (blog), November 11, 2011, http://moneyaware. co.uk/2011/11/25-euphemisms-for-youve-been-made-redundant.

68. *College English* (National Council of Teachers of English) 52, no. 1 (January 1990), p. 50, cited in Henry Beard and Christopher Cerf, *The Official Politically Correct Dictionary and Handbook*, updated edition (New York: Villard Books, 1994), p. 145.

69. Christopher Lane, "Shy on Drugs," *The New York Times*, September 21, 2007, www.nytimes.com/2007/09/21/college/coll21lane.html; and Christopher Lane, "Shy? Or Something More Serious?," *The Washington Post*, November 6, 2007, http://www.washingtonpost.com/wp-dyn/content/article/2007/11/02/ AR2007110201767.html.

70. "Varieties of English: Gobbledygook," FunTrivia.com, http://www.funtrivia .com/en/subtopics/Gobbledygook-315836.html.

71. Hanna Siegel, "Christians Rip Glenn Beck Over 'Social Justice' Slam," ABC News, March 12, 2010, http://abcnews.go.com/WN/glenn-beck-social-justice -christians-rage-back-nazism/story?id=10085008.

72. Hugh Rawson, *A Dictionary of Euphemisms and Other Doubletalk* (New York: Crown, 1981), p. 263.

73. Hugh Rawson, *A Dictionary of Euphemisms and Other Doubletalk* (New York: Crown, 1981), p. 263.

74. "Common Euphemisms to Refer to a Software Defect," Zuma Lifeguard's Wiki, retrieved from http://zumalifeguard.wikia.com/wiki/Common_euphemisms _to_refer_to_a_software_defect, July 20, 2014.

75. Rik Haynes, "10 Job Titles to Avoid on Your Business Card," *Print & Design* (blog), Solopress.com, January 16, 2013, http://blog.solopress.com/printing/ business-cards/10-job-titles-to-avoid-on-your-business-card.

76. Paul Wasserman and Don Hausrath, *Weasel Words: The Dictionary of American Doublespeak* (Herndon, VA: Capital Books, 2006), p. 162.

77. Martha Brooke, "Why David Segal Got Corporate-Speak & Our Authentic Answer," *InteractionThinking* (blog), Interaction Metrics, June 25, 2013, http://interactionmetrics.com/blog/?p=346.

78. Richard Mooney, "If This Sounds Slippery . . . How to Apologize and Admit Nothing," *The New York Times,* November 30, 1992, http://www.nytimes.com/ 1992/11/30/opinion/editorial-notebook-if-this-sounds-slippery-how-to -apologize-and-admit-nothing.html.

79. William Lutz, interviewed by Jamie Eckle, "CareerWatch: Combatting Doublespeak," *Computer World*, October 24, 2011, http://www.computerworld .com/article/2550212/it-management/career-watch—combatting -doublespeak.html.

80. Rob Hutton, "My 'Shameful Secret': I've Learnt to Love Clichéd Journalese," *The Telegraph*, September 8, 2013, http://www.telegraph.co.uk/culture/ 10288967/My-shameful-secret-Ive-learnt-to-love-cliched-journalese.html.

81. Jon Henley, "A Glossary of US Military Torture Euphemisms," *The Guardian*, December 12, 2007, http://www.theguardian.com/world/2007/dec/13/usa .humanrights.

82. Sue Horner, "Corporatespeak for Axed," Get It Write, November 19, 2010, http://getitwrite.ca/2010/11/19/axed.

83. Crawford Kilian, "The English Speaker's Guide to Political Journalese," *The Tyee*, April 27, 2013, retrieved from http://thetyee.ca/Mediacheck/2013/04/27/Guide-to-Journalese, July 8, 2014.

84. John Leo, "Euphemism, Double-Speak Marginalize the Language," *The Seattle Times*, August 15, 1995, http://community.seattletimes.nwsource.com/archive/?date=19950815&slug=2136517.

85. Erik. D. Olson, "Bottled Water: Pure Drink or Pure Hype?," Natural Resources Defense Council, April, 1999, http://www.nrdc.org/water/drinking/bw/chap5.asp.

86. Andrew Jacobs, "Tiananmen Square Anniversary Prompts Campaign of Silence," *The New York Times*, May 28, 2014, p. A4, http://www.nytimes.com/2014/05/28/world/asia/tiananmen-square-anniversary-prompts-campaign-of-silence.html; and Edward Wong, "China Moves to Calm Restive Xinjiang Region," *The New York Times*, May 31, 2014, p. A9, http://www.nytimes.com/2014/05/31/world/asia/chinas-leader-lays-out-plan-to-pacify-restive-region.html.

87. Glenn Beck, *Beck*, Fox News Channel, January 27, 2010, retrieved from http://mediamatters.org/video/2010/01/27/beck-social-security-medicare-should-have-never/159638.

88. Lucy Fisher, "Euphemisms II," *Wordly Wisdom* (blog), retrieved from http://wordlywisdom.net/Euphemisms-II.php, April 11, 2014.

89. Alex Hern, "Top Five Racist Republican Dog-Whistles," *New Statesman*, July 27, 2012, http://www.newstatesman.com/politics/2012/07/top-five-racist-republican-dog-whistles.

90. "Connotation and Denotation," p. 7, document posted by Jo Anna Bashforth, professor of English, California State University, Northridge, retrieved from https://www.csun.edu/~bashforth/098_PDF/06Sep15Connotation_Denotation.pdf, November 4, 2014.

91. Edward H. Crane, "Obama Is a Statist, Not a Socialist," *National Review*, April 29, 2009, retrieved from http://www.cato.org/publications/commentary/obama-is-statist-not-socialist, May 16, 2014; and "Statist," *Urban Dictionary*, August 31, 2008, http://www.urbandictionary.com/define.php?term=Statist.

92. Ashok Koparaday, "Medical Research Jargon," MyDoctorTells.com, October 12, 2013, http://mydoctortells.files.wordpress.com/2013/10/medical-research-jargon.jpg.

93. John Leo, "Journalese as a Second Tongue," *Time*, March 18, 1985, retrieved from http://bhs.cc/journalism/pdf/pw/journalese.pdf, July 7, 2014.

94. Monique van den Berg, "Revisiting Fat Euphemisms," *Big Fat Deal* (blog), August 18, 2010, http://www.bfdblog.com/mo-pie.

95. "Making Murder Respectable," *The Economist*, December 17, 2011, retrieved from http://www.economist.com/node/21541767, January 22, 2014.

96. Josh White, "Soldiers Facing Extended Tours: Critics of Army Policy Liken It to a Draft," *The Washington Post*, June 3, 2004; p. A01, http://www.washingtonpost.com/wp-dyn/articles/A10961-2004Jun2.html.

97. William Lutz, *Doublespeak* (New York: Harper Perennial, 1990), p. 108, cited in Henry Beard and Christopher Cerf, *The Official Politically Correct Dictionary and Handbook*, updated edition (New York: Villard Books, 1994), p. 145.

98. Ian Haney López, interviewed by Bill Moyers on "Ian Haney López on the Dog Whistle Politics of Race, Part I," *Moyers & Company*, American Public Television, February 28, 2014, http://billmoyers.com/episode/ian-haney -lopez-on-the-dog-whistle-politics-of-race; and "Faculty Profiles: Ian F. Haney López," *Berkeley Law, University of California*, retrieved from http:// www.law.berkeley.edu/php-programs/faculty/facultyProfile.php?facID=301, May 10, 2014.

99. Judith S. Neaman and Carole G. Silver, *Kind Words* (New York: Avon Books, 1991), p. 354, cited in Henry Beard and Christopher Cerf, *The Official Politically Correct Dictionary and Handbook*, updated edition (New York: Villard Books, 1994), p. 146.

100. Lucy Kellaway, "And the Golden Flannel of the Year Award Goes to . . . ," *Financial Times*, January 4, 2015, http://www.ft.com/intl/cms/s/0/8438a3ee -926a-11e4-b213-00144feabdc0.html#axzz3SRhpTKWQ.

101. Dan Clore, "Dubya's Doublespeak," Infoshop News, May 19, 2005, http://news .infoshop.org/article.php?story=20050519192522985.

102. William Lutz, cited in Gareth Branwyn, "This Shit Doesn't Stink. It Exceeds the Odor Threshold," *Stim* 8, no. 2 (January 24, 1997), http://www.stim.com/ Stim-x/8.2/doublespeak/doublespeak.html.

103. Andrew Jacobs, "For Prostitutes Jailed in China, Forced Labor with No Recourse," *The New York Times*, January 1, 2014, p. A1, http://www.nytimes .com/2014/01/02/world/asia/for-prostitutes-in-china-jail-with-no-recourse .html.

104. Paul Stainton, "Six Examples of Clever Marketing Messages Gone Wrong," *The Deluxe Blog*, April 29, 2014, https://ww.deluxe.com/blog/six-examples -clever-marketing-messages-gone-wrong.

105. William Lutz, *Doublespeak* (New York: Harper Perennial, 1990), p. 269, cited in Henry Beard and Christopher Cerf, *The Official Politically Correct Dictionary and Handbook*, updated edition (New York: Villard Books, 1994), p. 146.

106. "English: It's Abused in Business," *The Atlanta Journal and Constitution*, May 7, 1980, p. D 8, cited in Henry Beard and Christopher Cerf, *The Official Politically Correct Dictionary and Handbook*, updated edition (New York: Villard Books, 1994), p. 146.

107. Dale MacIntyre, "Annoying Euphemisms Part II: Substance Abuse," *On Being Relational Beings* (blog), November 5, 2013, http://dalemacintyre .blogspot.com/2013/11/annoying-euphemisms-part-ii-substance.html.

108. Lynn Schneider, "20 Examples of Great Euphemisms," December 23, 2011, http://lynnschneiderbooks.com/2011/12/23/20-examples-of-great -euphemisms.

109. Bruce Hilton, "Doublespeak Again Comes to the Rescue," *Chicago Tribune*, December 10, 1989, http://articles.chicagotribune.com/1989-12-10/features/

8903160824_1_doublespeak-awards-hospital-report-negative-patient
-care-outcome.

110. Steven Poole, "An A–Z of Modern Office Jargon," *The Guardian*, October
22, 2013, http://www.theguardian.com/money/2013/oct/22/a-z-modern
-office-jargon.

111. Mark Peters, "Pass the Strategic Dynamism Salts," Visual Thesaurus,
July 5, 2012, http://www.visualthesaurus.com/cm/evasive/pass-the
-strategic-dynamism-salts.

112. J. T. Mihalczo, "Super-Prompt-Critical Behavior of an Unmoderated,
Unreflected Uranimum-Molybenum Alloy Assembly," Oak Ridge National
Laboratory, U.S. Atomic Energy Commission, May 10, 1962, http://web.ornl
.gov/info/reports/1962/3445605700337.pdf; and Ann Larabee, *Decade of
Disaster* (Champaign: University of Illinois Press, 1999), p. 45.

113. Alisa Mariani, letter to *The New York Times*, published January 28, 2003,
http://www.nytimes.com/2003/01/28/opinion/l-war-and-diplomacy-a-week
-of-decision-on-iraq-057371.html.

114. Mark Peters, "Tender Undoing and Other Surface Coal," Visual Thesaurus,
August 6, 2014, http://www.visualthesaurus.com/cm/evasive/tender-undoing
-and-other-surface-coal.

115. Gai Beckerman, "Parsing the 'Surge,'" *Columbia Journalism Review*, January 9,
2007, http://www.cjr.org/behind_the_news/parsing_the_surge.php?page=all.

116. Rich Coffey, "Euphemisms Glossary," The American Empire, Vizettes.com,
retrieved from http://vizettes.com/kt/american_empire/pages/euphemisms
-glossary.htm, November 22, 2014.

117. "The Ridiculous Business Jargon Dictionary," *The Office Life* (blog),
retrieved from http://www.theofficelife.com/business-jargon-dictionary-S
.html, January 27, 2014.

118. Kate Sheppard, "Susan B. Anthony List Founder: Republicans Hijacked My
PAC!," *Mother Jones*, February 22, 2012, http://www.motherjones.com/poli
tics/2012/02/susan-b-anthony-list-sharp-right-turn-rachel-macnair.

119. "Suspended Campaign," Taegan Goddard's Political Dictionary, retrieved
from http://politicaldictionary.com, May 18, 2014.

120. John Leo, "Euphemisms," Townhall.com, February 23, 2004, retrieved from
http://townhall.com/columnists/johnleo/2004/02/23/euphemisms/page/full,
July 19, 2014.

121. Joe Saluzzi and Saul Arnuk, "The Mind-Numbing Euphemism: Providing
Liquidity," Business Insider, March 3, 2011, http://www.businessinsider
.com/the-mind-numbing-euphemism-providing-liquidity-2011-3.

122. "Swiftboating," Taegan Goddard's Political Dictionary, retrieved from http://
politicaldictionary.com, May 18, 2014; and Joe Conason, "Smear Boat Veterans
for Bush," *Salon*, May 4, 2004, http://www.salon.com/2004/05/05/swift_4.

123. "Nokia Siemens Networks Enters Final Stage of Synergy-Related Headcount
Restructuring," press release, Nokia Siemens Networks, November 11, 2008,
http://nsn.com/news-events/press-room/press-releases/nokia-siemens
-networks-enters-final-stage-of-synergy-related-h.

124. D. J. Kehl and Howard Livingston, "Doublespeak Detection for the English Classroom," *The English Journal,* July 1999, p. 80, retrieved from http://www.jstor.org/discover/10.2307/822191?uid=3739832&uid=2134&uid=2479801677&uid=2&uid=70&uid=3&uid=2479801667&uid=3739256&uid=60&sid=21103823248907, April 8, 2014.

t

1. Helen Pidd, "New All-White England Kit Could Highlight Stains of Defeat," *The Guardian,* March 29, 2009, http://www.theguardian.com/football/2009/mar/29/new-england-kit-white.
2. William Davis, "Interfacing with Biz Speak," *The New York Times Magazine,* June 8, 1986, http://www.nytimes.com/1986/06/08/magazine/interfacing-with-biz-speak.html.
3. Dave Barry, "Circumcision: Some Men Feel They Were Wronged by the Rite," *Orlando Sentinel,* December 9, 1991, http://articles.orlandosentinel.com/1991-12-09/lifestyle/9112070062_1_circumcision-recap-intact.
4. Chris Moody, "How Republicans Are Being Taught to Talk About Occupy Wall Street," Yahoo! News, December 1, 2011, http://news.yahoo.com/blogs/ticket/republicans-being-taught-talk-occupy-wall-street-133707949.html.
5. Sandra McCartt, "Jargon, Bizspeak, and Being Real," MyResourcer.com, January 20, 2011, http://www.myresourcer.com/blog/2011/01/20/sandra-mccartt-guest-blog-jargon-bizspeak-and-being-real.
6. Dwayne Mulder, "Further Examples of Euphemism/Dysphemism," Santa Rosa Junior College, September 27, 2013, http://online.santarosa.edu/presentation/page/?98555.
7. Dr. Daniela Ribtsch, "How Our Values Shape Our Views," *The Express* (Lock Haven, Pennsylvania), January 22, 2014, http://www.lockhaven.com/page/content.detail/id/549126/How-our-values-shape-our-views.html.
8. Norman Solomon, *The Power of Babble* (New York: Dell, 1992), p. 253.
9. Matthew Gentzkow and Jesse M. Shapiro, "What Drives Media Slant? Evidence from U.S. Daily Newspapers," *Econometrica* 78, no. 1 (January 2010), p. 44, retrieved from http://faculty.chicagobooth.edu/matthew.gentzkow/research/biasmeas.pdf, July 9, 2014.
10. Geoffrey Nunberg, "Compounding the Insults," *Language Log* (blog), July 16, 2006, http://itre.cis.upenn.edu/~myl/languagelog/archives/003354.html. Professor Nunberg was so impressed by the phrase referenced in this entry that he used it, in its entirety, as the subtitle of *Talking Right*, a book he wrote about the success of Republican "culture-stereotyping."
11. Daniel Okrent, "The War of the Words: A Dispatch from the Front Lines," *The New York Times*, March 6, 2005, http://www.nytimes.com/2005/03/06/weekinreview/06bott.html?pagewanted=1&_r=0&oref=login.
12. Steven Poole, "A Tax on Jobs," *Unspeak* (blog), May 21, 2010, http://unspeak.net/austerity-measures.

13. Matthew Gentzkow and Jesse M. Shapiro, "What Drives Media Slant? Evidence from U.S. Daily Newspapers," *Econometrica* 78, no. 1 (January 2010), p. 44, retrieved from http://faculty.chicagobooth.edu/matthew .gentzkow/research/biasmeas.pdf, July 9, 2014.

14. James A. Dorn, "Ending Tax Socialism," Cato Institute, September 13, 1996, http://www.cato.org/publications/commentary/ending-tax-socialism.

15. Steve Forbes, quoted in Joshua Green, "Meet Mr. Death," *The American Prospect*, December 19, 2001, http://prospect.org/article/meet-mr-death.

16. University of Oregon School of Journalism and Communication, "Euphemism—Definition and List," retrieved from http://journalism.uoregon .edu/~tbivins/J496/readings/LANGUAGE/euphemism_defandlist.pdf, January 15, 2014; the National Taxpayer Union website, http://www.ntu.org/ about-ntu, accessed February 27, 2015; and the U.S. Taxpayers Party website, http://www.ustpm.org/about/platform/36-platform.html, accessed January 15, 2014.

17. Andrew Jacobs, "For Prostitutes Jailed in China, Forced Labor with No Recourse," *The New York Times*, January 1, 2014, p. A1, http://www.nytimes .com/2014/01/02/world/asia/for-prostitutes-in-china-jail-with-no-recourse .html.

18. Steven Greenhouse, "Domino's Delivery Workers Settle Suit for $1.3 Million," *The New York Times*, February 1, 2014, p. A3.

19. "Your Silliest Job Titles," *BBC News Magazine*, March 17, 2010, http://news .bbc.co.uk/2/hi/uk_news/magazine/8570244.stm.

20. Chris Hiller, "Trust Me I Am a Spin Doctor," *Trade Secrets* (blog), Nature.com, October 26, 2012, http://blogs.nature.com/tradesecrets/2012/10/26/trust-me -i-am-a-spin-doctor.

21. D. J. Kehl and Howard Livingston, "Doublespeak Detection for the English Classroom," *The English Journal*, July 1999, p. 79, retrieved from http://www .jstor.org/discover/10.2307/822191?uid=3739832&uid=2134&uid= 2479801677&uid=2&uid=70&uid=3&uid=2479801667&uid=3739256&uid=60& sid=21103823248907, April 8, 2014.

22. Robert Todd Carroll, "Language and Critical Thinking," *Becoming a Critical Thinker* (New York: Pearson, 2004), p. 30, retrieved from http://www.skepdic .com/refuge/ctlessons/ch2.pdf, April 11, 2014.

23. John Leo, "The New Verbal Order," *U.S. News & World Report*, July 20, 1991, p. 14, cited in Henry Beard and Christopher Cerf, *The Official Politically Correct Dictionary and Handbook*, updated edition (New York: Villard Books, 1994), p. 146.

24. Paul Stainton, "Six Examples of Clever Marketing Messages Gone Wrong," *The Deluxe Blog*, April 29, 2014, https://ww.deluxe.com/blog/six-examples-clever -marketing-messages-gone-wrong.

25. *Quarterly Review of Doublespeak* (National Council of Teachers of English, Urbana, Illinois), April 1991, p. 6, cited in Henry Beard and Christopher Cerf, *The Official Politically Correct Dictionary and Handbook*, updated edition (New York: Villard Books, 1994), p. 146.

26. Mark Peters, "Tender Undoing and Other Surface Coal," Visual Thesaurus, August 6, 2014, http://www.visualthesaurus.com/cm/evasive/tender-undoing -and-other-surface-coal.

27. William Lutz, *Doublespeak* (New York: Harper Perennial, 1990), p. 67, cited in Henry Beard and Christopher Cerf, *The Official Politically Correct Dictionary and Handbook*, updated edition (New York: Villard Books, 1994), p. 147.

28. Keith Allan and Kate Burridge, *Euphemism & Dysphemism: Language Used as Shield and Weapon* (New York: Oxford University Press, 1991), p. 168, cited in Henry Beard and Christopher Cerf, *The Official Politically Correct Dictionary and Handbook*, updated edition (New York: Villard Books, 1994), p. 147.

29. Winston Churchill, speech in the House of Commons, February 22, 1906, quoted in *The Outlook* 17, no. 421, February 24, 1906, p. 250.

30. George Black, "Briefingspeak," anthologized in Micah Sifry and Christopher Cerf, *The Gulf War Reader* (New York: Times Books/Random House, 1991), p. 390.

31. Mark Peters, "One Man's Trash Is Another Man's Service Item," Visual Thesaurus, July 7, 2014, http://www.visualthesaurus.com/cm/evasive/one -mans-trash-is-another-mans-service-item.

32. Richard Price, quoted in Tim Sandlin, "Rejection, Hollywood Style," *The Huffington Post* (Canada): Living, November 18, 2013, http://www .huffingtonpost.ca/tim-sandlin/rejection-hollywood-screenwriting_b _4298062.html.

33. "Learn to Speak Editor in Just One Week!," *Editorial Anonymous* (blog), June 10, 2007, http://editorialanonymous.blogspot.com/2007/06/learn-to-speak -editor-in-just-one-week.html.

34. Adrian Chan, "Apple Store Employees Aren't Allowed to Say 'Unfortunately,'" *Gizmodo*, June 15, 2011, http://gizmodo.com/5812157/apple-store-employees -arent-allowed-to-say-unfortunately.

35. John Leo, "Brawley Case of the South," Townhall.com, August 10, 2007, http:// townhall.com/columnists/johnleo/2007/08/10/brawley_case_of_the_south.

36. "City Trying to Give Abandoned Hulks That 'Lived-in' Look," Associated Press, October 10, 1980, http://news.google.com/newspapers?nid=1346&dat= 19801010&id=HY8wAAAAIBAJ&sjid=HvsDAAAAIBAJ&pg=6817,3294255.

37. Jeremy Hobson, "The Best Corporate Spin of the Year," Marketplace: Business, January 17, 2012, http://www.marketplace.org/topics/business/ best-corporate-spin-year.

38. "Western Conservative Conference Features Antigovernment Hogwash and Crazy Conspiracy Theories," Southern Poverty Law Center, February 25, 2014, http://www.splcenter.org/blog/2014/02/25/western-conservative-conference -features-antigovernment-hogwash-and-crazy-conspiracy-theories.

39. "Therapeutic Misadventure," National Association of Personal Injury Lawyers, August 25, 2011, http://www.napil.net/2011/08/therapeutic-misadventure .html.; and William Lutz, *Doublespeak* (New York: Harper Perennial, 1990), p. 67, cited in Henry Beard and Christopher Cerf, *The Official Politically Correct Dictionary and Handbook*, updated edition (New York: Villard Books, 1994), p. 134.

40. Jessica Mitford, *Kind and Unusual Punishment: The Press Business*, quoted in Hugh Rawson, *A Dictionary of Euphemisms and Other Doubletalk* (New York: Crown, 1981), p. 14, cited in Henry Beard and Christopher Cerf, *The Official Politically Correct Dictionary and Handbook*, updated edition (New York: Villard Books, 1994), p. 147.

41. Jonny Geller, tweet to #publishingeuphemisms, February 23, 2012, https://twitter.com/search?q=%23publishingeuphemisms.

42. Damien Darlin, "Dell's Exploding Computer and Other Image Problems," *The New York Times*, July 10, 2006, http://www.nytimes.com/2006/07/10/technology/10dell.html.

43. William Lutz, cited in Gareth Branwyn, "This Shit Doesn't Stink. It Exceeds the Odor Threshold," *Stim* 8, no. 2 (January 24, 1997), http://www.stim.com/Stim-x/8.2/doublespeak/doublespeak.html.

44. Mark Peters, "Clear Communication That Didn't Get Accomplished," Visual Thesaurus, February 5, 2014, http://www.visualthesaurus.com/cm/evasive/clear-communication-that-didnt-get-accomplished.

45. Tim Sandlin, "Rejection, Hollywood Style," *The Huffington Post* (Canada): Living, November 18, 2013, http://www.huffingtonpost.ca/tim-sandlin/rejection-hollywood-screenwriting_b_4298062.html.

46. Andrew K. Dart, "Why Don't Liberals Just Say What They Mean?" akdart.com, http://www.akdart.com/libspeak.html.

47. Hal F. Rosenbluth and Diane McFerrin Peters, *Care to Compete? Secrets from America's Best Companies on How to Manage with People and Profits in Mind* (New York: Basic Books, 1999), p. 137.

48. Mark Neil, "The Science of Spending: Are You Frugal or Just a Cheapskate?," *Your Money and Your Life* (blog), August 28, 2012, https://yourmoneyandyourlifepdx.wordpress.com/2012/08/28/the-science-of-spending-are-you-frugal-or-just-a-cheapskate.

49. Jon Kelly, "The 10 Most Scandalous Euphemisms," *BBC News Magazine*, May 15, 2013, www.bbc.co.uk/news-magazine-2247069.

50. Anthony Weiner, tweet, May 28, 2011, https://twitter.com/repweiner/status/74337670263877632; and Michele Kim, "A Timeline of Weiner's Sexting Scandal," NBC News New York, July 29, 2013, http://www.nbcnewyork.com/news/local/Weiner-Timeline-Photo-Scandal-Women—123266188.html.

51. Ralph Keyes, *Euphemania: Our Love Affair with Euphemisms* (New York: Little, Brown, 2010), p. 27.

52. Nigel Rees, "In Other Words . . . ," *The Guardian*, October 13, 2006, retrieved from http://www.theguardian.com/money/2006/oct/14/careers.work, February 19, 2014.

53. Ralph Keyes, *Euphemania: Our Love Affair with Euphemisms* (New York: Little, Brown, 2010), p. 204.

54. Kate Zernicke, "Christie Faces Scandal on Traffic Jam Aides Ordered," *The New York Times*, January 8, 2014, p. A1.

55. Seth Fiegerman, "True Meanings of Real-Estate Buzzwords," MSN.com, retrieved from http://realestate.msn.com/true-meanings-of-real-estate-buzzwords, January 30, 2014.

56. Henry Blodget, "Euphemism of the Day: 'Transition from Homeownership,'" *Business Insider*, June 24, 2010, http://www.businessinsider.com/euphemism -of-the-day-transition-from-homeownership-2010-6.

57. A job title encountered by Shrewsbury (UK) resident Paul Pearson, as reported in "25 of Readers' Inflated Job Titles," *BBC News Magazine*, July 31, 2012, http://www.bbc.co.uk/news/magazine-18983009.

58. Erin McKean, "Frisky: The TSA Spawns Anger—and a New Lexicon," *The Boston Globe*, November 28, 2010, http://www.boston.com/bostonglobe/ideas/ articles/2010/11/28/frisky.

59. John Leo, "Reality Gets a Makeover with Words That Buff and Polish," Townhall.com, August 18, 2003, http://townhall.com/columnists/johnleo/2003/ 08/18/reality_gets_a_makeover_with_words_that_buff_and_polish/page/full.

60. Geoffrey Nunberg, "Simpler Terms; If It's 'Orwellian,' It's Probably Not," *The New York Times*, June 22, 2003, http://www.nytimes.com/2003/06/22/weekin review/simpler-terms-if-it-s-orwellian-it-s-probably-not.html.

61. Merriam-Webster.com, retrieved from http://www.merriam-webster.com/ dictionary/tree%20hugger, January 16, 2014.

62. Edward Harrison, "Dog Whistle Economics' Code Words," *Naked Capitalism* (blog), December 8, 2011, http://www.nakedcapitalism.com/2011/12/dog -whistle-economics-code-words.html.

63. "Euphemism Used in Dismissal," Baidu.com, retrieved from http://wenku .baidu.com/view/1c84df82e53a580216fcfe98.html, May 25, 2014.

64. "'T' Euphemisms," EuphemismList.com, retrieved from www.euphemismlist .com, January 24, 2014.

65. Stephen Colbert, "The Word—Truthiness," Comedy Central, October 17, 2005, retrieved from http://thecolbertreport.cc.com/videos/63ite2/the-word— truthiness, May 27, 2014; and Ben Zimmer, "On Language: Truthiness," *The New York Times Magazine*, October 17, 2010, p. MM22, http://www.nytimes .com/2010/10/17/magazine/17FOB-onlanguage-t.html.

66. Nigel Rees, "In Other Words . . . ," *The Guardian*, October 13, 2006, retrieved from http://www.theguardian.com/money/2006/oct/14/careers.work, February 19, 2014.

67. Luke Mullins, "The Real Estate Euphemism Pocket Translator," *U.S. News & World Report*: Money, September 9, 2008, retrieved from http://money.usnews .com/money/blogs/the-home-front/2008/09/09/the-real-estate-euphemism -pocket-translator, January 15, 2014.

u

1. Konstantin Kakaes, "Banishing the Word *Drone* Won't Solve the Unmanned Vehicle Industry's Real Problems," *Slate*, August 16, 2013, http://www.slate .com/blogs/future_tense/2013/08/16/banishing_the_word_drone_won_t _solve_the_uav_industry_s_real_problems.html.

2. David D. Kirkpatrick, "Historian Says Borrowing Was Wider Than Known," *The New York Times*, February 23, 2002, http://www.nytimes.com/2002/02/ 23/books/23BOOK.html.

3. Michael Lazzaro (aka "Hunter"), "Fox News Objects to Calling Michael Brown an 'Unarmed Teen,'" *Daily Kos*, August 25, 2014, retrieved from http://www .dailykos.com/story/2014/08/25/1324537/-Fox-News-objects-to-calling -Michael-Brown-an-unarmed-teen, August 27, 2014.

4. "Unassigned," *The Free Dictionary*, http://www.thefreedictionary.com/down size.

5. *Journal of Biomedical Materials Research Part B: Applied Biomaterials*, cited in Adam Marcus and Ivan Oransky, "The Euphemism Parade: What's Behind Paper Retractions?," *Lab Times*, July 2013, http://www.labtimes.org/ labtimes/ranking/dont/2013_07.lasso.

6. Cher Caldwell, "unSpun: Finding Facts in a World of Disinformation," Quizlet, retrieved from http://quizlet.com/6194441/un-spun-finding-facts-in-a-world -of-disinformation-flash-cards, April 17, 2014.

7. Jim Edwards, "A Layoff by Any Other Name: Merck Memo Uses 12 Euphemisms for Job Cuts," *CBS Money Watch*, September 19, 2011, http:// www.cbsnews.com/news/a-layoff-by-any-other-name-merck-memo-uses-12 -euphemisms-for-job-cuts.

8. U.S. secretary of energy Donald Hodel, quoted in William Lutz, *Doublespeak* (New York: Harper Perennial, 1990), p. 213, cited in Henry Beard and Christopher Cerf, *The Official Politically Correct Dictionary and Handbook*, updated edition (New York: Villard Books, 1994), p. 147.

9. William Lutz, *Doublespeak* (New York: Harper Perennial, 1990), p. 214, cited in Henry Beard and Christopher Cerf, *The Official Politically Correct Dictionary and Handbook*, updated edition (New York: Villard Books, 1994), p. 147.

10. *Quarterly Review of Doublespeak* (National Council of Teachers of English, Urbana, Illinois), October 1989, p. 4, cited in Henry Beard and Christopher Cerf, *The Official Politically Correct Dictionary and Handbook*, updated edition (New York: Villard Books, 1994), p. 147.

11. "NYC93FA166—National Transportation Safety Board, Airport Accident Report," Probable Cause Approval Date: September 13. 1994, retrieved from http://www.ntsb.gov/aviationquery/brief.aspx?ev_id=20001211X13217, October 31, 2014.

12. Paul Wasserman and Don Hausrath, *Weasel Words: The Dictionary of American Doublespeak* (Herndon, VA: Capital Books, 2005), p. 3.

13. Julian Sanchez, cited in James Joyner, "Poor Euphemisms," *Outside the Beltway*, August 7, 2007, http://www.outsidethebeltway.com/poor_euphemisms.

14. Lynn Schneider, "20 Examples of Great Euphemisms," December 23, 2011, http://lynnschneiderbooks.com/2011/12/23/20-examples-of-great-euphemisms.

15. "Code of Conduct for the International Space Station Crew," NASA, cited in Mary Roach, *Packing for Mars: The Curious Science of Life in the Void* (New York: W. W. Norton, 2010).

16. Mark Peters, "One Man's Trash Is Another Man's Service Item," Visual Thesaurus, July 7, 2014, http://www.visualthesaurus.com/cm/evasive/one -mans-trash-is-another-mans-service-item; and "Kourtney Kardashian's Unexpected Life Event," AOL.com, retrieved from http://features.aol.com/ video/kourtney-kardashians-unexpected-life-event, August 30, 2014.

17. Ron Grossman, "It's the Jargon, Stupid—and It Doesn't Belong in Business," *Chicago Tribune,* February 11, 2007, http://articles.chicagotribune.com/2007-02-11/news/0702110185_1_jargon-long-term-strength-vocabulary.

18. Rick Horowitz, "The Don't-Offend-the-Local-Hate-Group Award," *The Philadelphia Inquirer,* October 14, 1995, http://articles.philly.com/1995-10-14/news/25693183_1_klan-rally-project-lemonade-klan-members.

19. "Euphemistic Food Names," Chowhound Discussion, Chow.com, October 7, 2013, http://chowhound.chow.com/topics/919531.

20. Molly Ivins and Lou DuBose, *Bushwhacked: Life in George W. Bush's America* (New York: Random House, 2003), p. 261; Jon Rosenwasser, "The Bush Administration's Doctrine of Preemption (and Prevention): When, How, Where?," Council on Foreign Relations, February 1, 2004, http://www.cfr.org/world/bush-administrations-doctrine-preemption-prevention-/p6799; and Michael James Long, "A Political Glossary—Euphemisms—Double Speak," James Gang Publishing, retrieved from http://www.jamesgangpublishing.com/aboutus/opinion/opinion.html#Double%20Speak, November 23, 2014.

21. Glenn Thompson, "The 12 Most Horrifically Misleading Euphemisms," Cracked.com, December 16, 2008, http://www.cracked.com/article_16884_the-12-most-horrifically-misleading-euphemisms_p2.html.

22. "Examples of Doublespeak," YourDictionary.com, http://examples.yourdictionary.com/examples-of-doublespeak.html.

23. Luke Mullins, "The Real Estate Euphemism Pocket Translator," *U.S. News & World Report*: Money, September 9, 2008, http://money.usnews.com/money/blogs/the-home-front/2008/09/09/the-real-estate-euphemism-pocket-translator.

24. Committee on Public Doublespeak, National Council of Teachers of English, 1992 Doublespeak Awards, cited in Thomas J. Brady, "Our Language Never Seems to Get Much Past 1984," *The Philadelphia Inquirer,* November 22, 1992, http://articles.philly.com/1992-11-22/news/26009738_1_piper-national-service-national-guard.

25. Joanne Mariner, "A First Look at the Military Commissions Act of 2009, Part One," FindLaw, November 4, 2009, http://writ.news.findlaw.com/mariner/20091104.html.

26. University of Oregon School of Journalism and Communication, "Euphemism—Definition and List," retrieved from http://journalism.uoregon.edu/~tbivins/J496/readings/LANGUAGE/euphemism_defandlist.pdf, February 16, 2014.

27. Alfred Lambremont Webre, "Leuren Moret—Fukushima HAARP Nuclear Attack by CIA, DOE, BP for London Banks," YouTube, uploaded May 9, 2011, http://www.youtube.com/watch?v=htsWup50i3E.

28. Gary Haynes, "If a Lab Ruins or Loses Your Film, There's Little You Can Do About It," *The Philadelphia Inquirer,* January 26, 1989, http://articles.philly.com/1989-01-26/entertainment/26123667_1_film-roll-kodachrome.

29. "Making Murder Respectable," *The Economist,* December 17, 2011, http://www.economist.com/node/21541767.

30. "Uptitling: Who Pays the Piping Technologist?" *e-cyclopedia*, BBC News, March 7, 2002, http://news.bbc.co.uk/2/hi/uk_news/1859965.stm.

31. Robert Todd Carroll, "Weasel Words," *The Skeptic's Dictionary*, updated December 24, 2013, http://www.skepdic.com/weaselwords.html.

32. Deborah Meier, "'Urban' Schools and Other Euphemisms," *Education Week*, May 29, 2014, http://blogs.edweek.org/edweek/Bridging-Differences/2014/05/deborah_meier_continues_her_co_2.html

33. Shreshtha Ramsout, "Euphemisms and Hyperbole," September 2, 2012, retrieved from http://www.slideshare.net/Englishteacher87/euphemisms-and-hyperbole, January 17, 2014.

34. Troy A. Clarke, "A Letter from Troy Clarke to All of Our Loyal GM Vehicle Owners," General Motors North America, June 5, 2009, retrieved from https://www.facebook.com/notes/classic-chevrolet/a-letter-from-troy-clarke-to-all-of-our-loyal-gm-vehicle-owners/85486928603, November 2, 2014.

35. James Watt, testimony before a House panel investigating charges of influence peddling within the Department of Housing and Urban Development, June 9, 1989, quoted in *The New York Times*, June 23, 1989, retrieved from http://www.nytimes.com/1989/06/23/opinion/284089.html. September 24, 2014.

36. "On Euphemism," CCJK.com, June 29, 2012, http://www.ccjk.com/on-euphemism.

V

1. Jim Edwards, "A Layoff by Any Other Name: Merck Memo Uses 12 Euphemisms for Job Cuts," *CBS Money Watch*, September 19, 2011, http://www.cbsnews.com/news/a-layoff-by-any-other-name-merck-memo-uses-12-euphemisms-for-job-cuts.

2. Steve Rubin, "Uses and Abuses of Language," Santa Rosa Junior College, November 27, 2013, http://online.santarosa.edu/presentation/page/?30609.

3. William Lutz, *Doublespeak* (New York: Harper Perennial, 1990), p. 213, cited in Henry Beard and Christopher Cerf, *The Official Politically Correct Dictionary and Handbook*, updated edition (New York: Villard Books, 1994), p. 148.

4. "Welcome to Orinda Auto Detail & Car Wash," http://www.orindaautodetail.com.

5. "Vertical Transportation Condition Assessment," web page, Elevator Consulting Associates, Inc., http://elevatorconsultingassociates.com/our-services/vertical-transportation-condition-assessment.

6. Steven Roger Fischer, *A History of Language* (London: Reaktion Books, 2004), p. 192.

7. Colonel Frank Horton, quoted in "Reagan Is the Recipient of the 1983 Doublespeak Award," *Nashua Telegraph* (Nashua, New Hampshire), November 21, 1983, p. 14, retrieved from http://news.google.com/newspapers?nid=2209&dat=19831121&id=Q5krAAAAIBAJ&sjid=GPgFAAAAIBAJ&pg=1759,1797733, August 12, 2014.

8. "Making Murder Respectable," *The Economist*, December 17, 2011, http://www
   .economist.com/node/21541767.

9. James Jay Baker, "Research Shows Gun Control Only Breeds Crime," *Los
   Angeles Daily News*, March 14, 1993, retrieved from http://www.newspapers
   .com/newspage/18090962/, January 27, 2014.

10. Bill O'Reilly, "Has Liberalism Won in America?," *The O'Reilly Factor*, Fox
    News Channel, transcript, FoxNews.com, February 25, 2013, http://www
    .foxnews.com/transcript/2013/02/26/bill-oreilly-has-liberalism-won
    -america.

11. Tsafi Saar, "We Have Lied," *Haaretz*, October 7, 2011, http://www.haaretz
    .com/weekend/week-s-end/we-have-lied-1.388695.

12. Mike Huckabee, speech at the 2014 Winter Meeting of the Republican
    National Committee, Washington, DC, January 23, 2014, quoted in Alexandra
    Petri, "Mike Huckabee and Women's Uncontrolled Libido," *The Washington
    Post*, January 23, 2014, http://www.washingtonpost.com/blogs/compost/wp/
    2014/01/23/mike-huckabee-and-womens-uncontrolled-libido-or-uncle-sugar.

13. Mark Peters, "Ameliorating Vintage Replacements," Visual Thesaurus,
    October 5, 2011, http://www.visualthesaurus.com/cm/evasive/ameliorating
    -vintage-replacements.

14. "Title Pouches," National Vinyl Products, Inc., retrieved from http://www
    .nationalvinyl.com/industries-served.html, May 25, 2014; and "Common
    Window Terminology," Denco Windows, Inc., Slinger, Wisconsin, retrieved
    from http://www.dencowindows.com/terminology.htm, May 25, 2014.

15. Jeffrey Schrank, "The Language of Advertising Claims," *Teaching About
    Doublespeak*, ed. Daniel Dieterich (Urbana, IL: National Council of Teachers
    of English, 1976), retrieved from http://users.drew.edu/sminegar/English_1
    _FA08_Sect_003/The%20Language%20of%20Advertising%20Claims.htm,
    April 19, 2014.

16. Ron Nixon, "T.S.A. Expands Duties Beyond Airport Security," *The New York
    Times*, August 6, 2013, p. A11, http://www.nytimes.com/2013/08/06/us/tsa
    -expands-duties-beyond-airport-security.html.

17. *Quarterly Review of Doublespeak* (National Council of Teachers of English,
    Urbana, Illinois), July 1991, p. 1, cited in Henry Beard and Christopher Cerf,
    The Official Politically Correct Dictionary and Handbook, updated edition
    (New York: Villard Books, 1994), p. 148.

18. Michael Delahunt, ArtLex Art Dictionary, retrieved from http://artlex.com,
    February 18, 2014.

19. Kathy Kellerman, "Doublespeak," web document, ComCon: Communications
    Consulting, retrieved from www.kkcomcon.com/doc/KDoublespeak.pdf,
    October 31, 2014.

20. Sarah Kendzior, "Surviving the Post-Employment Economy," Al Jazeera
    America, November 3, 2013, retrieved from http://www.isidewith.com/
    article/surviving-the-post-employment-economy, January 14. 2014.

21. "New Vatican Document Seeks to Clarify Purposely Misleading U.N.
    Language," Life Site News, December 11, 2002, http://www.lifesitenews.com/
    news/archive//ldn/2002/dec/02121102, April 11, 2014.

W

1. Gary Krist, tweet to #pubcode, August 25, 2011, https://twitter.com/search?f= realtime&q=%23pubcode.
2. Michael Moynihan, "Exclusive! The Words That Journalists Overuse," *The Daily Beast*, February 1, 2013, http://www.thedailybeast.com/articles/2013/ 02/01/exclusive-the-words-that-journalists-overuse.html; and SuzieQ4624, "Romney Tries to Clarify 'Middle Income' . . . Fails . . . Again," *Daily Kos*, September 14, 2012, http://www.dailykos.com/story/2012/09/14/1131964/ -Romney-Tries-To-Clarify-Middle-Income-Fails-Again.
3. "Unequal Naming: The Gulf War 1991," *Guardian Weekly*, February 3, 1991, retrieved from http://www.myread.org/images/cloze/unequal_print.pdf, May 24, 2014.
4. Bill Hutchinson, "Nutty New NRA President Jim Porter Still Fighting War Against 'Northern Aggression,'" *Daily News* (New York), May 2, 2013, http:// www.nydailynews.com/news/national/nutty-new-nra-president-jim -porter-war-guns-article-1.1333864#ixzz2ynSXTpvR.
5. Jacob Levenson, "The War on What, Exactly?," *Columbia Journalism Review*, December 1, 2004, retrieved from http://www.alternet.org/story/20631/the _war_on_what,_exactly; and "White House Apologizes for Using 'Crusade' to Describe War on Terrorism," Associated Press, September 18, 2001, retrieved from http://www.freerepublic.com/focus/news/526718/posts, October 5, 2014.
6. Marin Cogan, "In the Beginning, There Was a Nipple," *ESPN Magazine*, January 28, 2014, http://espn.go.com/espn/feature/story/_/id/10333439/ wardrobe-malfunction-beginning-there-was-nipple.
7. Gulliver Ink Spots, "Pentagonese: A Primer," *Wired*, February 11, 2011, http:// www.wired.com/2011/02/pentagonese-a-primer.
8. Jon Kelly, "The 10 Most Scandalous Euphemisms," *BBC News Magazine*, May 15, 2013, http://www.bbc.co.uk/news/magazine-22470691; and "'Moments of Madness' That Ruined Ron Davies," *The Telegraph*, March 10, 2003, http:// www.telegraph.co.uk/news/uknews/1424188/Moments-of-madness-that -ruined-Ron-Davies.html.
9. Michael Manekin, interview with John Stauber in *Valley Advocate*, PR Nation, August 16, 2001, retrieved from http://www.ratical.org/ratville/ PRnation.html, April 11, 2014; and "Policy and Position Statements," Water Environment Federation, December 2, 2011, http://www.wef.org/ GovernmentAffairs/PolicyandPositionStatements.
10. William Lutz, *Doublespeak* (New York: Harper Collins, 1990), cited in Paul Cesarini, "Why Lutz?," Bowling Green State University, retrieved from http:// personal.bgsu.edu/~pcesari/722project1.html, May 24, 2014.
11. Vincent Iacopino, "A Memo on Torture to John Yoo," *The Guardian*, June 2, 2011, http://www.theguardian.com/commentisfree/cifamerica/2011/jun/02/ john-yoo-torture-waterboarding; and William Safire, "On Language: Waterboarding," *The New York Times Magazine*, March 9, 2008, http://www .nytimes.com/2008/03/09/magazine/09wwlnSafire-t.html.

12. Colin Randall, "'Let's Do Lunch': Putting a Name to an Insincere Phrase," *The National*, July 26, 2014, http://www.thenational.ae/opinion/comment/lets-do-lunch-putting-a-name-to-an-insincere-phrase.

13. Enid Nemy, "New Yorkers, etc.," *The New York Times*, May 22, 1988, http://www.nytimes.com/1988/05/22/style/new-yorkers-etc.html, reprinted in *Quarterly Review of Doublespeak* (National Council of Teachers of English, Urbana, Illinois), July 1990, p. 12, cited in Henry Beard and Christopher Cerf, *The Official Politically Correct Dictionary and Handbook*, updated edition (New York: Villard Books, 1994), p. 138.

14. Guy Winch, "The 10 Most Annoying Customer Service Practices" (blog post), GuyWinch.com, September 17, 2011, http://www.guywinch.com/10-most-annoying-customer-service-practices.

15. Colin Randall, "'Let's Do Lunch': Putting a Name to an Insincere Phrase," *The National*, July 26, 2014, http://www.thenational.ae/opinion/comment/lets-do-lunch-putting-a-name-to-an-insincere-phrase.

16. James A. Martin, Ph.D., CMA, "The Language of Politics: Political Euphemisms, Abstractions, and Weasel Words," *Management and Accounting Web*, retrieved from http://maaw.info/PoliticalLanguage.htm, February 22, 2014.

17. Spencer Ackerman, "Let's All Stop Saying 'Weapons of Mass Destruction' Forever," *Wired*, March 29, 2013, http://www.wired.com/2013/03/weapons-of-mass-destruction; and James R. Holmes, "Chemical Weapons Are NOT WMDs," *The Diplomat*, August 31, 2013, http://thediplomat.com/2013/08/chemical-weapons-are-not-a-wmd.

18. Richard Nordquist, "What Are Weasel Words," About.com, http://grammar.about.com/od/words/a/What-Are-Weasel-Words.htm.

19. John Pick, *The Modern Newspeak* (London: Harrap, 1998), p. 60, cited in Henry Beard and Christopher Cerf, *The Official Politically Correct Dictionary and Handbook*, updated edition (New York: Villard Books, 1994), p. 148.

20. "Your Silliest Job Titles," *BBC News Magazine*, March 17, 2010. http://news.bbc.co.uk/2/hi/uk_news/magazine/8570244.stm.

21. John Leo, "Journalese as a Second Tongue," *Time*, March 18, 1985, retrieved from http://bhs.cc/journalism/pdf/pw/journalese.pdf, July 7, 2014.

22. Lucy Fisher, "Euphemisms II," *Wordly Wisdom* (blog), retrieved from http://wordlywisdom.net/Euphemisms-II.php, April 11, 2014.

23. "Examples of Doublespeak," YourDictionary.com, http://examples.yourdictionary.com/examples-of-doublespeak.html.

24. "Making Murder Respectable," *The Economist*, December 17, 2011, http://www.economist.com/node/21541767.

25. Mark Peters, "One Man's Trash Is Another Man's Service Item," Visual Thesaurus, July 7, 2014, http://www.visualthesaurus.com/cm/evasive/one-mans-trash-is-another-mans-service-item.

26. Joan Healy, "Commentator Finds Examples of Government Doublespeak," WBFO News, Buffalo, New York, May 21, 2002, http://news.wbfo.org/post/commentator-finds-examples-government-doublespeak; and Adrianne Aron, "Haiti and the School of the Assassins," SOA Watch, January 18, 2007, http://

www.soaw.org/about-the-soawhinsec/236-latin-america-and-the
-soawhinsec/1475-haiti-and-the-school-of-the-assassins.

27. "Doublespeak," SourceWatch, Center for Media and Democracy, updated
August 30, 2009, http://www.sourcewatch.org/index.php/Doublespeak.

28. Jim Willis, "OH EPA Dings MarkWest Over Slurry Spills in OH Swamps,"
Marcellus Drilling News, August 2013, http://marcellusdrilling.com/2013/08/
oh-epa-dings-markwest-over-slurry-spills-in-oh-swamps.

29. Ashok Koparaday, "Medical Research Jargon," MyDoctorTells.com, October
12, 2013, http://mydoctortells.files.wordpress.com/2013/10/medical-research
-jargon.jpg.

30. "TINA's Glossary," TruthinAdvertising.org, retrieved from https://www
.truthinadvertising.org/tinas-glossary/#gs_index, February 15, 2014.

31. Rush Limbaugh, *The Rush Limbaugh Show*, Premiere Radio Networks, August
17, 2011, retrieved from http://mediamatters.org/video/2011/08/17/limbaugh
-christens-obamas-bus-tour-the-white-li/183007, October 31, 2014.

32. "Police Transcript: Audio Interview of Larry Craig," FoxNews.com, August 30,
2007, http://www.foxnews.com/story/2007/08/30/transcript-audio-interview
-sen-larry-craig.

33. Steve Rubin, "Uses and Abuses of Language," Santa Rosa Junior College,
November 27, 2013, http://online.santarosa.edu/presentation/page/?30609.

34. William Lutz, *Doublespeak* (New York: Harper Perennial, 1990), cited in
Henry Beard and Christopher Cerf, *The Official Politically Correct Dictionary
and Handbook*, updated edition (New York: Villard Books, 1994), p. 148.

35. Ralph Keyes, *Euphemania: Our Love Affair with Euphemisms* (New York:
Little, Brown, 2010), p. 79.

36. "Doublespeak," *Random Thoughts* (blog), March 28, 2006, retrieved from
http://markcbuffy.blogspot.com/2006/05/doublespeak-funny.html, April 8, 2014.

37. "Hardwood Inspired Tile Flooring: Doing What Wood Can't," TrendsinFloor
ing.com, April 25, 2012, http://trendsinflooring.com/hardwood-inspired-tile
-flooring-doing-what-wood-cant/188.

38. Rocky Smith, "Gobbledygook," *Mr. Write's Page* (blog), March 12, 2013, http://
rockysmith.wordpress.com/2013/03/12/gobbledygook.

39. John Leo, "On Society: Evasive Language Results in Suboptimal Outcomes,"
The Porterville Reporter, February 27, 2006, retrieved from http://www
.recorderonline.com/on-society-evasive-language-results-in-suboptimal
-outcomes/article_91862650-3314-558c-a0f8-c1c0a627beee.html, August 21,
2014.

40. Lucy Fisher, "Euphemisms II," *Wordly Wisdom* (blog), retrieved from http://
wordlywisdom.net/Euphemisms-II.php, April 11, 2014.

41. "Financial Dictionary," TheFreeDictionary.com, retrieved from http://finan
cial-dictionary.thefreedictionary.com/Work+Sandwich, January 26, 2014.

42. "Looking at the Layoffs at SIG-Sauer," *WeaponsMan* (blog), retrieved from
http://weaponsman.com/?p=16841, November 24, 2014.

43. Darryl K. Taft, "IBM Layoffs Begin in Workforce Rebalancing Effort," eWeek,
March 1, 2014, http://www.eweek.com/it-management/ibm-layoffs-begin-in
-workforce-rebalancing-effort.html.

44. Michael Daly, "Nisan Hadal's Murders Called 'Workplace Violence' by U.S.," *The Daily Beast*, August 6, 2013, http://www.thedailybeast.com/articles/2013/08/06/nidal-hasan-s-murders-termed-workplace-violence-by-u-s.html; Patrick Jonsson, "With Nidal Hasan Bombshell, Time to Call Fort Hood Shooting a Terror Attack?," *The Christian Science Monitor*, June 5, 2013, http://www.csmonitor.com/USA/Justice/2013/0605/With-Nidal-Hasan-bombshell-time-to-call-Fort-Hood-shooting-a-terror-attack; and "Barack Obama Says Since He Took Office, There Have Been No Large-Scale Attacks on the United States," PolitiFact.com (a project of the *Tampa Bay Times*), May 24, 2013, http://www.politifact.com/truth-o-meter/statements/2013/may/24/barack-obama/barack-obama-says-he-took-office-there-have-been-n/.

Y

1. Jeffrey Schrank. "The Language of Advertising Claims," *Teaching About Doublespeak*, ed. Daniel Dieterich (Urbana, IL: National Council of Teachers of English, 1976), retrieved from http://users.drew.edu/sminegar/English_1_FA08_Sect_003/The%20Language%20of%20Advertising%20Claims.htm, April 11, 2014.
2. Tim Wu, "Why Airlines Want to Make You Suffer," *The New Yorker*, December 26, 2014, http://www.newyorker.com/business/currency/airlines-want-you-to-suffer?intcid=mod-most-popular.
3. Reid Kanaley, "Web Winner," November 11, 2007, http://articles.philly.com/2007-11-11/business/24996434_1_jargon-watch-dilbert-lingo.
4. "The Lure of the Before and After," *Truth in Advertising,* January 10, 2012, https://www.truthinadvertising.org/the-lure-of-the-before-and-after.
5. "Running the Asylum," editorial, *The Augusta Chronicle* (Augusta, Georgia), December 26, 2011, http://chronicle.augusta.com/opinion/editorials/2011-12-26/running-asylum.

Z

1. Don Watson, *Watson's Dictionary of Weasel Words, Contemporary Clichés, Cant, and Management Jargon* (Sydney: Random House of Australia, 2004), p. 354.
2. "The Ridiculous Business Jargon Dictionary," *The Office Life* (blog), retrieved from http://www.theofficelife.com/business-jargon-dictionary-Z.html, January 11, 2015.
3. Serena Gordon, "Trans Fat on Food Labels: The New Math," *Prevention*, November 2011, http://www.prevention.com/food/smart-shopping/fda-sets-new-trans-fat-guidelines-food-labels.
4. Paul Wasserman and Don Hausrath, *Weasel Words: The Dictionary of American Doublespeak* (Herndon, VA: Capital Books, 2006), p. 195.
5. John Leo, "Reality Gets a Makeover with Words That Buff and Polish," Town hall.com, August 18, 2003, http://townhall.com/columnists/johnleo/2003/08/18/reality_gets_a_makeover_with_words_that_buff_and_polish/page/full.
6. Kate Sheppard, "Virginia Is for Zygote Personhood?," *Mother Jones*, February 14, 2012, http://www.motherjones.com/mojo/2012/02/virginia-zygote-personhood.

illustration credits

All line drawings © Ryan G. Smith

about the authors

HENRY BEARD attended Harvard, where he wrote for the iconic Ivy League college humor magazine, the *Harvard Lampoon*, rubbing shoulders, figuratively speaking, with towering literary figures from its storied past like Robert Benchley, George Santayana, and John Updike. After graduating in the top two-thirds of his class, he went on to become one of the founders of the *National Lampoon*, and served as its editor in the 1970s, during what several compensated endorsers have called its "golden age."

Beard is the author or co–exclusive coauthor of up to fifty humorous books, including the *New York Times* bestsellers *Miss Piggy's Guide to Life*, *The Sailing Dictionary*, *French for Cats*, *O.J.'s Legal Pad*, and *Leslie Nielsen's Stupid Little Golf Book*, as well as a number of verygoodsellers and evenbettersellers, like *Latin for All Occasions*, *Poetry for Cats*, *The Way Things Really Work*, *What's Worrying Gus?*, *The Dick Cheney Code*, and *The Official Exceptions to the Rules of Golf*.

Beard's most recent project is a unique philanthropic enterprise, often misinterpreted as a form of leisure, in which he uses the proceeds from sales of his semi-monumental masterwork, *Golf: An Unofficial and Unauthorized History of the World's Most Preposterous Sport*, to purchase golf balls and then distribute them, free of charge, in heavily wooded and overgrown grassy areas along the margins of local courses in the upscale undisclosed location where he resides.

CHRISTOPHER CERF is, among other things, an author, a composer-lyricist, a television and music producer, and a former contributing editor of the *National Lampoon*. Cerf has written more than three hundred songs for *Sesame Street*, and also co-created the PBS literacy education series *Between the Lions*—work which, in addition to winning multiple Emmy and Grammy awards, is frequently credited with playing a major role in the impressive 0.19-point average annual gain in reading scores that American fourth-graders have achieved since 1980 (a performance strong enough to earn the U.S. an eye-popping twenty-first place among the more than 195 nations competing for the top spot in literacy proficiency).

Similarly, his collaborations with Marlo Thomas and the Free To Be Foundation not only have produced a number-one *New York Times*–bestselling book and an Emmy Award–winning ABC special, but also may have been responsible for keeping the U.S. from falling below its stunning number 20 ranking on the World Economic Forum's Global Gender Gap Index.

Cerf also conceived and coedited *Not the New York Times*, a newspaper parody whose success led to the sustainable clear-cutting of several previously unspoiled, but arguably overgrown, forested areas; worked as a content supervisor at Random House, the laboratory for the written word founded by his father, the late Bennett Cerf; and partnered with Victor S. Navasky to compile *The Experts Speak*, which celebrated the incomplete success of statements and predictions made by the world's leading authorities on a dizzying array of topics.

Spinglish: The Definitive Dictionary of Deliberately Deceptive Language marks the sixth in a series of print collaborations between Christopher Cerf and his *National Lampoon* colleague Henry Beard. Previous joint projects include *The Pentagon Catalog*, *The Book of Sequels*, *The Official*

Politically Correct Dictionary and Handbook, *The Official Sexually Correct Dictionary and Dating Guide*, and *Encyclopedia Paranoiaca*, a collection of works so notable that one prominent New York book publisher (name withheld on request) was prompted to remark, "If there were a Nobel Prize for Satire, this gifted duo of comic geniuses would surely be on the shortlist for that coveted, though lamentably nonexistent, award!"